The Best Effect

The Best Effect

THEOLOGY AND THE ORIGINS OF CONSEQUENTIALISM

Ryan Darr

The University of Chicago Press   CHICAGO AND LONDON

The University of Chicago Press, Chicago 60637
The University of Chicago Press, Ltd., London
© 2023 by The University of Chicago
For more information, contact the University of Chicago
Press, 1427 E. 60th St., Chicago, IL 60637.
Published 2023
Printed in the United States of America

32 31 30 29 28 27 26 25 24 23   1 2 3 4 5

ISBN-13: 978-0-226-82997-5 (cloth)
ISBN-13: 978-0-226-82999-9 (paper)
ISBN-13: 978-0-226-82998-2 (e-book)
DOI: https://doi.org/10.7208/chicago/9780226829982.001.0001

Library of Congress Cataloging-in-Publication Data

Names: Darr, Ryan, author.
Title: The best effect : theology and the origins of consequen-
tialism / Ryan Darr.
Other titles: Theology and the origins of consequentialism
Description: Chicago : The University of Chicago Press, 2023. |
Includes bibliographical references and index.
Identifiers: LCCN 2023016551 | ISBN 9780226829975 (cloth) |
ISBN 9780226829999 (paperback) |
ISBN 9780226829982 (ebook)
Subjects: LCSH: Consequentialism (Ethics)—History. |
Consequentialism (Ethics)—History—17th century. |
Consequentialism (Ethics)—History—18th century. |
Religious ethics. | Ethics—Great Britain—History—
17th century. | Ethics—Great Britain—History—18th century.
Classification: LCC BJ1500.C63 D37 2023 |
DDC 171/.5—dc23/eng/20230512
LC record available at https://lccn.loc.gov/2023016551

♾ This paper meets the requirements of ANSI/NISO Z39.48-1992
(Permanence of Paper).

To my parents,
Kevin and Kathy Darr

Contents

Introduction

> But if someone really thinks, in advance, that it is open to question whether
> such an action as procuring the judicial execution of the innocent should be
> quite excluded from consideration—I do not want to argue with him; he
> shows a corrupt mind.

ELIZABETH ANSCOMBE, "MODERN MORAL
PHILOSOPHY"[1]

> There is prima facie a necessity for the deontologist to defend himself
> against the charge of heartlessness, in his apparently preferring abstract
> conformity to a rule to the prevention of avoidable human suffering.

J. J. C. SMART, UTILITARIANISM: FOR AND AGAINST[2]

The moral puzzles that a culture considers particularly interesting or
difficult offer a unique window into its ethical presuppositions. In the
Anglophone world, no moral puzzle has captured more attention in recent decades than the trolley problem. The philosopher Philippa Foot
first introduced a version of the problem in 1967 in order to gain insight
into the moral permissibility of abortion.[3] Since Foot's original paper, the
trolley problem has been applied to many other ethical problems, from
pandemics to climate change. "Trolleyology," moreover, has taken on a
life of its own and is now often treated as if it were more interesting in its
own right than the real-world problems it supposedly illuminates. While
trolleyology is not without detractors, it is pervasive in the academy. A
quick search of "the trolley problem" now brings up over seven thousand
academic texts, approximately half of which were published in the last four
years.[4] In many universities, undergraduate students puzzle over trolleys
in introductory courses in philosophy and ethics—and increasingly in
psychology as well. Nor is the trolley problem confined to the academy.

In the last several years, two books have been written on it for a popular audience.[5] And it is increasingly making its way into popular culture, from the TV show *The Good Place* to the board game *Trolley by Trial* to the countless trolley problem memes.[6]

For the uninitiated, the standard trolley problem goes like this. Consider the following two cases. In the first, a trolley is racing down a track out of control. You are standing nearby and realize that the trolley is about to hit and kill five people who are on the track. You also notice a lever beside the track. If you pull the lever, the trolley will be diverted onto a side track and avoid the five people. There is, however, one person on the side track who will be hit and killed. Do you pull the lever?

Now imagine a second case. Again, a trolley is racing down a track out of control, headed straight for five people. If you do nothing, all five will be killed. In this case, there is no lever and no sidetrack. You are instead standing on a footbridge that passes over the track. Near you on the footbridge is a large man—so large, in fact, that his mass would be sufficient to stop the trolley. If you push him off the bridge, he will fall in front of the trolley and stop it. He will be killed, but the five people on the track ahead will be saved. Do you push the man?

While judgments on these cases vary, the most common by far is to answer the first in the positive and second in the negative: pull the switch; do not push the man.[7] The rationale in the first case seems pretty straightforward: it is better for one person to die than for five people to die. The second case also seems rather clear. To push a man off a bridge in front of a moving train is widely considered murder, something that is never permissible, even when it is done for a good cause. What, then, is the problem? The problem arises when we make the parallels between the two cases explicit. In both cases, five people will die if you do not intervene. In both cases, the intervention that saves the five leads to the death of one. No one else is involved, and no other morally significant consequences follow. It would seem, then, that the answer to the two cases should be the same. What can justify the divergent moral judgments in the two cases, especially at the cost of four lives?

In the conclusion of the book, I consider how to address these cases ethically. For the moment, I want to focus on what we learn from their current intellectual and cultural prominence. In academia, their prominence highlights the continuing importance of the fundamental division between consequentialists, who make moral judgments solely on the basis of outcomes, and their non-consequentialist opponents. And the broader popularity suggests that this division reflects something in the wider culture. On this issue, scholarly debates in ethics are not out of touch with wider cultural views.

The popularity of the trolley problem does more than highlight an influential division between two competing ethical views. It also suggests that consequentialism has a certain advantage. Consider the two quotations in the epigraph above, which come from two very influential twentieth-century philosophers born just a year apart. Elizabeth Anscombe seeks to eliminate certain ethical possibilities, to place them outside the bounds of our consideration. For Anscombe, the fact that a consequentialist would consider performing a grave injustice (condemning and executing the innocent) to avoid seemingly worse consequences (say, a deadly riot) means that we should not even argue with him. He is too morally corrupt to be taken seriously. The same corruption, presumably, is present in the one who would seriously consider pushing an innocent man in front of a runaway trolley. Anscombe's view makes clear that even considering the trolley problem is already taking up a particular moral stance, one in which moral principles like those of justice can potentially be set aside when their results are undesirable. And the popularity of the trolley problem indicates that many now take precisely that stance.

But considering the trolley problem often does more than open up the possibility that common moral principles can be violated for the sake of better consequences. In the second quotation, J. J. C. Smart claims that the deontologist—that is, the one who believes we have moral duties that are independent of consequences—is at least prima facie heartless, choosing moral principles at the cost of real-world harms. The claim is an attempt to push the burden of proof onto consequentialism's opponents. Smart presses us to ask: Is the refusal to push the large man in front of the train just a prioritization of our own moral principles above human lives? If he is successful, we will begin to suspect that common moral principles are not standards of praiseworthy behavior but potential barriers to human compassion.

The trolley problem often functions to do just what Smart seeks to do: push the burden of proof onto the non-consequentialist. If you agree to pull the lever in the first case, then you presumably accept that the death of five people is worse than the death of one. The question, then, is why you would not do the same thing in the second case. Just as Smart intends, the non-consequentialist begins to look irrational. She is forced to rest significant weight on the differences between the cases, which the consequentialist will argue are insignificant. The burden of proof now lies with the non-consequentialist.

We can see the results of this shift in the burden of proof in trolley problem studies. Researchers find that most people reject consistently consequentialist views. The idea of pushing an innocent man to his death, even to save lives, is, to most of us, morally repulsive. When researchers ask participants in studies what they would do in trolley cases, consistently consequentialist answers are relatively rare. Matters are different, however, when it comes to moral reasoning. When participants give reasons for their judgments, they struggle to resist consequentialist reasoning. Joshua Greene, one of the most influential trolleyology researchers, writes:

> [I]n all my years as a trolleyologist, I've never encountered anyone who was not aware of the utilitarian rationale for pushing the man off the footbridge. No one's ever said, "Try to save more lives? Why, that never occurred to me!" When people approve of pushing, it's always because the benefits outweigh the costs. And when people disapprove of pushing, it's always with an acute awareness that they are making this judgment despite the competing utilitarian rationale. People's reasons for not pushing the man off the footbridge are very different. When people say that it's wrong to push, they're often puzzled by their own judgment ("I know that it's irrational, but . . ."), and they typically have a hard time justifying that judgment in a consistent way.[8]

Having relied on consequentialist logic to answer the first case, participants find themselves struggling to explain why they do not follow the same logic in the second. This, I think, is the most interesting insight we gain from the popular attention given to trolley cases: even among the majority who resist consequentialist conclusions, consequentialist reasoning is the only form of moral reasoning widely taken to be unproblematic.

How should we understand this result? Anscombe might say this: participants share her view that certain actions are simply off the table for consideration. Researchers then force them to put those actions back on the table, and the participants struggle to articulate considerations about the morally inconsiderable. Greene offers a very different explanation, which is drawn from the dual process theory of cognition. According to Greene, we have both a rational processing system and an emotional processing system. The rational processing system reaches consistently consequentialist conclusions. This rational system is what we use in the first trolley case. The emotional processing system, by contrast, reaches its judgments immediately and without rational reflection. When it is triggered—as it is in the second case by the thought of violently shoving a man to his death—it renders an immediate judgment about the act, which explains our revulsion at pushing the man. When we have to justify our negative answer to the second case, the rational processing system, which is consequentialist, struggles to justify the emotional judgment.

Greene's explanation builds the consequentialism/deontology divide into the human brain, effectively naturalizing it. Yet while both consequentialism and deontology become natural results of human cognition in Greene's theory, only consequentialism remains rational. The rational processing system, he claims, is "a cost-benefit reasoning system that aims for optimal consequences."[9] Any aversions to particular types of actions (e.g., executing the innocent or pushing a man to his death) are automatic and emotional. Thus practical rationality, when it is not overridden by emotion, is concerned only with consequences. And Greene, not surprisingly, goes on to endorse consequentialism.

Compelling as it is, Greene's explanation faces a serious objection. By reading current ethical categories into the very nature of cognition, Greene treats them as if they were universal and timeless. He is certainly not alone in doing so. The problem is this: how can we reconcile such a view with the historical and cultural particularity of these categories? Consequentialism, after all, is a relatively recent invention, a product of early modern and Enlightenment philosophy. The standard consequentialism/deontology division is even more recent. Studying the history of ethics should make us wary of explanations like Greene's.

On this point, however, our historical stories about consequentialism have failed us. Given the current sense, highlighted by Greene's research, that consequentialism is uniquely rational, it can be difficult to imagine that consequentialism had to be invented, and this difficulty has interfered with our stories of its origins. In the common imagination, utilitarianism—the "classical" form of consequentialism in which morality consists of maximizing happiness—is often seen as the paradigmatic secular ethic, the natural result of tossing off religious and cultural prohibitions. Notice the way Greene's psychological explanation precisely mirrors the historical narrative. In both cases, utilitarianism is what is left when we remove irrational moral inhibitions. The implicit assumption is that utilitarianism did not have to be invented, only liberated. While the common story is right to see classical utilitarianism as a secular reform project, the invention of consequentialism did not occur with the classical utilitarians. The invention of consequentialism is, in fact, more complicated—and more theological—than is often assumed. The story of its invention is the story told in this book.

According to the popular account, Jeremy Bentham is the founder of utilitarianism, which is taken to be the earliest form of consequentialism.

If utilitarianism names a British project of social and legal reform, Bentham has a claim to be its founder. But if utilitarianism names a position in moral philosophy—and especially if, as is now common, it is understood as a subset of consequentialism—the story is much more complex. Bentham is certainly not the inventor of consequentialism. If we read Bentham as the first consequentialist, we will be misled by the fact that consequentialist forms of thought simply appear as a naturally available resource to build a nonreligious ethic. For Bentham, they are simply available, but that does not make them natural. They had already been invented over a century before by explicitly theological ethicists.

Consequentialism relies on what I will call consequentialist moral rationality, that is, a way of understanding and assessing actions (as well as traits, rules, laws, etc.) by their causal relationship to better or worse outcomes.[10] This picture of moral rationality includes several features. One must, for example, see the good as a state of affairs to be realized, a view that differs sharply from dominant ancient and medieval views, as we will see in the first chapter. One must also see the good as subject to quantitative analysis such that one can rank or quantify particular goods and combine them to form sets or wholes that can also be ranked or quantified. All good states of affairs must therefore be commensurable. This, again, is by no means obvious, and it certainly was not intuitive before the seventeenth century (which, unsurprisingly, is also a period of the increasing financialization of many aspects of social life). Finally, one must have a notion of causal responsibility according to which it makes sense to attribute to an action not only the effects that it directly realizes but also further effects that would not have occurred had the action not occurred—even if these further effects are mediated by the actions of many other agents. None of these features is self-evident, and none is common before the seventeenth century.

Today, however, these forms of thought are commonplace, and they are often accepted even by those who reject consequentialism. Their prevalence explains why consequentialism carries an aura of being uniquely rational. As Samuel Scheffler writes, consequentialism is so compelling, despite its many unattractive implications, because it follows from "the canons of rationality we most naturally apply."[11] Scheffler's language is telling. Consequentialism does not follow from the only canons of rationality available or even from the most appropriate or convincing canons of rationality, but from those that we most "naturally" apply. We might naturally apply them because they embody the very structure of the human rational processing system, as Greene suggests. But given that they have not been applied by most people throughout most of history, it is more likely that they feel "natural" to us for social and historical reasons. Consequentialist moral rationality does indeed seem natural and intuitive, a fact which has made it difficult to see it as invented. By attending to its invention, we can recognize it as a particular, traditioned form of reasoning that many of us have inherited.

This book tells a new story of the origins of consequentialism, beginning with the early work of conceptual formation.[12] I argue that consequentialist moral rationality was invented through a series of subtle conceptual shifts in the seventeenth century and attained success originally for reasons very different from those that motivated utilitarianism's classical "founders." At the same time, it created new problems that drove its later development in the eighteenth century. By the time Bentham employed consequentialist moral rationality for his own aims, it had been around for a century and, for many moralists, was already largely taken for granted.

Part of the reason that this earlier history is often overlooked is that consequentialism in general and utilitarianism in particular is so often seen as a secular approach to ethics, while its earlier history is quite theological. Attending to the earlier conceptual development of consequentialism, then, helps us better understand something else: that the history of consequentialism is a theological history, a fact that remains true well into the nineteenth century. The essential role of religious concerns and theological debates in the formation of consequentialism have yet to be adequately understood.

Theology and Consequentialism in the History of Moral Philosophy

Despite the popular picture, it is well known among historians of moral philosophy that Bentham was preceded by a number of theological ethicists arguing that the right action is the one that produces the greatest happiness. These figures are most commonly known in the literature as "theological utilitarians." Their role in the existing histories of utilitarianism is complicated. Consider the two earliest English-language histories of utilitarianism, Leslie Stephen's *The English Utilitarians* (1900) and Ernest Albee's *A History of English Utilitarianism* (1902). Stephen's book consists of three volumes devoted to three classical late eighteenth- and nineteenth-century figures: Jeremy Bentham, James Mill, and John Stuart Mill. Despite his extensive attention to context—social, political, and intellectual—Stephen hardly mentions the earlier theological utilitarian tradition. Stephen does, however, have an explanation for the limited scope of his attention. He is concerned, he writes, "with the history of a school or sect, not with the history of the arguments by which it justifies itself in the court of pure reason."[13] His focus is not ideas but "men actively engaged in framing political platforms and carrying on agitations."[14] While this focus does not entirely justify the absence of the earlier theological figures, it certainly makes sense of Stephen's choice of main characters.

Albee takes the opposite approach. He is interested in the history of ideas. Utilitarianism, in his view, "has had both a perfectly continuous and a fairly logical development from the beginnings of English Ethics to the present time."[15] For this reason, Albee presents a strikingly different picture of the importance of Bentham. While Bentham is the central character of Stephen's first volume, he is a minor player in Albee's narrative. Indeed, Albee goes out of his way to diminish Bentham's role, arguing that Bentham "contributed almost nothing of importance to Ethics."[16] Theological utilitarianism occupies most of the first half of the book. Bentham does not show up until the middle of the book and receives only half of a chapter. Bentham, for Albee, was only a popularizer.

These two histories could hardly be more different. Albee's strong aversion to exaggerated pictures of Bentham's intellectual importance is matched by Stephen's blatant antipathy to theological utilitarianism. Yet despite their different approaches and different stances, Stephen and Albee do not disagree in any strong sense. Albee doubts Bentham's intellectual contribution but not his political influence. And Stephen's disregard of theological utilitarianism is not as stark when one discovers that he elsewhere describes it as the "dominant school" of ethics in the eighteenth century.[17] Both Albee and Stephen recognize that theological utilitarianism arose prior to its secular counterpart and was far more significant in the eighteenth century.

While the narrow scope of Stephen's book is explained by his focus on a political sect, later works adopted Stephen's narrow scope without his justification. In 1928, Élie Halévy's *The Growth of Philosophical Radicalism* appeared in English translation. Halévy treats utilitarianism as synonymous with "philosophical radicalism," arguing that "in Jeremy Bentham, Philosophical Radicalism had its great man."[18] In this way, Halévy intentionally limits his scope, but he also restricts the term "utilitarian" to a narrow tradition of thought.[19] Moreover, while he does briefly mention one theological utilitarian as a forerunner of Bentham, he immediately dismisses all theological elements as "foreign to the spirit of the doctrine."[20] Halévy's book was followed by John Plamenatz's *The English Utilitarians* (1949), an intellectual history of utilitarianism that almost completely ignores its theological proponents. Plamenatz takes Thomas Hobbes to be the primary precursor to Bentham. The one theological utilitarian discussed is William Paley, but he is dismissed as "a disciple of Hobbes" and only a "quasi-utilitarian."[21]

This mid-century narrative has become the popular picture, and the disregard for or dismissal of the theological proponents of utilitarianism remains surprisingly common. Consider two examples. Julia Driver's *Stanford Encyclopedia of Philosophy* article "The History of Utilitarianism" claims that Bentham gives "the first systematic account of utilitarianism." It contains a section on precursors that includes theological utilitarians, but it quickly dismisses their importance with the claim that theological utilitarianism is "not theoretically clean in the sense that it isn't clear what essential work God does, at least in terms of normative ethics."[22] Even if this claim were true, which it is not, it would hardly challenge their importance in the history of utilitarianism. Bart Schultz's recent book, *The Happiness Philosophers: The Lives and Works of the Great Utilitarians*, scarcely mentions the theological utilitarians. Schultz is quite careful about his language. He is interested in "classical" or "nontheological" utilitarianism. Most often, he just qualifies his objects of study as the "great" utilitarians. But while he is careful not to claim that Godwin or Bentham were "founders" of utilitarianism, his book gives that impression by playing into the standard picture. Indeed, three of the four blurbs on the back of the book describe it as an account of the lives of the "founders" of utilitarianism.

Even when taken more seriously, theological utilitarianism is too often treated as an attempt to synthesize Christianity and utilitarianism. Frederick Rosen, in an otherwise important book, argues that William Paley, the most famous theological utilitarian, attempts a synthesis between secular utilitarianism and Christianity.[23] This sort of picture accounts for theological utilitarianism as an attempt to absorb an influential secular ethic into Christianity, disregarding the intellectual tradition on which Paley draws.

The failure to attend to the theological proponents of utilitarianism, which Philip Schofield has recently described as a "significant gap in historiography," remains a problem in the history of moral philosophy.[24] The most important scholar calling attention to this problem has been James Crimmins.[25] Crimmins has for several decades insisted upon the importance of the theological utilitarians and sought to make their works available.[26] Crimmins's efforts have more recently received additional support from the appearance of Niall O'Flaherty's *Utilitarianism in the Age of Enlightenment*, which marks an important moment in the process of historical correction.[27] O'Flaherty demonstrates with force and clarity the importance of a tradition of eighteenth-century theological utilitarianism, which culminates in the work of William Paley, whose influence in the late eighteenth and early nineteenth centuries far overshadowed the almost unknown works of Bentham.

The work of Crimmins and O'Flaherty ought to change the way the history of utilitarianism is taught. Yet, as all good scholarship should, these works raise new questions. Theological utilitarianism is historically prior to its "classical" counterpart; the former was also intellectually dominant over the latter well into the nineteenth century, both in academic respectability and social influence. How, then, did theological utilitarianism originate? What motivated Christian ethicists to develop a utilitarian theory of morality? Theological utilitarianism is not an odd hybridity created by the synthesis of a "secular" ethical system with Christian ethics. It is, rather, a development internal to Christian ethics. This seemingly strange development within the Christian moral tradition requires more scholarly attention.

Crimmins and O'Flaherty demonstrate the importance of the eighteenth-century tradition of theological utilitarianism. This book seeks to uncover its theological roots. Moreover, it widens the scope of attention from utilitarianism in particular to consequentialism in general. I am interested, as I explained above, in consequentialist moral rationality, a form of rationality that predates eighteenth-century theological utilitarianism. To see the innovations that made theological utilitarianism possible, we must begin in the seventeenth century. By uncovering the theological roots of consequentialism, we gain not only a more accurate history but also a better sense of the contingency of widely influential forms of thought.

While this book offers a novel intellectual origin story, it does not do so according to some of the common norms of the origin-story genre. For this reason, some readers have questioned whether the book is an origin story at all.[28] Intellectual origin stories often break views down into their component parts and seek out the earlier developments of those parts among "precursors" to the view. They then trace the evolution of the component parts until they are synthesized in the work of the "founder" of the view. My approach is quite different. I begin not with parts but with wholes, which I call moral cosmologies. My story starts with a widespread seventeenth-century theological moral cosmology and traces its development into a new, consequentialist alternative. Instead of focusing on separable components, I focus on conceptual developments that transform the structure of the whole.

I have no objection to breaking down views into component parts and seeking out precursors that develop and transmit those parts. I have

learned a great deal from origin stories of this type. In the case of consequentialism, though, such an approach has one very notable flaw: it
systematically occludes the larger theological context in which the components develop and to which they are meant to contribute. In order to
understand the theological development of consequentialism, I focus primarily on that which is missing from earlier work. For this reason, some
component parts may receive less attention than they might otherwise
have, but the result is a more expansive view of the whole.

Teleology, Consequentialism, and Modern Morality

Despite the shortcomings of the history of moral philosophy literature
just surveyed, the idea that modern morality has theological roots is quite
common in many fields of study. One might think that we could find a
better account of the theological origins of consequentialism by turning
from the works of historians of philosophy to the works of theologians
and other scholars with explicit theological interests. Unfortunately, even
among those who explicitly argue that modern morality has theological
roots, one finds a striking lack of attention to consequentialism.

Theological stories of modern morality are found most notably among
scholars who employ them in order to critique modern moral and political
thought. Often building on the works of Elizabeth Anscombe and Alasdair
MacIntyre, these scholars tell theologically rich stories in which medieval
teleological virtue ethics, which was founded on the rational pursuit of
common goods, gives way to modern ruled-based ethics, which is at best
unable to achieve rational consensus and at worst outright incoherent—
and in either case ultimately reducible to the will to power.

The movement known as Radical Orthodoxy has perhaps been the
most notable example of this project among theologians. The problems
of modern moral and social thought, according to John Milbank, can be
traced back to errors in late medieval theology: the univocity of being, voluntarism, and nominalism.[29] And religious philosophers and theologians
are not alone in seeking the origins of modern morality in theology. The
Catholic historian Brad Gregory has argued that modern morality, which
he considers fundamentally incoherent, is an unintended byproduct of
the Protestant Reformation.

These big narratives generally agree that the problem—or at least a
central problem—with modern morality is its rejection of teleology, that
is, an approach to ethics centered on the pursuit of an end or ends. Ancient and medieval morality, they argue, was centered on the rational and

common pursuit of the good. Modern morality subordinates and often subjectivizes the good. It treats morality as a system of rights and obligations meant to prevent harm and ensure social peace among those unable to agree on goods and ends worth pursuing together. But these rights and obligations, the critics argue, are rationally indefensible. Anscombe famously argues that modern talk about obligation exists as a holdover from Christian notions of divine law. Modern moral philosophers, she claims, continue to argue about our moral obligations without realizing that talk of moral obligation shorn of a divine legislator is fundamentally incoherent.[30] MacIntyre develops a similar argument, mocking modern moral philosophy as an attempt to justify irrational cultural taboos and comparing human rights to witches and unicorns.[31] Moral obligations and rights used to make sense, according to MacIntyre, within a teleological context of a community pursuing the good together. But absent such a teleological context, modern moral philosophy has been unable to justify them.

Picking up from Anscombe and MacIntyre, Gregory and Milbank tell similar stories. Gregory claims that "a transformation from a substantive morality of the good to a formal morality of rights constitutes the central change in Western ethics over the past half millennium, in terms of theory, practices, laws, and institutions."[32] Gregory's story begins from MacIntyre's observation that modern moral debates appear to be intractable. The reason, for Gregory as for MacIntyre, lies in the decline of Aristotelian teleology. Rights, he goes on to argue, were originally rooted in a teleological morality oriented to the individual and communal good. The Reformers transformed the notion of rights by turning it against the Roman church and insisting on the priority of individual conscience. Nonetheless, rights remained rooted in a vision of the good, which, despite religious disagreement, was widely accepted into the nineteenth century. While the focus on rights marginalized the good, rights remained implicitly rooted in shared convictions about the good. Only when a substantive percentage of people in formerly Christian societies rejected Christianity did it become clear that formal rights alone cannot be rationally justified. Moral philosophers have, Gregory contends, failed to justify human rights, and no other foundation of morality has been found. As a result, morality has been reduced to expressions of individual preference without rational grounding. Gregory agrees with MacIntyre: belief in human rights is comparable to belief in unicorns or witches.

Milbank, too, offers a variant of this story. Modern social thought, in Milbank's telling, "begins with human persons as individuals and yet defines their individuality essentialistically, as 'will' or 'capacity' or 'impulse to self-preservation.'"[33] This conception of persons, according to Milbank, has its roots in late medieval conceptions of God, which were then applied to human beings. In the heightened importance of divine freedom and power among the late medieval voluntarists—and especially in the centrality of the limitation of God's *potentia absoluta* through covenant—one finds the roots of a view of the self defined ultimately by power but socially limited through contractual rights and obligations. The ethical and political enterprise is then best understood as the imposition of contractual limits on the exercise of individual will and power. Moral philosophy, instead of beginning from the good, becomes a project of negotiating the clash of individual wills. The centrality of rights in modern morality stems from a new vision of social life as a contractual creation of otherwise free individuals, each of whom chooses to give up some autonomy for the sake of the support and protection of society. The goods individuals pursue within the realm of their rights are subjective and private.

The increased focus on rights in modern moral philosophy is indubitable. Yet the common claim that an ethics of rights has replaced an ethics of the good in modern morality completely ignores consequentialism, which has been one of the most influential views in Anglophone moral philosophy for centuries. Indeed, the claim that belief in rights is unjustified was made perhaps most famously by Jeremy Bentham, who, long before MacIntyre, called natural rights "nonsense upon stilts."[34] Among the figures just discussed, only MacIntyre gives any real attention to utilitarianism, but he ignores its theological roots and treats its classical expression as simple incoherence.

In contrast to these big theological narratives, the brief account of the origin of consequentialism by John Perry is the best theological work available on the topic. Utilitarianism, he argues, "was originally a Christian endeavor, and its earliest systematic defenses were works of moral theology."[35] It emerged as one teleological approach to ethics among others. He is exactly right on both points. But Perry's aim is to reduce the distance between utilitarianism and other teleologies, presenting them as a single family of views. The only real difference, he suggests, is that utilitarianism becomes a reform project. The value of Perry's argument is that it displays the parallels between consequentialism and other teleologies, encouraging a richer dialogue between views that are often seen as opposing. Yet in doing so, Perry misrepresents the differences between consequentialist teleology and its competitors.

Consequentialism is one teleological approach among others, but it is a distinctive way of thinking about goods, ends, and our relationship to them. These differences must be understood. Still, as Perry helps us to see, the persistence of consequentialism in modernity belies the idea that

modern morality is only about subjective rights and contractual obligations. For almost two centuries after Aristotelian natural teleology lost
its prestige in most elite academic circles, theological consequentialism
remained an important intellectual force. Secular consequentialism continues to shape moral and political thought to this day. Attending to the
history of consequentialism, then, allows us to see the ongoing importance of teleology and the good in modern ethics.

Even more importantly, attending to the persistence of teleology is crucial to the effort in which these scholars are engaged: critically evaluating
modern moral thought. Attending to consequentialism as the major form
of modern teleology allows us to recognize shifting ways of conceiving
goods and ends and their relationships to human agency and rationality.
Teleology does not simply persist; it changes. These shifts remain with us
and are crucial to understanding the sense, discussed above, that consequentialist forms of thought are uniquely rational. When big theological
narratives of modern morality ignore consequentialism, they fail to include these shifts. Indeed, some of those seeking to recover pre-modern
natural teleology fail to recognize how much their view of goods, ends,
agency, and rationality is shaped by the consequentialist tradition. By attending to the history of consequentialism—and particularly the earliest
theological development of consequentialism—we can better understand
the limits and possibilities of teleological ethics today.[36]

Terminology and Definitions

How one tells the history of consequentialism depends in significant part
on what one takes consequentialism to be. As with utilitarianism, one can
define it so generally that one can find it in antiquity—an approach that
has been attractive to utilitarians[37]—or one can use it to pick out a view
that emerges in early modernity. I am interested in the latter usage. Consequentialism is now generally taken to be the family of views of which
utilitarianism is one member.[38] How broadly it ought to be defined is a
matter of some disagreement. The broadest definition, which is also one
of the more common, is this: consequentialism is a view according to
which all moral properties depend on consequences. Such a definition is
reasonable but also quite expansive. As is sometimes observed, it includes
absurd views, such as the view that the morality of acts depends solely
on their contribution to the number of goats in Texas.[39] A more precise
specification will better highlight the distinctive view that emerges in the
seventeenth century and remains attractive to so many today.

I will add two further qualifications to the above definition. First, moral properties depend not simply on consequences but on the *value* of consequences. A consequentialist view, in my terminology, is one that judges acts, rules, laws, or character traits by their causal contribution to valuable or disvaluable states of affairs. While I will call a view consequentialist even if it does not require the maximization of valuable consequences, all of the views discussed in this book are maximizing views, largely because they begin with divine morality. It might be reasonable to think that an act is good if it produces some good consequences or slightly more good than bad consequences, but if good consequences are what make an act good, then the act with the best consequences seems to be best. And God, naturally, is thought to do what is best. Consequentialist views that begin with God tend to conclude that we, too, ought to do what is best.

A second qualification: I will only call a view consequentialist if the value of the consequences is treated agent-neutrally. This qualification rules out egoistic views. Some, for example, will call egoistic hedonism—a view according to which one should always do what maximizes one's own pleasure in the long run—a consequentialist view. I will not. Grouping egoistic views with agent-neutral views occludes what is interesting and distinctive about the innovations that occur in the seventeenth century— for example, the construction of the very idea that the states of affairs that result from actions are bearers of value that can be calculated impersonally and that morally good actions are those that contribute to this value.

The question of what makes particular outcomes valuable remains open under the definition I have provided. For the thinkers discussed in this book, the answer is generally either total happiness or total perfection or both. Following standard terminology, when the view specifies that happiness is the good and that happiness is to be maximized, I will call that view utilitarianism. Hence, my terminology will shift over the course of the book. The first two parts speak primarily of consequentialism. In part III, I begin to speak of utilitarianism. I could, in order to maintain more consistency, use the term "hedonistic, maximizing consequentialism" instead of utilitarianism. But I prefer the simpler term and the one that more obviously calls attention to the close connection between the theological traditions I will be discussing and the later tradition of "classical" utilitarianism.

I have been saying that consequentialist views determine "moral properties" by the agent-neutral value of consequences. Most contemporary consequentialist views determine all moral properties by looking to consequences. The seventeenth- and eighteenth-century views I will discuss, by contrast, do not always determine *all* moral properties by consequences. In particular, some believe that actions are good or bad due to their consequences but that those actions do not become obligatory until God commands them. Such views might be seen as hybrids of consequentialism and divine command theory. Since I am focused on consequentialism, I will refer to these views as consequentialist throughout the book. I do not mean to discount the importance of divine command to these thinkers, only to call attention to the fact that their views are essential to the tradition of theological consequentialism. Moreover, while human morality depends in these views at least partially on the addition of divine command, divine morality is sensitive only to goodness and is thus consequentialist without qualification.

Let me also clarify my use of the term "teleology." I will call an ethical view teleological if moral properties depend on a relation to an end. Consequentialism is a version of teleology, one that takes the end to be the realization of agent-neutral value and the relation to the end to be one of causal promotion.[40] Eudaimonistic views, according to which moral properties depend on the relationship to an agent's happiness or perfection, are also teleological. Chapter 1 discusses a broad family of non-consequentialist teleological views according to which the end is God and moral properties depend on relation to God. One goal of this book is to call attention to the fact that there are many different teleological views. Though consequentialism is a latecomer to the club, it tends to dominate the terrain, often occluding other alternatives.

One final term requires an introduction: "consequentialist moral cosmology." While the aim of the book is to explain the emergence of consequentialism in the form we recognize today, the primary focus of the book—the main character, we might say—is the consequentialist moral cosmology. The consequentialist moral cosmology, I argue, is the larger theological vision in which consequentialist ideas first emerge, and it is a predecessor to utilitarianism, both theological and classical. It is a view that encompasses theology, ethics, and cosmology. It includes the following three elements: (1) A consequentialist view of human morality according to which the right action is the one that contributes most to a maximally good state of creation. (2) A view of divine morality according to which God acts according to the same consequentialist moral principles that bind human beings. (3) An account of divine authority over rational creatures grounded in the fact that God shares the same moral aim as rational creatures and is best able to direct them on how to pursue it. Rational creatures ought to obey God because God knows best how to realize maximal goodness in creation. An implication of these elements is that God and rational creatures form a single moral community founded on shared moral principles and a shared end. While nonrational creatures do not act on moral principles, they too are ordered to the same end, something we can infer from the fact that God does all things to maximize goodness in creation. The whole cosmos, then, is ordered to the realization of maximal goodness.

I call the conjunction of these three views a "cosmology" rather than an "ethic" or even a "moral theology" because it encompasses a comprehensive picture of the cosmos as a single moral system directed to a single moral end: the realization of maximal goodness. God pursues this end perfectly. Rational creatures pursue it when they act according to reason and when they obey God. The rest of creation pursues it inadvertently under the guidance of divine providence. By calling it a cosmology, I aim to highlight the way it functions as a successor notion to the dominant medieval, Renaissance, and Reformation view of the entire cosmos as a single system oriented toward God as its end, which I discuss in more detail in the first chapter. Let us call this earlier view, by contrast, a theocentric moral cosmology.

I want to be clear that "consequentialist moral cosmology" is an invented term of art. Its function in the story I tell is like that of a Weberian ideal type. While several figures hold the views that together constitute the consequentialist moral cosmology, no one names the view or actively defends it as such. I use the term to illuminate a distinct trajectory of thought and trace its development over time. The three elements of the consequentialist moral cosmology come together in the work of the figures discussed in part I, Henry More and Richard Cumberland. They remain attractive to the figures discussed in part II, but tensions begin to arise between the three elements and as a result of their implications. While no figure is explicitly defending or modifying the consequentialist moral cosmology, keeping these three elements in view allows us to see key dynamics in the development and evolution of theological consequentialism.

The Rise and Fall of the Consequentialist Moral Cosmology

If the consequentialist moral cosmology is the main character, the narrative arc of the book is the story of its rise and fall. The consequentialist moral cosmology arises in the mid-seventeenth century among the originators of consequentialism. It faces mounting pressure over several decades, driven largely by theological concerns about evil, and it is finally abandoned in the early to mid-eighteenth century. Its demise, however, does not mark the end of consequentialism. Instead, consequentialism takes new forms—in particular, a view I will call, following Colin Heydt, Anglican utilitarianism[41]—and only grows in influence.

Part I tells the story of the invention of consequentialist moral rationality and the consequentialist moral cosmology in the mid-seventeenth century. Consequentialism, I argue, arises from an attempt to defeat voluntarist theological and ethical views, which were quite influential in early modern thought. Rather than reclaiming the dominant forms of anti-voluntarist theology and ethics, which were broadly Aristotelian, seventeenth-century thinkers like Henry More (chapter 2) and Richard Cumberland (chapter 3) drew from newly ascendant forms of thought—most notably the geometric and the mechanistic—in order to construct a new approach to moral rationality and a new theological picture of the cosmos. The result is the consequentialist moral cosmology.

Today, consequentialism is considered a revisionary approach to morality. Rather than seeking to affirm intuitive moral judgments, it subjects all moral intuitions to rigorous, rational analysis. It can generate counterintuitive results, including approval of the violation of cherished moral principles (e.g., a prohibition against pushing people in front of trolleys). The early consequentialist theological tradition, by contrast, was not particularly interested in revising Christian morality. For More and Cumberland, consequentialism provides a new justification for Christian morality. The commands of the Decalogue and Jesus's teachings about neighbor love are taken to be the divine commands by which God governs creation for the best consequences. And theological beliefs about divine providence function to ensure that obedience to God is never ultimately wrong.

Crucial to the development of consequentialism as a new justification for morality is the invention of consequentialist moral rationality. Many of More's and Cumberland's innovations are subtle, but they are also profound. We see in More and Cumberland the development of new ways of conceiving goodness, ends, and agency. We also see the development of a new picture of causal responsibility that grants heightened moral significance to efficient causation. These innovations are missed by those stories of modern morality that ignore the persistence of teleology. Much of part I is focused on tracing and understanding these developments. Those only interested in the invention of consequentialism need only read part I. Those interested in the further development of the theological consequentialist tradition—and especially in how it became what we now call utilitarianism—will want to read the remaining two parts of the book.

While More and Cumberland were extremely influential on subsequent generations, the story of part II is the story not of the triumph of the consequentialist moral cosmology but of its breakdown. Though the focus of this book is on British theology and ethics, part II begins with an intrusion from the continent. In 1697, Pierre Bayle published the first edition of his *Dictionnaire historique et critique*. Bayle's *Dictionnaire* is a massive achievement, covering topics from nearly every realm of human knowledge, but the work achieved instant notoriety and controversy due in particular to a few key theological issues. None was more important than Bayle's treatment of evil, which is the subject of chapter 4. Bayle argued at length and in multiple articles that no rational explanation can be given for the existence and extent of evil in a world created by a perfectly good God, especially the God of Christianity. The controversy over the work quickly reached Britain.

The controversy about evil had important implications for the consequentialist moral cosmology of More and Cumberland. In their desire to defeat voluntarism, More and Cumberland treat God as one moral agent among others in the moral community, subject to the same moral or rational necessities. What Bayle presses over and over again is that God is not simply one moral agent among others. For Bayle, God is responsible not only for God's actions but for everything, including the actions of free creatures. If God is morally bound to realize the best possible state of creation, then creation must be as perfect as it can be. The apparent imperfections of the world become evidence against the anti-voluntarist cause.

Those attracted to the consequentialist moral cosmology did not remain silent. Indeed, Britain produced the first two major responses to Bayle: that of William King and that of Lord Anthony Ashley Cooper, who is better known simply as Shaftesbury. The fifth chapter centers on King's *De origine mali* and the sixth on Shaftesbury's *Characteristicks of Men, Manners, Opinions, Times*. Chapter 7 turns to the appropriation of Shaftesbury's theodicy and ethics by one of his most important intellectual descendants, Francis Hutcheson. King, Shaftesbury, and Hutcheson, I argue, are all intellectual descendants of More and Cumberland, defending central elements of the consequentialist moral cosmology. At the same time, they each introduce innovations motivated largely by the attempt to respond to Bayle's arguments about evil. As a result, the moral community between God and creatures that is so important to More and Cumberland begins to break down as a product of efforts to defend God's moral perfection by consequentialist standards.

The result of the struggle with evil discussed in part II is the decline of the consequentialist moral cosmology. Its distinctive combination of elements, which proved so effective in combating seventeenth-century voluntarism, were ultimately unable to account for the existence and extent of evil in the world. The later inheritors of consequentialism reject central aspects of More and Cumberland's project, including their anti-voluntarism, their commitment to divine-human moral community, and their account of divine authority.

The rejection of these key features of More and Cumberland's project, however, is not the rejection of consequentialism. The major tradition of eighteenth-century consequentialism, Anglican utilitarianism, carries forward many of More and Cumberland's innovations. Above all, consequentialist moral rationality, with its new picture of goods, ends, agency, and causation, is not only embraced but largely taken for granted. What was innovative in the mid-seventeenth century is, by the mid-eighteenth century, commonplace.

Part III centers on the birth of Anglican utilitarianism in the works of Edmund Law and his circle at Cambridge from the 1720s to the 1740s. Chapter 8 treats John Gay's initial articulation of the ethical position, and chapter 9 situates it in its larger context in Edmund Law's comprehensive rational theology in his *An Essay on the Origin of Evil*, a translation of King's *De origine mali* filled with extensive notes. Anglican utilitarianism, I argue in these two chapters, arises in large part as a synthesis of the works discussed in part II. The context in which Anglican utilitarian ethics gains its appeal is provided by a rationalist theology that seeks to reconcile a morally perfect consequentialist Creator with a world marked by sin, pain, and death. It includes features such as egoism and hedonism that are surprising occurrences within the Christian moral tradition. These features appear to lend credibility to the idea that theological utilitarianism is an attempt to accommodate a secular position within Christian theology. Situating these features within the larger Anglican utilitarian theological project, however, belies such a view. They are perfectly intelligible in light of Law's effort to develop a rationally satisfactory theodicy on consequentialist grounds. In their efforts to preserve the moral perfection of God as a consequentialist, the Anglican utilitarians ultimately reject human moral community with God, arguing that human beings could not possibly be motivated by the same end or the same reasons as God. Human beings can only be moved by the prospects of their own pleasure; God alone ensures that universal pleasure is maximized. Voluntarism makes a surprising return in a tradition founded on its rejection.

The end of the consequentialist moral cosmology, then, is not the end of consequentialism. From the breakdown of the consequentialist moral cosmology emerges a new form of consequentialism, Anglican utilitarianism. Here we reach the terrain covered by the histories of utilitarianism discussed above. Building on the work of Crimmins and O'Flaherty, I argue for the historical importance of the theological tradition of utilitarianism. No history of utilitarianism is complete without understanding these earlier sources and their role in transmitting consequentialist ideas into the nineteenth century. The story of this book ends with Anglican utilitarianism, the last significant school of theological consequentialism.

The book concludes by returning to the present and reconsidering debates about consequentialism in light of its theological origins. Contemporary consequentialism, I argue, bears the traces of its history. The standard critiques of consequentialism result from the elimination of the theological premises from which it was constructed. One possible response to this recognition is a return to theological consequentialism, which resolves some—though not all—of the problems posed by the objections. Ultimately, though, I argue that a better way forward is to rethink the early modern innovations regarding goods, ends, and agency, which first gave rise to consequentialist moral rationality. I illustrate by returning to the trolley problem.

PART I

*The Consequentialist
Moral Cosmology*

1

God and Morality in the Seventeenth Century

Colin Heydt begins his essay "Utilitarianism before Bentham" by listing the challenges and advantages of telling the history of utilitarianism.[1] One advantage, according to Heydt, is that the origin of utilitarianism, unlike that of many long-standing positions, can be dated. Utilitarianism, he writes, began in Britain between 1660 and 1730. Despite common tendencies to date the origin of utilitarianism to Bentham's writings or to find it in the ancient world, Heydt rightly insists on a late seventeenth- to early eighteenth-century range.[2] Even so, the story of utilitarianism—and, with it, the story of consequentialism—cannot be quite so neatly contained. While the major works in which utilitarianism began to take shape were written after 1660, those works cannot be properly understood apart from an intellectual context with a much longer history. This chapter sketches the relevant intellectual context, beginning where many stories about modern morality begin: with the rise of voluntarist theology in the late medieval period.

While the rise of voluntarist theology is widely cited as a crucial factor in the emergence of modern morality, the role of voluntarist theology has been described in many different ways. For some, as I discuss below, modern morality is essentially voluntarist. The explanations vary. Modern morality is voluntarist because of its emphasis on freedom and autonomy or because of its focus on law and obligation or because of its vision of social life as defined by contractual relations. In stark contrast, others describe modern morality as anti-voluntarist. In this view, the project of modern morality—or at least of the most significant branches of it—arises from efforts to find an alternative to voluntarist theology.

The fundamental reason for these disagreements, I argue, is a lack of clarity on the meaning of the term "voluntarism." The first task of this chapter, therefore, is to clarify the multiple meanings of the term in order to begin to get a handle on its significance. Once we have a clear picture of what voluntarism means, we can begin to inquire into its relationship to consequentialism. At this point, I turn to J. B. Schneewind's article "Voluntarism and the Origins of Utilitarianism." Schneewind is among those who see modern morality as a product of the rejection of voluntarist theology. Like many others, he conflates different ideas under the term "voluntarism," which complicates his argument about the anti-voluntarist origins of modern morality. Nonetheless, once we have sorted out the relevant meanings of voluntarism, I argue that we can affirm Schneewind's thesis that the development of utilitarianism in particular and consequentialism in general is motivated, at least in part, by a reaction against certain aspects of voluntarist theology.

Schneewind, therefore, points us in the right direction. His argument, however, has a fundamental flaw. As I explain below, Schneewind takes it for granted that consequentialist moral rationality was already available as an option—indeed, he suggests that it was the only option—for early modern ethicists looking for an account of divine teleological rationality with which to counter voluntarism. In doing so, Schneewind presupposes precisely what he should be explaining. Moreover, he demonstrates what I claimed in the introduction: that the seeming naturalness of consequentialist moral rationality interferes with our histories of its emergence. Schneewind is right that the early consequentialists were seeking an account of teleological moral rationality to make sense of divine action, but he is wrong to think that no other alternatives were available.

This point is essential for the argument of the book. Only once we understand the nature of the available seventeenth-century alternatives can we see consequentialist moral rationality as an invention rather than a natural way of thinking that was simply latent, waiting for someone to employ it in ethics. I therefore spend the remainder of the chapter briefly surveying three seventeenth-century alternatives to voluntarist theology, each of which employs a non-consequentialist form of teleological rationality. More than three alternatives were available. My choice is strategic. Because I argue in the next chapter that the Cambridge philosopher and theologian Henry More first develops consequentialist moral rationality, I center my survey on the anti-voluntarist traditions to which More had the most direct access: Thomistic, Reformed, and Platonic. In each case, I begin by describing More's relationship to the tradition. This approach has the additional purpose of introducing More's intellectual background, which will be important for the argument of the next chapter.

One additional flaw in Schneewind's picture is his assumption that the voluntarism versus anti-voluntarism debate is a debate about whether or not God and human beings share a "moral community"; that is, whether or not God and human beings are subject to the same moral principles. This claim, again, is a product of the failure to attend to the wider set of alternatives available in the seventeenth century. While I highlight differences between the three non-voluntarist views surveyed below, I also argue that they share a common structure regarding the relationship between divine and human morality. In this common structure, God and human beings share an end without sharing moral principles. God is thus neither inside Schneewind's moral community nor outside of it. This shared view of divine and human morality, I argue, is part of a larger cosmic vision, which I call the theocentric moral cosmology.

Within the larger argument of the book, this chapter functions primarily to contextualize Henry More and the other early consequentialists in order to better understand their works and specify how their views differ from important seventeenth-century alternatives. But it also has an additional purpose. It demonstrates that three major seventeenth-century views are all versions of the theocentric moral cosmology, a view which will serve throughout the book as a fruitful contrast with the consequentialist moral cosmology developed by Henry More and Richard Cumberland. And in the book's conclusion, I return to these seventeenth-century alternative approaches to moral rationality, arguing that they offer insights with which the now dominant consequentialist approach to moral rationality ought to be supplemented.

Voluntarism and Modern Morality

I begin with the history and meaning of voluntarism. The term "voluntarism" generally indicates an elevation of will over intellect. While the term is vague, it no doubt names a meaningful development in late medieval thought. What happened? We still lack an adequate account of the intricacies of late medieval theology. Francis Oakley, however, has painted an obviously simplistic but still insightful picture of the history of Christian theology that illuminates the emergence of late medieval voluntarism. Oakley's picture, in brief, is this.

The first several centuries of the Common Era witnessed a remarkable fusion of ideas about the divine from multiple sources: the demiurge of Plato's *Timaeus* was fused with Aristotle's unmoved mover to create a new picture of the divine. Plato's forms were then reinterpreted as ideas in the divine mind. Thus, Oakley writes, "emerged the notion of a transcendent God, at once the highest good or final cause to which all things lovingly aspire" and "the first efficient cause to which all things owe their existence."[3] Then, in "a further and quite stunning conflation," this philosophical God was identified with the biblical God of Abraham, Isaac, and Jacob. Philo blazed this trail, and Augustine completed it.

This synthesis, while of enduring influence, was not, according to Oakley, stable. The Greek notions of the divine, which tended to identify God with the rational order of the cosmos, were not easily reconciled with the biblical God of freedom and almighty power. The tension, already present in Augustine, was greatly heightened in the twelfth and thirteenth centuries by the recovery of the Aristotelian corpus together with its Islamic interpreters. Aquinas sought to incorporate the new Aristotelian ideas into Christian theology. In the years after his death, a negative reaction followed.[4] For many theologians, Aquinas's eternal law, which is the very reason of God by which creation is governed, threatened to subordinate God to the rational order of the cosmos. His thirteenth- and fourteenth-century critics, "taking the omnipotence of God as their fundamental principle," increasingly emphasized divine freedom from and power over the rational order of creation.[5] God's *potentia absoluta*, previously understood as an abstract possibility of a power that was decisively determined as *potentia ordinata*, became the real, looming possibility that God might at any moment override the natural order. Everything not logically impossible had to remain within the absolute power of God, and the desire to protect divine omnipotence tended to expand the conceived realm of logical possibility. One result was nominalism, a view that rejected the metaphysics of essences and thus further expanded the sphere of divine freedom. Another was a move toward an ethics centered on obedience to the divine will rather than on the rational pursuit of creaturely perfection in accordance with the rational order of creation.[6]

In Oakley's picture, the rise of voluntarism has its roots in the worry that the biblical God was being limited by the Aristotelian vision of a rationally ordered cosmos. The effect of the increasing emphasis on divine freedom and power in the late medieval period was profound precisely because so much philosophical thought was built on Greek foundations. The elevation of God's freedom rendered the order of creation—including its moral order—increasingly contingent. Ethics, for some voluntarist theologians, is rooted not in a fixed rational order but in the commands freely willed by God. Moreover, voluntarist theologians tended to elevate the will in human beings as well, emphasizing human freedom and individuality. Human will, like divine will, took on a new significance.

The idea that modern morality is a product of late medieval voluntarism is a common scholarly narrative, and any attempt to understand the theological roots of a modern approach to morality like consequentialism must reckon with it. Consider, for example, the work of John Milbank. Modern social thought, as John Milbank puts it, "begins with human persons as individuals and yet defines their individuality essentialistically, as 'will' or 'capacity' or 'impulse to self-preservation.' "[7] This view differs from ancient and medieval teleological views of the human person. How did this view of human beings arise? The answer is that it was "theologically promoted" by a late medieval voluntarist view of God in which unconstrained divine will and power were elevated above divine rationality and goodness.[8] The new vision of the human person followed in the image of the new vision of God. And this new vision of the human person came along with a new vision of social life as formed by contractual constraints on the radically free human will, which is oriented toward private goods. Modern morality took these views of individuals and societies for granted, working out the conditions of fair cooperation among free individual subjects. For this reason (among others), Milbank dates the advent of modernity back to late medieval voluntarism.

Milbank's story of modernity, which traces modernity back to the medieval voluntarist theology of John Duns Scotus, builds on earlier scholarship, but his version has been particularly influential. In his book-length critique of Milbank's "Scotus story," Daniel Horan traces its influence, finding it repeated by theologians, philosophers, literary theorists, historians, and writers of popular books.[9]

The political theorist Michael Gillespie offers a different but related view of the relationship between voluntarist theology and modernity. One finds among the late medieval voluntarists, Gillespie argues, "the birth or rebirth of a different kind of God, an omnipotent God of will who calls into question all of reason and nature and thus overturns all eternal standards of truth and justice, and good and evil."[10] This new view of God, he argues, destroyed medieval philosophy and theology. It also gave rise to a "new conception of man." In so doing, voluntarist theology became "the foundation for modernity as the realm of human self-assertion."[11]

In stories like those told by Milbank and Gillespie, one gets the impression that modern morality is essentially voluntarist. The modern self is the voluntarist self in whom will triumphs over nature and reason. Modern morality then arises as a system meant to constrain the radically free will for the sake of social peace. Virtues, final ends, and common goods are subordinated or dismissed, and law and obligation, which function to limit the realm of individual assertion, become the operative moral categories.

One finds a quite different picture of the significance of voluntarist theology for modern morality in the work of J. B. Schneewind. In his essay "Voluntarism and the Foundation of Ethics," Schneewind argues that many of the major theories of ethics "originated in the struggle against voluntarism."[12] Schneewind agrees that voluntarist theology plays a significant role in modern ethics, but he sees its primary role negatively: it was an opponent to be overcome. As an opponent, voluntarist theology set the terms of debate in certain ways and thus exerted an important, if inadvertent, influence. But the ethical views that ultimately triumphed in modern moral philosophy were anti-voluntarist.

So which is it? Is modern morality voluntarist (Milbank, Gillespie) or anti-voluntarist (Schneewind)? How are we to understand the existence of these two contrasting views of the role of voluntarism in modern morality? In outline, both are quite plausible. Modern morality is indeed marked by an emphasis on individuality, freedom, obligation, and social cooperation, and these features do reflect aspects of late medieval voluntarist theology. At the same time, many of the most notable early modern ethicists were vehement opponents of voluntarism, and their arguments clearly shaped the most important views in modern moral philosophy. But how can modern morality be both voluntarist and anti-voluntarist?

The problem with these disagreements is that they arise from a distinct lack of clarity about the term "voluntarism." The great Reformation historian Heiko Oberman, writing in 1963, expressed his doubt that the term was "at all helpful."[13] The situation has not notably improved. The term, Davey Henreckson writes, "gets bandied about with disconcerting ease" while its meaning "shifts in unpredictable ways."[14] None of the above sources grapples with the multiple related but different meanings of the term, leaving readers to fill in the silences. Given this state of affairs—and given the fact that the term "voluntarism" was only coined in the nineteenth century and played no role in these earlier debates[15]—the idea of dropping the term altogether is tempting. But it is now too important to the literature to ignore, and it does name something important, at least when suitably clarified.

When it comes to the emergence of consequentialism, Schneewind's view is the more insightful one: consequentialism has its roots in an anti-voluntarist reaction. The insight, though, can only be appreciated by clarifying the meaning of the term. In the essay "Voluntarism and the Foundation of Ethics," in which he argues for the anti-voluntarist roots of modern moral philosophy, Schneewind applies the term "voluntarism" to a number of related but importantly different ideas. In the very first paragraph alone, all of the following ideas are called voluntarist: (1) No cause or ground determines what God wills; (2) our moral obligations are explained solely by divine will; (3) God is incomprehensible to us; (4) God predestines who will be saved; (5) eternal truths such as those of mathematics are only true because God eternally wills them to be true.

Each of these ideas (except perhaps the third) is related to some important emphasis on the divine will. They are not, however, mutually entail-
ing. One can hold some without others. Grouping them together under
the single term "voluntarism" and then discussing its influence on modern
moral philosophy is sure to cause problems, as we can see in the drastically different accounts of what does or does not make modern morality
voluntarist.

Let us, therefore, distinguish several different meanings of the term.
While the term has been applied in many areas, including metaphysics and
epistemology, I focus only on the meanings of voluntarism most directly
relevant to ethics. Let us distinguish a few relevant meanings with four
different terms—"agential voluntarism," "ethical voluntarism," "legislative
voluntarism," and "soteriological voluntarism"—a list that is not meant to
be exhaustive.[16] The first term names a view about agency:

> *Agential voluntarism*: The will in itself is indifferent to the judgments of
> reason about the good to be done and the evil to be avoided. *Radical
> agential voluntarism* asserts that the will is capable of freely making its
> objects good or bad.

Agential voluntarism can, with some care, be applied to God. When applied to God, it tends to come packaged with the idea there are no standards of good or evil prior to the act of divine will and thus is a form of
radical agential voluntarism.[17]

The next two terms, ethical voluntarism and legislative voluntarism,
are views about the source of morality:

> *Ethical voluntarism*: The good to be done and the evil to be avoided are
> determined solely by the will of God, which chooses freely and not from
> prior or independent rational or moral standards.[18]

> *Legislative voluntarism*: All moral obligations arise from the commands
> of God.

These latter two views about morality can be placed on a spectrum. Ethical voluntarism is an extreme view that traces all normative judgments
about action back to a free, ungrounded, and inexplicable act of divine
will. Legislative voluntarism is a more moderate view. Legislative voluntarism is compatible with the view that some normative judgments
about human actions are founded on nature or reason. For example, human actions may be naturally good or bad independently of divine will.

They may even be morally good or bad independently of divine will.[19] But nothing, in this view, is morally obligatory unless God commands it. The other end of the spectrum can be called "ethical intellectualism." For the ethical intellectualist, all moral properties, including those that arise from divine commands, are ultimately grounded in reason or nature (which may include divine reason or divine nature). A command, including a divine command, can only make actions good or bad if reason or nature gives the commander the authority to do so. Ethical voluntarist and intellectualist views about morality are not, as is sometimes imagined, a simple dichotomy.

Finally, let us add one further term, which concerns the freedom of divine choice concerning salvation:

> *Soteriological voluntarism*: Nothing requires God to save creatures. God freely chooses whether to save creatures and, if so, which creatures to save.[20]

It is important to emphasize that this view does not entail that God chooses arbitrarily or lacks any reasons for one choice or another. It is only a denial of the necessity to save. Soteriological voluntarism is thus fully compatible (and often held together with) the rejection of all three forms of voluntarism listed above. Unlike the other forms of voluntarism, it is not particularly characteristic of late medieval theology. Rather, it is widely seen as orthodox because it ensures the gratuity of salvation by denying that God is in any way bound to save creatures. In fact, soteriological voluntarism is different enough from the other forms of voluntarism that its inclusion in the early modern debates about voluntarism causes quite a bit of confusion. Even in the seventeenth century, many of the critics of voluntarist theology—especially Henry More and other Cambridge Platonists—lumped all four of the above voluntarisms together. Anyone affirming soteriological voluntarism (with the general target being Calvinists) was assumed to be an agential and ethical voluntarist as well. Leaning on these sources, Schneewind repeats the mistake. To determine which aspects of his argument are correct, we must maintain the above distinctions. With this terminology in hand, let us turn to Schneewind's argument about the anti-voluntarist origin of utilitarianism.[21]

Utilitarianism and the Rejection of Ethical Voluntarism

Schneewind begins his essay by asking how and why utilitarianism arose in modern thought. "A quick answer," he writes, "would be: Utilitarianism is what you get when Christian love is combined with a strong rational decision procedure."[22] The importance of Christian love in early modern European thought requires no explanation. The question, then, is why morality would require a strong rational decision procedure. Schneewind answers that the need for a strong rational decision procedure arose from Christian opposition to voluntarism.

In this essay, Schneewind's two examples of voluntarists are René Descartes and Thomas Hobbes. Descartes's voluntarism lies in his claim that eternal truths, including those of mathematics, depend on the contingent and free will of God.[23] This view does not neatly fit my definitions above, but it does entail ethical voluntarism: truths about good and evil are true only because God wills them to be true. Hobbes's voluntarism lies in his claim that God's ability to determine moral standards depends solely on God's absolute power over us.[24] This view of the source of morality is quite different from Descartes's, but it, too, is a form of ethical voluntarism. While Schneewind uses the term loosely, let us focus on ethical voluntarism, which was the real target of the seventeenth-century anti-voluntarists who developed consequentialist moral rationality.

Schneewind's essay is not an attempt to sketch the full origin story of utilitarianism. He is only seeking to specify the intellectual and motivational sources behind it. As such, he illustrates the important role of anti-ethical-voluntarism with two examples: Richard Cumberland and G. W. Leibniz. A more complete picture would have to include Henry More, who, I will argue in the next chapter, is the first consequentialist. Fortunately, More, too, fits nicely in Schneewind's picture of the anti-ethical-voluntarist roots of utilitarianism.

More's rejection of ethical voluntarism was closely bound with his rejection of soteriological voluntarism. Indeed, he saw no difference between the two. He was raised, according to his autobiographical preface to the Latin edition of his works, "under *Parents* and a *Master* that were great *Calvinists*."[25] But from a young age, he was unable to "swallow down that hard Doctrine concerning *Fate* . . . or *Calvinistick Predestination*," a fact which earned him the rod. As More tells it, he rejected the doctrine of predestination due to "firm and unshaken Perswasion of the *Divine Justice* and *Goodness*," which, he insists, arose from "an *internal Sensation*" and was not "*ex Traduce*, or by way of *Propagation*."[26] Calvinists, of course, agree that God is perfectly good and just. Yet More believes that they attribute to God acts (i.e., creating people destined for damnation) that cannot be reconciled with divine goodness. For More, such a God can only be called good if goodness is determined solely by God's will. Soteriological voluntarism is thus linked to ethical voluntarism, which is the real target of his ire. In his 1668 theological dialogue, *Divine Dialogues*, More is harshly critical of "the Religion of the *Superlapsarians* [that is, predestinarians] the Object whereof is *Infinite Power* unmodified by either *Justice* or *Goodness*." He here attributes the Hobbesian God to Calvinists. He then goes on to argue that worshipping a deity with the power to arbitrarily determine what is good and evil is worse than worshipping the devil.[27]

More, we can see, shares in the adamant rejection of ethical voluntarism. How, then, does the rejection of ethical voluntarism lead to utilitarianism? To counter ethical voluntarism, Schneewind argues, its opponents claimed that God acts according to eternal moral truths. For the argument to succeed, the opponents of ethical voluntarism could not simply posit the existence of eternal moral truths. They had to identify those moral truths. Otherwise, God's actions and God's commands would appear entirely arbitrary to us, a result that would be practically indistinguishable from ethical voluntarism. These seventeenth-century moralists came to believe that defeating ethical voluntarism required an account of what Schneewind calls in *The Invention of Autonomy* a "moral community" between God and rational creatures. A moral community is one in which "members are mutually comprehensible because they accept the same principles," which means that moral principles "are valid for God as well as for us."[28] To secure such a community, Schneewind argues, one needs an account of the rationality of divine action. He continues:

> A teleological model of rationality was the only model available. We act rationally when we act deliberately to bring about some good end. If God acts rationally, that is what he does as well. When one possible action promises more good than the alternatives, the rational course is to pursue the greater good. If some single course of action produces more good than any of the others, then the most rational action is the one that maximizes good. If God is rational, then he wills to bring about the greatest good. And if morality requires us to do what God necessarily does, then we are on the road to utilitarianism.[29]

Divine rationality, in other words, takes the form of consequentialist moral rationality. The problem with Schneewind's argument is that he presupposes what he should be explaining, namely, the existence of consequentialist moral rationality. He believes that the only available account of divine rationality is a teleological one—that is, an account in which the rationality of action is derived from its orientation toward an end—and the only teleological option is consequentialist. If divine moral rationality is consequentialist, and if the moral standards for God are the same as those for human beings, then we are, as Schneewind says, "on the road to utilitarianism." Yet given the fact, never mentioned by Schneewind, that opposition to ethical voluntarism was not new in the seventeenth century, other models of the rationality of divine action must have been available. Schneewind may be right that the only models of rationality available were teleological, though this state of affairs would soon change. But teleological models of rationality are not necessarily consequentialist. In fact, different versions of teleological rationality were on offer among the major existing ethical intellectualist alternatives to ethical voluntarism.[30] When we recognize these alternatives, Schneewind's argument becomes implausible. The early consequentialists did not simply turn to an existing form of teleological rationality, much less the only available one. They invented a new one.

Attending to these ethical intellectualist alternatives challenges Schneewind's picture in another way. As we will see, these alternatives do not conform to Schneewind's characterization of ethical intellectualism because they do not place God inside the moral community, at least according to Schneewind's way of doing so: God does not share the same moral principles as human beings. Yet these alternatives do not place God outside of the moral community, either. The dichotomy between placement in and out of the moral community is a false one—or, perhaps better, it is one that only comes into being in the latter part of the seventeenth century. The early consequentialists like Henry More do indeed place God "inside" the moral community, arguing that God and human beings share eternal, immutable moral principles. But this move is itself an innovation. It is not essential to ethical intellectualism as such.

In order to demonstrate the innovative character of Henry More's approach to both moral rationality and divine-human moral community— the topic of the next chapter—I first briefly survey some already existing ethical intellectualist paths that he does not take. I will discuss the three that are most obviously available to him: Thomist, Reformed, and Platonic. All three, I will argue, provide an account of divine moral rationality that is teleological but not consequentialist. Moreover, all three fail to conform to Schneewind's either-or picture of divine-human moral community. In fact, all three share a similar structure: God and human beings act teleologically for the same end but not according to the same principles of action.

Each of the next three sections treats one of the available ethical intellectualist options. I begin each section by discussing More's connection to the relevant tradition, and then I briefly characterize the tradition's account of divine and human teleological rationality and divine-human moral community. By the end, the structure shared by all three should be evident.

Divine and Human Morality in Thomism

Ethical voluntarism, a late medieval development, had opponents from its inception. The established scholastic tradition of opposition to ethical voluntarism generally took the form of Thomism. While the Reformation transformed much about the late medieval intellectual world, it also left much in place, a fact that is perhaps especially true of the universities. More's education at Cambridge would have been decidedly Protestant but still deeply scholastic. Both the structure and the content of the bachelor's degree remained largely continuous through and beyond the English Reformation. Aristotle dominated the curriculum in both the arts and the sciences, though the Aristotle received was refracted through the great medieval scholastics, many of whom continued to be read and discussed.[31]

The theology curriculum, as one would expect, changed more after the Reformation than other fields of study did. In a random sampling of questions treated in the surviving notebooks from Cambridge at the start of the seventeenth century, William Costello finds that the majority of them take "specifically Protestant" positions. Nearly half of the questions, moreover, concern central topics of the Reformation: grace and justification.[32] That these questions rose to prominence and displaced earlier questions is significant. It does not, however, make the disputes any less scholastic. Not only did the methods of inquiry remain similar, but the categories employed were largely continuous with those of medieval scholasticism. And as John Patrick Donnelly has written, "Insofar as the roots of Protestant scholasticism go back to the Middle Ages, they tend to go back to the *via antiqua* and Thomism."[33] More's education would have introduced him to scholastic ethical intellectualism and thus, at least in some form, to Thomism.[34]

Let us, therefore, briefly consider how Thomism provides an ethical intellectualist alternative to ethical voluntarism.[35] For Aquinas, good and evil logically precede God's will, and God's will is moved by the good. Indeed, to possess a will is simply to be moved by the good that one intellectually apprehends.[36] What, then, is the good that moves God's will? In *Summa contra gentiles* I.72.4, Aquinas writes:

> [F]or each being endowed with a will the principal object willed is the ultimate end. For the end is willed through itself, and through it other

things become objects of will. But the ultimate end is God Himself, since He is the highest good, as has been shown. Therefore, God is the principal object of His will.

The principal object of God's will, which is God's final end, is the highest good, namely, Godself. There is no choice here between alternative ends. God necessarily (though also freely) wills Godself as final end.

The claim that God necessarily wills Godself as an end does not entail that all divine action is necessitated. God immediately and perfectly attains this end and is thus perfectly happy. Nothing is needed to complete the divine happiness, and God is in no way bound to create anything. God can choose freely whether to will Godself by creating or to will Godself without creating. And if God chooses to will Godself by creating, nothing requires the creation of one world or another. Aquinas has no problem saying that God could have created a better world.[37] But if God does choose to create, certain necessities follow. Most importantly, God can only will to create for Godself, meaning that God will be the final end of all creatures.[38] Human beings and all other creatures, therefore, have God as their final end. Human action is teleologically ordered as well, and good and evil in human actions depend on the relationship between those actions and the final end.

Aquinas, then, falls firmly on the side of ethical intellectualism. God does not choose what is ultimately good or evil for human beings or for Godself. But importantly, Aquinas offers a teleological view of moral rationality different from the one that Schneewind characterizes as the only option. Teleological moral rationality, for Aquinas, does not require God to "bring about the greatest good," since the greatest good (Godself) already necessarily exists.[39] The final end of God and all creatures is not a state of affairs to be realized; it is the best thing, the ultimate object of love, which draws every appetite in all their movements. The exercise of agency is not first and foremost to realize the good but to respond to it.

Some readers may doubt that what I have just described is genuine teleology. To act for an end, it is usually thought, is to aim to bring about some good. Aquinas certainly recognizes that seeking one's end does entail acting to realize goods. Above all, seeking God as one's end entails acting in ways conducive to attaining union with God. When discussing the final end, he distinguishes between the "for which" and the "by which," or, as he also puts it, the "thing itself in which is found the aspect of good" and the "use or acquisition of that thing."[40] For the miser, Aquinas writes, the thing itself is money, and the acquisition is possession. When it comes to the final end, God is the thing itself. All things desire and act for the sake of God. All things do not, however, share the same mode of "acquisition" of that thing. Rational creatures attain their end through contemplating God in the beatific vision. Nonrational creatures, by contrast, cannot attain union with God through contemplation.[41] Their mode of acquisition is the realization of some aspect of divine goodness in the perfection of their form. In this way, Aquinas affirms that God and all creatures act for the sake of the same end without concluding that all do so in the same way or by seeking the same outcome.[42]

What does this teleological picture of moral rationality entail practically? Aquinas has a great deal to say about what it means for human beings to act for their final end. Human action ought to be shaped by the virtues, those natural and supernatural habits by which human beings are perfected according to their kind and elevated by grace to union with God. The virtues play a particular role in the lives of human beings, creatures whose perfection requires the formation of habits directed toward the attainment of their end. Aquinas's picture of human morality fits with his more general view that the way each thing acts for its end depends upon the sort of thing it is. Human beings act for the end in a human way, loving and ultimately attaining God in the way appropriate for creatures of our nature (as elevated by grace). Angels also act for the sake of God, and their end resembles ours. Still, angels act for the end in a manner appropriate to their kind, not in a human way. Likewise, nonrational creatures act for the sake of God, and each does so in its species-characteristic way. Despite the shared end, there is no single principle or standard of action applicable to every creature.

Something analogous is true of God. God shares our end, but this does not mean that God acts according to the moral rules, principles, or virtues of human beings. Because God is rational, God has free choice. But God also always acts for God's end in accordance with the divine nature. Just as we can make reasonably accurate judgments about how, for example, a badger will act for its end once we have a grasp of the sort of creature a badger is, so, in principle, we could do the same with God.[43] The problem, however, is that, as Aquinas repeatedly insists, we can know *that* God is, but we cannot know *what* God is.[44] While we know that God will act perfectly for God's end, we cannot know exactly how God will do so.

Aquinas accepts that we can speak of God as, for example, just, merciful, and charitable. Yet, for Aquinas, moral language about God—like all language about God—is analogous. It both does and does not mean the same thing it means when used of creatures. God certainly does not possess the human virtues, which are habits by which human beings reach their perfection. Because of Aquinas's view of teleological rationality, his claim that God and rational creatures share one and the same end does not entail that they are subject to the same moral principles.[45]

What, then, does this view mean for human moral community with God? While God and human beings share a moral community in one important sense—that is, by sharing a common end—they do not share Schneewind's moral community, which includes shared moral principles. Borrowing a phrase from Jennifer Herdt, we can call this picture of the human moral relationship to God "moral community with God without common measure."[46] God is not a member of the human moral community with its shared standards and common principles. In one sense, our relation to God is analogous to our relation to nonhuman creatures, who share our end without sharing our morality. But God is also much more intimately related to the human moral community. God not only shares our end; God is our end. All human moral action is moved ultimately by the goodness of God and toward union with God.

In Aquinas, we find a view of human and divine moral rationality that is neither ethical voluntarist nor consequentialist. Schneewind is correct that opposition to ethical voluntarism is a central motive for the development of consequentialism. He is wrong, however, to imagine that consequentialism was the only option available for the anti-ethical-voluntarist. Thomism, we have seen, offers a non-consequentialist approach to teleological rationality, one which was highly influential. Anti-ethical-voluntarism, then, does not entail consequentialism.

Divine and Human Morality in Reformed Scholasticism

While More was educated in scholastic theology, his was a distinctly Protestant and largely Reformed scholasticism. More was educated at Christ's College Cambridge. Beyond Emmanuel College, Christ's was the college most influenced by the Puritans. The great Puritan theologians William Perkins and his student William Ames were both educated at Christ's. Perhaps, one might think, the Reformed tradition in which he was trained was ethical voluntarist. His critiques of the "Calvinists" and the "Superlapsarians" suggest as much. And perhaps the ethical voluntarism of his education occluded the scholastic intellectualist option. But the picture More's later writings give of Reformed theology is quite misleading. In fact, the Reformed tradition provided another ethical intellectualist option with which More could have opposed ethical voluntarism.

Though John Calvin did not work out his views in scholastic terminology, the Reformed tradition soon did.[47] And entering into the scholastic disputes, the early modern Reformed theologians confronted the multiple scholastic options on the relationship between divine will and morality. For one assessment of the results, consider one of the most famous works of seventeenth-century Reformed theology, Francis Turretin's *Institutio theologiae elencticae*. In his discussion of law, Turretin raises the question of "the nature of the moral law."[48] This question, as he understands it, is about whether the precepts of the moral law are of natural right and thus necessary, or whether they are of positive right, meaning that they depend upon God's good pleasure and can be dispensed if God so wills.[49] It is, in other words, a question about ethical voluntarism and intellectualism. Following an established tradition, Turretin lists three "celebrated opinions." The first, which he attributes to the scholastic theologians William of Ockham and Jean Gerson, holds that the precepts of the moral law are of positive right and thus potentially subject to dispensation. This opinion is a version of ethical voluntarism. The second, which he attributes to Duns Scotus and Gabriel Biel, holds that the second table of the Decalogue is of positive right, while the first table, which concerns duties to God, is of natural right.[50] It is, in Turretin's scheme, an intermediate position.[51] The third is the view of Aquinas:

> The third is the opinion of those who hold that the moral law as to all its precepts is simply indispensable because it contains the intrinsic reason of justice and duty; not as proceeding from the law, but as founded on the nature of God and arising from the intrinsic constitution of the thing and the proportion between the object and act, compared with right reason or the rational nature. Thomas Aquinas, with his followers (ST, I–II, Q. 100, Art. 8), Altissiodorensis, Richard of Middleton, Peter Paludanus and many others, thinks thus.[52]

Turretin goes on to argue in favor of Thomistic ethical intellectualism. And while he recognizes that some members of "our party"—that is, the Reformed—embrace each of the first two options, he asserts confidently that the Thomistic view is "the more common opinion of the orthodox."[53] In his treatment of God, moreover, Turretin follows Aquinas almost exactly, arguing that God necessarily wills Godself as an end and creates creatures for the sake of the very same end.[54]

Turretin's claim that the Thomist option is the "more common opinion of the orthodox" strongly suggests that More did not have to reject Reformed theology in order to reject ethical voluntarism. He could have found an alternative within his own tradition. To see this, consider a source proximate to More, William Ames, a fellow of Christ's College three decades before More and perhaps the most influential seventeenth-century English Puritan theologian. In the 1620s, Ames wrote *Medulla theologiae*, a standard work among English Puritans, which was meant to serve as a manual of Reformed theology.[55] Ames does at first sound as if he embraces ethical voluntarism: "the rule of virtue is the revealed will of God."[56] But the will of God, Ames quickly clarifies, is not different from the "intellectualist" rule of right reason. He writes:

> That which is said to be right reason, if absolute rectitude be looked after, it is not else-where to be sought for then where it is, that is, in the Scriptures: neither doth it differ from the will of God revealed for the direction of our life. *Psal.* 119.66. Teach me the excellency of reason and knowledge: for I believe thy precepts. But if those imperfect notions concerning that which is honest, and dishonest, be understood, which are found in the mind of man after the fall: seeing they are imperfect and very obscure, they cannot exactly informe virtue; neither indeed doe they differ any thing from the written Law of God, but in imperfection and obscurity only.[57]

The same point occurs elsewhere as well. For example, he argues that while the efficient cause of obedience to God is sanctifying grace mediated by faith, one of the "adjuvant causes" is the perfect conformity of the things commanded with reason and conscience, a point he makes together with the classic natural law citation of Romans 2. The will of God is our standard of virtue, Ames argues, because right reason has been damaged by the fall. Ames may take a slightly lower view of our postlapsarian faculties, but he stands in basic agreement with Aquinas on this point.

If we consider the question of divine and human teleological rationality, Ames's picture is somewhat different from Aquinas's, but it retains a similar structure. God, according to Ames, creates and governs by divine decrees, which are expressions of divine power in agreement with divine nature. The end of every divine decree is "the glory of God himself."[58] Having been created by God and for God's glory, "all created things in their natural manner tend to God from whom they came."[59] Of human virtue, Ames writes that "the chiefe end is Gods glory." Human salvation is the "lesse principall end," because obedience merely for reward would be mercenary. Virtue consists not simply of obedience to God but of obedience to God for the sake of God's end.

For Ames, then, God and human beings share the same end, God's glory. What, then, is God's glory? He describes it as "that goodnesse, or perfection of God which is made manifest by his Efficiency, and shines forth in his works."[60] God's glory, in other words, is simply God's goodness or perfection, which is manifested in creation. For God to act for God's glory is not, as some critics have worried, for God to vaingloriously seek fame or praise.[61] Indeed, God's glory does not depend on human beings at all. This point is emphasized in the Westminster Confession of Faith, composed shortly after Ames's death, which states that God "is alone in and unto Himself all-sufficient, not standing in need of any creatures which He hath made, nor deriving any glory from them, but only manifesting His own glory in, by, unto, and upon them."[62] God's glory is perfectly secured by God's goodness and perfection. God creates and governs not to attain something in addition to God's goodness and perfection but simply as expressions of goodness and perfection.

Given that creatures are made for the glory of God, they unsurprisingly share the same end. Creatures exist for God's glory and ought to act for the sake of it. And it is important to recognize that while the end is theocentric—it is God's glory and not their own that creatures are to pursue—the end is not something entirely external to creatures. Creatures are themselves manifestations of that very glory. Moreover, salvation, for Ames, culminates in "glorification" by which creatures are invited into friendship with God and share in glory through Christ. This idea, too, is echoed in the Westminster Confession, which repeatedly describes salvation in terms of "communion in glory with Christ."[63] Human happiness is to share in God's glory through Christ.

In Ames, then, we find an analogous picture to that of Aquinas. God and human beings share one and the same end, but God and human beings act for the sake of that end in different ways. For God to act for God's glory is simply to act in accordance with divine goodness and perfection. Human creatures are to act for the sake of God's glory by submitting themselves to God in obedience, which, after the fall, is the only sure way of acting according to right reason. By obeying God, they become manifestations of God's glory, and they enjoy that same glory in communion with God through Christ. God and rational creatures thus form a sort of moral community founded on a shared end. But Ames's picture, like Aquinas's, does not fit Schneewind's dichotomy. God, who shares our end, is not beyond the moral community, but God and human beings do not act according to a shared set of moral principles.

Moreover, the end for which both God and human beings act is not an end in need of realization. The end is not produced by divine or human agency. It is eternal and perfectly realized in the divine nature. The end, rather, is a prior goodness to which agency is responsive and by which it is drawn. The rationality of divine and human action is teleological but not consequentialist.

More criticizes the Reformed tradition for reducing God to sheer will and power without goodness. In light of Turretin's judgment about the Reformed tradition and the example of Ames's influential theology, it is difficult to understand More's critique. Perhaps he is simply reacting to the theology of his father, who as we have seen was a Puritan minister. When his critiques are read in light of the major Reformed theologians of the day, More appears to simply be conflating soteriological voluntarism with ethical voluntarism.[64] Beyond the conceptual mistake, the problem with conflating the two is that it renders Aquinas[65]—and, indeed, the entire Augustinian Christian tradition—ethical voluntarist, a completely implausible result.

However we understand More's thinking, it is clear that he decisively rejects Reformed theology in particular and scholastic theology in general. Instead, he turns to the Christian Platonic tradition. Despite its many important differences, I will now argue, the Christian Platonic account of divine and human teleological rationality and divine-human moral community shares a formal structure with the Thomistic and Reformed alternatives.

Divine and Human Morality in Christian Platonism

As More tells it in his autobiographical preface, his encounter with scholasticism produced nothing but "mere *Scepticism*."[66] After four years of study, he writes, "I look'd upon my self as having plainly lost my time in the Reading of *such* Authors." More's skepticism about scholasticism may have been, as he implies, a product of his innate leanings, but it was certainly in line with emerging trends of his age. For many, the critique of scholasticism by, among others, Descartes and Hobbes made the simple repetition of scholastic alternatives to ethical voluntarism seem problematic. Despite his forceful criticisms of Descartes and Hobbes, More followed their lead in seeking alternatives to scholasticism. Rather than looking to Thomistic and Reformed theology for an alternative to ethical voluntarism, More discovered another option in the revival of Platonism in the Italian Renaissance.

More goes on in his autobiographical preface to say that his disappointment with his scholastic education turned out to be a great good because it led him to doubt that "the *Knowledge* of things was really that *Supreme Felicity* of Man." Instead, he came to believe that felicity is attained through spiritual purification. Around this time, he began reading "the *Platonick* Writers, *Marsilius Ficinus, Plotinus* himself, *Mercurius Trismegistus*, and the *Mystical Divines*." Above all, he says, he was affected by the anonymous work *Theologica Germanica*, which taught him to "*extinguish our own proper Will; that being thus Dead to our selves, we may live alone unto God.*"[67] The embrace of Platonism, for More, was part of a spiritual awakening, which included the rejection of philosophical speculation divorced from moral purification. The good cannot simply be understood; it must be loved, and only the one who loves the good can understand it.[68] As the *Theologica Germanica* puts it, "no one can be illumined before becoming purified."[69] This insight, More tells us, set him on a course of spiritual transformation, marked by conflict between God's will for perfection and his own will and self-love.

In addition to their emphasis on spiritual purification, More embraces the "Platonick Writers" because they, modifying Plato's form of the good, identify goodness as the central attribute of the divine essence. This view of God generates a picture of divine moral perfection that More finds appealing. In Plato's *Timaeus*, the character Timaeus explains to Socrates why the divine artificer framed the world: "He was good, and one who is good can never become jealous of anything. And so, being free of jealously, he wanted everything to become as much like himself as was possible."[70] For Plato, the artificer of the world needs nothing for himself. He acts only to share his goodness, making the world of matter as good as possible. The artificer, Plato writes, "wanted nothing more than to make the world like the best of the intelligible things, complete in every way."[71]

Plato's picture is developed by Plotinus, a key source for More. Plotinus writes of the One: "due to its neither seeking anything, nor having anything, nor needing anything, it in a way overflows and its superabundance has made something else."[72] Echoing Plato, he says that for the One to remain within itself would be a kind of jealous grudging.[73] And this "something else" that the One produces, in turn, produces something else lower than itself. The chain of emanation goes on as far as possible because there is no jealous grudging at any step.[74] The cosmos, therefore, contains the fullest possible distribution of divine goodness. Plotinus argues at length in his treatise on providence that the world is as good as it could possibly be.[75] When Neoplatonic thought is Christianized in Pseudo-Dionysius, this non-jealous distribution of the good becomes divine love:

> And we may be so bold as to claim also that the Cause of all things loves all things in the superabundance of his goodness, that because of this goodness he makes all things, brings all things to perfection, holds all things together, returns all things. The divine longing is Good seeking good for the sake of the Good. That yearning which creates all the goodness of the world preexisted superabundantly within the Good and did

not allow it to remain without issue. It stirred him to use the abundance of his powers in the production of the world.[76]

Breaking with Plotinus, Pseudo-Dionysius claims that the Good does have yearning, or *eros*, which is the divine love that creates to share goodness for the sake of the Good. In this way, Pseudo-Dionysius puts more of an agential twist on the emanationist paradigm.[77]

In the Christian Platonic tradition, we find an account of divine teleological action as the selfless and abundant overflow of divine goodness, which is given maximally to creation. Very little emphasis falls on the freedom of God. God is, above all, pure goodness, giving itself abundantly. Christian Platonism entered medieval theology through Pseudo-Dionysius, among others. Aquinas cites Pseudo-Dionysius regularly and embraces the view that God shares God's goodness with creation for the sake of God's goodness. Aquinas's view, however, opens more space for divine discretion, insisting that God might not have created or might have created a better or worse world. Ensuring divine discretion was important for most Christian theologians. Marsilio Ficino, the most influential figure in the fifteenth-century Platonic revival and an early influence on More, follows Aquinas's account.[78] More, by contrast, enthusiastically embraces the overriding emphasis on divine goodness with little interest in leaving space for divine discretion. More is convinced that God's freedom is found precisely in always producing as much goodness as possible.

In his embrace of the Christian Platonic tradition, moreover, More finds a way to address his preoccupation with the question of salvation. He objects, as we have seen, to the dominant Augustinian view of soteriological voluntarism. This objection applies as much to Thomism as it does to the Reformed tradition. Plotinus believes that all things ultimately return to the One, and Pseudo-Dionysius states in the quote above that God not only creates all things but also "perfects" and "returns" all things. More is attracted to this universalist strand of thought, including in the version embraced by the "*Mystical Divine*," Origen, who More calls "that Miracle of the Christian World" and from whom he borrows heavily, though he does not ultimately appear to fully embrace Origen's doctrine of universal salvation.[79]

In More's embrace of Christian Platonism, we can see seeds of his later consequentialism: God's goodness is identified with God's maximally communicating the divine goodness, producing the best possible world. Yet despite the fact that at least some in the Platonic tradition understand divine perfection to entail God's realization of a maximally good world, one does not find a consequentialist approach to human ethics in ancient, medieval, or Renaissance Platonism. One reason is that the goodness God communicates maximally to creation is divine-likeness, which is very different from later consequentialist accounts of goodness and not something that humans can obviously communicate to others. A second reason is just as important: in Platonism in general and Christian Platonism in particular, divine and human morality are not taken to be the same.[80]

The formal structure of the Christian Platonic view of divine and human morality is much like the one we find in Aquinas and Ames. We can see this alignment in Pseudo-Dionysius. God's creation of and care for the world are described as "Good seeking good for the sake of the Good."[81] God overflows and shares God's goodness for the sake of God's goodness. All creatures, too, act for the sake of God's goodness:

> All things are returned to [the Good] as their own goal. All things desire it: everything with mind and reason seeks to know it, everything sentient yearns to perceive it, everything lacking perception has a living and instinctive longing for it, and everything lifeless and merely existent turns, in its own fashion for a share of it.[82]

God and creatures share an end, the Good, which is God. But as in the other alternatives discussed, God and creatures do not act for the good in the same way. God acts for God's own goodness by overflowing into creation and drawing all things back to God. Each type of created thing acts for God's goodness by striving to attain that goodness in its proper manner, which depends on the kind of thing it is. If God's "morality" is best described in quasi-consequentialist terms as bringing about maximal goodness in creation, creaturely morality is certainly not. Creatures do act teleologically, yearning for God's goodness as their end. But, again, this end is not something to be realized. The teleological rationality is not consequentialist.

We find another version of a broadly Platonic view in More's friend and colleague, Ralph Cudworth. Cudworth, like More, adamantly rejects ethical voluntarism, which he characterizes as a view according to which there is "nothing so essential to the Deity as uncontrollable power and arbitrary will, and therefore that God could not be God if there should be anything evil in its own nature which he could not do."[83] Instead of picturing God as "nothing else but will and power," Cudworth offers a different image:

> His nature is better expressed by some in this mystical or enigmatical representation of an infinite circle, whose inmost centre is simple good-

ness, the radii [or] rays and expanded area (plat) thereof all compre-
hending and immutable wisdom, the exterior periphery or interminate
circumference, omnipotent will or activity by which everything without God is brought forth into experience.[84]

The point of this image is twofold: first, to emphasize that all divine action
originates in pure goodness; and second, to insist that the rays run from
God's goodness to God's power and not the opposite, so that God's will
acts on the world but does not act inwardly to determine God's goodness
or wisdom. God's will is simply the way God's power acts to disseminate
God's goodness shaped by wisdom. The implication, for Cudworth, is
that God necessarily creates the best possible world: "if the world could
be better," he writes, "there is no God."[85]

God's perfection, then, requires the production of maximal goodness.
What about human morality? Cudworth does not provide a developed
account of normative ethics, but it seems unlikely that human moral goodness for Cudworth would take the same shape as divine goodness.[86] Echoing his image of God, Cudworth argues that human beings, too, have a
love of goodness at the very "centre of the soul." But drawing from Plato's
Symposium, Cudworth maintains that our love of the good is different
from God's:

> That which moveth in us, and is the spring and principle of all delib-
> erative action, can be no other than a constant, restless, uninterrupted
> desire, or love of good as such, and happiness. This is an ever bubbling
> fountain in the centre of the soul, an elator or spring of motion, both
> a *primum* and *perpetuum mobile* [first and perpetual mover] in us, the
> first wheel that sets all the other wheels in motion, and an everlasting
> and incessant mover. God, an absolutely perfect being, is not this love
> of indigent desire, but a love of overflowing fulness and redundancy,
> communicating itself. But imperfect beings, as human souls, especially
> lapsed, by reason of the *penia* which is in them, are in continual inquest,
> restless desire, and search, always pursuing a scent of good before them
> and hunting after it.[87]

We are by now familiar with this idea. God and creatures are moved to
act for the sake of the very same good, namely, God's own goodness. But
the fact that we act for the sake of the same good does not mean we relate
to it in the same way. God, who is perfect goodness, acts for the sake
of this good by overflowing and sharing it with creatures. We, who are
marked by lack, are moved by the longing to attain and unite with this

good. Thus, while divine action takes a quasi-consequentialist form, human moral action does not. Had More followed Cudworth in making this contrast between divine and human love of the good, he would not likely have invented consequentialist moral rationality. But on this point, More breaks with Cudworth and the larger Platonic tradition. As we will see in the next chapter, he assimilates human morality to divine morality.[88]

Theocentric Moral Cosmologies

I began this chapter with an overview of recent disagreements about the relationship between voluntarist theology and modern morality. These disagreements, I argued, arise from imprecision about the meaning of "voluntarism." After having specified several meanings relevant to ethics, I focused primarily on ethical voluntarism, a view according to which the good to be done and the evil to be avoided are determined solely by the will of God, which chooses freely and not from prior or independent rational or moral standards. With this definition in view, I argued that Schneewind is right that consequentialism arises from the rejection of ethical voluntarism.

Schneewind's argument, though, has several important problems. He claims that in order to defeat ethical voluntarism, the anti-ethical-voluntarists need to provide moral principles applicable to both God and human beings such that God and human beings form a single moral community. Moreover, he claims that doing so requires an account of divine teleological rationality and that a consequentialist account is the only option. Both claims are false, a fact which can be seen by attending to other ethical intellectualist alternatives to ethical voluntarism available in the seventeenth century. Much of this chapter has been occupied with displaying the existence and character of these alternatives, with a focus on those available to Henry More.

The Thomistic, Reformed, and Platonic ethical intellectualist alternatives make two things clear. First, consequentialist moral rationality was not the only option for those seeking a teleological account of divine rationality. The Thomistic, Reformed, and Platonic traditions all offer teleological accounts of divine and human rationality, none of which is consequentialist. Schneewind falsely assumes that any account of teleological rationality will begin with assessing the goodness of outcomes to be sought. But these traditions do not conceive ends first in terms of outcomes or states of affairs. Ends, rather, are the goods for the sake of which an agent acts. The ultimate end, for these traditions, is God (or, to say the same thing differently, God's goodness or God's glory).

Second, the idea that God is either in the human moral community (meaning that God is subject to the same moral principles as us) or outside of the human moral community (meaning that God's ungrounded will is the absolute source of all morality) is a false dichotomy. According to the formal structure shared by all three ethical intellectualist options discussed above, God necessarily shares the same end as human beings—an end whose goodness is not a product of unconstrained divine choice—but God does not act for the sake of the end according to the same principles as human beings. The fact that this view is shared by all three ethical intellectualist traditions surveyed suggests that it is the dominant view of the seventeenth century.

Having surveyed these ethical intellectualist options, we are now in a position to recognize what Schneewind does not: that More and other early consequentialists did not simply turn to the only form of teleological rationality available. They invented a new form of teleological rationality. Consequentialist moral rationality is not the sole form of teleological rationality, and it was not simply lying around, waiting for anti-ethical-voluntarists of the seventeenth century. It was created by conceptual innovation.

In addition to showing that More's employment of consequentialist moral rationality was not necessary, our survey of the other ethical intellectualist options serves an additional function. I have argued that all three options share a formal structure regarding human and divine morality. For all three, God (or God's goodness or God's glory) is the final end of both God and all created things. Each thing acts for the sake of the shared end. The way each thing acts for the sake of the shared end, though, depends on the type of thing it is, meaning that human moral principles do not apply to God and nonhuman creatures.

I will say that a view with this formal structure has a theocentric moral cosmology. I have already introduced the notion of the consequentialist moral cosmology, and the next two chapters trace its creation. This theocentric moral cosmology will serve as a contrast point through which I will highlight the distinctive features of the consequentialist moral cosmology, which includes a different picture of goods, ends, and agency as well as a different relationship between God and human morality. To the emergence of consequentialist moral rationality and the consequentialist moral cosmology in the work of Henry More we now turn.

2

Virtue and the Divine Life

HENRY MORE'S MORAL THEOLOGY

Though he is not particularly well known today, Henry More was a tower-
ing intellectual figure in seventeenth-century England. In his own day, he
was, as Jasper Reid notes, "arguably the leading philosophical authority in
Britain."[1] He engaged almost all the most notable European philosophers
of the seventeenth century. He exchanged letters with Descartes that were
published and widely read. He wrote the first full-length critique of Spi-
noza's *Ethics*. He also persistently criticized Hobbes, who apparently said
that he would embrace More's views if he ever had to reject his own.[2] In
addition, More was arguably the original source of the rise of Platonism
in mid-seventeenth-century Cambridge, and he was certainly the most
prolific of those figures now known as the Cambridge Platonists.[3]

More, I claimed in the previous chapter, departs from the major theological traditions of the early seventeenth century by applying the same
moral principles to both God and rational creatures. In his effort to articulate the eternal moral principles that apply to God and rational creatures,
More invents consequentialist moral rationality. This chapter develops
and defends these claims. It also argues that More's invention of consequentialist moral rationality occurs as part of the development of a new
moral and theological vision of the cosmos, which I call the consequentialist moral cosmology and which plays a central role in the remainder
of the book.

For More, human beings possess a "most divine Faculty of the Soul"
called the boniform faculty.[4] The boniform faculty is a rational appetite,
which More says "much resembles that part of the Will which moves towards that which we judge to be absolutely the best."[5] It desires "with an
unquenchable thirst and affection . . . that which is absolutely and simply
the best."[6] More's boniform faculty echoes Cudworth's notion, discussed
in the previous chapter, that human beings, like God, have a love of the
good at our center. Like Cudworth, More describes this principle as

occupying in our souls the very same place as pure goodness does in the divine: the boniform faculty "seems to supply the same place in [the soul], as the essential Good of the *Platonicks*, is said to do in the Deity."[7] But while Cudworth immediately follows this comparison with a contrast— God's love of the good is an overflowing communication while ours is an erotic longing driven by lack—More makes no such contrast. For More, the boniform faculty's love of the good is the same as God's.

In this way, More develops a different view of the moral community between God and creatures. If God's goodness consists of the maximal realization of goodness in creation, so does ours. This conclusion is precisely what we find in More's eternal moral principles, which he calls moral axioms. The axioms specify the boniform faculty's object, that which is absolutely and simply the best. They do so by defining good and evil and interpreting them according to a logical structure that enables one to judge not only what is good but also what is absolutely best. And the logical structure of the axioms, I argue, is consequentialist. In More's axioms, we find the first articulation—inchoate and not entirely consistent—of consequentialist moral rationality.

More's account of the boniform faculty and the moral axioms occurs in his ethical treatise, *Enchiridion ethicum* (1667), which is the only ethical treatise published by one of the Cambridge Platonists.[8] Cudworth's ethical writings remained unfinished and were not published until the eighteenth century.[9] Yet More's *Enchiridion*, despite its widespread adoption as a textbook in the seventeenth and eighteenth centuries, has received surprisingly little attention.[10] Much of this chapter focuses on the *Enchiridion*, especially the boniform faculty and the moral axioms. Before turning to More's ethical treatise, however, I begin with his most systematic theological text, *The Grand Mystery of Godliness* (1660), which was published seven years earlier. In *Grand Mystery*, More provides an outline of his ethics together with the theology that motivates it. After considering *Grand Mystery*, we will be able to more fully understand *Enchiridion ethicum*, including the points at which it marks a development in More's thinking.

The Gospel and the Triumph of Divine Life

More began his publishing career in the 1640s with a series of Platonically inspired poems on the soul and its spiritual assent. The poems, according to Robert Crocker, present a sophisticated psychology, metaphysics, and epistemology "that consciously opposed both the apparent implications of the Calvinism of his upbringing and the scholastic philosophy he had first imbibed at Christ's [College]." These poems, Crocker continues, "might be described as the first philosophical production of Cambridge Platonism, a first 'manifesto' of considerable intellectual sophistication" as well as "a first attempt at stating the philosophical theology that he was to develop later in the more trenchant, controversial prose of his works of natural theology."[11]

More's transition from poetry to these "more trenchant" philosophical works began in 1650 with his polemical response to the work of Thomas Vaughan, a fellow Platonist as well as an alchemist. As More tells it, his polemical response was driven by the concern that his work (and Platonic theology in general) would be associated with Vaughan's writings and dismissed. Vaughan's magical and alchemical approach to illumination offered More a chance to clarify and differentiate his own approach to illumination through spiritual purification. This process of differentiating himself from other proponents of illumination continued well beyond the dispute with Vaughan. The term "enthusiasm"—a passionate but not rational religious impulse—became important for More as a term of abuse and an eventual object of philosophical reflection in *Enthusiasmus triumphatus* (1656). More came to believe that defending his Platonically inspired spiritual vision required the elaboration and defense of a metaphysics and epistemology, a task to which he gave increasing attention in the 1650s in major works of natural theology, *An Antidote against Atheisme* (1652) and *The Immortality of the Soul* (1659).[12]

His first major work of theology, *An Explanation of the Grand Mystery of Godliness*, appeared in 1660. Before *Grand Mystery*, More writes in the preface, his published writings had been primarily philosophical, addressing the two philosophical "pillars" on which religion stands: the existence of God and the immortality of the soul. In *Grand Mystery*, he turns to theology, "the very chief and top bough of that Tree of Knowledge," developing his alternative to Reformed theology.[13] The two core themes of the work echo those of the Cambridge Platonists more generally. The first is the reasonableness of the gospel. Rejecting any sharp dichotomy between faith and reason, More asserts that the gospel, while not knowable apart from revelation, is eminently reasonable. *Grand Mystery* presents "an orderly Exhibition of the Truths [of the gospel], that the *Scope of the Whole* being understood, the *Reasonableness of the Particulars* thereunto tending may clearly appear."[14] The second is that the aim of the gospel is godliness. In contrast to what he considers an excessive focus on justification in Reformed theology—being made right before God by the imputation of Christ's righteousness rather than by one's own—More insists that the gospel makes us righteous not only through imputation but also and more importantly through moral and spiritual transformation.

The central claim of the work, which unites the two core themes, is that "the *End* to which all *Parts* of the Christian Mystery point at is *the Advancement and Triumph of the Divine Life.*"[15] According to More, God creates human beings to share in the divine life. Sharing in the divine life is the end of the gospel and of all true religion. And the divine life, for More, is not simply a supernatural gift made available by grace. It is also a constitutive principle of our natures. The souls of human beings and angels possess "*a twofold Principle of Life*," divine and animal.[16] These two principles have a natural relation of authority: the divine rules the animal. But in a cosmic fall, the souls of men and many angels chose to immerse themselves in the immediate pleasures of the animal life without regard for the divine.[17] In so doing, they threw both their souls and the cosmos out of harmony. Human life is now marked by a struggle between the divine principle of life and the animal principle of life. The gospel of Jesus Christ enters into this disordered world as both a revelation of the truth of our natures and a "kind of Engine to raise the *Divine life* into those Triumphs that are due to it, and are designed for it from everlasting by the all-seeing Providence of God."[18]

Since the two principles of life also structure More's ethics, let us consider them more closely. The animal principle of life is shared by all animals. Its root, according to More, is self-love, and its "*Branches* are all the *Animal Passions*, such as *Anger, Fear, Sorrow, Joy*, all the necessary *Desires* of the Body, to keep it in Being, such as are *Hunger*, and *Thirst*, and *Sleepiness*."[19] Animal life, More insists, contains "simply no *Evil* but *Good*."[20] And if there is no poison in the root, he adds, there is none in branches either.[21] Only undue or immoderate use of the senses and passions is sinful. Indeed, the animal principle of self-love, which reigns among all nonrational animals, is a clear sign of divine design, since no animal can care for its needs better than itself. While nonrational animals act only from self-love, general providence ensures that they do what is best for the whole.[22] Animal passion, for More, is an expansive category. It includes not only affective movements but also the exercise of crafts for self-preservation, an obscure sense of religion, and political affection. Even the natural cardinal virtues of political justice, temperance, fortitude, courage, and friendship are animal passions.[23]

In human beings, reason elevates animal life, but reason is not itself divine life. Reason is, according to More, "a *Middle Life* or *Facultie* of the Soul of Man betwixt the *Divine* and *Animal*."[24] Reason is neither good nor evil in itself. It can be good if joined to the divine principle and evil if subjected to the animal principle. When serving the animal principle, reason can still do remarkable things: it can amass riches; it can achieve the heights of philosophy, arts, eloquence, and political success; it can even write beautiful hymns of praise to Christ.[25] After detailing the possibilities of animal life informed by reason, More notes that he has "advanced *the Animal life so high*, by adding this *Middle Nature* to it, that you may perhaps marvail upon what I shall pitch that may seem more precious or desirable" when advancing to the divine life.[26] But, he says, this question would only occur from the perspective of animal life. From the perspective of animal life, the divine life will not appear as an elevation. The root of divine life is "*an obediential Faith and Affiance in the true God*," and its branches are the divine virtues of charity, humility, and purity as well as divine versions of the cardinal virtues.[27]

Echoing Augustine's theology of two cities, More argues that because human beings and angels are social beings, they form polities based on their principle of life.[28] Since the fall into sin, there have arisen

> two distinct *Kingdoms*, the one of *Darkness*, (whose Laws reach no further than to the Interest of the *Animal life*,) the other of *Light*, which is the true Kingdom of God, and here the *Animal life* is in subjection, and the *Divine life* bears rule; as the *Divine life* is trodden down in the other Kingdom, and the *Animal life* has the sole jurisdiction.[29]

The two kingdoms, founded on different principles, are necessarily at odds, and the struggle between them is the central tension of history until the final triumph of the divine principle in the kingdom of God.[30]

Religion, for More, is a passion of the animal life, and all religions before Christianity rose no higher than animal life. This is true, he argues, not only of paganism but also of Judaism. More, following a common trope, believes that Judaism presented divine truths but under the images of worldly things. At the same time, all religion—and Judaism above all—prepares the way for the coming of the gospel: "*Christianity* is not only the *Compleatment* and *Perfection* of *Judaisme*, but also of universal *Paganisme*; the Summe or Substance of whatever was considerable in any Religion being comprehended in the Gospel of Christ."[31] The preparatory nature of Judaism goes beyond that of other religions due to Mosaic revelation. More claims the same for the highest expressions of Greek paganism. Following an ancient tradition, he traces a line of transmission from Moses through the Pythagorean and Platonic traditions. Though these philosophical sources distorted aspects of the ancient teaching or cabbala, they contain deposits of truths. The coming of Christ and Christianity, for More, is the decisive moment in the history of the progress of the divine life. The gospel, he argues, is a "*Seven-fold Engine*," that is, an engine with seven powers: the call to be inwardly and truly righteous, the extraordinary degree of righteousness, the promise of the Spirit, the example of the life of Christ, the passion of Christ, the resurrection and ascension of Christ, and the final judgment of Christ. Together these powers are able "to beat down every stronghold of sin, and to raise up the *Divine Life* and Spirit of Righteousness in us."[32] All aspects of the gospel conspire to this end. The gospel, in More's reading, does not free us from the righteousness of the law but calls us to a higher kind of righteousness. Christ freely takes away our sins, not to allow us to remain in our vices but to draw us to a higher righteousness. The coming of Christ and the introduction of the sevenfold engine of the gospel inaugurates a new era in history. Christianity, according to More, "*is that Period of the Wisdome of God and his Providence, wherein the Animal life is remarkably insulted and triumphed over by the Divine.*"[33]

In *Grand Mystery*, we find an outline of More's moral theology. Our souls contain two principles, divine and animal, which in our fallen condition stand at odds with one another. We become godly when, by the power of the sevenfold engine of the gospel, we join reason with the divine principle and subordinate the animal life. We can already see in his early moral theology how More might assimilate human morality to divine. Human morality, after all, is living according to the divine principle of life. But in *Grand Mystery*, More does not assimilate the two. More argues that the divine life in human beings, rooted in "*an obediential Faith and Affiance in the true God*," exhibits different virtues from the divine life of God. The virtues of the divine life in human beings are called divine "not so much because they imitate in some things the Holy Attributes of the Eternal Deity, but because they are such as are proper to a Creature to whom God communicates his own nature so far forth as it is capable of receiving it."[34] Sharing the divine life is not sharing divine virtues. On this point, however, More's views began to change. While his writings of the later 1660s, *Enchiridion ethicum* and *Divine Dialogues*, continue to describe the animal principle in the same terms, they shift the description of the divine principle, resulting in the assimilation of human virtue to divine virtue.

Happiness and Virtue in *Enchiridion ethicum*

In 1667, seven years after *Grand Mystery*, More published his only work of moral philosophy, *Enchiridion ethicum*. He wrote this treatise, he says in the preface, only due to pressure from his friends. His hesitation arose from the belief that virtue cannot be attained by definitions and divisions.

Spiritual purification, not intellectual clarification, is the route to virtue. But his friends eventually convinced him that many in the present age could be moved to recognize the existence of moral truths by nothing but the compulsion of rational necessity.[35]

Enchiridion ethicum is a work of moral philosophy. More does not cite scripture, and he develops his argument almost exclusively through conversation with ancient pagan philosophy, above all Aristotle.[36] Nonetheless, the theological convictions already discussed—especially the centrality of the contrast between animal life and divine life—are crucial for understanding an otherwise unusual and surprising approach to moral philosophy. And More states clearly in the preface that his treatment of virtue in the *Enchiridion* is equivalent to his treatment of grace and the divine life in his theological work, writing that despite their different names, "*Virtue, Grace,* and *the Divine Life* . . . are all but one and the same Thing."[37]

Ethics, More writes in the opening line, is "*the Art of Living well and happily.*"[38] The distinction between living well and living happily is meant to recognize with Aristotle and against the Stoics that happiness depends not only on virtue but also on circumstances beyond one's control. To live well is to live virtuously. Happiness, by contrast, is "*that pleasure which the mind takes in from a Sense of Virtue, and a Conscience of Well-doing; and of conforming in all things to the Rules of both.*"[39] Like Aristotle, More thinks of pleasure as the flower that completes the activity of virtue; unlike Aristotle, he equates happiness with the pleasure itself.[40] He does so because he believes that happiness must be something affective rather than intellectual. The prioritization of affect over intellect reflects More's elevation of spiritual purification over knowledge. He argues that because we are moved to objects not as intelligible but as good, happiness cannot lie in the mere intellectual grasp of the supreme object.[41] It must lie in the affective movement toward the object.

More is here stepping into a scholastic debate that goes back to the latter part of the thirteenth century. All parties in this debate agreed, following Aristotle, that happiness lies in the highest activity of our highest power with respect to its proper object.[42] All also agreed that God is the proper object of the highest activity of the highest power. The dispute was over which power is higher: intellect or will.[43] This disagreement closely tracked disagreements about what I have called agential voluntarism.[44] Aquinas argued that happiness lies in the intellect's contemplation of God. His later critics—most notably Duns Scotus—argued that happiness lies in the will's love of God.[45]

More cites Aristotle to the same effect: happiness lies in the highest activity of the best thing in us.[46] Having rejected the idea that happiness

consists of an activity of the intellect, we might expect him to conclude
that happiness is found in the activity of the will. As we have seen, however, More is highly averse to elevating the will, which, he believes, frees it
from conformity to wisdom and goodness and renders its movements arbitrary, leading to voluntarism. The will, for More, is the faculty by which
we are the masters of our actions. It provides a sort of freedom, but this
freedom (*liberum arbitrium*) is imperfect because it includes the capacity
to do evil.[47] Divine freedom consists not simply of authoring actions but
of authoring actions that are only for the best.[48] The will, like the intellect,
is part of the middle life of the soul.

If the highest faculty is neither intellect nor will, what remains? More
resolves the problem by introducing a new faculty, the boniform faculty.
He gives surprisingly few details about this new faculty. He once asserts
that it is divine (*"plane divina est"*) but most often speaks of it as a most
divine faculty of soul (*"facultas divinissima"*).[49] In light of his theology, we
should not be surprised to find an affective faculty that is elevated above
both animal passions and reason and is described as divine. Here we have
the psychological locus of the divine life. After introducing the faculty,
he describes it as

> that faculty which tastes that which is simply and absolutely best, and
> rejoices in it to a singular degree. Indeed, that faculty is closely related
> to that part of the will that is carried to what is absolutely best, dragged
> off by inextinguishable thirst and passion for so pleasing an object, and
> possessing it is flooded with ineffable joy and pleasure.[50]

The boniform faculty, More writes, "seems to supply the same place in [the
soul], as the essential Good of the *Platonicks*, is said to do in the Deity."[51]
Goodness, for the "*Platonicks*," is the essential feature of the divine. Aristotle, according to More, wrongly elevated divine intellect, but he "should
have remembered, that the divine life was not a matter of sapience only,
but was principally to consist in love, benignity, and beneficence or well-
doing."[52] In human beings, the boniform faculty is one appetite among
many, but it is the highest. Its appetite, which More calls "*Intellectual Love*,"
is always for that which is absolutely and simply the best.[53] To live according to the boniform faculty is to live a divine life.

Happiness, then, is the pleasure of living virtuously and well, and it
resides in the boniform faculty of the soul. More's definition of virtue is
a natural result of the argument so far: "*Virtue is an intellectual Power of
the soul, by which it over-rules the animal Impressions or bodily Passions; so
as in every Action it easily pursues what is absolutely and simply the best.*"[54]

Virtue is a power of the intellectual part of the soul—the middle part that includes intellect and will—by which one is able to overrule [*dominare*] the animal life and pursue only the object of the boniform faculty, that is, to pursue what is absolutely and simply the best.

But what is absolutely and simply the best? More explains what he means by referring to "that famous distinction of the good" between that which is good or better simply [*simpiciter bonum vel simpliciter Melius*] and that which is good to some person or particular affect of a person [*alicui personae vel alicui particulari alicujus personae affectui bonum vel Melius*].[55] The paragraph that follows reveals that the distinction More has in mind comes from Aristotle. In several works, Aristotle distinguishes between good without qualification and good in some respect. The distinction occurs in *Nicomachean Ethics* in order to resolve a dispute between those who argue that wish or rational desire [*boulēsis*] is for the good and those who say it is for the apparent good. Because both carry unappealing consequences, Aristotle suggests instead that "without qualification and in reality, what is wished is the good, but for each person what is wished is the apparent good."[56] He explains the idea by analogy with bodies. That which is healthy to a healthy body is healthy without qualification, even though it may not be healthy to a sick body. What is healthy to a sick body can be called healthy, but only in some respect. The same, he suggests, is true of the relationship between character and the good. Every person wishes for that which appears good. The good without qualification is what is wished for by a person of excellent character. Those of less than excellent character wish only for that which is good in some respect.[57]

Aristotle's distinction explains how some things can be good without qualification even while not everyone perceives them as good or desires them. The solution appeals to the character of the desirer. Rather than following Aristotle's use of the distinction, though, More actually follows Aquinas's somewhat expanded use. Explaining how sin is possible given that appetite is always for the good, Aquinas employs the distinction between the good simply [*bonum simpliciter*] and the good in some respect [*bonum secundum quid*] to explain that different things can be good to different appetites—rational, sensitive, bodily—such that even to the virtuous not everything that is good in some respect is good simply.[58] Likewise, More emphasizes that we have different inclinations which draw us to different particular goods and that virtue directs us only to that which is good simply. For More, that which is good simply corresponds to one inclination in particular: "what we hold to be the *absolute Good, or better thing*, is that which proves grateful or more grateful, to *the Boniform Faculty of the Soul*, which we have already pronounced to be a *Thing Divine*."[59]

At this point, we find ourselves in a circle: the boniform faculty desires that which is absolutely and simply the best, and that which is absolutely and simply the best is that which the boniform faculty desires.[60] But More does not leave matters here. While the boniform faculty knows what is good and best, it knows by taste, not judgment.[61] The function of judging what is best falls to reason: "that certainly is *absolutely and simply the best, which according to the Circumstances of the Case in question, comes up closest to Right Reason*, or is rather consentaneous with it."[62] Right reason, according to More, is "*a sort of Copy or Transcript of that Reason or Law eternal which is registered in the Mind Divine.*"[63] While More suggests in *Grand Mystery* that reason can be joined to either animal or divine life, here he clarifies that *right* reason accords only with the divine. And right reason, for More, is simply reason untainted by the animal passions. When the passions are controlled, he contends, reason will not fail to judge what is best. Just as an unblemished eye can easily distinguish colors, so a mind freed from animal passions can "naturally discern" what is best.[64]

From the very beginning of the work, More expressed skepticism that reason alone can make one virtuous. Virtue comes not from knowledge but from conforming to our highest appetite. Nonetheless, we see here that reason plays an important role. Indeed, More believes that right reason can discern self-evident, universal moral principles, which he calls *noemata* or moral axioms. While More is convinced that these axioms are of little use to the spiritually impure, he nonetheless insists that they are "immediately and irresistibly true."[65] The axioms of practical reason are as undeniably true as those of mathematics. The proper understanding of these axioms can in principle lead even those with no awareness of the boniform faculty to right judgments about what is best.[66]

Practical Reason and the Moral Axioms

Having argued that virtue pursues that which is absolutely and simply best, More introduces the moral axioms, which allow us to determine what is absolutely and simply best. These axioms function as the principles of the boniform faculty. When More discusses the virtues in later chapters, he specifies which of the axioms are relevant to each virtue. Each virtue, for More, arises from and can be resolved into the intellectual love of the boniform faculty, with the axioms as mediating principles.[67] Let us, then, consider the logic of the axioms.

More lists twenty-three moral axioms. The first twelve concern duties to ourselves, and they specify the principles of the first three cardinal virtues: prudence, fortitude, and temperance. *Noema* I defines good: "Good is what to some perceptive living being of some rank is grateful, pleasant, or congruous, and connected with the perceptive being's conservation."[68] Evil, defined in *Noema* II, is the opposite. This definition both expands and constricts common scholastic definitions. It is an expansion insofar as More, perhaps simply through lack of precision, refuses to choose between alternative positions. Is the good the desirable? Is it the agreeable? Is it the pleasant?[69] More appears willing to include them all. On the other hand, it is a constriction in that it limits the good to *perceptive* beings. This limitation is perhaps a result of More's desire to link the good to happiness and his explicit definition of happiness in terms of pleasure.

Once good has been defined, most of the remaining axioms specify ways of judging and comparing goods. One way to do so is by the nature of the living being involved: "Of the species or ranks of perceptive life which are found in the universe of things," More writes in *Noema* III, "some are superior and more excellent than others." The implication, More clarifies, is that goods for higher beings are better than goods for lower beings. And the excellence of the being is not the only way to rank goods. *Noema* IV states: "One good can be greater than another by nature, duration, or both." Duration is quite straightforward. It includes both the limited duration of temporal goods and the difference between temporal and eternal goods (*Noemata* VII, X, XI). More never explains "nature," but his short gloss suggests that he means the rank or excellence of the being for whom something is a good. Moreover, goods can be ordered by "weight [*pondus*] and duration" (*Noema* VII). Weight is a matter of *how* grateful, pleasant, or congruous something is. Though More gives no details about how to determine weight, he presumably thinks that goods that are grateful to higher faculties (e.g., the boniform faculty) have greater weight than those grateful to lower faculties. When beings of the same kind are considered, goodness is judged only by weight and duration. Temporal distance from the present does not affect the degree of goodness: "That which is certain in the future ought to be accounted as present" (*Noema* VIII). Goods can in this way be identified and ranked. The good is to be chosen, *Noema* V states, and the greater good is to be preferred over the lesser.

One important point to consider is how More is conceiving of a good. In the axioms, he simply refers to a good [*bonum*] or goods [*bona*]. What kind of thing does he have in mind? A good is clearly not a desirable object itself. A good, rather, is the state of affairs in which a perceptive living thing attains some desirable object, outcome, or end. More does not use this language, but it is implicit in the axioms. A good obviously includes a relation, since "good" is defined by gratefulness, pleasantness, or congruity to a perceptive living being, but it is not merely a relation. Since it can be judged by the temporal duration during which it obtains, it is better understood as the state of affairs in which a being is so related to that which is grateful, pleasant or congruous.[70] This way of conceiving goods as states of affairs, which is quite foreign to the dominant Aristotelian tradition, has profound implications, especially as we turn to the second set of axioms.

The second set of axioms concerns duties to others, including God, and it specifies the principles of the virtues of sincerity, justice, gratitude, mercy, and piety. Some of the axioms in this set are traditional principles of justice: give to others what is due to them; obey the magistrate; obey God above the magistrate (*Noema* XX–XXII). Others are quite different. More begins by stating that our affection toward any good ought to be proportional to its degree of goodness: "We ought to pursue the highest and most absolute good with the highest affection, the middle goods with medium affection, and the lowest goods with lowest affection" (*Noema* XIII). This axiom is presumably also a principle of prudence, but its location at the beginning of the axioms on duties to others is important. It implies that one is to pursue goods based on their nature, weight, and duration, not based on whether they are good for oneself or others. And this implication is reinforced in the next axiom, which is More's version of the golden rule (*Noema* XIV).

Even more importantly, More considers states of affairs containing multiple goods and treats them by summing up all the goods contained. These more complex states of affairs can also be ranked. Rather than an abstract treatment, he gives an example: "If it is good that to one man is supplied that by which he lives well and happily, it plainly follows by a certain analogy and by mathematics that it is twice as good that it is supplied to two men, three times as good to three, a thousand times as good to a thousand, and thus hereafter" (*Noema* XVIII). One is not, therefore, to determine the greatest single good for a single being and pursue that above all. One is, rather, to engage in a complex set of calculations by which one determines which total quantity of good one can realize by realizing goods for many different beings. More recognizes that calculations of this sort will also have to evaluate evils that result and engages in some comparisons between goods and evils, writing, for example, that "it is better for one man to live without pleasure than for another to live terribly and miserably" (*Noema* XIX).

The second set of axioms is especially important. The first set can be seen as a more sophisticated version of the argument of Socrates in *Protagoras*.[71] According to Socrates, because good is pleasure and evil is pain, all goods and evils are commensurable. With no regard for whether the pleasure and pain are present or future, one ought to add up the pleasure and pain caused by different courses of action and choose the one in which pleasure most exceeds pain. Though it is certainly questionable whether pleasure and pain can indeed be treated quantitatively as Socrates suggests, hedonistic accounts of the good have always been prone to this sort of logic. More's innovation in the first set of axioms is to apply this logic to a more complex account of the good. With the second set of axioms, he transforms the structure of reasoning by treating goods impersonally and summing them across subjects. Now the goods to be realized are the goods of all perceptive living beings, ranked not only by weight and duration but also by the excellence of the nature of the being. Though goods and evils come in many degrees across many subjects, all are commensurable.

Taken together, the axioms provide a rational procedure for distinguishing what is good in some respect, which More sometimes calls a relative good, from what is absolutely and simply the best. I can first rank those things that are grateful, pleasant, or congruous to me by their weight and duration. Each is a relative good, but some are better than others. But identifying the good of greatest weight and duration for me is not enough. What is most grateful, pleasant, or congruous to me is not yet what is best. The same sort of judgments must be made about what would be good for others. My action is good if it procures me some good, but my action is better if it does so for others as well. This logic leads to the conclusion that what is best is not just for me to attain a good of greatest weight and duration but for as many sentient beings as possible to attain such goods—and especially beings of higher natures. To do that which is absolutely and simply the best is to realize the states of affairs that contain the most possible goodness. The moral logic of the axioms is consequentialist.

The consequentialist logic of the axioms can be seen clearly in More's critique of Hobbes. When Hobbes says the good is simply what is desired, according to More, he is judging by the animal appetite. The same is true when he affirms a right in the state of nature to do whatever one judges necessary for one's survival. Right reason reaches a different conclusion. To judge, as Hobbes does, that one's own life and preservation is an exceedingly high good comes with several logical entailments:

> If according to them, Life and Conservation be so valuable, it must also follow, that the more durable these are, they are so much the better, and that the most durable is best of all. Furthermore, if such self-conservation of one man be really good, it is doubly so to preserve two men, and thrice as much to save three, and so forward. Whence by the Light of Nature, it is manifest, that every intellectual Creature stands bound to provide, both in present and in future, for his own, and his

Neighbor's Preservation, so far forth as in him lies, and as it may consist without doing prejudice to a third.[72]

In this way, the logic of the axioms rules out merely relative judgments about good and evil and renders the Hobbesian agent irrational. If my preservation is a great good, the preservation of all is many times greater. Because I ought to pursue goods with a zeal corresponding to their degree of goodness, I ought to pursue the preservation of my neighbor as equal to my own and the preservation of all with far greater zeal.[73]

We can see in this argument how the axioms provide a set of rules by which that which is absolutely and simply the best can be distinguished from that which is good in some respect. But notice that this distinction, as it is made by the axioms, is different from the distinction More cites in Aristotle. When More first introduces the distinction between what is good in some respect and what is simply and absolutely best, he uses an Aristotelian distinction with a Thomistic nuance: that which is grateful to any one faculty is good in some respect, while what is grateful to the boniform faculty is absolutely and simply the best. The axioms, however, make the distinction in a different way. Anything grateful, pleasant, or congruous to any sentient being is, according to the axioms, good. Yet to pursue some good just because it is good for oneself, no matter which appetite it suits, is to pursue what is only good in some respect. That which is absolutely and simply the best is the realization of the most possible goodness.

More, then, makes two different distinctions using the same language. But, importantly, there is no contradiction here. More may be conflating these two distinctions, but they are not incompatible. In fact, they serve different functions. The first distinction explains why virtue is conducive to happiness. The answer is that it is pleasing to the highest appetite of the soul, the boniform faculty. The second distinction explains why virtue is morally good. It is a distinction between the different outcomes that one might choose to pursue: that which contains some good for oneself and that which includes the most good for all. The fact that an action brings about what is best explains its moral goodness.

In fact, not only are the two distinctions compatible; they align perfectly due to More's account of the two principles of life. The animal life necessarily pursues all things only in relation to one's own sensitive appetites. That which the animal passions pursue is a relative good in both senses: it is good relative only to a lower faculty in us, and it is a relative good insofar as it is pursued only as good for oneself. The divine life, by contrast, aims only for the realization of the greatest degree of goodness, which is precisely what the boniform faculty relishes. Pursuing the realization of the most goodness always conforms to that which is best in us.

Virtue, therefore, aims for the realization of maximal goodness, not for any particular being, but as a sum across all perceptive living beings. This conclusion raises two further questions. The first is how More came to these axioms. Because he takes them to be self-evident, he does not think any explanation is required. Yet their innovative character belies the claim of self-evidence. I have already suggested Plato's *Protagoras* as one possible source. Another factor that likely shaped the character of the axioms is More's understanding of self-evident truth. His most extended treatment of the subject is found in his argument that the idea of God is innate, in the first book of *An Antidote against Atheisme*. By "innate ideas," More means "an active sagacity in the Soul, or quick recollection as it were, whereby some small businesse being hinted unto her, she runs out presently into a more clear and larger conception."[74] "Innate" does not mean present from birth but immediately evident to the soul by its active powers when appropriate stimuli are present.[75] Sense provides the occasion but not the ideas themselves.

More's short argument for innate ideas relies primarily on examples, which he divides into two classes. The first is geometrical figures, which are known by reflection but never perfectly realized in the world. The second class of examples is a set of concepts More calls "*Relative Notions or Ideas*."[76] Relative notions involve the logical relation of terms: cause, effect, whole, part, like, unlike, proportion, symmetry, and so on. These ideas, More argues, cannot be products of sense. They are, rather, ideas that the intellect actively supplies upon encountering the relevant sense experience.[77] And importantly, More argues that relative notions can be combined into self-evident propositions, such as: "*The whole is bigger than the part: If you take Equall from Equall, the Remainders are Equall; Every number is either Even or Odde*."[78]

An Antidote against Atheisme never mentions good and evil as relative notions, but More seems to have thought of them this way. His friend and colleague Cudworth, in his unfinished work *A Treatise Concerning Eternal and Immutable Morality*, treats good and evil as self-evident relative notions.[79] Cudworth aims to show that morality is not the product of will or convention but of reason. And Cudworth understands self-evident notions much the same as More does. They are ideas that come from the active powers of the mind. If the mind were a blank slate, Cudworth concludes, "there could not possibly be any such thing as moral good and evil, just and unjust."[80] Cudworth's treatise ends with these conclusions, and the details of our innate notions of good and evil, justice and injustice,

remain unspecified. Nonetheless, we see in Cudworth an argument for
the innateness of moral notions as relative. We cannot know if this sort of
argument is behind More's axioms, but it certainly fits. Indeed, the innovative characteristics of More's self-evident axioms are not hard to explain
if the axioms are an effort to work out the implications of interpreting
good and evil as relative notions. Many of the more innovative axioms,
especially those that employ consequentialist logic, can be reasonably understood as an attempt to treat good and evil as relative notions and to
combine them into self-evident propositions.

The second question is this: If the normative ethics of the axioms is
consequentialist, why is More's description of the virtues so traditional?
While More does make some innovations in the structure and description
of the virtues, he goes out of his way to argue that the difference between
his treatment of the virtues and that of many ancient moralists is simply
verbal.[81] The answer is quite straightforward, and it is one that we will see
repeated again and again. It depends on More's view of general providence.
Consider the animal passions, which have thus far figured into More's ethics only negatively as that which must be overruled. As we saw in *Grand
Mystery*, More considers the animal passions to be good in themselves.
They are part of God's general providential ordering for the best. Though
animal passions are rooted in self-love, they are providentially ordered to
the good of the whole.[82] They are "imperfect Shadows and Footsteps of the
Divine Wisdom and Goodness," which are to be illuminated and perfected
through reason.[83] More treats the passions at length in *Enchiridion*, closely
following Descartes's *The Passions of the Soul*.[84] His aim is to "interpret the
Voice of Nature in them all" by determining "the end unto which Nature,
or rather God, who is the Parent of Nature, has destined each of them."[85]
The details are far too numerous to discuss, but a few instances will suffice.
Some are quite obvious: from hunger, we know that we are to nourish ourselves. Others are more complex: from esteem and disesteem toward the
self, we learn that we are to respect one another; from veneration, we learn
that we are to obey political and religious authorities; from remorse, we
learn that we are free agents. Every passion, even jealousy and cowardice,
has its providential function.[86]

While the animal passions are providential guides and important
sources of moral reasoning, they also cause problems. Not only do they
tend to be excessive, but they also aim only for relative goods. To correct
these problems, right reason and virtue are required. Yet the transformation is not as significant as one might think. While virtue reorients one
from one's own relative good to that which is absolutely best, it does not
thereby reject the insight of the passions. The passions, too, are directed by

divine providence to that which is absolutely best. Reason is to control the passions but also to recognize their providential guidance. Therefore, to judge that the life and preservation of all is a far greater good than my own life and preservation does not require that I give no more thought to my own life and preservation than to anyone else's. It requires, rather, that I recognize through my passions a particular office to care for myself and my family above others, not because their lives and preservation are any better than the lives and preservation of others, but because this is how God would have me do my part to achieve that which is best. Learning from the passions, reason recognizes that achieving maximal preservation occurs when each is especially concerned with their own. It still may happen that my preservation directly conflicts with the preservation of a greater number, in which case I presumably ought to choose the latter. Nonetheless, the revisionist potential of More's normative ethics is largely tempered. While consequentialism will eventually become a reformist project, the early consequentialists do not employ it this way. Consequentialism is, given certain providentialist assumptions, consistent with acting largely in conformity with our natural desires.

Divine Morality and the Kingdom of God

In *Grand Mystery*, More says that human beings, even when they live according to the divine life, have different virtues than God. *Enchiridion ethicum* does not directly address this question, but it does give the impression that More has changed his view. More states repeatedly that we are to imitate and resemble God. Virtue is "a thing Divine, and God's true Image."[87] To be virtuous is "to imitate the Divine Wisdom, and the Divine Goodness, with all our Might."[88] And right reason, we have seen, is described as "*a sort of Copy or Transcript*" of immutable divine reason.[89] In his brief discussion of the natural law, More even states quite explicitly that it applies to God: "There is therefore a Law, which is eternal and immutable, and in some sort common both to God and Men."[90] That law, the law of right reason, is articulated in the axioms, even if some of the axioms are clearly applicable only to human beings (e.g., obey the magistrate). The implication is that divine action will also conform to the self-evident and eternal moral truths to which the axioms give voice. And this is precisely what we find in More's next major work.

The year after the appearance of *Enchiridion ethicum*, More published a fictional theological dialogue between seven friends called *Divine Dialogues* (1668). *Divine Dialogues* returns to many of More's favorite themes: the goodness of God, the perfection of divine providence, the preexistence of the soul, and the two principles of life. The topic of *Divine Dialogues* is the kingdom of God: its nature, origin, progress, and end.[91] Before the dialogue begins to address these topics, one character expresses doubt about the existence of God and providence, a doubt which occupies the entire first volume. Providence, in particular, receives extended attention. The key question concerns "the *Measure of God's Providence*, namely, Whether the *Rule* thereof be his *pure Goodness*, or his *mere Will and Sovereignty*."[92] More defends the former against the latter, which is his characterization of ethical voluntarism, a characterization that he regularly attributes to Calvinism but that is best seen as a Hobbesian view. Divine providence, the dialogues conclude, always does what is absolutely best. This theme is certainly not new for More. He defends it throughout his corpus. He even uses it as a premise to argue for other positions. In *The Immortality of the Soul* (1659), More offers a "demonstration" of the preexistence of the soul from the goodness and wisdom of God. He writes:

> if it be good for the Souls of men to be at all, the *sooner* they are the *better*. But we are most certain that the *Wisdome* and *Goodness* of God will doe that which is the *best*; and therefore if they can enjoy themselves before they come into these terrestrial Bodies (it being better for them to enjoy themselves than not) they must *be* before they come into these Bodies.[93]

We already see here the idea that the degree of goodness depends in part on duration and thus that God will maximize duration. In *Divine Dialogues*, the logic of the axioms shapes More's thinking about divine providence even more clearly. Critiques of the goodness of divine providence, the dialogues argue, are founded on the failure to recognize that the evils of the world "are not *really* so in themselves, but onely *relatively*."[94] The problem is not providence but the way our animal passions lead us to focus on the badness of particulars rather than the goodness of the whole. When we instead judge according to right reason, we see otherwise, "for the Divine Wisdome freely and generously having provided for the whole, does not, as Man, dote on this or that Particular, but willingly lets them go for a more solid and more Universal good."[95] More's overall argument is perhaps best summarized in this passage:

> there are no Evils in the World that God foresaw (and he foresaw all that were to be) which will not consist with this Principle, *That God's Goodness is the Measure of his Providence*. For the nature of things is such, that some Particulars or Individuals must of necessity suffer for

the greater good of the Whole; besides the manifold *Incompossibilities* and *Lubricities* of *Matter*, that cannot have the same conveniences and fitnesses in any shape or modification, nor would be fit for any thing, if its shapes and modifications were not in a manner infinitely varied. . . . Forasmuch as those *Incompossibilities* in *Matter* are unavoidable; and what-ever designed or permitted Evil there seems in Providence, it is for a far greater good, and therefore is not properly in the summary compute of the whole affairs of the Universe to be reputed evil, the loss in particulars being so vast a gain to the Whole. It is therefore our Ignorance, *O Hylobares*, of the truth Law of Goodness (who are so much immersed into the Life of *Selfishness*, which is that low Life of Plants and Animals) that makes us such incompetent judges of what is or is not carried on according to the law of that *Love* or *Goodness* which is truly Divine.[96]

The distinction between what happens to particulars and what happens on the "full compute of all circumstances" echoes the axioms and their distinction between relative goods and what is good on the whole. Here the emphasis falls not on comparing goods but on comparing goods and evils. And God, we are told, maximizes the good. The goodness that is the measure of God's providence, it seems, is itself measured by consequentialist standards.

When, in the second volume of *Divine Dialogues*, More returns to the topic of the animal life and the divine life, we discover that More has indeed changed his view. In *Grand Mystery*, the root of the animal life is self-love, and the root of the divine life is an "obediential faith and affiance in the true God." [97] In *Divine Dialogues*, the root of animal life remains self-love, but the root of divine life becomes "the pure love of God, or of that which is simply and absolutely good."[98] This brings the root of the divine life into conformity with *Enchiridion ethicum*. It also sharpens the parallel with Augustine. More, like Augustine, now argues that two loves give rise to two kingdoms. Unlike Augustine, however, More does not define the love that orders the kingdom of God simply as the love of God. He adds: "or of that which is simply and absolutely good." A natural way of reading the disjunction would be as two ways of saying the same thing: what is simply and absolutely good is God. By now, however, we know that he has another notion of "simply and absolutely good" in mind. According to this notion, to love what is simply and absolutely good is to love as God loves, loving no goods as relative but only as aspects of what is absolutely best. More maps the distinction between loving relative goods and loving absolute goods onto the distinction between loving oneself and loving God.

More's revised account of the divine life allows an innovative picture of the kingdom of God. Philotheus, More's spokesperson in the dialogue, distinguishes between several different meanings of the kingdom of God, the most general of which is: "*The Kingdome of God is the Power of God enjoyning, exciting, commissioning, or permitting his creatures to act according to certain Laws, which, considering all circumstances, or upon the compute of the whole, are for the best.*"[99] Hylobares then asks what justifies God's right to be sovereign over the kingdom, noting that others (e.g., Hobbes) justify it by God's infinite power. Hylobares is here raising an important challenge to More's view. Divine authority over creation is too important to the biblical tradition to be ignored, and ethical voluntarists have a straightforward explanation of it: good and evil are determined solely by unconstrained divine will. More needs to show that he can offer an alternative explanation. Philotheus answers:

> [F]rom these three, his infinite *Goodness, Wisdome* and *Power*, issue out all the Orders of the Creation in the whole Universe. So that all the Creatures being his, and his Goodness being so perfect, immutable and permanent, as never out of any humour, (as I may so speak) vacillancy, or supine indifferency, to be carried otherwise than to what is the best, and his Wisdome never at a loss to discern, nor his Power to execute it; we see the clearest foundation imaginable of the *Right* of the *absolute Sovereignty* we acknowledge in God. For is there not all reason, that he that is so immutably Good, that it is repugnant that he should ever will anything but what is absolutely for the best, should have a full right of acting merely according to the suggestions and sentiments of his own minde, it being impossible but that they should be for the best, he having proportionable *Wisdome* also and *Power* adjoyned to this infinite *Goodness*, to contrive and execute his holy, just and benign designs?[100]

The right of God to be sovereign over the kingdom rests, according to More, on the fact that God always wills what is absolutely best and has the wisdom and power to achieve it. How does this fact justify the right of sovereign authority? The question of the right to sovereignty is most fundamentally about God's authority to command rational creatures. For More, God has the authority to command rational creatures because God is most perfectly able to direct them to that which they are already rationally and morally bound to pursue: the realization of that which is best. Nothing will more effectively achieve this end than obedience to God. In *Enchiridion*, More writes that human right reason is "consonant to *Divine Reason*, which does nothing partially for the sake of this or that particular:

but as she generously dictates, like to a common *Parent*, such Laws as tend, in their own Nature, to the Happiness of all Mankind."[101] Here we see the implications. Because God perfectly realizes the same end that creatures are bound to pursue, the kingdom of God is a community founded on a single shared pursuit, the realization of which is best achieved when God commands and creatures obey.

While More's distinction between the two principles in *Divine Dialogues* echoes Augustine's two loves, More overlays the distinction between the love of self and the love of God with the distinction between the love of relative goods and the love of the best. In the kingdom of darkness, each one loves all goods only as relative to the self. In the kingdom of God, each one loves only that which is absolutely the best, not for anyone in particular, but "upon the compute of the whole."[102] God rules over this kingdom because God can perfectly direct all members in their pursuit of the best. Ultimately, the shared aim of realizing that which is absolutely and simply the best is the fundamental principle of the kingdom of God. Rational creatures love and serve God as the one most capable of directing all things to the best.

More's Consequentialist Moral Cosmology

In the previous chapter, I argued that the major non-ethical-voluntarist options available to More—Thomistic, Reformed, and Platonic—all hold a view in which the highest good is also the shared end of God and rational creatures. This shared end is God. More agrees with these views that God and rational creatures all ought to act for the sake of the highest good, which becomes their shared end. But in More, the shared end is a state of the created world, namely, one in which maximal goodness is realized. We could call More's revision a shift from a theocentric to a cosmocentric vision of the end. But it is not simply the object of the end that changes. It is also our relationship to it. If the end is God, the end is not produced by divine or human activity. It is an object that precedes activity and calls it forth by attraction. When the end is a state of the created world, by contrast, it is conceived as a product of our activity. The point of moral agency is to produce the end, a view which I will call a productivist picture of agency.[103]

In addition to reconceiving the end shared by God and rational creatures, More also reconceives the moral relationship between God and rational creatures. The principles that direct our pursuit of our end are self-evident, immutable principles that apply to both God and rational creatures. We have here a moral community between God and human beings in Schneewind's sense of a community of shared moral principles. God, who is perfectly good, always acts to realize the best. We, too, act to realize the best when we act virtuously, conforming our will to the desires of the boniform faculty. The fact that God and rational creatures are all bound to act to realize the same end allows More to explain God's authority over rational creatures. God, simply put, is best able to direct the shared pursuit of the end. God's commands are therefore to be obeyed.

This combination of views about human morality, divine morality, divine-human moral community, and the nature of divine authority is what I am calling the consequentialist moral cosmology.[104] More is the first to defend this combination of views, which, like the theocentric moral cosmology of the other seventeenth-century intellectualists, forms a coherent theological, moral, and cosmic vision. More's path to the consequentialist moral cosmology was marked by particularities that would not be repeated. His path, though, was not the only possible path. The consequentialist moral cosmology soon found an unexpected ally in the natural lawyer Richard Cumberland.

Teleology Transformed

RICHARD CUMBERLAND'S
PERFECTIONISTIC NATURAL LAW

Five years after the appearance of Henry More's *Enchiridion ethicum*, Richard Cumberland published his massive moral treatise, *De legibus naturae*. The relationship between the two works remains unclear. Cumberland mentions More once but does not cite *Enchiridion ethicum*. Yet there are striking similarities between these two texts that are otherwise radically different in argument and aim. Indeed, the similarities are strong enough that Jon Parkin considers *Enchiridion ethicum* a probable source for *De legibus*.[1] For my purposes, however, what matters is how ideas we have seen in More appear in Cumberland in a new and significant way.

De legibus presents a theory of the natural law formulated explicitly against Thomas Hobbes. Cumberland, like More, is an adamant critic of ethical voluntarism, especially as articulated by Hobbes. Cumberland believes that truths about goodness and badness are natural, not a product of will and convention. But Cumberland does not go quite as far as More in his anti-voluntarism. He accepts legislative voluntarism, the view that moral obligation requires divine command. While actions are good or bad by nature, they are not *morally* good or bad by nature. Morality requires the command of a legitimate authority, which adds the obligation to perform or avoid the action. The task of *De legibus* is to demonstrate that some actions are naturally good or bad and that God's commands have rendered the naturally good actions morally obligatory and the naturally bad actions morally impermissible.

Cumberland, unlike More, is commonly recognized as a source for later utilitarianism. Indeed, due to his insistence that the natural law requires the promotion of the common good of all rational beings, he is sometimes called the first utilitarian.[2] In one of only two book-length treatments of Cumberland's ethics in English, Linda Kirk argues that his legislative voluntarism is merely a concession to religious authorities that masks the radical nature of his utilitarian ethic.[3] According to Kirk, there are two accounts of the natural law in Cumberland: one legislative voluntarist and one utilitarian. Jon Parkin, in the other English-language book on Cumberland's ethics, responds that there is indeed a tension between two different aspects of Cumberland's theory of the natural law, the naturalist and the legislative voluntarist, but that the whole point of *De legibus* is to demonstrate the consistency of the two.[4] Parkin is right, and I want to take his argument a step further. Not only is Cumberland's legislative voluntarism not intended to mask his consequentialism; the consequentialist elements in his thought are a product of his method of proving the reality of a divinely commanded natural law.

Cumberland frames his treatise as a contribution to another anti-ethical-voluntarist approach to ethics, one which I did not discuss in chapter 1: the Grotian natural law. Hugo Grotius's views had come under attack from ethical voluntarists—most notably Hobbes—and Cumberland steps in to defend Grotius. Yet while Cumberland frames himself as a defender of Grotius, his version of the natural law differs substantially from Grotius's. Cumberland's natural law is better read as a modification of the scholastic approach to natural law in the broadly Thomistic tradition, a fact which is occluded not only by Cumberland's self-presentation but also by his English translator's explicit attempt to *"free him from as many of his Scholastick Terms as I could."*[5] In this chapter, I argue that Cumberland's innovations within the Thomistic moral tradition mirror More's innovations in the Christian Platonic moral tradition. The result is another version of the consequentialist moral cosmology.

Cumberland and the Natural Law: Scholastic and Modern

Cumberland explicitly situates his work in the natural law tradition stemming from Hugo Grotius. He begins by noting that the natural law can be deduced in two ways: either from its effects or from its causes. The former method, he claims, is that of Grotius and Robert Sharrock.[6] The highest praise in this endeavor goes to Grotius, and Cumberland defends the value of Grotius's approach against its critics.[7] Yet he also takes objections to Grotius's work very seriously. He is particularly concerned about the objection from both John Selden and Hobbes that Grotius's account of the natural law does not justify its authority as a law. This objection stems from the conviction that law, properly speaking, requires the command of a superior. According to Selden, Grotius's problem can be solved in one of two ways: either by establishing that God gave the natural law to Adam and Noah, who passed it down by tradition, or by proving that God has made the natural law available to all by reason.[8] Selden only fully develops the former method, which, Cumberland objects, cannot serve as grounds for a universal natural law (Intro.iii). Cumberland takes up the second method. Grotius, arguing only from effects, proved the universality of the natural law. Beginning from causes, Cumberland aims to complete Grotius's work by demonstrating the natural law's authority.

Grotius, Selden, and Sharrock are all natural lawyers whose work is to be furthered and perhaps completed by Cumberland. Hobbes, by contrast, figures into Cumberland's project negatively. Indeed, much of *De legibus* is spent refuting Hobbes in great detail. Why is refuting Hobbes so important to Cumberland? One reason in particular is worth highlighting because it stems from the distinctive character of the Grotian natural law. While the relationship between Grotius and the scholastic natural law tradition is a complicated matter, Grotius's early readers agreed that Grotius's *De jure belli ac pacis* marks a new beginning in the natural law tradition. Schneewind offers one insightful account of the distinctiveness of Grotian natural law.[9] Grotius, according to Schneewind, is the first natural lawyer to take skepticism seriously. Whereas Francisco Suárez and Richard Hooker, the last great natural lawyers in the scholastic tradition, take many theological convictions for granted, Grotius aims to assume only what cannot be denied by the skeptic. Rather than inquiring into contentious topics like perfection, happiness, or the final end, Grotius begins with what he takes to be two undeniable features of human beings: we seek our own preservation and benefit, and we desire social life. These two features give rise to the problem that the natural law is meant to solve, which Schneewind calls the Grotian problematic:

> We are self-preserving and quarrelsome beings; but we are also sociable. These two aspects of human nature make the problem of maintaining the social order quite definite: how are quarrelsome but socially minded beings like ourselves to live together? What limits must we place on our tendency to controversy in order to satisfy our sociable desires? Grotius's central thought is that the laws of nature are empirically discoverable directives that show us how to solve this problem.[10]

While this new conception of the natural law avoids some problems, it also creates a new problem, which Hobbes skillfully exposes. If the natural law is a rational solution to the Grotian problematic, an individual should rationally only conform to it if all others do. Without universal conformity—which, Hobbes argues, can only be ensured by an absolute sovereign—the natural law rationally binds no one.

Though Cumberland defends Grotius, he does not treat the natural law as a solution to the Grotian problematic.[11] For this reason, positioning himself as a defender of Grotius is more of a rhetorical than a substantive move. Cumberland instead returns to the scholastic perfectionist approach stemming from Aquinas and running through Francisco Suárez, rooting the natural law in a teleological vision of the cosmos in which all creatures are ordered to the highest good. The return to a perfectionistic and cosmological natural law provides Cumberland with a way around the Hobbesian subversion of the Grotian natural law because it grounds the natural law in something beyond social coordination. It does not, however, address the other issue raised by Hobbes and Selden, the problem of obligation. The problem, according to the critics, is that an action can be rational without being morally obligatory. According to this view, which Cumberland accepts, obligation requires the command of a legitimate authority together with the imposition of sanctions. With this background, Cumberland's primary aim now clearly comes into view: to prove that God is a legitimate authority who has commanded and forbidden the actions that reason judges to be good and bad.

In his attempt to hold together a perfectionistic, ethical intellectualist account of natural good and evil with a legislative voluntarist account of obligation, Cumberland follows in the footsteps of Francisco Suárez, who developed a "middle way" in the scholastic tradition. For Suárez, agreement with rational nature is what determines the goodness and badness of human actions but not what makes them obligatory. To be morally binding, good and bad actions must be commanded and forbidden by God.[12] As creatures, Suárez argues, we require moral government by our Creator.[13] Being perfectly good, God could not fail to command that which naturally conforms to human nature.[14] The natural law is the result. Cumberland is not the first in England to adopt Suárez's approach. He was preceded by Nathaniel Culverwell, who is often associated with the Cambridge Platonists.[15]

While Cumberland follows Suárez and Culverwell in outline, he departs sharply from them in detail. Cumberland, like Grotius, aims to prove even to the skeptic or Epicurean that God commands and prohibits what is naturally good and evil. Revelation must be bracketed.[16] Moreover, Suárez's argument that God must have commanded whatever right reason judges to be good no longer strikes Cumberland as tenable after Hobbes. Hobbes accepts that reason can give us universally true propositions like those of the natural law, but he systematically undermines any attempt to determine divine commands. Cumberland, therefore, seeks to develop a new rational demonstration that the natural law is commanded by God, which he undertakes through a philosophical and scientific exploration of the created order. Laws, according to Cumberland, are "nothing but *practical Propositions, with Rewards and Punishments annex'd, promulg'd by competent Authority*" (Intro.vi). Hobbes granted that reason gives us practical propositions; the challenge for Cumberland is to show that God is a legitimate authority who has promulgated these rational propositions and annexed sanctions to them.

Cumberland's key argument is that the rewards and punishments of the natural law are built into the causal structure of the universe. This argument echoes the commonplace that virtue is its own reward and vice is its own punishment, and Cumberland draws upon a long history of argumentation. At the same time, by arguing that virtue and vice are linked to happiness and misery through the causal structure of the universe, now understood in mechanistic terms, Cumberland structurally transforms the tradition on which he draws. The remainder of this chapter traces the structural transformation and its implications. Given the disordered and often rambling character of the massive text, I will present the argument of the work logically rather than following Cumberland's presentation. I begin with Cumberland's account of the final end.

Natural Goodness and the Final End

Cumberland follows the scholastic tradition by structuring his ethical inquiry around the question of the final end. Aquinas begins the second part of the *Summa theologica*, which covers human action and morality, with a treatise on the final end.[17] Our final end, according to Aquinas, is God, and all human action is assessed by its relation to this end. Good acts are directed or referred to the final end, and bad acts are not. And for Aquinas, who is not a legislative voluntarist, the goodness or badness of human action is moral simply because human actions "proceed from a deliberate will."[18] No command is necessary.

For Cumberland, too, the goodness or badness of human action depends on its orientation to or deviation from the final end. But Cumberland's effort to prove that the natural law includes natural sanctions requires him to introduce two key innovations. We must make these explicit before discussing his account of the final end. The first innovation concerns the relationship between happiness and the final end. For Aquinas, "happiness means the acquisition of the last end."[19] For Cumberland, by contrast, happiness cannot mean attaining the final end. Happiness must be the reward for the pursuit of the final end. If it were also the object or aim of such actions, his argument would reduce to this: God causally imposes the reward of happiness for the proper pursuit of happiness. Though Cumberland maintains that happiness is found in the final end, he needs happiness to be distinct enough from the final end to plausibly be a reward "annex'd" to the pursuit of it (Intro.vi).

A second difference concerns the framing of the question of the final end. The Thomistic argument that we must have a final end goes back to Aristotle: desire must rest somewhere.[20] If we had no final end, we would have to give an infinite series of reasons for our actions: this is for the sake of that, which is for the sake of that, ad infinitum. Cumberland agrees that rational action must aim at some ultimate end: "All agree," he writes, "that whoever acts *deliberately*, must (1) propose an *End* to himself, then (2) search out, chuse, and apply the *Means*, by which it may be obtain'd" (V.iv). Right reason, therefore, demands that we first determine the "*Best End.*" Cumberland then introduces a crucial innovation:

> But, because the words, *End* and *Means*, are of very doubtful significa-
> tion, and suppose the *free*, the *mutable*, intention of a rational Agent,
> which can *never be certainly known*; and because they, consequently,
> present to our minds a matter *not so proper for Demonstration*; I thought
> it fit, *without changing* the matter in hand, to consider it *under another
> notion*; that is, because the *connexion* is more *conspicuous*, and perfectly
> *inseparable*, between *Efficient Causes*, and their *Effects*, and continual
> experience and frequent observation plainly discover, *what* Effects will
> follow Causes assign'd, therefore "I have laid down the Definition, the
> *Publick Good* as the *Effect*, our *Actions* and *Powers*, from which anything
> of that kind is hop'd for, as the *Efficient Causes*." (V.iv)

Though Cumberland claims that this shift is made "*without changing* the matter in hand," the change is in fact quite significant. By shifting the account of human action from means–end to efficient cause–effect, Cumberland transforms the question of the final end. The question of our final end becomes, in Cumberland's hands, the question of the "*best Effect* in our power" (I.ix). The significance of this change is most obvious in the fact that the Thomistic answer (along with the Reformed and Platonic answers) is automatically ruled out: God cannot be our final end because God cannot be the effect of our actions. We could, of course, say that what Aquinas describes as the acquisition of our end—that is, the eternal con-templation of God in the beatific vision—might be an effect in our power. As we will see, however, conceiving the end as the best effect makes this answer seem implausible.

Why does Cumberland shift the terms in this manner? The reason he gives is that the relationship between an efficient cause and its effect is capable of demonstration while that between means and end, which depends on the intention of free and mutable beings, is not. We cannot always know human intentions, but we can be certain about the interactions between efficient causes and effects. Cumberland argues that though our actions stem from free decisions, "after we have *determin'd to act*, the *connexion* between our *Actions* and all the *Effects* thence depending, is *necessarily* and plainly natural and, therefore, *capable of Demonstration*" (V.iv). He does not doubt the reality of freedom and intentional action for ends, but his Cartesian body-soul dualism allows them to be sharply distinguished from the mechanistic world of causes and effects. Empirical demonstration is limited to bodies.[21] And why is strict demonstration so important? The answer, once again, returns us to the central aim: to prove that the natural law is a legitimate law with sanctions. Cumberland needs to show that particular act-types have fixed, empirically demonstratable effects, effects that are the divine sanctions through which God enacts the natural law. Cumberland sees the shift in interpreting human action from means–end to efficient cause–effect as a necessary step in this demonstration.[22]

The question of our final end, then, is the question of the best effect in our power. Once we know the best effect, we can determine the content of the natural law by determining which actions are conducive to it. What is the best effect in our power? To answer this question, we need Cumberland's account of natural goodness. While Cumberland limits moral goodness to actions in conformity with a law imposed by the command of a legitimate authority, he considers natural goodness to be a rationally discernible feature of the natural world. The naturally good, according to Cumberland, is "*that which preserves, or enlarges and perfects, the Faculties*[23] *of any one Thing, or of several*" (III.i). The natural good that primarily concerns Cumberland is that which is naturally good for human beings, but the definition is more general.

Immediately following his definition, Cumberland notes that goodness is a sort of *convenientia* or agreement, which is how Suárez defines the good.[24] But, again, Cumberland worries that the term is of "very uncertain signification." Agreement, too, must be reformulated in a manner that permits demonstration. Rather than concerning himself with the intrinsic suitability or fittingness between things, Cumberland focuses on the effects of one thing on another: "For we do not otherwise use to judge whether the nature or essence of anything agrees [*conveniat*] with another or not than by the effects of the actions thence proceeding" (III.i).

Cumberland does not deny intrinsic agreement but asserts that intrinsic agreement is known only by the effects of one thing on another.

This account of natural goodness is explicitly framed against Hobbes. For Hobbes, natural good and evil are determined by individual desires.[25] I call that which I want good; you do the same. There is no reason to expect us to agree. Cumberland's definition also grants a certain relativity to the meaning of "good." "Good" first of all means "good for," or, as Cumberland puts it, "*good*, to the Nature of this thing, rather than of others" (III.i). But he disagrees with Hobbes on two fundamental points. First, Cumberland claims that Hobbes gets the relationship between desire and reason backward. We do not desire something and therefore judge it to be good; rather, we desire it because we judge it to be good (III.ii). Second, he argues that "good for" is an objective relationship. That which preserves or perfects a person depends not on desire but "upon the *natural Powers* of things," which cannot "be chang'd at the *Pleasure of Men*." If a man in the state of nature were to desire wolfsbane (a poison) for the sake of health and nourishment, it would still kill him (I.xxviii).

Importantly, Cumberland's definition also includes what preserves or perfects aggregates. An aggregate can include anything which reason can consider "under an indefinite Notion, equally applicable to all [such that] it can also unite them into *one* general Body, in order to discover what is Good or Evil for it" (III.i). One example is all animals of a species. Another is all rational beings, an aggregate that, due to its indefinite characterization, even includes God (III.i).

We can now return to the question of the final end as the best effect. The best effect in our power will be the greatest natural good in our power. While Cumberland accepts that we all necessarily desire our own happiness, he argues that our happiness is not the best effect in our power. The happiness of one rational being is a rather limited natural good. The best effect, rather, is the common good of all rationals, which he describes as "the Aggregate or sum of all those good things, which, either we can contribute towards, or are necessary to, the Happiness of *all* rational Beings, consider'd as collected into one Body, each in his proper order" (V.viii). Cumberland never clearly states the reasoning by which he comes to this answer, but it appears to be this: the best effect is what is best for the best thing, and the best thing is the aggregate of rational beings, including God.[26] The best effect, therefore, is what is best for the aggregate of all rationals, which is the sum total of everything that is naturally good for this aggregate, as an aggregate, taken in its proper order. Instead of summing the goods of individual beings, as More does, Cumberland conceives the best effect as the good of an ordered whole.[27]

Natural Goodness and Human Action

Having determined the best effect, the next question is how we are to understand the relationship between the best effect and particular actions. Before addressing this question, however, let us consider a possible objection, namely, that the common good of all rationals cannot possibly be in the power of any particular rational creature. This objection illuminates another way in which Cumberland's teleological natural law modifies the Thomistic tradition. The end is not, for Cumberland, the best effect in the power of any one rational being. It is, rather, the best possible effect of the actions of all rational beings together. Why does Cumberland consider the best effect in these terms?

Cumberland, as noted above, contrasts his account of natural goodness with Hobbes's. Because Hobbes thinks goodness is determined by our desires, he argues that we only pursue that which we consider good for ourselves: "The object of the will is that which every man thinks good for himself."[28] For Cumberland, by contrast, "good for" is an objective relationship. For this reason, nothing prevents one person from recognizing what is good for another (III.iv). He continues:

> Nor see I any thing to hinder, but that what I judge agreeable to any Nature, I may desire should happen to it; nay, that I should endeavour, as far as in me lies, that it should be effected. But whatever any Faculty (and, consequently, the Will) can be employ'd about, is included in the *adequate Object* of that Faculty. (III.iv)

Cumberland accepts the scholastic dictum that the object of the will is the good. If the intellect can recognize any natural good, then, Cumberland thinks, the will can pursue it. We can, according to Cumberland, will goods for other people, for animals, for aggregates, and even for inanimate beings capable of preservation and perfection (III.i).

This account of goodness and its relationship to the will enables a further argument against Hobbes. To pursue one's own good alone, according to Cumberland, is a rational contradiction. It is to be inconsistent with oneself (I.vi). If I treat my happiness as the best effect, I will judge all things as good or bad only insofar as they are good or bad for me. I will judge your regaining health as bad if you are my competitor. But your regaining health is an objective natural good. I thus fall into rational contradiction, treating what I know to be good as bad. One could reply, however, that I do not have to deny that your health is good for you to think that it is bad for me. But Cumberland rejects the idea because it would allow different people to have different final ends. He writes:

> *Reason* will not suffer, that the greatest *Private* Good should be propos'd as the *ultimate End*. For, since that *Action* is certainly *Good*, which will lead directly, or the shortest way, to that *End*, which is truly *ultimate*; supposing *different ultimate Ends*, whose causes are *opposite*, *Actions* truly *Good* will be in *mutual opposition* to one another, which is impossible . . . For [two different men judging that his own happiness is the ultimate good] contain a manifest Contradiction; and, therefore, one only of these Dictates can be suppos'd true. But, since there is no Cause, why the Happiness of one of these should be his ultimate End, rather than the Happiness of another should likewise be his ultimate End; we may conclude, that Reason dictates to neither, that he should propose to himself his own Happiness only, as his greatest End, but to everyone, rather his own in conjunction with the Happiness of others; and this is that *Common Good*, which we contend is to be sought after. (V.xvi)

Actions are good when they promote the ultimate end. If different people have different ultimate ends, then one person's good actions will be in opposition to another person's good actions, which Cumberland thinks is impossible. If my ultimate end is my happiness, I might rightly seek some position of social prestige in order to attain greater happiness. You might do the same. But if we seek the same position, we will be in opposition, even while we both act rightly, a result that Cumberland considers rationally contradictory. If we are both acting rightly, our actions must seek the same outcome. Because the point of an action is its effect, Cumberland thinks that all good actions must ultimately "intend one and the same Effect" (V.xvi). Only in this way can there be a single, shared standard for the goodness and badness of all human actions (V.xvi).

At this point, we can see why the best effect must be universally shared. We can also now see how the best effect provides the standard for the natural goodness and badness of human action. Those actions are naturally good "which, from their own *natural* Force or Efficacy, are apt to promote the common Good." Moreover, Cumberland adds, those actions are naturally right which "take the shortest way to this Effect, as to their End" (Intro.xvi). Neither natural goodness nor natural rightness on its own entails moral goodness. Moral goodness requires the command of a superior. Before turning to moral goodness, let us pause and take note of a key feature of this account of the natural goodness of human actions.

Cumberland, I have been arguing, is best understood as modifying a Thomistic account of the natural law in the legislative voluntarist tradition of Suárez and Culverwell. Like Suárez and Culverwell, he argues that acts are naturally good and evil but that moral obligation depends upon divine command. Within this general agreement, however, lie important differences. One difference concerns what precisely is natural and what depends upon divine command. All agree that action is naturally good and bad and that moral obligation depends upon divine command. The disagreement lies where one draws the line around morality. Terence Irwin offers a helpful summary of this disagreement.[29] For Suárez, moral obligation is not the entirety of what is morally good or right. He distinguishes moral obligation from moral goodness. The former depends upon divine command, but the latter does not. Cumberland, by contrast, argues that nothing can be morally good apart from divine command. The boundaries of morality, for Cumberland, are identical to the boundaries of obligation. Culverwell falls between these two positions, equating morality with divinely imposed obligation but allowing for a natural *honestas* or natural obligation that does not depend upon divine command.[30]

Even more important is the question of the grounds of the natural goodness of an action. In Suárez's metaphysics, goodness is a transcendental attribute that is extensionally equivalent with being but adds the aspect of agreeability.[31] Many things can be agreeable to human nature. Following Aristotle and Aquinas, Suárez divides these into the pleasant, the useful, and the honest. The morally good is equivalent to the honest. It expresses a particular kind of agreeability with human nature, namely, an agreeability with rational nature.[32] Culverwell likewise speaks of the "convenience" and "irreconcilable disconvenience" that an action can have to human nature as the grounds of a natural obligation.[33]

Very similar language is repeated by Cumberland (IV.ii). Irwin cites this similarity to demonstrate Cumberland's continuity on this point with Suárez and Culverwell. Yet Cumberland's traditional affirmation should not mask a more important discontinuity. While he accepts that naturally good action agrees with human nature, he does not take agreement with human nature to be the criterion of natural goodness for human action. For Cumberland, the criterion of natural goodness for human action is the relationship between an act as an efficient cause and the common good of all rationals as an effect. Those acts which causally contribute to the common good of rationals are good; those that causally hinder it are evil.

Recall that Cumberland defines natural goodness as that which preserves and perfects any being. Preserving and perfecting, he acknowledges, is a kind of fittingness. In this way, his general picture of goodness resembles Suárez's. But for Cumberland, the fittingness that matters for the goodness of human action is the fittingness between human action and the aggregate of all rationals. In what sense, then, is naturally good action fitting with human nature? For Cumberland, fittingness is determined by effects. One thing is fitting with another if it tends toward its preservation or perfection. Good actions may be defined by agreement with the aggregate of rationals, but Cumberland is seeking to demonstrate that, as a result of the causal structure of the universe, they tend also toward the preservation and perfection of the agent. Fittingness with human nature, then, is not essential to the goodness of human action; it is the reward.[34]

Moral Goodness and the Natural Law

The naturally good actions that promote the common good are the same actions that God commands. In this way, Cumberland follows Suárez and Culverwell. But unlike Suárez and Culverwell, Cumberland is not satisfied to argue only on rational grounds that God commands what is naturally good. Arguing with Hobbes, he does not expect arguments about what God's goodness necessitates to carry much weight. He seeks to demonstrate empirically that naturally good and bad actions are enforced by naturally occurring sanctions.

The natural law, Cumberland claims, can be stated as a single proposition. His two expressions of this proposition are slightly different. I quote both:

> The Endeavour, to the utmost of our power, of promoting the common Good of the whole System of rational Agents, conduces, as far as in us lies, to the good of every Part, in which our own Happiness, as that of a Part, is contain'd. But contrary Actions produce contrary Effects, and consequently our own Misery, among that of others. (Intro.ix)

> The greatest Benevolence of every rational Agent towards all, forms the happiest State of every, and of all the Benevolent, as far as in their power, and is necessarily requisite to the happiest State which they can attain, and therefore the common Good is the supreme Law. (I.iv)

In these statements of the natural law, Cumberland links particular human actions with the best effect: actions that arise from the greatest benevolence causally promote the best effect. It is important to note that Cumberland uses the term "benevolence" in a particular way. Benevolence (*benevolentia*) is commonly used for a desire for the well-being of others in contrast to that of the self.[35] For Cumberland, benevolence simply means willing something good:

> But seeing *only voluntary* Actions can be govern'd by human *Reason*, and *those only which regard intelligent Beings*, are consider'd in *Morality*; and seeing the Object of the Will is *Good*, (for *Evil* is rated from the Privation of Good;) it is *evident*, "That a more general Notion of such Actions cannot be form'd, than what falls under the Name *Benevolence*," because it comprehends the *Desire* of all kinds of *good Things*, and consequently the avoiding all kinds of *Evils*. (I.viii)

Benevolence is not a particular kind of aim or desire in contrast to another. Because all voluntary actions aim for some good, all voluntary actions are benevolent. The emphasis is not on benevolence as one kind of aim over against another, but on the *degree* of benevolence. "Greatest benevolence" (*benevolentia maxima*) simply means the pursuit of the greatest good. That is why the other formulation can replace "greatest benevolence" with "Endeavour, to the utmost of our power, of promoting the common Good."[36]

Cumberland calls the proposition stating the natural law a practical proposition (Intro.xi). The subject of the proposition consists of actions in our power, and the predicate consists of the consequence of those actions. The proposition states that there is a natural causal connection between the subject and the predicate. Universal benevolence, Cumberland contends, is the intrinsic cause of the present common good and the efficient cause of the future common good (I.iv). This causal connection is the "foundation of the truth of the proposition," and much of *De legibus* is dedicated to its proof (Intro.xv). The connection, he argues, is imprinted on our minds by the nature of things, that is, by experience and observation of the outcomes of actions. There is no need for an appeal to innate ideas (Intro.v).[37]

The causal connection between the greatest benevolence and the common good suffices for Cumberland to demonstrate that actions stemming from the greatest benevolence are naturally good. Demonstrating that the same actions are morally obligatory requires him to prove that they are commands promulgated by God and enforced by sanctions. The will of God, Cumberland argues, determines the causal connection between acts and consequences. This fact, combined with the way natural causal consequences imprint themselves on our minds, establishes divine promulgation of the natural law. The sanction comes from the fact that the full happiness of any individual rational being is found only in the common good. Those acts that tend toward the common good tend also toward the happiness of the actor, while those that hinder the common good also hinder the happiness of the actor. These features together allow Cumberland to conclude, without appeal to revelation, that the natural law is divinely imposed.

Virtue, Happiness, and Sanctions

The upshot of Cumberland's argument appears to be that the one who pursues the common good with utmost endeavor will be rewarded with happiness. But, one might object, the conclusion is obviously false; it runs into the old problem of the suffering of the virtuous and triumph of the wicked. Cumberland's scattered responses to this objection illuminate important aspects of his view. Recall, first of all, that Cumberland's natural law proposition is collective. The argument is not that a single individual, striving with all her might, can produce the common good of which her happiness is a part. The only cause that can produce the common good is the utmost endeavor of all rational beings. The argument principally addresses humanity as a whole, and Cumberland regularly makes analogies with physical systems:

> The whole Race of Mankind ought to be consider'd as one System of Bodies, so that nothing of any Moment can be done by any Man, relating to the Life, Fortune, or Posterity of any one, which may not some way affect those things which are alike dear to others; as the Motion of every Body, in the System of the World, communicates its Motion to many others, especially neighbouring ones. (II.xiv)

He makes a similar analogy to animal bodies. The body maintains the good of each part, but always for the sake of the good of the body. And each part can have no good unless the life of the body is maintained (Intro.xxii).

Cumberland, then, does not posit a strict correlation between individual benevolence and individual happiness. He posits a causal relationship between two states of affairs, one of universal benevolence and the other of the greatest happiness of all rationals.[38] This causal connection, for Cumberland, is sufficient to pick out benevolence as the naturally good principle of all human action. He does not seem to think, however, that it is sufficient to prove that the natural law contains sanctions. The proof of the existence of sanctions requires more careful attention to the results of individual actions. Here Cumberland comes face to face with the problem that virtue does not always seem to result in happiness.

Let us first clarify what Cumberland means by happiness. We all, according to Cumberland, naturally and necessarily desire our own happiness. Happiness lies in the full realization of our natural powers, which brings with it the greatest pleasure and peace of mind. Some have argued that Cumberland is a hedonist, but he explicitly refuses to prioritize pleasure.[39] Happiness includes both perfective and affective components: "I have no inclination, very curiously to *inquire*, 'Whether the *Happiness* of Man be an Aggregate of the most vigorous *Actions*, which can proceed from our Faculties; or rather a most *grateful Sense of them*, join'd with Tranquility and Joy, which by some is call'd *Pleasure*.' These as inseparably connected, and *both necessary* to Happiness" (V.xiii).

The argument that virtue produces individual happiness is twofold: virtue produces both immediate and mediate effects (V.xii). The immediate effects are those of virtue itself. Maximal benevolence, when guided by prudence, is itself the whole of virtue, and virtue is a necessary part of our happiness. To act with our greatest effort for the greatest good is to maximally exercise our powers. To do otherwise is to fail to realize ourselves to the fullest extent and is to miss the "vast *Pleasure*" therein (V.xv). Moreover, to pursue anything other than the best end is, as we have seen, to fall into practical contradiction, which "greatly *hurts* the Soundness, Peace, and *Contentment* of the Mind in its Actions." Virtue, by contrast, produces "greatest *Tranquility*" (V.xvi). Finally, only virtue allows proper governance of the passions, which otherwise lead to uncontrolled actions and the constant frustration of desire.[40]

Mediate effects are the external effects of our actions concerning those goods of body and mind necessary for happiness. Virtue, he argues, has naturally good mediate effects for us, which "we may, with *certainty*, expect from *God*, and, with greater *probability*, hope to obtain from *Men*" (V.xviii). The certainty of divine sanctions can be inferred from what we know of the divine will from the nature of creation (V.xix–V.xii). These sanctions occur after death. The reality of postmortem sanctions, which will fill in the deficiencies of the sanctions imposed by created effects, is crucial to Cumberland's argument. But these sanctions cannot be observed and thus cannot serve as evidence of the natural law.[41]

Cumberland appeals principally to the social effects of human action. The argument is clearest regarding negative sanctions. He offers three arguments that those who do what is naturally bad should expect punishment. First, human beings are incited to action by what he calls "meritorious causes." Blameworthy acts trigger responses from others in a manner that is "altogether as Real, as any Impulse from external Objects upon our Senses" (V.xxxvi). Hindering the common good provokes the wrath of others just as surely as the smell of food provokes their hunger. Second, "every Action proceeding from Malevolence towards others, has a natural endless Tendency to produce other Malevolent Actions of the like kind" (V.xxxvii). Evil acts, for example, cause other evil acts through example. In this way, the evil acts of any individual tend to destabilize society and thwart the common happiness, including that of the actor. Finally, because human beings have reason, we can recognize the harmful effects of evil and be vigilant in punishing it. In cases in which evildoers are more likely to avoid detection, we make the punishments even more severe to deter these evil acts (V.xxxix).

Even given these features of the world, the mediate effects may not be realized. Since virtue alone is not sufficient for happiness, virtue without the mediate effects, may not produce happiness. How, then, can Cumberland hold to his statement of the natural law? To address this problem, he relies on two crucial distinctions: first, between that which is in our power and that which is not; second, between the natural consequences of acts and those that are accidental.

The first distinction allows Cumberland to limit the realm of effects in question. The natural law concerns only our actions. Therefore, the effects that communicate divine sanctions are only the effects of those actions. The connection between virtue and divine sanctions, he argues, "is somewhat obscur'd by those evil Things which happen to the Good, and those good Things which happen to the Evil." Evil things which happen to the good (and vice versa) are not usually the direct consequence of their actions:

> In comparing the Effects of good and evil Actions, those good or evil Things, which can neither be procur'd nor avoided by human Industry, are not to be taken into Account. Such are those which happen by natural Necessity, or by mere Chance, from external Causes: for these both may, and do, happen alike both to good and bad. We shall therefore here consider those only, which can be taken care of by human Reason, as in some measure depending upon our Actions. (Intro.xvii)

This distinction allows Cumberland to rule out of consideration many of the events most destructive to happiness. The good and the bad alike suffer from frailty, sickness, pain, and death. The same would be true even if all rational beings acted with the greatest benevolence. The natural order is not constituted to ensure the happiness of the virtuous. The importance of natural sanctions is not their sufficiency as sanctions but the fact that they make God's commands known to us. The natural connection between virtue and happiness confirms that the natural law is a law, even when the virtuous are oppressed by evils beyond human power. And lest anyone have too great a hope of achieving happiness through virtue, Cumberland is quite frank: those things which are not in our power "are by far the greatest, and the most, of those Motions which we daily perceive in the Universe, which we (little Animals) cannot obstruct, and . . . which are the continual Sources, even to Men themselves, of the Vicissitudes of Adversity and Prosperity, Birth, Maturity, and Death" (I.xxi).

This first distinction certainly makes Cumberland's case more plausible, but it remains insufficient. Even the argument about the effects of our own actions can be at best probable. Cumberland never disputes the fact that virtue can itself result in pain, suffering, and death—a fact that is certainly unavoidable for a Christian for whom Jesus is the exemplar of virtue. How, then, can we be sure that merely probable outcomes are indeed divine sanctions? At times, Cumberland speaks as if probability were itself sufficient. He appeals to emerging markets in reversions in which a contingent future benefit is given a definite present price. The same, he argues, is true with the probable outcomes of our actions: we can render them as a definite but lesser present value (V.xxvi). In this way, probable sanctions can be reinterpreted as definite.[42]

But Cumberland does not leave the matter at simple probability. He relies on a distinction—never clearly articulated but implicit throughout—between natural effects and accidental effects. Cumberland, as we have seen, is keen to reinterpret Aristotelian and scholastic categories in mechanistic terms. The same applies to the notion of the nature or essence of a thing. The nature of a thing is known by its characteristic effects: "The effects are what disclose the hidden powers and inward constitution of all things" (III.i). He applies the same approach to human actions. Act-types are defined not by the intention or understanding of the agent, which Cumberland brackets, but by their characteristic effects. Virtuous actions are those with the characteristic effect of promoting the common good of rationals.

Cumberland allows for accidental deviations from these characteristic effects. We are naturally inclined to breathe, and air is good for us—yet, when contingencies intervene, it is occasionally harmful. Meat, drink, and exercise are also naturally good for us—except, again, when they are accidentally bad for us (Intro.xxi). The same is true with virtue. Virtue naturally causally contributes to the common good of rationals as well as the happiness of the virtuous. When accidents intervene, virtue may not have its characteristic effects.[43] God commands what naturally promotes the best effect, not whatever might accidentally do so in a given case. One would be wrong to execute the innocent, even if it happened to promote the best effect in a given case. The fact that it naturally hinders the best effect demonstrates that God forbids it.

These two distinctions together allow Cumberland to recognize that virtue does not always cause happiness without abandoning his argument about natural sanctions. Amidst the external causes and diseased elements that obscure the divinely ordained sanctions, Cumberland isolates the natural effects of human actions—which are, when the "entire *adequate Causes*" are considered, "wholly *immutable*" (I.xxvi)—and locates rewards and punishments here. In creating the causal nexus of the world, God has "attached" happiness and misery to commanded and forbidden actions, a fact that is communicated to us by the nature of things.

Divine Authority and Moral Obligation

Laws, according to Cumberland, are "nothing but *practical Propositions, with Rewards and Punishments annex'd, promulg'd by competent Authority*" (Intro.vi). We have now seen how Cumberland understands the promulgation and sanctions of the natural law. The final element required is to show that God is a legitimate authority.

Not everyone agrees that Cumberland considers this final step necessary. Some have argued that moral obligation for Cumberland is simply the necessity of an act to one's happiness.[44] In this view, the fact that virtue is the best means to happiness suffices for moral obligation. But this view confuses obligation with morality. Cumberland wants to do away with the metaphorical language with which obligation is often defined. To say that obligation is a "bind" or a "tie" is not to make it any less obscure. What these terms are trying to grasp, he thinks, is the necessity or force of obligation, and here he appeals to the sanctions: "The whole force of *Obligation* is this, *That the Legislator has annex'd to the observance of his Laws, Good; to the transgression, Evil*" (V.xi). Sanctions explain the force imposed by obligation—the way in which it "binds" or "ties" those subject to it. This force, however, is not what makes the act morally good. Otherwise, we would be morally obligated by anything that turns out to be necessary to our happiness. God's legitimate command makes actions morally good or bad, and the sanctions add the bind that we refer to when we call the actions obligatory.

Those who have recognized this account of morality in Cumberland have tended to see a different problem: how to ground divine authority.[45] Divine authority, as I noted in the previous chapter, is one point on which the ethical voluntarist seems to have an upper hand. The authority of God is easy to explain if God's will is the source of truths about good and evil. Cumberland rejects this solution. One common anti-ethical-voluntarist approach (that of Suárez and Culverwell) is to ground divine authority on the right of a Creator. Cumberland, who is skeptical of this view, instead follows the outlines of More's view. Cumberland's argument for divine authority goes like this. God's own determination of an end and the best means to it are analogous to a law in God. Echoing Aquinas, he calls it the eternal law. God, by rational necessity, wills the best end—that is, the best effect, the common good of all rationals—as well as the best means to it. Among the best means is God's own governance of creation, and this conclusion provides the grounds for God's authority. Therefore, God enacts the natural law by promulgation and sanctions. As rational creatures, we too can recognize that God's governance of creation is the best means to the best effect. We thus have rational grounds for submitting to divine authority. Upon discovering the precepts and sanctions of the natural law promulgated and imposed through the nature of things, we recognize ourselves to be bound to conform to the natural law.[46]

The problem, according to some interpreters, is that Cumberland, against his own principles, ultimately reduces morality to a rational dictate of practical reason. Because all rationals, God and creatures, can recognize the necessity of divine governance as a means to the best effect, all judge that God must rule and creatures obey. This judgment seems to make divine commands superfluous. Instead of commanding, God could just inform rational creatures about how to best pursue the common good of all rationals, which they are already rationally bound to do. The distinction between command and counsel seems to disappear. Stephen Darwall argues that obligation in Cumberland must just mean the necessity of practical reason.[47] Terence Irwin finds Cumberland's position doubtful without an account of natural (that is, premoral) obligation.[48] Darwall and Irwin are right to see that Cumberland accounts for divine authority in terms of rational necessity. Like More, Cumberland ultimately grounds divine authority in the claim that we are rationally bound to pursue the same end as God. This shared endeavor commits all parties to following the dictates of the one most capable of directing the common pursuit. Despite the critiques, Cumberland's view is consistent on his own terms. Practical reason and moral obligation are supposed to align. Cumberland's argument explains why they do. It allows him to do precisely what he set out to do: demonstrate that naturally good actions are also morally obligatory.

Cumberland's Transformation of the Perfectionistic Natural Law

Cumberland's account of the natural law was among the most significant in seventeenth-century Europe. Its influence spread not only throughout Britain but also to the continent. Samuel Pufendorf adopted key elements of Cumberland's argument to overcome critiques of his own position.[49] In England in the decades following the publication of *De legibus*, two abridged translations of the work appeared, the first by Samuel Parker and the second by James Tyrrell. Both had the express intent of popularizing Cumberland's argument.[50] The entire text was translated into English in 1727 by John Maxwell and into French in 1744 by Jean Barbeyrac. Through these and other channels, Cumberland's arguments reached a wide audience.

De legibus, then, was profoundly influential on eighteenth-century moral philosophy, but not in the way Cumberland might have expected. The heart of *De legibus* is the reconciliation of a rational and perfectionistic natural law with legislative voluntarism. Its central contribution is to argue that the promulgation and sanctions of the natural law can be found in the causal structure of the created order. Cumberland's argument, I have just argued, succeeds on its own terms—if, that is, its empirical claims and its picture of goods, ends, and agency are granted. Yet despite a few early enthusiasts, Cumberland convinced few people of his big ideas. His greatest impact must be found elsewhere: in the many subtle but profound ways in which he shifted features of the perfectionistic natural law tradition in order to demonstrate the existence of divinely imposed sanctions. The most important is the way he shifts the structure of teleology by changing the final end to the best effect. This move mirrors the same shift we saw in More. Rather than a theocentric picture, Cumberland gives us a cosmocentric one. The highest good and object of all striving is not God but the common good of all rationals. Together with this move from the final end to the best effect, Cumberland introduces a series of subtler shifts in the perfectionist natural law tradition.

First, Cumberland implicitly embraces a productivist picture of human agency.[51] Cumberland, I have noted, brackets "internal" movements of the soul such as intention and desire. While human action is free, movements of the body, once freely chosen, enter into a world of mechanical necessity, causing certain effects, including rewards and punishments. The relationship between bodily movements and their effects is central to his argument. One problem with this picture is that while bodily movements may mechanistically produce effects, bodily movements are not

themselves human actions, a fact that Cumberland does not recognize.[52]
While bracketing intention and desire, Cumberland continues to refer
to bodily movements as human actions, that is, he continues to refer to
them in intentional terms. To make this work, he has to interpret human
action in a particular way. Causal effects must not only be the product
of external bodily movement; they must also be the object of intention
and desire. By implicitly interpreting human action in this way, Cumberland can speak of bodily movements both as actions and as efficient
causes. The result of his effort to bracket intention and desire, then, is
that they sneak back in but under different terms. All human action, in
these productivist terms, has as its aim and object an effect produced in
the world.

Cumberland believes that he is clarifying traditional conceptions of
human action. His brief discussion of ancient moral philosophy demonstrates that he is wrong. The ancients, he says, considered happiness to be
the final end. We have seen why this is problematic in Cumberland's terms.
But rather than rejecting all ancient moral thought, Cumberland decides
that the ancients can be read charitably as saying something different:

> [W]hen *Moral Writers* speak of *every Man's Happiness* as *his ultimate
> end*, I would willingly *interpret* them in this sense, "That it is the chief
> End among those, which respect the Agent himself only"; and I doubt
> not, but that every *Good Man* has an End, that is, intends an Effect, that
> is greater, namely, the Honour of God, and the Increase of other Mens
> Happiness. (V.xlvii)

It is not hard to see how Cumberland's account of human agency distorts
his reading of ancient ethics. Aristotle means to say neither that one's own
happiness is the only effect one intends nor that it is the effect one intends
with respect to oneself only. For the ancients, the virtuous do aim to bring
about effects beyond their own happiness, including perhaps the honor of
God and the happiness of others, but the question of which effects they
ought to cause is not the same as the question of the final end. The view we
now call eudaimonism becomes very difficult to understand when agency
is construed in Cumberland's productivist terms. Indeed, eudaimonism
becomes essentially indistinguishable from egoism. Difficulty making
sense of ancient eudaimonism will be a lasting problem for those who
accept, implicitly or explicitly, a productivist picture of human agency. By
the time we reach the moral debates of early eighteenth-century Britain,
eudaimonism holds no conceptual space beyond egoism.[53]

The second and closely related conceptual shift is the way he conceives the grounds of natural goodness. Cumberland, as we have seen, accepts that natural goodness is a kind of *convenientia*. While this claim echoes that of Suárez, Cumberland introduces subtle but profound differences. One has already been highlighted. Cumberland changes the grounds of the natural goodness of actions from their agreement with human nature to their agreement with the aggregate of all rationals, which is understood in terms of the actions' causal promotion of the common good of all rationals. The other is even more subtle but no less important. *Convenientia* in Suárez is, according to Jorge Gracia and Douglas Paul Davis, best translated as "agreeability" rather than "agreement" because it is a feature of something in virtue of which that thing is desirable.[54] Though Cumberland does not use the same metaphysical terminology, I want to suggest that he thinks of *convenientia* as "agreement" rather than "agreeability," that is, as an act or event in which one thing preserves or perfects another.[55] Thus the highest good, in Suárez's account, is that which is maximally agreeable (God), while the highest good, on Cumberland's, is that state in which maximal agreement is realized (the common good of all rationals). This shift in the nature of natural goodness is closely related to the shift in the nature of human agency. If all action aims at effects, and if all action also aims at some natural good, then natural goodness must be the sort of thing that can be the effect of an action. Like More, then, Cumberland treats the good as a state of affairs to be achieved.

Finally, Cumberland, absorbing ideas from Hobbes even as he criticizes them, grants a heightened moral significance to efficient causality. One way he does this is simply by conceiving of acts principally as efficient causes for the sake of effects. More subtly, he also develops the notion that particular act-types have natural causal consequences. He treats human society on the model of a material system in which the same act-types have invariant natural effects, even while accidents sometimes intervene (I.xxvi). In his concrete arguments to this effect, he treats the actor as an agent and the rest of society mechanistically.[56] The agent in question acts; others respond naturally to, for example, "meritorious causes" or negative examples. Despite his focus on the common good, then, there is something profoundly apolitical in Cumberland's moral philosophy. Individual moral agents ought to consider how others will instinctively react to their actions, but moral agents do not genuinely act together. While all aim at the realization of the same effect, each considers only the particular causal trajectory of their own actions.

Cumberland's innovations in the perfectionistic natural law tradition mirror More's innovations in the Christian Platonist tradition. Cumberland conceives the end as a state of affairs to be realized. He argues that good actions are those that causally promote that state. He thinks that God seeks to realize the same end as rational creatures. And he claims that divine authority derives from God's superior capacity to guide the shared pursuit of the end. Cumberland, in other words, embraces the consequentialist moral cosmology.

Epilogue to Part I

In his *Outlines of the History of Ethics*, Henry Sidgwick writes that the Cambridge Platonists and Richard Cumberland offer the two most important responses to Hobbes in the subsequent generation.[1] Both seek to counter what they see as the corrosive effects of Hobbes's moral and political philosophy.[2] The contribution of More and Cumberland, according to Sidgwick, was to provide a "counter-exposition of orthodox doctrine" about the good against Hobbes.[3] If Sidgwick means that More and Cumberland both assert against Hobbes that the good is natural and not a product of will and power, then his claim is perfectly accurate. It is, nonetheless, misleading. While More and Cumberland both challenge Hobbes's ethical views, including his ethical voluntarism, they do not simply reassert an earlier ethical orthodoxy. If they are orthodox in their defense of the objectivity of the good, they are also highly innovative in how they understand the good.

When we compare More and Cumberland to the alternative seventeenth-century ethical intellectualist options surveyed in chapter 1, we find a starkly different picture. According to those earlier intellectualist options, the highest good and final end of the moral life is God. God and rational creatures act for the sake of this end, though in different ways and without shared moral principles. For More and Cumberland, the end shared by God and creatures is not an object but a desired outcome: the realization of maximal goodness in creation. This shift is particularly lucid in Cumberland's linguistic shift: the final end becomes the best effect. The moral life is structured not by one's orientation to the highest good, God in Godself, but by one's causal production of the best effect, the common good of all rational beings.

This revised conception of the good and the final end naturally pairs with a new picture of human agency. Again, this shift is particularly clear in Cumberland, who implicitly embraces a productivist picture of human agency according to which the object and purpose of action is the causal production of states of affairs. The notion that God could be the end becomes quite difficult to understand since God is not a state of affairs to be realized. An important concomitant of this conception of the end to which both God and rational creatures relate primarily by causal production is that God and rational creatures share the same moral principles of action. More elaborates a set of axioms, while Cumberland reduces all morality to the principle of benevolence. In each case, the principle or principles apply to God as well as to rational creatures.[4]

One strength of ethical voluntarism is that it makes sense of God's moral authority to command creatures, an authority presupposed by the biblical texts. Rejecting the idea that God determines good and evil by will, the anti-ethical-voluntarist must provide a different explanation of God's authority to command rational creatures. More and Cumberland offer an innovative solution to this problem. God, they argue, is most capable of directing the shared pursuit of the best effect. For this reason, God ought to issue commands to rational creatures, and rational creatures ought to obey God's commands. God's commands are binding because God commands the best means to the end that we are already bound to pursue.

One can see in these shifts the emergence of consequentialist moral rationality. In the introduction, I listed three features of consequentialist moral rationality: (1) the good is a state of affairs to be realized; (2) the goodness of different states of affairs is always commensurable and subject to ranking or quantitative analysis; and (3) moral agents should see themselves as causally responsible not only for the immediate effects of their actions but also for the more distant effects, including those mediated by the actions of others. These features are now all in place. The first two are evident in More. The third only comes clearly into view in Cumberland. In the works of More and Cumberland, we can see consequentialist moral rationality emerge through subtle but profound conceptual innovations.

More and Cumberland also disagree on several important points. More, for example, believes that moral principles are innate and self-evident. Cumberland believes they are learned by experience, though he thinks the cosmos is designed in such a way that we cannot avoid learning them. In addition, Cumberland embraces legislative voluntarism, and More does not. That disagreement, however, is not particularly significant. It reduces to this: For More, God only commands us to do that which we are already morally required to do. For Cumberland, God only commands us to do that which is already naturally good and rational to do but not yet morally required. Without God's commands, we would still have a decisive reason (just not a moral reason) to do the same thing. Both More and Cumberland agree that God only commands us to do that which maximally conduces to the realization of the greatest good of creation. Both also agree that God necessarily acts according to the same principles that bind human beings, even if Cumberland would say that God's reasons for doing so are only moral in an analogical sense because no higher authority commands God.

One other difference deserves comment. More and Cumberland both seek to maintain a teleological picture of morality that differs from earlier scholastic views. In their efforts to move beyond scholastic Aristotelianism, they turn to new paradigms of thought. Given his commitment to eternal, self-evident truth, More is unsurprisingly drawn to a mathematical paradigm, and his axioms are clearly modeled on mathematics.[5] Cumberland, by contrast, is drawn to the mechanistic paradigm that was increasingly dominant in natural philosophy. A turn to mechanism might at first seem anti-teleological. But just as in most natural philosophy of the time, Cumberland could interpret mechanistic processes as processes designed by God for the sake of God's ends in creation. Despite their different paradigms, More and Cumberland end up with very similar views, a fact which is less surprising when one remembers that mechanistic processes were increasingly being understood mathematically. If we step back from many of the details and take in the larger moral vision, the similarities are striking. Moving forward, I will largely set aside More and Cumberland's differences and focus on the shared moral vision, the consequentialist moral cosmology.

The term "consequentialist moral cosmology" names a view that encompasses theology, ethics, and cosmology. The following elements are central: (1) A consequentialist view of morality according to which the right action is the one that contributes most to a maximally good state of the world.[6] (2) A view of divine morality according to which God acts according to the same consequentialist principles as rational creatures. (3) An account of divine authority over rational creatures grounded in the fact that God shares the same end as rational creatures and is best able to direct them on how to pursue it. Rational creatures ought to obey God because God knows best how to realize maximal natural goodness in creation. An implication of these elements is that God and rational creatures form a single moral community founded on shared principles of action and a shared end.

I call the conjunction of these three elements a "cosmology" rather than an "ethic" or a "moral philosophy" because it encompasses a comprehensive picture of the cosmos as a single moral system directed to a single moral end: the realization of maximal goodness in creation. God pursues this end perfectly. Rational creatures pursue it when they act according to reason and when they obey God. The rest of creation pursues it inadvertently under the guidance of divine providence. The goal of calling it a cosmology is to highlight the way it functions as a successor notion to the dominant medieval, Renaissance, and Reformation theocentric moral cosmology, a view of the entire cosmos as a single system oriented toward God as its end.

*****

The story of the invention of consequentialist moral rationality and the consequentialist moral cosmology is now complete. The story of theological consequentialism, however, has just begun. If the book ended here, the link between theological consequentialism and classical utilitarianism would remain opaque. The next two parts of the book, therefore, trace the development of theological consequentialism into the eighteenth century. Eighteenth-century theological consequentialism looks quite different from its seventeenth-century predecessor—and much more like the views now known as classical utilitarianism.

The importance of the consequentialist moral cosmology for the following generations of British moralists is difficult to overstate. More and Cumberland, as Sidgwick says, were perhaps the two most influential British moral philosophers of the generation after Hobbes. The fact that they reach very similar conclusions is not mentioned by either of them, but it was soon observed by their readers. James Tyrrell, the author of one of the two abridgments of Cumberland's treatise, certainly noticed the affinities between Cumberland's position and More's. In his abridged translation of *De legibus*, he lists several of More's moral axioms to fill out the details of what can be demonstrated by Cumberland's method.[7]

Yet while the consequentialist moral cosmology of More and Cumberland was highly influential on the following generations, the story of part II is not the story of its triumph. Instead, part II sets the scene for its rejection by most eighteenth-century theological consequentialists. As with the decline of any once-compelling moral vision, the reasons are multiple, including not only intellectual reasons but also social and political reasons. In what follows, I focus in particular on one problem that was integral to the breakdown of the consequentialist moral cosmology: a new and particularly pernicious version of the theological problem of evil. Pierre Bayle articulated this problem in an especially forceful manner that required response (chapter 4). Those who sought to address the problem within the general framework of the consequentialist moral cosmology struggled to do so without abandoning core elements of the view.

The consequentialist moral cosmology, as I noted in the introduction, is a term of art that functions as an ideal type. None of the figures discussed in chapters 5–7—William King, Shaftesbury, and Francis Hutcheson—defends it as such. But King, Shaftesbury, and Hutcheson are anti-ethical-voluntarists who have been influenced by More and Cumberland. They believe that God maximizes goodness in creation and that we ought to pursue the same end. They share the vision of a moral community between God and rational creatures. Yet they are also preoccupied with the issue of evil. In each case, I argue that their attempts to resolve the challenges posed by the existence and extent of evil in the world ultimately require them to abandon core aspects of the consequentialist moral cosmology. Chapters 5–7 can thus be read as three independent attempts to answer Bayle's challenge about evil within the broad framework provided by the consequentialist moral cosmology. None, I argue, is successful.

The failure of the consequentialist moral cosmology, however, was not the failure of consequentialist moral rationality. Even when the consequentialist moral cosmology was ultimately abandoned in the eighteenth century, the key innovations of More and Cumberland—innovations about goodness, ends, agency, and causality—not only survived but were increasingly taken for granted. One result, as we will see in part III, was eighteenth-century utilitarianism.

PART II

Evil and the Divine Consequentialist

4

Evil and the Consequentialist Moral Cosmology

PIERRE BAYLE AND BRITISH ETHICS

In *Evil in Modern Thought*, Susan Neiman challenges the standard story of modern philosophy. The problem of evil, according to Neiman's intriguing view, "is the guiding force of modern thought."[1] The enterprise of philosophy, she writes, is often thought to begin with epistemology: what if appearance is different from reality? Philosophy arises as a way to resolve the problem. Neiman doubts this story because she doubts that the epistemological worry provides a compelling motive for philosophy. The worry that drives philosophy, she writes, is "*not* the fear that the world might not turn out to the be way it seems to us—but rather the fear that it would."[2] Questions posed by the experience of evil, she argues, lie at the very heart of modern philosophy.

One need not accept Neiman's thesis to find her arguments illuminating. Evil is no doubt a central issue for modern philosophers, especially in the eighteenth century. One text in particular stood at the center of eighteenth-century debates about evil: Pierre Bayle's *Dictionnaire historique et critique*.[3] For this reason, Neiman dates the advent of the Enlightenment to the publication of Bayle's *Dictionnaire* in 1697. Beginning the story of modern philosophy with any single text is at least somewhat artificial, and Bayle's treatment of evil was certainly indebted to an already contentious debate about evil on the Continent.[4] Nonetheless, Neiman is correct to highlight its importance. Bayle's *Dictionnaire* quickly found its way to the center of nearly all philosophical and theological disputes about evil.

Bayle's central contention about evil is clear: human reason can find no justification for God's decision to create and govern a world so full of horror. He seeks to systematically undermine every attempt to morally justify God. Then, just as the reader might expect skeptical or atheistic conclusions, Bayle instead concludes that human reason is inadequate. We must simply fall back on faith and trust scripture, even though its doctrines are logically contradictory according to human reason.

Many readers took Bayle's explicit conclusions as a disingenuous attempt to avoid persecution. The implicit skeptical or atheistic conclusions seemed more compelling and likely the real motivation. But whether or not Bayle is taken at his word, his text offers a forceful critique of all attempts to subject God to any moral standard comprehensible to human reason. The implications of the critique, however, depend on one's views about the relationship between God and morality. Not everyone wants to subject God to moral standards. For the ethical voluntarist, Bayle's arguments about evil pose no threat. God's choice to create and govern this world is good because God willed to do so. For the intellectual heirs of Henry More and Richard Cumberland, by contrast, Bayle's challenge was too significant to ignore. Part II demonstrates that Bayle's arguments about God and evil challenged and ultimately transformed the consequentialist moral cosmology of More and Cumberland.

Contemporary discussions of the challenge evil poses to theism tend to frame it as a singular and straightforward problem: *the* problem of evil.[5] In fact, there is no singular or straightforward problem of evil. This is true in part because, as some have noted, the challenge evil poses is practical before it is theoretical. But even at the purely theoretical level, the nature of the challenge posed by evil—if, indeed, there is a challenge—depends on a wide variety of other beliefs. Amélie Oksenberg Rorty comments that the way the passions are conceived in early modern thought tends to "sensitively reflect gerrymandering shifts in power elsewhere."[6] The same can be said about evil and its theological implications. Whether and how evil presents a problem depends on beliefs about a wide variety of other issues, including the nature of God, the relationship between God and the world, the nature and ends of creation, the historical narrative of divine and human activity, the nature of morality, and God's relationship to morality.

A key theme of part I was the role of shifting conceptions of the good in seventeenth-century ethics. Because evil is usually understood to be the opposite of good, shifting conceptions of good are likely to have implications for evil. Yet conceptions of evil are also sensitive to a different set of concerns, especially in the context of broadly theistic belief. This chapter frames the debate about evil in the late seventeenth and early eighteenth centuries. I begin by contextualizing it within both the Augustinian tradition in general and post-Reformation theological polemics in particular. I then trace the unique contours of the early modern debate, which differ in important ways from earlier debates. Finally, I consider Bayle's understanding of the problem evil poses to theism, which sets the terms in which the issue is taken up in early eighteenth-century Britain. This chapter prepares the way for the next three chapters, which consider three separate responses to Bayle's challenge by British thinkers, each of which maintains key features of the consequentialist moral cosmology while also modifying it to address Bayle's arguments about evil.

Evil in the Augustinian Tradition

No thinker has been more important in shaping the Western Christian understanding of evil than Augustine. Augustine wrestled with the subject of evil throughout his life, from his early days as a Manichean to his late writings on the Pelagian controversy and the fall of Rome. His works on the nature and source of evil profoundly shaped theological orthodoxy in the Latin West until at least the seventeenth century. Augustine was perhaps nowhere more innovative than on the topics of sin and evil, but his innovations must be understood against the background of an already well established debate about evil.

The problem of evil, as it is commonly named, is now generally posed as a skeptical challenge, whether logical or evidential, to the existence of God. The first formulation is usually attributed to Epicurus. The surviving quotation comes from Lactantius's *De ira rei*:

> God either wishes to take away evils and he cannot, or he can and does not wish to, or he neither wishes to nor is able, or he both wishes to and is able. If he wishes to and is not able, he is feeble, which does not fall in with the notion of god. If he is able to and does not wish to, he is envious, which is equally foreign to god. If he neither wishes to nor is able, he is both envious and feeble and therefore not god. If he both wishes to and is able, which alone is fitting to god, whence, therefore, are there evils, and why does he not remove them?[7]

Whether or not this argument originates with Epicurus—and there are some compelling reasons to think that it does not[8]—it was an important argument in antiquity. A similar argument, Mark Larrimore notes, is also attributed to the Gnostic Marcion and used by Sextus Empiricus in *Outlines of Pyrrhonism*. While today the argument is taken to be an atheistic challenge to theistic belief, none of these three ancient sources used it this way. In fact, it served a different purpose for each. Sextus used it, together with many other sets of seemingly incompatible propositions, to induce the reader to embrace a general practice of withholding assent. Marcion employed it against a single first principle of all things and in favor of Gnostic dualism. Even Epicurus had no interest in rejecting belief in the gods. For Epicurus, the argument, if he used it, would have been against divine providence, not against the existence of the gods. The rejection of providence was linked to his positive moral vision: just as the gods enjoy happiness apart from the cares of the world, so too should human beings.[9]

A modified variant of the dualist challenge was the most important version of the argument in Augustine's time, not only for Augustine but also for the ascendant philosophy of Neoplatonism. The dualistic challenge, for both Plotinus and Augustine, came from the Manichean sect.[10] Plotinus's response to dualism proved to be quite influential on Augustine. For Plotinus, evil is not a reality equal to and opposite of good. Evil, rather, is an absence or lack of measure, form, or determination. Evil is to good, he says, as nonmeasure is to measure. And Plotinus argues that there is a reality that corresponds to this essence, namely, matter, the very end of the chain of emanation.[11]

Augustine, bound by scripture to affirm the goodness of creation, could not follow Plotinus' assertion that matter is evil. Matter, for Augustine, does not follow necessarily by emanation from the divine. Matter is the product of a free divine choice—and thus a good part of creation. Nor does Augustine believe that matter is the source of moral evil. The immaterial angels required no connection with matter to fall. Still, Augustine takes a great deal from Plotinus, including the view that evil is an absence or lack of being.

Evil, for Augustine, is a privation of goodness. The Augustinian view echoes Plotinus, but we must distinguish Augustine's view of evil as privation from Plotinus's view, which we could call evil as limitation.[12] The distinction, to put it simply, is this: on the latter view, any lack of good is evil; on the former, only the lack of a due good is evil. The good that is due is determined by the kind of thing under consideration. According to Augustine, the inability to speak is evil for a human being but not an elm tree. The inability to fly is evil for a falcon but not a human being. Creaturely limitation as such is not evil. Each thing is good in its specific way as the kind of thing it is. Evil, therefore, is not necessary for Augustine as it is for Plotinus. But if evil does not have its source in an evil principle, matter, or creaturely limitation, what is the source of evil? Augustine's famous answer is that evil originates in the free decision of rational creatures. His first major work on this is *De libero arbitrio voluntatis*, which he began just two years after his conversion but did not complete until approximately 395.[13]

De libero is a dialogue between Augustine and Evodius, which begins with Evodius saying: "Tell me, please, whether God is not the cause of evil."[14] Augustine responds by distinguishing between two kinds of evil: evil done and evil suffered. God, he says, "is the cause of the second kind of evil, but not of the first."[15] God causes the second kind of evil as punishment for the first. What, then, is the cause of the first kind of evil? In book I, Augustine convinces Evodius that the cause of evil is the creaturely will. The good is right order, which, in the case of human beings, is the reign of reason. Reason, according to Augustine, cannot be overcome by the force of the passions. Evil action only occurs when one wills against right reason, as when one wills that which is temporal over that which is eternal.

In book II, Evodius raises a new line of inquiry. If the creaturely will is the source of all evil—directly of evil done and indirectly of evil suffered by provoking just punishment—then why did God give us freedom of will? Augustine answers that human beings are only capable of living rightly by willing to do so. For this reason, freedom of will is a condition of all right living. If God had not given us freedom of will, we could not live rightly. Evodius pushes back that the will does not need to be capable of misuse. Augustine responds that many good things (e.g., all corporeal things) are capable of misuse. Why, then, is it so objectionable that the will is capable of misuse? Only the highest goods cannot be misused. As an intermediate good, the will can be misused, and its misuse is an evil, which is to say, a loss of order and thus of being. Evil done is a defective movement, a failure of the human being to realize its perfection. As a defective cause, the movement of the will away from the good cannot be explained. Nonetheless, it is voluntary and thus attributable to the created agent.[16]

Augustine's views did not remain static over time, though how precisely they changed is a matter of debate.[17] Interpreters tend to agree that the most important stimulus for Augustine's evolving views on evil was the Pelagian controversy during which Augustine began to argue unequivocally that human beings after the Fall of Adam and Eve are incapable of willing the good without the grace of God. Jesse Couenhoven has persuasively argued that the late Augustine abandons what is now called "the free will defense": the view that the goodness added to creation by giving some creatures the free choice between good and evil explains why God exposes creation to the risk of sin and its consequences. Augustine, according to Couenhoven, comes to explicitly reject the idea of a neutral will equally able to choose good and evil. The created will is made to will the good. The human capacity for evil, according to the late Augustine, arises from the fact that human beings are created from nothing. Having been created from nothing, they are capable of slipping back toward nothingness. This is not an explanation of sin but the condition of its possibility. Sin has no explanation; it is absurd. Why, then, does God allow evil? The only answer is that God permits evil in order to ultimately bring greater good from it. The Fall is a felix culpa, a happy fault.[18]

Augustine's influence over both scholastic and Reformation theology is unrivaled. Both his early and later views were deeply influential in the history of Christian theology in the West. His distinction between evil done and evil suffered remained standard, as did the justification of the latter as punishment for the former. However its nature and role are understood, the creaturely will was taken to be the source of all moral evil and the reason that God punishes creatures with other evils. Even for Bayle, the broadly Augustinian approach remains the most reasonable attempt to explain evil.

This is not to say, of course, that no developments occurred on the topic between Augustine and the seventeenth century. It is only to say that developments took place within a broadly Augustinian framework. One of the most important developments for our purposes is that arguments like those of Epicurus, Sextus, and Marcion were put to new uses. For example, Aquinas appears to be the first thinker in the Latin West to raise the question of whether the existence of evil implies the nonexistence of God. Aquinas, of course, answers that it does not. Brian Davies has argued that Aquinas raises the question not because he takes it seriously, but simply because the dialectical structure of his *Summa theologica* requires objections to every assertion, including the existence of God.[19] In any case, by the time of Bayle, arguments like the one attributed to Epicurus were generally taken to be atheistic in implication. Just as importantly, arguments about the difficulty of adequately accounting for evil found an additional purpose in the theological polemics following the Reformation.[20] The charge, for example, that a rival ecclesial tradition made God "the author of sin" was a common objection, the point of which was not to reject theism or even Christianity but to reject a competing branch of increasingly divided Christendom. According to Bayle, not a year had passed since the time of Luther and Calvin in which the charge of making God the author of sin was not leveled against them and their followers.[21] This charge was raised most forcefully against the Reformed tradition in the sustained polemics against its particular formulation of soteriological voluntarism. According to the polemicists, Reformed soteriological voluntarism entails that God not only permits but wills and causes sin. This sort of critique was meant to support the superiority of alternative soteriologies, some of which, as we saw with Henry More, modified or rejected soteriological voluntarism.

Evil and Moral Community with God

A central theme of this book is the importance of how one conceives the moral relationship between God and human beings, which I have discussed using Schneewind's language of moral community between God and human beings. Ethical voluntarists tend to elevate God above the moral community. God is the source of morality, not a subject of morality. God freely chooses what is good and obligatory for human beings. Ethical intellectualists, by contrast, reject the idea that God freely chooses what is good and obligatory for human beings—or at least that God freely chooses everything that is good and obligatory for human beings. Morality, for the ethical intellectualist, depends not ultimately on the free commands of God but on reason and nature, both divine and created.

As Schneewind frames the debate, the ethical intellectualist believes in eternal and immutable moral principles, which apply to God as well as human beings. Yet as we have seen, the major traditions of ethical intellectualism in the seventeenth century do not defend the existence of moral principles that God and human beings share in common. I argued in chapter 1 that Thomist, Reformed, and Platonic ethical intellectualist views assert that God and human beings share the same ultimate end but not the same principles or standards for pursuing that end. On these views, God and human beings share a kind of moral community founded on a shared end—which, following Jennifer Herdt, I call "moral community without common measure"—but not a common morality.

For More and Cumberland, by contrast, God and human beings form a single moral community founded on shared principles of action. More defends the existence of self-evident, eternal moral principles by which one can determine what is absolutely and simply the best. God and human beings ought to conform to these immutable principles in pursuit of the best. Likewise, Cumberland reduces all morality to maximal benevolent striving for the realization of the best end. While only humans are morally bound by this law, God is rationally bound by it. More and Cumberland, then, articulate principles of action that bind not only human beings but also God.

The issue of how God relates to human morality is closely related to the issue of the theological challenge posed by evil. The problem of evil, as it is now typically construed, presupposes that morality applies to God. If morality does not apply to God, the problem may just disappear. Consider how Hobbes handles the issue. In his controversy with Bishop Bramhall, published over several years in the 1650s, Hobbes argued that freedom simply means the power to do what one wants to do, not the power to do other than what one does. Freedom is opposed to constraint but not to necessity. Bramhall objects, predictably, that this view makes God the author of sin—the very sin for which God punishes creatures. Hobbes responds:

> The power of God alone without other help is sufficient justification of any action he does. That which men make amongst themselves here by pacts and covenants and call by the name of justice, and according whereunto men are counted and termed rightly just or unjust, is not that by which God Almighty's actions are to be measured or called just, no more than his counsels are to be measured by human wisdom. That which he does is made just by his doing it: just, I say, in him, not always just in us by the example.[22]

Hobbes, admittedly, is an extreme case. Few, if any, adopt his version of ethical voluntarism. Nonetheless, his response here is quite instructive. In Hobbes, we see that an ethical voluntarist, at least of a certain stripe, has a simple response to challenges about evil. If everything God does is made just by God's doing it, then "the problem of evil" does not get off the ground. God can be the author of sin, and the world can be filled with evils. God remains just.

In rejecting ethical voluntarism, More and Cumberland take on the burden of reconciling divine moral perfection with the existence of sin and evil. But the problems posed by evil are also not the same for all ethical intellectualists. I argued that the views of Aquinas, Ames, and Cudworth have a common structure according to which God and rational creatures share a common end but not a common set of moral principles. Take Aquinas. In his view, God and all creatures have the same end, God. For rational agents, an act is good if it is appropriately ordered to this end. Importantly, however, what it means to act appropriately for the sake of this end depends upon what sort of thing one is. Human beings are to act for the sake of this end in one way; God does so in another way.

Aquinas's way of conceiving the cosmos as a moral community between God and rational creatures does not include self-evident principles of action equally applicable to all rational beings. Aquinas, therefore, does not need to show that God acts according to the moral principles of human beings. God is not virtuous in the way human beings are because human virtues are the habits that perfect human beings in their pursuit of the end. God's way of acting for the end of God's own goodness depends upon the sort of thing God is—and Aquinas denies that we can know what God is.[23] When Aquinas seeks to show that God does not cause moral evil, his concern is not primarily moral but metaphysical. The problem is not that we would know God did wrong if God caused moral evil but that moral evil is a privation that, unlike natural evil, is not caused by the agency of some other created being.[24]

More and Cumberland, by contrast, give us the principles of divine action, which are the same as the principles of human action. More and Cumberland thus need to show that the evils of the world are compatible with the existence of a God acting according to known principles. And not only are the standards that guide God's activity precisely specified; those standards are consequentialist in nature. Given this view, it is difficult to avoid the conclusion that God must create and govern the best possible world. For those convinced by More and Cumberland, the existence of evil begins to pose a new threat. One has to wonder: Does God truly realize as much goodness as possible? Is this world really as good as it can be?

The consequentialist moral cosmology shapes the nature of the challenge posed by evil in another way as well. If we are to share with God in the effort to realize the greatest possible goodness in creation, God's providential aims must be largely comprehensible to us. Otherwise, the idea of a shared pursuit with a shared end is hard to sustain. How are we to join in God's providential promotion of the best if God's ways are opaque to us? Thus, the reasons for the existence of various evils must also be at least broadly comprehensible. We cannot simply trust that God inscrutably works all things for the good because we cannot join God in what we find inscrutable. We must be able to follow the workings of divine providence, including the divine permission of evil. What we find, then, is that the challenge posed by the existence of evil takes a new and particularly pernicious form in light of the consequentialist moral cosmology.

Bayle on Reason, Faith, and the Inexplicability of Evil

Henry More recognized the threat that the existence and extent of evil poses to his theology and ethics, and he wrote about it extensively. In *Divine Dialogues* (1668), he adopts an approach inspired by Origen, explaining the present state of the world as one moment in a larger cosmic narrative that begins with the fall of preexistent souls. More's approach to explaining the state of the world was controversial, but many readers saw no problem dismissing his views about the preexistence of souls while embracing his larger theological and ethical program. Cumberland never raised the question of the compatibility of his view of divine aims with the evils of the world. Indeed, evil was not widely felt to pose a pressing problem among most Anglican thinkers until the first decade of the eighteenth century. The event that sparked this change was the appearance of Pierre Bayle's *Dictionnaire historique et critique* in 1697. Before we can understand how engaging this issue shaped British ethics, we must consider the work of Bayle.

Bayle is a notoriously difficult author to interpret, especially regarding his most notorious claim: that it is impossible for Christians to rationally account for evil. Evil, as Thomas Lennon writes, "is a problem that plagues Bayle, appearing with greater frequency than any other in his work."[25] In the words of Jean-Pierre Jossua, Bayle's work is marked by "l'obsession du mal."[26] Bayle's most influential treatment of evil occurs in the *Dictionnaire*. The interpretive difficulty with Bayle is how to determine the aim of his arguments. Long regarded as an irreligious skeptic, Bayle has recently been treated as a more complex figure. Elizabeth Labrousse argued in 1964 that Bayle is not an irreligious skeptic but a faithful Calvinist who employed skepticism in order to induce his readers to abandon hopes of a rational theology and fall back on faith.[27] This reading has been influential but also contested, and many alternatives have been proposed. The problem has even been given a name: the Bayle enigma.[28]

Fortunately, however, Bayle's aims are less important for present purposes than the way his arguments were received. When we set aside his aims, Bayle's arguments turn out to be relatively straightforward. Each of his detailed discussions of evil in the *Dictionnaire* occurs in the extensive remarks included in one of his articles on an ancient or medieval dualistic sect that attributed the existence of the world to two principles, one good and one evil ("Manichees," "Marcionites," and "Pauliciens"). Bayle's position is the same in every case. He affirms that, on a priori grounds, theism is rationally superior to dualism. But for a theory to be convincing, he argues, it must be able to account for experience. The strength of the dualists lies in a posteriori arguments. Traditional theism, he contends, cannot account for the experience of evil because all rational explanations for the existence of evil in a world created by a perfectly good God fail. Again and again, he concludes that theism—and especially Christianity—is incapable of providing a rational explanation for the experience of evil in the world. Then, in the final paragraphs, he uses this conclusion to implore his reader to give up rational argumentation and turn to revelation.

Debates about the relationship between God and evil, as I have noted, were at this time caught up in and shaped by post-Reformation theological polemics. Bayle's writings on evil must be read in this context. Bayle was raised a Calvinist and was a close friend of Pierre Jurieu (until, that is, they became bitter enemies in the 1690s). Jurieu, a Reformed theologian and apologist, was deeply engaged in the theological polemics of the time. Notably, Jurieu addressed the common charge that Reformed theology makes God the author of sin in his 1686 work *Jugement sur les méthodes rigides et relâchées d'expliquer la providence et la grâce*. In response to this criticism, Jurieu defends the Reformed position by arguing that no alternative theological explanation of sin and evil is any more rationally or morally defensible. By arguing that evil presents a problem for every theological position, Jurieu aimed to diffuse a major objection against Reformed theology and move the debate to friendlier terrain.[29]

Bayle quotes Jurieu at multiple points in his discussions of evil. In many cases, he does so positively, following a similar strategy of showing that no rational explanation of evil is available. Jurieu's argument in *Jugement sur les méthodes* concludes that the Reformed account of evil is to be preferred simply because it is the one that most elevates God. In another treatise on the same theme published the following year, Jurieu explicitly rejects rational grounds for theology: "Je crois les mystères de l'Évangile, non par conviction, mais parce que je les veux croire."[30] On this point, too, Bayle's discussions of evil follow Jurieu's example, turning away from reason and embracing scripture on faith alone.

If Bayle's arguments follow the trajectory of Jurieu's, why were they so much more explosive? There are at least three reasons. First, Bayle seems to relish vivid descriptions of the many evils of the world. History, he writes, "is properly speaking nothing but a record of the crimes and misfortunes of humankind."[31] Moral goodness among human beings is "infinitely less" than moral evil.[32] Bayle at times appears to mock creation, treating it as an embarrassment and a moral disaster, only to conclude with an appeal to revelation that it is not hard to see as disingenuous. Second, Bayle, unlike Jurieu, argues that there is one theological position that can account for the experience of evil, namely, Manichean dualism. His frequent assertion that dualism best explains our experience of the world as well as his use of fictional dialogues in which the dualist always manages to embarrass the theist struck many as heretical. Third, Bayle regularly compares God with immoral human beings: a tyrant, an uncaring mother, an evil gift giver, a passive observer of a crime. The images are striking, and so is the collapse of the moral distance between God and creatures. Through these comparisons, Bayle implicitly insists that any rational defense of God must hold God to at least as high a moral standard as human beings—a standard that, as Bayle sees it, God does meet.

Bayle typically argues by imagining the objections a dualist would raise against a theist. *Unde malum*? The theist's most reasonable answer, Bayle thinks, is precisely the one Augustine gave: evil is not created by God but introduced by creaturely freedom. The natural evils that pervade the world are the punishments that result from the moral evil of rational creatures. Bayle agrees that this is the most plausible thing Christians (and theists in general) can say about evil.[33] He never seriously questions this answer as a historical account of the source of evil. Instead, he tries to show that it fails to morally justify God.

Bayle's arguments are scattered across his responses to several different articles. Instead of summarizing each, I am going to reconstruct his arguments, focusing on those most relevant to the next three chapters. Bayle's most relevant arguments can be divided into two sets with two different aims. The first set of arguments I will discuss aims to establish that creatures do not have freedom of indifference, that is, the capacity to choose among different options, including the capacity to choose against what one knows to be best.[34] Freedom of indifference can be described as a version of agential voluntarism, though with the additional element of libertarian freedom: one must be able to act other than one does.[35] These arguments are meant to show that evil cannot be explained by indeterminate creaturely choices that go against divine ends. God must have willed the fall of creatures. The second set of arguments aims to show that nothing can justify God in willing the fall of creatures.

The first set of arguments can be divided into three types: metaphysical, theological, and ethical. The metaphysical argument, which I will not discuss in any depth, is that freedom of indifference is incompatible with the notion of continuous creation. Because human beings are continuously and totally supported by God at every moment, our wills may be free in the sense that they are capable of making a variety of choices, but not in the sense of genuine self-determination.[36] He denies that we could ever have a distinct idea of a self-determining being that is not self-existent.[37] And a being that lacks self-determination must also lack freedom of indifference. The appeal to a lack of distinct ideas is a clear reference to Descartes, who sought to limit the boundaries of knowledge to clear and distinct ideas—though even Descartes made an exception in the case of God and was willing to affirm what he saw as the inconceivable combination of the freedom of human will and the determination of all things by divine decree.[38]

The theological argument is that any theologically acceptable notion of creaturely freedom must be compatible with divine determination for soteriological reasons: the saints in heaven must be both determined to the good and nonetheless free. The primary target here is the idea, which Bayle finds among some theologians, that true and valuable creaturely freedom is impossible without the real capacity to choose evil. The argument is supposed to establish that God had to grant freedom of indifference—and with it the possibility of sin—in order to create creatures with true and valuable freedom. Again and again, Bayle responds to such arguments by pointing to the saints in heaven. If, as St. Basil insisted, the freedom to sin is necessary to truly love God, then, Bayle replies, the saints in heaven would either be capable of falling back into sin or cease to love God.[39] He would presumably make a similar reply to Augustine's early argument that God allows the possibility of sin because all lower creaturely goods can be misused.[40]

The third and most sustained argument is moral. Even if the freedom of indifference were metaphysically possible, and even if it were a very valuable gift for creatures, God would be wrong to give it to us since God knows that we will misuse it. Bayle's strategy in his moral arguments is to evaluate God's acts by comparing them with analogous human actions. Imagine a father preparing a gift for his child. The gift may be a great good. Nonetheless, if the father knows that the gift will bring about the ruin of the child, the father would be wrong to give it. Likewise, God would be wrong to give the gift of freedom of indifference to a human being whose ruin it will cause.[41]

One might respond that God does not simply give the destructive gift. God gives it together with a clear warning about its misuse. Unimpressed, Bayle turns to a new analogy. God would then be like a mother who allows her daughter to go to a dance knowing that the daughter will commit sexual sin. The mother exhorts her daughter about the importance of purity. Yet if the mother sends her anyway with full knowledge of what will happen, then she does not truly care about her daughter or about purity.[42]

One further response would be to deny that God has foreknowledge of free creaturely choices, a view Bayle attributes to the Socinians. This view, Bayle says, comes closest to exonerating God, but it too fails. Even if God were to lack foreknowledge, God would still be choosing to risk the possibility of sin and the great flood of evils it unleashes. Such a God is still no better than the mother who sends her daughter to the dance. Perhaps, in this case, the mother does not know for sure what the daughter will do. But if a caring mother were, like God, watching the daughter the entire time, she would certainly know that sin was coming before the moment it occurred, and she would intervene.[43] To respond that God does not intervene in order to respect our freedom is still, according to Bayle, to attribute to God a morally bad omission. The value of respecting human freedom has limits. Even human observers are morally bound to intervene if they see a person engaging in a self-destructive act like suicide.[44] For God to passively allow a much greater evil, the fall of the entire human race, is morally reprehensible.

If the first set of arguments is accepted, Bayle's opponent must abandon the idea that rational creatures possess freedom of indifference, which can explain evil and exonerate God. The result is that any defensible notion of creaturely freedom must be compatible with divine determination. Even if, as Augustine argued, the possibility of sin is a metaphysical necessity for creatures, God can ensure that the possibility is not realized. The importance of this result for the issue of evil is clear: creaturely freedom cannot be used to argue that the world is other than God willed it to be. The world we have, in other words, is the world God wants. God's intentions have not been foiled. God willed a world full of evil.

Those familiar with these disputes will notice an ambiguity in the previous sentence. What does it mean to say that God willed a world full of evil? Does it mean that God causes it or that God allows it? This sort of distinction has been crucial in the history of theology: God permits sin but does not cause it. For Bayle, though, the distinction loses a great deal of its importance. Bayle sees little difference between causing and permitting. In either case, God creates a world that God knows will end up full of evil, even when other options were available, including refusing to create altogether. The question of God's causal relation to evil fades into the background, and the question of God's moral responsibility for the state of the world becomes primary.

In light of the first set of arguments, one obvious option available to Bayle's opponents is to give up on the freedom of difference as Augustine did. Perhaps God does intend the fall, but God does so because the fall and its attendant evils are necessary for the attainment of some greater goods in creation. Here, again, we find different types of arguments. One is both metaphysical and theological. Bayle argues forcefully against the view that evil is necessary in order for God to communicate any good to creatures. This argument occurs in the course of his remark on Lactantius's explanation of evil. Lactantius, he says, argued that God permits evil because it is necessary to wisdom, which is itself necessary to virtue and to the attainment of the highest good. Bayle reacts with outrage. The idea that God could not have communicated wisdom—or, indeed, any good—without the existence of evil is, according to Bayle, heretical. Are the angels not virtuous? Do they not enjoy God? What about Adam and Eve? The assertion, according to Bayle, destroys the Christian narrative. Moreover, it subjects God to the necessity of evil in communicating the greatest goods, including the enjoyment of Godself. This sort of view, Bayle argues, falsely generalizes experiences from the world. We cannot achieve wisdom or virtue without some suffering, but this fact is a result of sin, not a metaphysical necessity.[45]

If evil cannot be necessary for communicating the good to creatures, perhaps, then, it is necessary for some further aim of God's. God may allow sin because God intends to display God's own mercy, justice, and providential wisdom through redemption. And the display of God's attributes may be part of God's larger end in creation: God's own glory. To this argument, Bayle objects on moral grounds. Once again, he turns to unflattering comparisons with analogous human actions:

> This is to compare God to a father who allows his children to break their legs in order to show to the whole city his skills in rejoining the bones or to a monarch who allows sedition to show his power in crushing it. The conduct of this farther and this monarch is so contrary to the clear and distinct ideas by which we judge goodness and wisdom, and in general to all the duties of a father and a king, that our reason cannot comprehend that God can use the same conduct.[46]

Bayle is no doubt misconstruing what theologians mean when they say that God acts for God's glory, but the rhetorical power of the comparisons is undeniable.

Bayle, in his extensive struggle with the existence of evil, in some ways resembles Augustine. Indeed, in a sense, Bayle ends up at the same point as the late Augustine. For Bayle, as for the late Augustine, free will may be the historical source of evil, but it cannot itself be the justification for evil. Augustine, according to Couenhoven, ultimately concludes that God creates us with a will with no defects, perfect in its love of the good. Sin cannot be explained by a choice freely made between two alternatives but by an inexplicable slip back toward nothingness, a possibility that arises not from the nature of the created will but from creaturehood itself. Augustine accepts that God foresees and does not prevent the fall. In the end, he is content to attribute evil to an inexplicable deficient cause that God chose to permit. Where, then, is the disagreement? Why does Augustine consider this conclusion sufficient while Bayle does not? Ultimately, I think, it comes down to an assumption Bayle consistently makes but never defends, namely, that fallen creation, even after the incarnation, is an unmitigated disaster. Life, for Bayle, is worse than nonexistence, and death, for the vast majority of human beings, will be far worse than life. Whereas Augustine and other Christian theologians believed that they could see enough of the goodness of God in creation and in Christ to trust in the goodness of what they could not understand, Bayle cannot see beyond the horror. For Bayle, even if, against all logic, God were incapable of creating a better world, God could have at the very least refrained from creating at all, a choice Bayle sees as obviously superior.[47]

Bayle returns to the topic of evil repeatedly in the *Dictionnaire*. In each case, he brings the discussion to the point at which theism or Christianity is trapped in a rational bind, unable to answer the challenges posed by its dualist opponents. He then concludes that the problem is not theism or Christianity but the attempt to defend God on rational grounds. "I do not believe that I am deceived," he writes, "if I say of natural revelation, that is, of the light of reason, what the theologians say of the Mosaic economy": its function is to "make known to human beings their powerlessness" and thus drive them to submit themselves in faith to divine revelation.[48] Whatever Bayle's motivation, his conclusion is that the rational inexplicability of evil—which is only one manifestation of the more general incapacity of reason to grasp the higher truths of God—should strengthen rather than weaken faith in God. If Bayle's goal was to elevate revelation over reason, he ironically sparked greater interest in rational theodicy, a result which, as we will see, became an increasingly important factor in ethics.

Bayle and Eighteenth-Century Theodicy

Bayle's treatment of evil set the terms of the enterprise that in the following decades would come to be known as "theodicy," a term coined by G. W. Leibniz.[49] Bayle's stark distinction between faith and reason, together with his insistence that reason will always leave one with a morally indefensible God, was one way in which he set the terms of the debate in the early eighteenth century. The mainstream position on evil before the seventeenth century combined rational explanation and faith. For Augustine, evil is finally inexplicable, but the inexplicable nature of evil does not preclude rational probing. Augustine explores the existence of evil at length, combining scriptural interpretation with philosophical reflection on morality, agency, and creatureliness. Similar things can be said of other major theologians such as Thomas Aquinas and John Calvin. But Bayle presents the Christian with a much starker choice: either work out a fully developed and defensible theodicy or abandon rationality and turn to revelation. It is no surprise, then, that many of Bayle's critics would leave behind the mainstream tradition and seek to exonerate God on rational grounds.

Posing such a stark division between rational theodicy and irrational faith was perhaps the most important way Bayle shaped debates about evil in the following generation, but a few other ways should be mentioned.

First, Bayle's focus is quite different from that of many of his predecessors. The worries driving scholastic treatments of evil are primarily metaphysical and causal. Evil is formally a privation and thus neither created nor directly caused by God. While Bayle touches on these issues, he shows little interest in them. When he does discuss metaphysical issues, the point is generally to establish God's moral responsibility for evil rather than God's causal relationship to it. The primary question, for Bayle, is not what evil is or how it is caused.[50] The primary question is why a good God would have created such a wretched world. For Bayle, the problem is a decidedly moral one.[51]

Second, Bayle assumes that any rational solution to the problem would have to exculpate God on moral grounds that apply equally to any moral agent. As we have seen, he repeatedly draws parallels between God's creative or providential acts and acts of human beings. In each case, Bayle assumes without argument that God can only be considered morally good if God acts in a way that a good human being would act in a similar situation. Good human beings do not give destructive gifts, send others into foreseeable evil, or destroy their subjects for their own glory. A rational theodicy must show that God is at least as good as a good human being. In his later work, *Réponse aux questions d'un provincial*, Bayle makes this presumption more explicit. He writes:

> One must not here claim that the goodness of God is not subject to the same rules as the goodness of the creature; for if there is in God an attribute which can be called goodness, it is necessary that the characteristics of goodness in general agree with it. Yet when we reduce goodness to the most general abstraction, we find it to be the will to do good. Divide and subdivide this general goodness into as many species as you want—infinite goodness, finite goodness, royal goodness, the goodness of a father, the goodness of a mother, the goodness of a master—you will find that the will to do good is an inseparable attribute of each.[52]

Divine and human goodness, for Bayle, must ultimately mean the same thing.[53]

Third, Bayle raises new challenges for the view that the value of the freedom of indifference is sufficient to explain the existence of evil. While this view is not, as Bayle recognizes, the position of many major theologians (Augustine, Aquinas, Luther, or Calvin), it is the position of many of the rationalist philosophers and theologians of the seventeenth century. Bayle puts the rationalist trend in theology on the defensive by rejecting its explanation of evil. While Bayle never questions the idea that creaturely wills are the source of evil in the world, he denies that freedom can in any way justify the existence of evil. Before Bayle, the defense of freedom of indifference was seen as a way to make Christianity more rational; after Bayle, the defenders of freedom of indifference look no more rational than any other theologians. Bayle's critics had to explain anew why freedom of indifference justifies its evil consequences and why God would not create free creatures that always choose the good—or, as we will see below, they had to rethink the place of freedom in the Christian story.

Bayle in Britain

Bayle was read widely in Britain. According to Elizabeth Labrousse, Bayle's works were more widely available in English than in any other language.[54] And Justin Champion, in a provisional survey of the records of sales of private libraries in England in the eighteenth century, found that 57 percent contained works by Bayle. Almost nine in ten of those included the *Dictionnaire*.[55] Bayle's importance for eighteenth-century British thought is hard to overestimate.

When it comes to the relationship between God and evil, an issue that received significant attention in the decades after the *Dictionnaire*, Bayle shaped the debate in a particular way. There is nothing necessary about the way he frames the issue. He presents a particular picture of rationality, of the nature and activity of God, of the relationship between divine and creaturely agency, and of the relationship of God to human morality. Yet in their responses, few British authors challenge Bayle's framing of the issue, in part because it fits well with their own assumptions. Bayle's frequent comparisons between God's actions and human actions would not likely move the authors discussed in chapter 1 for whom divine goodness is not the same as human moral goodness. But for the intellectual descendants of More and Cumberland, with their embrace of a particular vision of divine-human moral community, Bayle's arguments from human cases had to be addressed.

The remainder of part II considers the works of three of the most significant British thinkers to address Bayle's critiques in the early decades of the eighteenth century: William King, Shaftesbury, and Francis Hutcheson. All three, I argue, defend a view that broadly mirrors the consequentialist moral cosmology of More and Cumberland. God, they contend, wills and realizes the best possible world, and rational creatures ought to will the same end as God. In detail, however, they depart in important respects from More and Cumberland, departures which are required by their attempts to explain evil. The modifications to the consequentialist moral cosmology, I conclude, ultimately make it unstable, leading eventually to the surprising return of ethical voluntarism in the consequentialist tradition. I begin in the next chapter with the first full-length response to Bayle's arguments about evil to appear in Britain, Archbishop William King's *De origine mali* (1702).

The Ethics of Archbishop
William King's De origine mali

Pierre Bayle's writings quickly found their way to Britain. His three major works were all translated into English in the first decade of the eighteenth century. Once you start looking for Bayle in eighteenth-century England, writes Justin Champion, "he's to be found everywhere."[1] His works sparked significant interest among British publishers, politicians, and audiences from the early years of the eighteenth century. Because Bayle was widely read as an atheist seeking to undermine faith, many leading philosophers and theologians responded critically.

This chapter and the next treat perhaps the two most important works on God, morality, and evil to emerge in Britain in the early years of the eighteenth century, both of which were profoundly shaped by critical engagement with Bayle's arguments about evil. The first, which is the topic of this chapter, is the 1702 treatise *De origine mali*, by William King, the Archbishop of Dublin. The second is the work of Lord Anthony Ashley Cooper, Earl of Shaftesbury, written primarily over the course of the first decade of the eighteenth century and published as *Characteristicks of Men, Manners, Opinions, Times* in 1711.

While the consequentialist moral cosmology is my own construct, it is nonetheless a set of ideas that together form a consistent theological and ethical picture of the cosmos. That set of ideas exerted a significant influence. King and Shaftesbury each defend views that closely follow the outlines of the consequentialist moral cosmology. God, both argue, seeks the realization of the greatest possible goodness in creation. Rational creatures ought to seek to realize the same end as God and do so in conformity with God's commands. At the same time, King and Shaftesbury each introduce important innovations to address the problems raised by Bayle, problems that are especially troubling for the consequentialist moral cosmology. Ultimately, I argue, their moral justifications of God according to consequentialist standards undermine the idea that human beings ought to seek the realization of the same end as God.

King's *De origine mali* is not well known today. Even in much of the literature on theodicy and optimism in the eighteenth century, King's treatise maintains only, as Uta Golembek puts it, "a shadow existence in asides and notes."[2] It was, however, widely read in the eighteenth century.[3] In England, Edmund Law translated it into English in 1731, and it went through five editions over the course of the eighteenth century. It was also an important source for Alexander Pope's famous *Essay on Man*.[4] On the continent, it was reviewed in major intellectual journals: *Nouvelles de la republique des lettres*, *Journal des scavans*, and *Acta eruditorum*. Pierre Bayle, working only from Jacques Bernard's review of the work, wrote a long critique of it in *Réponse aux questions d'un provincial* (1706). Leibniz included a critical assessment of it as an appendix to *Théodicée* (1710). In Germany, it was critically engaged by, among others, Christian Wolff.[5] Arthur Lovejoy claims, not implausibly, that *De origine mali* was "perhaps, when both its direct and indirect influence are considered, the most influential of eighteenth-century theodicies."[6]

King began his treatise in 1697, the same year Bayle published the *Dictionnaire*. Whether or not he originally conceived it as a response to Bayle, the final product was certainly crafted to respond to Bayle's arguments.[7] The idea for the work was originally generated, he tells us, in conversation with Robert Southwell—the father, it is worth noting, of Edward Southwell, who translated Henry More's *Enchiridion ethicum* into English in 1690—and the work is dedicated to him.

While King seeks to defend orthodox Christianity, he is quite innovative in his theology. Accepting many of Bayle's critiques, King abandons the dominant Augustinian account of the origin of evil. The existence of evil, for King, does not have its historical source in the misuse of creaturely freedom. It is, rather, a necessary feature of the finite, corporeal world. And King argues for a new view of the nature and function of creaturely freedom according to which freedom is a capacity given to rational creatures to allow them to cope with their necessary subjection to evil. This new account of freedom is quite successful in addressing many of Bayle's arguments. It also has notable moral implications. Indeed, a significant portion of *De origine* is about morality, as any serious theodicy must be.

The ethics of *De origine*, I argue, is more consistently consequentialist than that of More or Cumberland. It also takes an important step toward utilitarianism—that is, toward identifying the good with happiness conceived hedonistically.[8] But while King takes up and develops More and

Cumberland's approach to divine and human morality, his theological and ethical view of the cosmos differs from that of More and Cumberland. King's innovative account of freedom, which is central to his new explanation of evil, introduces a division between the divine and human pursuit of the best outcome. He continues to maintain that rational creatures ought to will the same end as God, the greatest happiness of all creatures. Yet he cannot ultimately hold that God and rational creatures will the same end for the same reasons. God's reasons to do so are rooted in God's goodness. Ours stem from the task, benevolently commanded by God, of achieving our own happiness. In King's *De origine*, the pressures of theodicy begin to drive divine and creaturely morality apart.

Evil of Imperfection and Natural Evil

King sets up the problem to be addressed in the first chapter of *De origine* by establishing the existence and attributes of God, including the classical divine attributes that create the standard contemporary philosophical picture of the problem of evil. He displays no interest in complicating the matter by introducing mystery or uncertainty about God's aims.[9] In everything God does, God perfectly expresses power and goodness. God, therefore, expresses power and goodness in creation, "for since the Exercise of the Divine Power, and the Communication of his Goodness, are the Ends for which the World is fram'd, there is no doubt but God has attain'd these Ends." To say that God creates for God's glory is, according to King, only a human way of speaking. God's glory is nothing other than "to have created a world with the greatest goodness."[10]

What, then, does it mean to create a world with the greatest goodness? King clarifies: "By good, I here understand that which is convenient [*conveniens*] and commodious, that which is correspondent to the appetite of every creature" (I.iii.11).[11] This definition is too vague to say much at this point. I will return to it below. But it is sufficient, at least, to place King in proximity to More and Cumberland. Drawing the logical conclusion from combining the account of the attributes and aims of God with the above definition of the good, we have King's central thesis:

> God therefore created the world with as great convenience [*convenientia*] and fitness [*commoditate*], with as great congruity [*congruentia*] to the appetites of things, as could be effected by infinite power, wisdom, and goodness. If then anything inconvenient or incommodious be now, or was from the beginning in it, that certainly could not be hindered or removed. (I.iii.11)

In these lines—including in the Latin terms[12]—we can hear echoes of More and Cumberland. God's aim is not simply to create a good world but to realize as much goodness in the world as possible. The challenge, then, is to explain why none of the seemingly countless evils of the world can be "hindered or removed."

King begins the argument by defining and categorizing evil. Both good and evil, he argues, arise from the relationships things have with one another: "Since there are some things which profit and others which prejudice one another; since some things agree, and others disagree; as we call the former good, so we style the latter evil" (II.1). Like Cumberland, King insists on the objectivity of judgments of good and evil. Some things agree with one another; others disagree. At the same time, King leaves more room than Cumberland for subjectivity. Evil is not only that which frustrates an implanted appetite. It is also "whatever forces any person to do or suffer what he would not" (II.1). The disagreement between two things can be a disagreement with either implanted appetite or a chosen preference.

King divides evil into three species, evil of imperfection, natural evil, and moral evil: "By evil of imperfection, I understand the absence of those perfections or advantages which exist elsewhere or in other beings; by natural evils, pains, uneasinesses, inconveniences and disappointments of appetites, arising from natural motions; by moral, vicious election, that is, such as are hurtful to ourselves or others" (II.2).[13] King's argument for the necessity of evil takes each kind of evil in turn.

The easiest to address is the evil of imperfection or, as he sometimes calls it, the evil of defect. Perfection, according to King, entails necessary existence. Because no creature can have necessary existence, no creature can be perfect. Imperfection, therefore, is a necessary feature of creation. If the evil of imperfection were a reason not to create, then God could create nothing. Between God and nothingness, King argues, is an infinite spectrum. No matter how high a being stands on the spectrum, an infinite distance will remain between the creature and God. If the evil of imperfection were a reason for the creature to complain against the Creator, complaints of a human being would be no more or less justified than the complaints of the lowest piece of matter or the highest angel.

If imperfection is unavoidable, one might think, God could at least have avoided creating lower beings. King responds to this objection by arguing that the whole of creation must be composed of various parts, and parts can never be equal to the whole in perfection. Equality of perfection, therefore, is inconsistent with the creation of a whole. Moreover, even if God could have created only the highest beings, why not also create lower beings? As long as the addition of lower beings does not conflict with the good of the higher beings, their creation only adds to the goodness of the cosmos.[14]

King's treatment of the evil of imperfection is a relatively successful way of disarming one set of critiques of creation. Why, it has often been asked, are humans born so helpless? Why are we so weak and vulnerable? King responds that all creatures necessarily fall short of perfection. Imperfection is no reason for God not to create creatures in every station in such a way as to form an excellent whole. What King does not but perhaps should say is that evil of imperfection is not truly evil at all. Bayle makes this point in response to King: "Evil, properly speaking, is contained only under physical and moral evil."[15] Good and evil in general, King says, "arise from the Relation things have to one another." He concludes his general discussion of evil with this: "Whatever therefore is *incommodious* or *inconvenience* to itself, or anything else; whatever becomes *troublesome*, or frustrates any *Appetite* implanted by God; whatever forces any Person to do or suffer what he would not, that is *Evil*" (II.1).[16] This general account of evil is difficult to square with King's metaphysical description of the evil of imperfection, which seems to echo Plotinian themes. If imperfection is evil, it is perhaps best seen as evil only for creatures like us who are capable of wishing for greater powers than we have. Or perhaps King would say that a mouse's inability to fly is evil when the mouse is unable to escape a hungry cat through the air. In any case, he sometimes employs Neoplatonic ideas that are difficult to integrate with the rest of his thought.

The second kind of evil is natural evil. King's view of natural evils, which echoes More's *Divine Dialogues*, draws upon new possibilities introduced by mechanical philosophy, especially regarding the nature and properties of matter.[17] King introduces the necessity of natural evil in a parallel manner to the necessity of the evil of imperfection: "As all created beings are made out of nothing, and on that account are necessarily imperfect; so all natural things have a relation to, or arise from, matter, and on that account are necessarily subject to natural evils" (III.i.2). The point here is not Plotinian. Matter is not evil. Matter simply has physical properties that necessitate creatures with material bodies to suffer frustrations of appetite. In particular, the mechanical laws of matter, though designed by God in the best possible way, will always have the unintended effect of producing natural evils.[18] God's situation concerning natural evil is similar to that concerning evil of imperfection: either create beings subject to evil or avoid creating them at all. And just as the evils of imperfection do not prevent God from the greater good of creating beings from nothing, so natural evils do not prevent God from the greater good of creating corporeal beings (III.i.2).

King's argument relies on a particular view of the nature of matter. Composing creatures from matter requires forming matter into parts and putting the parts in motion, a process that will necessarily lead to "clashing and opposition, comminution, concretion and repulsion, and all those evils which we behold in generation and corruption" (III.i.4). Even the best mechanical laws cannot avoid this result. Disease and death are a product of the necessary dissolution of material bodies. To stave them off as much as possible, God gives creatures a strong appetite for self-preservation. Pain is a necessary byproduct of this appetite. Moreover, because the continued existence of creatures, given their necessary dissolution, requires continual generation, God also gives creatures an appetite for reproduction. All passions, with both their good and evil effects, arise from the two basic inclinations to self-preservation and generation (III.vi.7). As with mechanical laws, these appetites are as perfectly designed as possible to achieve their intended effects, but they have unintended side effects that are naturally evil.[19]

Freedom, Undue Elections, and Moral Evil

King's treatment of the final type of evil, moral evil, takes up well over half of the treatise, and it is his most important and most innovative contribution to the project of theodicy. It is here that we find the treatise making contributions to ethics. Moral evils, he writes, are "those inconveniencies of life and condition which befall ourselves or others through wrong elections" (V.intro). Moral evils are, like all evils, inconveniencies. What distinguishes moral evils is that they, unlike many other evils, are a product of free human choices. Note that moral evils, according to this definition, are not wrong elections themselves. They are those evils that "befall ourselves or others" through those elections. Moral evils, then, are a subset of natural evils. While King is not unique in treating moral evils as a subset of natural evils—the same is true, for example, of Aquinas—King's way of doing so is original. For Aquinas, following Augustine, moral evils are natural evils because they are privations of the goodness a created thing should have. Moral evils are those natural evils that are privations of a particular kind of thing: human actions.[20] For King, by contrast, moral evils are not bad human elections or actions at all; they are the inconveniences that arise from human elections or actions. King's language, however, is not entirely consistent. He sometimes also speaks of the elections themselves as moral evils. Still, when he speaks of the elections as evil, he is clear that they are evil precisely because they cause natural evil.

The justification for the existence of moral evils begins with an exploration of the nature of elections or acts of the will. King rejects two common
views of election. The first is a rough characterization of John Locke's
view in *An Essay Concerning Human Understanding* according to which
the will is determined not by the goodness of the object but by the uneasiness that arises from its absence. King argues that this view precludes
genuine freedom.[21] While it preserves freedom from external constraint,
it does not allow freedom from necessity. For this reason, King argues, it
destroys morality, praise, and blame (V.i.i.12–17). King also adds a second
critique. This view, he argues, leaves us with only fixed appetites, whether
intellectual or sensual. Given the necessary results of even the best physical laws, not all fixed appetites can be satisfied. A creature with only fixed
appetites can thus attain only very limited happiness. God would surely
also give us a free appetite, which can find satisfaction in any physical
circumstances (V.i.i.18).[22]

King finds the second view more plausible. According to this view,
which is a characterization of a common scholastic view, we necessarily
desire the highest good, and we desire all other goods only in reference
to it. Because the highest good is supernatural and transcendent, all ordinary choices are between lower goods, none of which can compel the
will. Freedom arises from the choice among inferior, worldly goods. King
accepts that this view grants genuine freedom. His objection to this option
is principally that of Bayle: we cannot explain why God would have given
us this sort of freedom. For King, the problem lies in its realism about the
good. The goodness or badness of any choice, in this view, is an objective
reality grasped by the intellect, meaning that there are always better and
worse choices. If the will is an appetite for the good, why would God make
it free? It would be better for the will to simply follow the intellect like an
instinct. If this view is correct, King thinks, God would be wrong to give
us free will (V.i.ii).

For King, this sort of problem arises for any view according to which
the will is an appetite for an objective good. Freedom in the pursuit of
an objective good simply opens up the possibility of failure. King instead
proposes a more radical distinction between the will and other powers,
faculties, and appetites. All other powers, faculties, and appetites, he argues, have fixed objects. For this reason, they are passive. Sight senses
only light. Hunger is satisfied only by food. The understanding grasps
only intelligible objects. In the presence of its proper object, each passive
power, faculty, or appetite is moved to its proper act. It receives pleasure
from its exercise of its proper act in the presence of its proper object,
and displeasure from that which opposes or hinders its act. Each passive

power, faculty, and appetite, then, has an object that is objectively good for it. According to King, if all powers, faculties, and appetites were passive, as in the second view, then freedom could have no positive value. It would be nothing but the power to fail to pursue happiness. The will must be an altogether different type of appetite.

Notice that King objects to both views of freedom on the grounds that they undermine the attainment of happiness: the first, because it treats all appetites as fixed and thus subject to unavoidable frustration; the second, because it grants us the power to choose lesser goods. We can see here how the context of theodicy—together with the presumption that God's aim must be the greatest happiness of creatures—profoundly shapes his approach to human freedom. For King, if all our appetites were determined to pursue their objects, we would lack the necessary flexibility to be happy in this world. The power to freely act for lesser objective goods only makes matters worse. The only option is to fundamentally rethink the nature of the will as an appetite, an undertaking that will inevitably have moral implications.

Though all other powers, faculties, and appetites have fixed objects and acts, King argues, the will does not. Instead, the will, as an active power, determines its own object. No property in things themselves can move the will because nothing is objectively good or bad for it. Good and bad for the will arise solely from its own free choice (V.i.iii.4). Yet like all other powers, once it has a determinate object, it takes pleasure in its act. If the will elects to sing, then singing brings pleasure and being prevented from singing brings pain. Moral agents, in this view, are self-active, determining themselves through the will (V.i.iii.16). King's term for self-determination through the will is "election." One might be tempted to ask what determines election, but King refuses the question. The will determines itself. Any other answer, he argues, destroys freedom (V.i.iii.17).

Human beings have many fixed appetites. The will does not remove these appetites, but it can choose against them. Fixed appetites can also oppose one another. A starving man, King writes, will find pleasure in eating bitter food. Even if he receives two degrees of uneasiness from the bitterness, he might eliminate three degrees of uneasiness by satiating the hunger. In this way, he finds mixed pleasure in eating. The will, too, can oppose fixed appetites, and it can do so even more powerfully. One can, for example, elect to endure hunger. While hunger will cause increasing uneasiness, the satisfaction of the will can outweigh the discomfort of hunger such that the agent finds a mixed pleasure. Indeed, because the will is the highest power we have, it has the capacity to find a pleasure greater than any other appetite. It thus allows us to achieve at least a mixed pleasure in anything that we freely determine to be an object of will—if, that is, we attain the object (V.i.iii.11).

Bayle, I argued in the previous chapter, raises significant problems for appeals to agential voluntarism and libertarian freedom in the context of theodicy. Rather than retreating from the appeal to free choice, King radicalizes the account of freedom. He defends a version of what I have called radical agential voluntarism.[23] The will is not simply neutral with respect to the judgments of reason regarding the good. It is capable of freely rendering its objects good—that is to say, of rendering them good for it, capable of satisfying it and thus bringing pleasure. When it comes to theodicy, King argues that his account of the will succeeds where the alternatives fail. God's aim, as we have seen, is to create a world with maximal satisfaction of creaturely appetites. Because of the qualities of matter, some degree of natural evil is unavoidable. Appetites will be frustrated. Given this fact, the value of free will is obvious:

> If good and evil proceed from nature, and be inherent in objects, so as to render them agreeable or disagreeable, antecedent to the election, the happiness of this agent will also depend upon them; and unless the whole series of things be so ordered that nothing can happen contrary to his appetites, he must fall short of happiness. For his appetites will be disappointed, which is the very thing that we call unhappiness. But if objects derive their agreeableness or disagreeableness from the choice, 'tis clear that he who has his choice may always enjoy the thing chosen, unless he choose impossibilities, &c. and never have his appetite frustrated, i.e. be always happy. (V.i.iii.20)

Free will, then, is of immeasurable value. It can render any object good, including the natural evils (i.e., frustrations of other powers, faculties, and fixed appetites) to which one is necessarily subjected as a corporeal being. One might, for example, be subject to an injury that causes pain when one moves. If one nonetheless freely wills to walk through the pain, one's will can be satisfied, causing a pleasure that can overbalance the pain. The will is above all a power to make oneself happy—or at least reasonably happy—in any circumstance.

King's view has obvious advantages for theodicy. One question, though, is whether a free appetite of this kind is even possible. King argues that it must be possible because it is actual in at least one case: "we must necessarily believe that God is invested with it" (V.i.iv.1). God is perfectly happy and sufficient: "He has no appetite to gratify with the enjoyment of things without him. He is therefore absolutely indifferent to all external things.

Nothing can benefit or harm him. What then should determine his will? Nothing without. He determines himself by creating an appetite in himself" (V.i.iv.2). Attributing radical agential voluntarism to God seems to risk ethical voluntarism. King does not intend this implication. We have already seen that King thinks that God cannot but have created a world with the greatest possible goodness, a conclusion foreign to ethical voluntarism. Indeed, King defends his view of the will precisely in order to show that God maximizes goodness. In applying this view of the will to God, his primary aim is to prove that a free appetite is possible. Secondarily, he aims to show that God is free not to create. If creation satisfied any fixed appetite in God, King thinks, then creation would be necessary. Only a free appetite in God can ensure the contingency of God's choice to create.[24]

How, then, can King square radical agential voluntarism with his argument about God's purpose in creation? Let us first clarify what it means that God freely makes the objects of God's will good, a question which King does not answer. If there are three kinds of evil, are there three kinds of goodness? And if so, which kind of goodness is determined by God's will? If there is a goodness of perfection—which, as I noted, would be difficult to fit under King's definition of good and evil—it could not depend on God's will. The perfection or imperfection of a creature, as King sees it, lies simply in the magnitude of its faculties and powers. The goodness in the case of divine will, as in the case of human will, must be natural goodness. God's free choice determines whether anything beyond Godself is pleasing to God. God has chosen to make the world as we find it pleasing and thus naturally good to Godself. To accommodate the divine appetite into his schema, King introduces a distinction between primary and secondary natural goodness. Primary natural goodness is determined by conformity to divine will. Secondary natural goodness is determined by conformity to creaturely appetites and wills.

When King writes that God creates a world "with the greatest goodness," which kind of goodness does he have in mind? It cannot be primary natural goodness, since any world God creates would have the same primary natural goodness due to its conformity to free divine election. He must mean secondary natural goodness. This conclusion certainly fits best with his claim, quoted above, that God "created the world with as great convenience and fitness, with as great congruity to the appetites of things, as could be effected by infinite power, wisdom, and goodness" (I.iii.11). Nevertheless, a worry remains. The primary/secondary distinction seems to indicate order of priority: natural goodness to God is more important than natural goodness to creatures. Could God not have elected to create a miserable world (as Bayle argues that our world is)? If God were to elect a miserable world, it would still have primary natural goodness, despite its secondary natural badness. How can King be so sure that a God with such radical freedom would create a world that is good for creatures?

King's solution is to argue that in electing to create a creature, God necessarily rejects all things inconsistent with that election. In electing to create human beings, for example, God necessarily wills a soul, a body, reason, senses, and everything else included in human nature. Moreover, King argues, God also necessarily wills all those things "as tend to promote [man's] benefit and happiness, as far as they can be made consistent with the benefit of the whole" (V.i.iv.14). Finally, in the same election God necessarily wills that human beings be perfected as far as possible: "By that very act of constituting him of such a nature and condition, 'tis plain, God also willed that he should be pious, sober, just and chaste" (V.i.iv.16). He goes on: "These and the like Laws of Nature then are immutable, *viz.* conformable to the Will of God, and contain'd in the very first Act of Election wherein he determin'd to create Man. Nor is God at liberty not to will these during his purposes to continue Man such as he is" (V.i.iv.16).

God's choices, then, are limited by the necessary entailments of the election to create. King does not tell us what kind of necessity is at stake. When he says that electing to create human beings entails willing that they have bodies and souls, he is presumably thinking of logical or metaphysical necessity. But when he says that electing to create human beings entails willing everything conducive to their happiness, he appeals to God's goodness. The necessity here appears to be moral, though King does not explain. The thought might be that goodness is a fixed appetite in God such that no act of the free divine appetite can fail to conform also to this fixed appetite. In any case, King seeks to drastically limit the implications of his radical agential voluntarism by loading the election to create with significant entailments.[25] In this way, he ensures that God does indeed will to realize as much happiness as possible—at least for those creatures God freely elects to create. He can also affirm the classical ethical intellectualist view that God could not change the natural law, a result he achieves by insisting that the election by which God enacts the natural law is necessarily contained in the very same election by which God creates.

King's embrace of radical agential voluntarism creates complications for his view of divine goodness, but it has a clear function: to prove that the existence of a free appetite is possible. And if it is possible, King argues, then God would surely have given it to creatures to increase their happiness. God, he suggests, must have multiplied creatures with free appetites as far as the system and order of the whole allowed (V.ii.1). Our happiness lies above all in the proper use of the will. Because the will pleases itself in any object it chooses, free creatures can be happy in any circumstance. This, he argues, is why scripture commands us to conform ourselves to the will of God. The one whose will remains conformed to the will of God is pleased by whatever occurs (V.ii.5). Even though one's fixed appetites will be frustrated, one's free appetite, which is greater, will remain pleased.[26]

God gave us the will to allow us to be happy in a world that will necessarily frustrate our appetites. Because this is the will's proper role, any election by the will that causes unhappiness is an undue election. He explains:

> From hence it is sufficiently evident what kind of elections are to be called undue: for it appears that God has given us this faculty of choosing that we may please ourselves in the use of it and be happy. Whensoever we make a choice as not to be able to enjoy the things chosen, it is plain that we choose foolishly and unduly: for we bring upon ourselves unnecessary misery. (V.iii.1)

An election that will be frustrated is undue. Undue elections are for that which is impossible, inconsistent with other elections, or not in our power. They could also be for that which is already lawfully occupied by the elections of other free beings. Finally, an election is undue if it unnecessarily opposes our other appetites, leading to avoidable pain (V.iii). Why, if we have the power to be happy in any situation, would we ever cause ourselves misery? King thinks reasons are not hard to find: ignorance, negligence, levity, habit, or other appetites (V.iv).

We are finally in a position to raise the question of why God allows moral evil. Moral evil has always raised the greatest challenge. The same is true for King, although in a unique way. The particular problem posed by moral evil, for King, is this: moral evils, unlike other natural evils, are not a necessary result of corporeality. In the case of both evil of imperfection and natural evil, King argues that God does as much as is logically or metaphysically possible to reduce evil. Moral evils are different. Moral evil is not necessary for creatures, even free creatures (V.v.i.1). In this case alone, God permits unnecessary evils. But King argues that each of the ways in which God might have eliminated moral evil would lead to greater evils.

King never seriously considers the idea that God might be able to providentially govern free creatures in and through their freedom without diminishing it. King's view of the relationship between divine and creaturely agency is, in Kathryn Tanner's terms, competitive.[27] For King, it would be logically impossible for God to move the creaturely will without destroying its nature. For a thing that moves itself to be moved by another, he says, is like a square circle (V.v.iv.5). King recognizes Bayle's argument that the saints in heaven are both free and incapable of sinning, but he attributes this to the absence of temptation.

The intellectual world has its own laws. God governs the material world through the laws of nature, which, for King, are Newtonian. These are the appropriate laws with which to govern matter, which is entirely passive. The intellectual world, by contrast, is composed of self-active creatures. For God to govern these creatures as if they were passive—that is, for God to move them or allow them to be moved from without—would be a contradiction. Instead, God governs them through laws appropriate to free creatures, namely, through moral laws that include rewards and punishments. King argues that the will can no more be moved by physical laws than matter can be moved by rewards and punishments (V.v.iii.3). If God were to govern the will by physical laws, it would no longer be a will.[28]

Removing moral evil, according to King, would end up causing even more evil. King employs many different arguments, the details of which are not worth repeating. The importance of the arguments for our purposes lies in the relationship it assumes between natural and moral evil. I have already observed that King takes moral evil to be a subset of natural evil. In the course of defending God's creation of free beings, King expresses the relation in a slightly different way:

> It must be observed that elections are therefore esteemed evil because they lead us into natural evils. For if an election contains nothing absurd or prejudicial, it is not a wrong one. Hatred of God, rebellion against his commands, murder, theft, lying are sins because they are hurtful to ourselves or others, because they deprive us of natural good and lead into evil. Elections therefore are wrong and undue on account of the natural evils which sometimes attend them; natural evils are greater than moral: for that which makes anything bad must necessarily be worse itself. (V.v.ii.8)

In this passage, in contrast to others, King identifies moral evil with undue elections and contrasts these with the natural evils that result. But the terminological shift should not hide the basic continuity of thought. God is concerned with natural evils. Undue elections are only a problem due to the resulting natural evils. The elections are themselves indifferent. For King, God's choice to allow undue elections results from weighing only two considerations: the natural evils caused by undue elections and the natural goods made possible by free appetites. The latter, he argues, decisively outweighs the former.[29]

King and the Augustinian Tradition

Let us now step back and contextualize King's innovations, first in the long Augustinian tradition on evil and then in the ethical tradition of More and Cumberland. King's treatise is full of echoes of the Augustinian approach to evil, which remained dominant. John Hick, for example, takes King to be simply rehearsing old Augustinian themes: "King was not an original thinker; but precisely for this reason his clear and uncritical exposition presents the Augustinian themes as they had become detached from the more creative minds that first produced them."[30] King, however, is far more original than Hick recognizes.

Consider, first of all, the division of evils into types. Augustine's key argument is that evil is a privation of some good due to a particular creaturely nature. There is, for Augustine, no evil of imperfection or defect as such. The simple lack of a possible good is not evil. A lack is only evil if it is a lack of a natural perfection—if, that is, it is a privation. King, by contrast, makes no distinction between those capacities that are proper to a being and those that are not. The inability to fly in a chipmunk is an evil of the same kind as the inability to fly in a robin. Still, as I noted above, the evil of imperfection is probably best not called evil according to King's own definition. But even if we limit King to natural and moral evil, his view remains very different from Augustine's. Because the evil of imperfection includes all the privations an Augustinian would have called natural evil, King's category of natural evil cannot be the same as Augustine's. Instead, natural evil is the frustration of appetite—and thus is very nearly reducible to subjective displeasure.[31] Bayle reaches the same conclusion in his critique of King. In King's view, according to Bayle, "To be lame is an evil only in so far as one has grief or one suffers pains and inconveniencies. A lame person who would be content with his condition would be happier than a man well made who would not be content with his."[32] Likewise, King's account of moral evil differs significantly from Augustine's. Moral evil, too, is a privation in the Augustinian tradition, namely, a privation of right love and action. For King, moral evil is a product only of the causal consequences of volition.

Beyond these shifts in terminology and categorization, King also departs from Augustine on a fundamental point: the rationale for the existence of evil. In the Augustinian tradition, moral evil presents the most significant problem for two reasons. First, all evil originates with moral evil. This raises difficult questions about why God would have made creatures with the capacity to introduce such devastating evils into creation. Second, moral evil is, at least for those uncorrupted by original sin, unintelligible. All natural evils are justified punishments for sin, but moral evil serves no function and achieves no end. It seems to be the sort of thing that has no place in God's good creation. Augustine himself recognizes this problem. He ultimately rejects the idea that God creates human beings with an indifferent will that is equally free to do both good and evil, and thus renders the introduction of moral evil inexplicable.[33] Aquinas echoes a long tradition when, in response to the question "whether pain [*poena*] or fault [*culpa*] has more the nature of evil," he answers that fault has more of the nature of evil than pain.[34] Bayle, likewise, concluded that the existence of moral evil is inexplicable. Bayle's argument rests on the Augustinian view that natural evil stems from moral evil, and moral evil is both unnecessary and unintelligible. Because moral evil is absurd, Bayle argues that a good God would never even allow its possibility.

King seeks to change the nature of the debate by rethinking the relationship between natural and moral evil, and he sees a new possibility with an appeal to mechanical philosophy.[35] If the nature of matter explains why corporeal beings are necessarily subject to natural evil, then natural evil is not a punishment for moral evil.[36] In creating corporeal beings, God cannot avoid natural evil. Corporeal beings must have certain faculties and appetites, yet the nature of matter ensures that these faculties and appetites will face a degree of pain and disappointment. The greatest gift God could give to corporeal beings is an appetite, stronger than all the rest, that is free to take pleasure in anything and therefore never subject to necessary pain or disappointment. The downside of this gift is that it opens up the possibility of misuse, that is, the possibility of causing unnecessary natural evils.

In King's account, the relationship between natural evil and moral evil is, in a certain sense, reversed. In the Augustinian picture, natural evil serves to justly punish sinners and, with the help of grace, rehabilitate them. Natural good and evil, we could say, are ordered to moral good, at least in this life. Natural evils are justified insofar as they punish or correct moral evils. King switches the relationship between natural and moral evil. Natural evils are inevitable but to be minimized. Creaturely freedom— and with it the possibility of both moral good and evil—is the most effective way to reduce natural evils. For King, in contrast to Aquinas, pain has more of the nature of evil than fault. As King puts it, "Natural evils are greater than moral: for that which makes anything bad must be worse itself" (V.v.ii.8).[37]

King's reordering of the relationship between natural and moral evil changes the nature of theodicy. Moral evil matters only instrumentally. Natural evil is the real problem. And natural evil is taken to consist above all in subjective displeasure. Because theodicy, as we have seen, is inextricably bound up with ethics, these changes in the problem of theodicy bear ethical implications. Let us turn to these implications.

The Moral Theology of *De origine mali*

King's God acts as a perfect consequentialist, weighing the goodness of different possible worlds and creating the one with maximal goodness. Human morality, too, is consequentialist. The point of human freedom—which, for King, is the condition of morality—is to increase human happiness by permitting human beings to be happy despite the inevitable frustration their fixed appetites will face. Because the purpose of freedom is human happiness, a free act that causes natural evil must be evil. The criterion for judging acts, then, is straightforwardly consequentialist: the moral goodness or badness of any act is determined entirely by the natural goodness or badness of its consequences.

Indeed, King's view in this sense goes further toward contemporary consequentialism than More's or Cumberland's. Though More and Cumberland judge actions to be good or bad by their consequences, both still attribute some inherent value to good actions themselves. For Cumberland, moral goodness consists of the conformity of an act to the divine will. And More insists that a good act is not simply one that realizes the best consequences but one that does so from the intellectual love of the boniform faculty. While More and Cumberland both believe that the right action is the one that maximizes good consequences, they do not determine the goodness of actions solely by consequences. King, by contrast, treats elections and actions entirely instrumentally. Their moral status depends solely on their contribution to natural goods and evils.

In addition, King takes an important step toward utilitarianism—that is, hedonistic consequentialism—which makes him, as we will see, a crucial source for Anglican utilitarianism. Though King's language at times echoes More's and Cumberland's, King's view of happiness is not perfectionistic. Why not? We have already seen the primary reason: the distinction between evil of imperfection and natural evil means that a lack of perfection is not a natural evil. But there is an additional reason. King's account of nonrational creatures contains a sort of perfectionism insofar as the appetites of nonrational creatures are given for definite ends, meaning that the natural goodness of satisfying appetites aligns precisely with the perfectionistic ends of the creature. Human beings, however, have an additional appetite with no object. The primary human appetite, then, has no connection with perfection in order to ensure that happiness is possible even when creaturely ends are frustrated, as they inevitably are. Free creatures can, simply by an act of will, please themselves in deformity, in failure, or in the completely trivial. They do so not, as with the Stoics, in recognizing that their true good lies in virtue rather than in circumstances, but rather in making their circumstances naturally good by freely willing them. God, we could say, created the will precisely in order to separate happiness from perfection. For this reason, the natural goodness to which moral goodness is ordered is essentially affective and not perfective. Human beings, like God, are to maximize subjective pleasure.

King further develops his moral philosophy in an appendix he includes on divine law. The topic of divine law became an inevitable part of theodicy after Bayle. Bayle's arguments about evil often take the form of imagined dialogues between a dualist and a pre-Christian theist. After the theist fails to resolve the problems raised by the dualist, Bayle would often add that Christianity, with its doctrines of divine law and eternal sanctions, makes theism's problem even harder. If God knew that human beings would disobey, why did God give commands in the first place? They do nothing but multiply evil by adding punishment.[38] King's appendix responds to this charge.

Echoing Cumberland, King defines law as "the will of a superior sufficiently promulgated to an inferior, and attended with the hope or fear of reward or punishment" (A.i.1). In contrast to Cumberland, however, King shows no interest in the problem of authority (A.ii.1). He divides divine law into two kinds: natural and positive. Natural law, he says, is that which God has implanted in the nature of every being. All bodies and all animals are subject to it. The natural law of bodies is Newtonian, and the natural law of animals concerns self- and species-preservation. Human beings, as free creatures, are subject to an additional law: "that they shall please themselves by election" (A.i.3). Divine positive law, by contrast, is that which is promulgated by God in revelation. God adds divine positive law for the simple reason that "it was impossible for nature to acquaint us with all the consequences which attend our actions in an infinite train and continuance of things" (A.i.3).

But why does God impose laws that will inevitably lead to punishment and thus add natural evils to the world? These laws, according to King, do not impose unnecessary sanctions. Rather, they are "means of acquainting free agents with what is expedient for them, and of moving them to the choice of it" (A.i.4). Because, as we have seen, free creatures cannot be compelled, the most effective way to bring them to their happiness is through laws that teach human beings their true interest. Despite his notion of divine governance by law and sanction, then, King denies that the natural evils that follow from breaking divine law are punishments, except perhaps in extreme cases. For King, scriptural language about punishments is just a more rhetorically forceful way of communicating to us the natural consequences of undue elections. Through divine law, God tells us how to avoid causing ourselves natural evil. The same, King argues, can be said of eternal punishments. Eternal punishments are known not by natural reason but by revelation. Our understanding of them is therefore limited. Nevertheless, King contends that they are the natural consequence of undue elections of which divine law seeks to warn us. They follow not from divine vengeance but from the laws of a created order containing the greatest goodness. Divine law, therefore, is nothing more than a set of truths about the consequences of our elections, some of which are known by natural reason and the rest revealed by God. It adds no evils to the world: it only warns about the natural consequences of actions.

King and the Consequentialist Moral Cosmology

While King's aim is to provide a theodicy, he cannot do so without addressing the nature of morality, both human and divine. In *De origine*, the pressures of theodicy—and particularly of a theodicy meant to demonstrate that God creates a world with the greatest goodness—shape the account of morality. Let us now consider how the moral theology of *De origine* compares to the consequentialist moral cosmology of More and Cumberland.

King does not cite More or Cumberland, though he sometimes conspicuously echoes More. Whether or not he knows their work, he has certainly been touched by their influence, which, as I have noted, was quite extensive. The important issue is not historical influence but the way in which the effort to address the problems raised by Bayle affects the combination of views that constitute the consequentialist moral cosmology. In King, we find our first example.

King's view broadly conforms to the consequentialist moral cosmology on the question of divine and human moral ends. God, according to King, wills the realization of the greatest goodness in creation. Human beings should also will this end. Human beings, according to the natural law, "shall please themselves by election" (A.i.3). The best way to please oneself, King argues, is to conform one's will to God's. To conform one's will to God's is to will whatever happens, knowing that God has arranged all things for the sake of the greatest goodness. Human beings are thus to will the realization of the greatest goodness in conformity with God's will. King, likewise, echoes the consequentialist moral cosmology in his discussion of law, arguing that human beings ought to obey God's natural and revealed commands, which inform them about how to contribute to the realization of the greatest goodness.

Yet while King's view conforms to the consequentialist moral cosmology in outline, his views about both divine and human morality are importantly different from those of More and Cumberland. The primary reason stems from his radical agential voluntarist account of the will. From King's perspective, both More and Cumberland hold problematic views of freedom, which opens them up to Bayle's argument that freedom is a harmful gift that a good God would never give. King's alternative account of freedom, when combined with his larger explanation of the origin of evil, successfully avoids this critique. Its moral implications, however, are significant.

In the case of God, King's radical agential voluntarism could easily lead to ethical voluntarism about divine morality, though King clearly is not interested in this result. He avoids it with a robust account of what is entailed in God's free choice to create together with what appears to be an appeal to a fixed divine appetite for goodness. In willing to create even one creature, God also wills everything necessary to the flourishing of that creature, which turns out to be a great deal. Indeed, Leibniz, in his assessment of *De origine*, argues that King's view leads to the conclusion that if God wills to create anything, God must will to create the best possible world.[39] King does not make the same argument as Leibniz, but he seems to want essentially the same result—though, of course, with a different notion of what makes a world the best.

The case of human morality is even more complicated. King is committed to the existence of a free appetite in human beings for its role in explaining evil. Our primary appetite, for King, has a single function: to allow us to be happy in a world that frustrates all fixed appetites. And because the function of the will is to be happy, King concludes that the natural law dictates that we please ourselves through election. King is then able to move from this principle to the conclusion that we ought to join our wills to God's will. Human beings ought to conform their wills to God's and thus share God's end, the realization of the greatest goodness. Nonetheless, we cannot avoid the conclusion that God and human beings will the same end for different reasons. Given that God freely elects to create, God wills the realization of the greatest goodness necessarily as an entailment of the will to create. Human beings will the realization of the greatest goodness because an omnipotent being does. We do not will this end due to any of its qualities but because we know God will realize it, thus rendering us happy. Indeed, we ought to will whatever we know will happen. Therefore, we will the realization of the greatest goodness only contingently. If we found ourselves in a world ruled by a cosmic demon, we ought to share the demon's end in order to please ourselves. This conclusion is unattractive but follows naturally from his description of the natural law. For More and Cumberland, by contrast, the goodness of the "*best Effect*" is itself a decisive reason for us to pursue it. If a demon ruled the cosmos, we would still have reason to pursue the same end and not obey the demon.

King's distance from the consequentialist moral cosmology is also apparent in his lack of concern for divine authority. King does not attempt to ground divine authority over creation. Rather, he reinterprets divine law in such a way that divine authority is unnecessary. God's commands, as King interprets them, function as counsels about the natural consequences of actions. We are to follow divine positive law in order to better secure our happiness. Once again, these innovations in ethics stem directly from theodicy. King is trying to avoid Bayle's argument that the imposition of divine law makes the world worse, an argument that could have caused problems for More and Cumberland. If divine law is instead nothing but a set of warnings about the natural consequences of acts, as King says, God does not harm us but increases our prospects for happiness.

In all these ways, we can see that King holds to an outline of the consequentialist moral cosmology while transforming its structure. The radical agential voluntarism and the new account of divine law, while both successful strategies against Bayle, are ultimately irreconcilable with the consequentialist moral cosmology as formulated by More and Cumberland. In the end, King maintains the moral perfection of God by consequentialist standards only by giving up the notion that we, too, can and should will the same end as God for the same reasons. A perfect, consequentialist God, King believes, would not burden us with the task of maximizing goodness for its own sake. A perfect, consequentialist God would rather give us the tools to be happy and instruct us about the best way to do so. Giving up the idea that God and human beings pursue the same end is not necessarily a problem for King on his own terms. He is not concerned with the consequentialist moral cosmology as such. Seeing how his theodicy shapes the moral relationship between God and creatures, however, helps us see why the consequentialist moral cosmology becomes difficult to maintain in light of Bayle's arguments about evil.

King is the first example of a figure who responds to Bayle while defending a view that broadly mirrors the consequentialist moral cosmology. The fact that King ends up breaking in crucial respects with the consequentialist moral cosmology in order to more successfully respond to

Bayle is not accidental. We will find a similar result—though with quite different details—in each of the next two chapters. The fact that it proves so difficult to explain the existence and extent of evil in the world within the framework of the consequentialist moral cosmology will ultimately lead to an unexpected result: a turn in the consequentialist tradition to its original opponent, ethical voluntarism. We will see this turn in the Anglican utilitarians in part III.

King's *De origine mali* was the first major response to Bayle in Britain. It was soon followed by another major work, Shaftesbury's *Characteristicks of Men, Manners, Times, Opinions.*

6

Shaftesbury the Theologian

VIRTUE AS FRIENDSHIP WITH GOD

In his first publication, a collection of Benjamin Whichcote's sermons, Shaftesbury calls Whichcote "the preacher of good-nature."[1] Whichcote, who spent much of his life at Cambridge, including as vice-chancellor during the interregnum period, was closely associated with Henry More and Ralph Cudworth and has often been called the leader of the Cambridge Platonists.[2] Though he did not publish in his lifetime, Whichcote expressed his views through his sermons, which exerted a lasting influence. Whichcote's sermons, according to Shaftesbury, provide an alternative to the common attempt to degrade human nature in order to elevate the need for divine grace and revelation. Shaftesbury's implicit target is the Reformed theological tradition. It is a strange thought, he contends, that a rational creature derived from "a Supreme Power acting with the greatest Goodness, and without any Inducement but that of Love and Good-will" should be either incapable of goodness or unable to act virtuously without the promise of heavenly reward.[3] In a religion in which "charity (or kindness) is made all in all," human beings must be naturally capable of generous affections.[4]

Shaftesbury's interest in "good-nature" shapes much of his published work. As his early preface to Whichcote's sermons suggests, Shaftesbury insists on an inference from the nature of God to the nature of humanity. In doing so, Shaftesbury carries forward ideas from Whichcote and the Cambridge Platonists.[5] We have seen, for example, that Henry More also considered goodness the defining characteristic of both God and, due to the divine faculty within, human beings. Indeed, with his emphasis on the good affections, Shaftesbury echoes no earlier thinker more than More, whose *Enchiridion ethicum* Shaftesbury calls "a right good piece of sound morals."[6] In his embrace of Whichcote and More and his antagonism to Reformed theology, Shaftesbury locates himself in the tradition of Latitudinarian theology that, by his day, was ascendant in the Anglican Church.[7]

Yet while Shaftesbury's early preface starts down a well established
path, the obstacles facing him were not the same as those of his predecessors. Of particular importance for present purposes is the fact that Shaftesbury's major works were written in the decade following the publication
of Bayle's *Dictionnaire*. Shaftesbury owned a copy of the *Dictionnaire*, and
he knew Bayle personally. They met during Shaftesbury's first retreat to
Holland in 1698–1699, and Shaftesbury, in a letter written shortly after
Bayle's death, speaks fondly of his friendship with Bayle, even while noting "the continuall differences in Opinions and the constant disputes
that were between us."[8] Shaftesbury's thought is deeply marked by the
attempt to overcome the philosophical and theological problems posed by
evil. The same is true of Henry More, though as we have seen, the problem looks somewhat different after Bayle, and this difference is notable
in Shaftesbury. In particular, Shaftesbury, like Bayle, has no patience for
More's appeal to creaturely freedom to explain the existence of evil. Shaftesbury takes a radically different approach from the dominant Augustinian
tradition—and, as we will see, from King. In his major work on the topic,
The Moralists, Shaftesbury argues, against appearances to the contrary,
that there is, in fact, no evil in the world, a view that was already present
in and integral to his earliest philosophical treatise, *An Inquiry into Virtue
and Merit*, first published in 1699. Indeed, his entire moral philosophy
depends upon the nonexistence of evil.

Shaftesbury offers an alternative defense of divine goodness against
Bayle's arguments about evil. William King, we saw in the previous chapter, developed one possible response to Bayle by rethinking the nature of
freedom and God's reasons for granting it to creatures. King's theodicy, I
argued, is quite effective as a response to Bayle. God's goodness by consequentialist standards remains. But in King's moral theology, God and
human beings no longer pursue the same end for the sake of its goodness,
as in More and Cumberland. The moral community between God and
creatures begins to break down. This chapter argues that a similar result
occurs with Shaftesbury.

For Shaftesbury, whose theology is more Stoic than Christian, the rational defense of the perfect goodness of God is paramount. While Shaftesbury is not properly called a consequentialist, his theological and ethical
vision of the cosmos closely mirrors the consequentialist moral cosmology. Shaftesbury defends divine goodness by arguing that God always acts
for and achieves the greatest natural good: the good of the cosmos as a
whole. Moreover, Shaftesbury understands our moral perfection to consist
in willing the very same end as God. Because we share the same end as
God, we are to submit our wills in all things to God's. In all these ways,

Shaftesbury sounds like More and Cumberland. Yet despite his claims to the contrary, I argue that Shaftesbury's attempt to eliminate evil from the cosmos ultimately makes it impossible for him to maintain that rational creatures can share God's end and thus God's morality.

Shaftesbury's major work, *Characteristicks of Men, Manners, Opinions, Times,* consists of five treatises, each of which has a different literary form, as well as a series of "Miscellaneous Reflections." While the attention of later ethicists has generally fixed upon the penultimate treatise, *Inquiry into Virtue and Merit,* Shaftesbury's ethical and theological vision is most fully articulated in the final treatise, *The Moralists.*[9] This chapter begins with the key elements of the *Inquiry,* which set up the major problems that *The Moralists* seeks to resolve. I then turn to *The Moralists,* arguing that Shaftesbury understands friendship with God—friendship founded on a shared end—as both the human good and the practical solution to the problem of evil. Finally, I argue that these two functions of friendship with God generate a tension that ultimately undermines the possibility of sharing God's end and thus of friendship with God. Shaftesbury provides a second example of the difficulty of addressing Bayle's argument within the broad framework of the consequentialist moral cosmology.

Morality and Religion in the *Inquiry*

Shaftesbury's earliest philosophical treatise, *Inquiry into Virtue and Merit*—published, he later said, in an unfinished form against his will[10]—appeared originally in 1699 and was revised and republished as part of *Characteristicks* in 1711.[11] The aim of book I of *Inquiry* is to consider the relationship between virtue and religion. Virtue and religion, Shaftesbury writes, are often so closely associated that they are presumed inseparable. Yet because all know of those who are religious but lacking virtue, or virtuous but lacking religion, one can ask how far religion influences or implies virtue, and whether virtue without religion is possible.[12] The very presupposition of the treatise—that there is such a thing as virtue independent of religion—would, Shaftesbury knew, be contentious, a fact that he attributes to the anxiety among many over the perceived rise in deism and atheism.[13] In response, he positions himself as the voice of moderation between the extremes of those who see no virtue in religion and those who see no virtue outside of religion, a defender of religion against the former and of natural virtue against the latter (I, 238–39).

As Shaftesbury frames the treatise, the real controversy is over whether virtue can be defined independently of religion. While this issue was a matter of controversy, Shaftesbury was by no means innovative in defining virtue without reference to religion. The much more striking feature of Shaftesbury's treatise is the way he defines religion.[14] Shaftesbury divides religious belief into four options: theist, atheist, polytheist, and daemonist. He writes:

> To believe therefore that everything is governed, ordered, or regulated for the best, by a designing principle or mind, necessarily good and permanent, is to be a perfect Theist. To believe nothing of a designing principle or mind, nor any cause, measure, or rule of things, but chance, so that in nature neither the interest of the whole nor of any particulars can be said to be in the least designed, pursued, or aimed at, is to be a perfect Atheist. To believe no one supreme designing principle or mind, but rather two, three, or more (though in their nature good), is to be a Polytheist. To believe the governing mind, or minds, not absolutely and necessarily good, nor confined to what is best, but capable of acting according to mere will or fancy, is to be a Daemonist. (I, 240–41)

While Shaftesbury is on the surface simply providing a method of classifying religious beliefs, his intent is more subversive. Religious classification comes not by tradition or confession but by how one conceives the order of the universe. The revisionist implications of this approach become particularly clear when Shaftesbury notes that few people consistently fall into a single category. One may spend one's life as a practicing Christian, but insofar as one continues to attribute anything in the universe to chance or an imperfectly good power, one is not properly a theist (I, 241).

The account of religion is revisionist in other ways as well. For Shaftesbury, theism, as the belief in a single perfectly good designing principle, necessarily entails that "there is no such thing as real ill in the universe, nothing ill with respect to the whole" (I, 239). Anyone who believes anything in the universe could be better believes in "ill with respect to the whole," which, for the rest of this chapter, I will simply call evil. Such a person is not, strictly speaking, a theist. Moreover, anyone who believes that the governing mind is capable of acting in any way at odds with the perfection of the universe is not a theist but a daemonist. We can recognize the latter as a shot at ethical voluntarists—one which, in outline, Henry More made before him.[15] Many Christians will end up, by Shaftesbury's lights, daemonists.

Religion, then, is defined by habitual opinions about the ordering principle of the universe. What is virtue? Shaftesbury begins with a general account of good and ill. Nature, he argues, compels each creature to seek a particular state of its constitution, which is its end. The good of every creature is the end to which everything in its constitution naturally refers. Shaftesbury simply takes for granted that such an end exists and, at least in most cases, can be determined. Anything that furthers the creature's end is good for it, and anything that opposes the end is ill for it. At this stage of the analysis, Shaftesbury sounds like More or Cumberland: the good of any being is that which preserves or perfects it.

Shaftesbury, however, does not stop here. To say something is good or ill for a creature is to refer to the private good or ill of that creature. We can also ask if the creature is good or ill, which is to refer to something beyond private good or ill. Shaftesbury imagines a perfectly solitary creature that greatly enjoys its condition and wants nothing. Can we call this creature good? He thinks not. We might, he writes, acknowledge a kind of goodness if the creature were "absolute and complete in himself, without any real relation to anything else in the universe" (I, 244). In reality, however, no creature is complete in itself. The structure of each creature "points beyond himself," revealing him to be "part of some other system" (I, 245). And if a creature's constitution reveals it to be a component of a larger system, its goodness as a creature depends on its functioning in proper relation to that system.

According to Shaftesbury, each creature is a component of its species; its species, of the system of all living things; and the system of living things, of the globe, sun, planets, and galaxy. If, he writes, "it be allowed that there is in like manner a system of all things, and a universal nature, there can be no particular being or system which is not either good or ill in that general one of the universe" (I, 246). Because each creature is a component of systems that are themselves components of the universal system, true good and ill must be good and ill for the universal system.

For Shaftesbury, then, the question of whether any creature is good or ill is a question not of private good but of the way in which the creature functions for the good or ill of the cosmic whole. In the case of sensitive creatures, a further nuance is required: only those acts that stem from an affection count toward the creature's goodness or lack of goodness.[16] In nonrational creatures, affections move the creature toward its good. The affections themselves are good when they are for the creature's good in a way that is consistent with or contributes to the good of the whole. For Shaftesbury, the link between the affection and the good or goods it intends must be natural and not accidental. Excessive affections may accidentally cause public good but are not for that reason good.

The same basic principle applies to rational creatures, although the matter is more complicated. Rational creatures are capable of forming general notions, which creates the possibility of new objects of affection. They are capable of reflecting on their own affections, "so that, by means of this reflected sense, there arises another kind of affection towards those very affections themselves, which have been already felt, and are now become the subject of a new liking or dislike" (I, 251). Shaftesbury draws here on an analogy with aesthetic judgment. Any object, he writes, will give rise to affections responding to its beauty or deformity, "according to the different measure, arrangement, and disposition of their several parts" (I, 251). The same phenomenon occurs with regard to the measure, arrangement, and disposition of human affections. We find harmonious affections agreeable and admirable and dissonant affections disagreeable and worthy of scorn. Because a rational creature can recognize the order of her affections and their integration into larger systems, she will approve of those affections that are harmonious with the public good and disapprove of those that are not. She is now not only good or ill but also virtuous or vicious, deserving of merit or demerit. In this way, she can "attain the speculation or science of what is morally good or ill" (I, 252).

Due to Shaftesbury's language about affection, one might be surprised by the reference here to "speculation or science." Shaftesbury speaks about moral judgment in aesthetic terms, and scholars have argued for his historical influence on aesthetic theory.[17] Yet Shaftesbury is often mistakenly read as a sentimentalist in the mold of later figures like Francis Hutcheson and David Hume. The fact that Shaftesbury describes moral judgment in affective terms does not mean that he takes it to be arational. One should not read the opposition between affect and reason, which is characteristic of some of his intellectual descendants, into his work. Shaftesbury stands in the Stoic and Platonic traditions in which affective judgments have rational content, even if it is inchoate.[18] One who is able to make proper affective judgments, then, has attained the science of morality.

Virtue in a rational creature consists of affections that are harmonious with one another and with the various systems of which the creature is a part. Vice is a lack of harmony. The question now is: How do virtue and vice relate to religion? For Shaftesbury, virtue is the natural state of the creature. Religion reinforces virtue when it reinforces our harmonious integration with the whole, as theism does by teaching that the whole is perfectly good. All other religious options, by contrast, interfere with natural virtue by giving us a false view of the whole as unintegrated and disordered. He concludes that religion strengthens virtue when it is theistic and weakens it otherwise.

A careful reader is likely to come away from the argument dissatisfied. A sleight of hand has occurred. Shaftesbury tells us that he will treat virtue and religion independently in order to determine the relationship between them. In fact, his account of virtue implicitly presupposes the truth of theism. He begins his account of virtue with an argument for the existence of a universal system of which every creature is a part. Moreover, he presupposes that the affections of each creature are naturally aligned not only with the creature's own good but also with the good of the whole. Without these theistic presuppositions, his picture of virtue is implausible. Shaftesbury has only shown us that theism supports virtue when virtue is implicitly theistic.[19]

This conclusion is only further reinforced in book II of the *Inquiry* when Shaftesbury addresses the question of "what obligation there is to virtue, or what reason to embrace it" (I, 280). The reason Shaftesbury gives is that virtue is the advantage and vice the disadvantage of every creature (I, 282). The force of the argument lies in the claim that human happiness is found in the harmonious operation of the affections. Shaftesbury interprets the structure of the mind by an analogy with the structure of the body: "'Tis certain that the order or symmetry of this inward part is in itself no less real and exact than that of the body" (I, 284). What is needed, he argues, is an "anatomist" of the mind who can ascertain the effect of "straining an affection, indulging any wrong passion, or relaxing any proper and natural habit or good inclination" (I, 284). The mind, for Shaftesbury, is a whole with mutually supporting parts like the body. Just as excessive use of one part of the body has implications for the whole, so any excessive passion affects the whole of the mind.

Both virtue and individual happiness are found in the harmonious operation of the natural affections. Any deviation from natural harmony is at once both a source of misery and a departure from virtue. While deviations can come in many forms, Shaftesbury focuses on three characteristic flaws in human affections—weak public affections, excessive private affections, and unnatural affections—arguing that each detracts from happiness. The greatest pleasures, according to Shaftesbury, are found in the operation of the social affections. We delight in the good of others and in their esteem for us. Moreover, even many bodily pleasures, such as a good meal or sex, are pleasurable largely because of their integration with social affections. All enjoyments are enhanced when shared. According to Shaftesbury,

> were pleasure to be computed in the same way as other things commonly are, it might properly be said, that out of these two branches (viz. community or participation in the pleasures of others, and belief of meriting well from others) would arise more than nine-tenths of whatever is enjoyed in life. And thus in the main sum of happiness

there is scarce a single article but what derives itself from social love, and depends immediately on the natural and kind affections. (I, 299)

Private affections also have an important role in one's happiness. But when they become excessive, they cause misery rather than happiness. Importantly, because Shaftesbury appeals to the desire for happiness as a motivation for virtue, he does not think of this desire as one of the self-affections. The self-affections, rather, are affections for particular private goods, such as long life, money, possessions, individual success, and individual rest or leisure.[20] Each of these affections can play a harmonious role in one's mental anatomy as long as it maintains its proper strength.

The argument certainly makes plausible the conclusion that human happiness depends in large part on relationships and social life and thus on social affections. Yet it hardly proves, as Shaftesbury puts it in the conclusion, that "virtue is the good, and vice the ill of everyone." The argument linking virtue and happiness is probabilistic at best, even granting its theistic premises. But Shaftesbury's intention is not to fully resolve the issue of happiness and the human good in the *Inquiry*. The aim of the *Inquiry*, according to the philosophical hero of *The Moralists*, is to reconcile his readers to moral realism so that "by this means a way might be laid open to religion." Indeed, realism in morality, he argues, requires realism in divinity. While the *Inquiry* is concerned above all with realism in morality, *The Moralists* completes the project by defending realism in divinity. In doing so, it completes the argument of the *Inquiry*, proving that virtue is the path to happiness. But to defend realism in divinity, Shaftesbury must address one major hurdle. He has asserted that theism entails the nonexistence of evil. Realism in divinity, then, requires a response to Bayle. Shaftesbury's approach to this issue, as we will see, is very different from King's.

Friendship and the Human Good

The Moralists, Shaftesbury's only philosophical dialogue, takes up both tasks just listed: it defends the nonexistence of evil, and it supplies Shaftesbury's full account of happiness and the human good. The dialogue is recounted in a letter from Philocles, a nondogmatic skeptic, to Palemon, a nobleman with philosophical interests. Philocles is writing in response to a previous conversation in which Palemon lamented the "wretched state of mankind." Mankind, Palemon complained, is "ill to himself, and cause of ill to all" (II, 10). All of creation except humanity is beautiful. Perhaps, he suggested, there is some Prometheus, some intermediary between God and the world that introduced such corruption. Philocles, however, quickly dispelled the hope of an intermediary, which only raises the problem of corruption one level higher. One must still affirm either that God could have prevented the corruption and did not or that God could not have prevented it. Both options are unacceptable to the theist.

The echoes of Bayle are clear, and Philocles has even been identified with Bayle.[21] Philocles, though, refused to respond on the terms set by Palemon. He asserted: "Much is alleged in answer to show why Nature errs, and how she came thus impotent and erring from an unerring hand. But I deny she errs" (II, 22). If human beings are components of a universal system, then what seems ill to human beings is not truly ill, that is, not evil. The universal system requires subordination of parts to one another and to the whole:

> Thus in the several orders of terrestrial forms a resignation is required, a sacrifice and mutual yielding of natures one to another. The vegetables by their death sustain the animals, and animal bodies dissolved enrich the earth, and raise again the vegetable world. The numerous insects are reduced by the superior kinds of birds and beasts, and these again are checked by man, who in his turn submits to other natures, and resigns his form a sacrifice in common to the rest of things. And if in natures so little exalted or pre-eminent above each other, the sacrifice of interests can appear so just, how much more reasonably may all the inferior natures be subjected to the superior nature of the world! (II, 22)

Philocles is obviously echoing the views of the *Inquiry* and using them to dissolve the problem posed by the existence of evil. But Shaftesbury does not position Philocles, who generally tends toward skepticism, as the philosophical hero of the story. Philocles goes on to explain how he came to these views after encountering the true philosophical hero of the work, Theocles. Most of the work, then, centers on the story of how a skeptic was converted to Shaftesbury's theism.

Interestingly, when Philocles begins to tell the story of his conversation with Theocles, we discover that the topic is not evil but the human good. The reason for the change of topics, I think, is quite clear. Shaftesbury wants to highlight that the dialogue addresses the question of evil, and he does this through the initial framing, which provides the rationale for the work. But for Shaftesbury, philosophy is about happiness, not mere speculation. He wants the philosophical hero of the story, Theocles, to focus on the human good. The final answer to the question of the human good does also resolve the question about the existence of evil, but it does so, so to speak, as a byproduct, and its solution is more practical than speculative. Shaftesbury thus centers the dialogue on the human good while using the introductory material to signal that the question about evil will be addressed along the way. To see how Theocles resolves the problem of evil through his argument about happiness, we will have to follow the trajectory of the dialogue.

Philocles tells us that he first raised the issue of the human good with Theocles in despair. There can be no human good, he lamented, because nothing in human life is constant. Theocles accepts the challenge of proving that there is a constant good that constitutes happiness, and he quickly begins to echo the *Inquiry*. "Tell me, my friend," he asks,

> if ever you were weary of doing good to those you love? Say when you ever found it unpleasing to serve a friend? . . . What would it be, therefore, if all life were in reality but one continued friendship, and could be made one such entire act? Here surely would be that fixed and constant good you sought. Or would you look for anything beyond? (II, 36)

Philocles agrees that he would not look further: a permanent friendship in which one could always do good for one's friend would be a "fixed and constant good." The challenge, then, is to find an object of permanent friendship. Theocles proposes two options: mankind and nature. For Philocles, however, these objects are too abstract: "this was too mysterious, too metaphysical an object for me" (II, 39). But Philocles is forced to admit that he already loves an abstract object: the ancient Roman people. "You might," Theocles says, "have the same indulgence for Nature or Mankind as for the people of old Rome [whom you love] under the representation of a beautiful youth called the Genius of the People" (II, 39). Perhaps, Theocles suggests, these higher objects can be loved in the same way. If a people have a "Genius" that can be loved, perhaps nature does as well. The Genius of Nature, as we will see, is Shaftesbury's (Stoic-inflected) version of God.

Friendship with the Genius of Nature

The argument that nature has a genius again echoes the *Inquiry* but in a new key. Beginning from the unity of a tree, which consists of "a sympathising of parts . . . a plain concurrence in one common end, and to the support, nourishment, and propagation of so fair a form," Theocles argues that nature as a whole must form a similar unity (II, 100). And because so many lesser forms are not only provident for themselves but also intelligent, the form of nature as a whole cannot lack these properties. Nature, too, has a genius, a divine provident mind governing the whole. Philocles is carried along through this argument, at once rational and enthusiastic, and he forgets the point—until, finally, Theocles brings him back to the original question, asking whether "the sovereign genius [is] . . . an object capable and worthy of real enjoyment" (II, 128). Philocles, full of enthusiasm, claims himself a proselyte. There is, after all, a true good for human beings: friendship with God, the Genius of Nature. Because we are always with God and always capable of doing good for the whole system of nature, "all life [can be] in reality but one continued friendship" (II, 36).

Theocles provides surprisingly few details about friendship with God. In his most explicit statement about the human relationship to God, Theocles says that we ought to conform our minds to the divine mind, which is achieved by "co-operat[ing] with it to the general good, and striv[ing] to will according to the best of wills" (II, 106). In other words, to be friends with God is to cooperate with God toward God's end, willing according to God's will. And God's end is always for one thing: "its own advantage and good, the good of all in general; and what is for the good of all in general is just and good" (II, 107).

The discovery of an object of constant and unending social affection, of continuous friendship, is the discovery of the good for human beings, a permanent source of happiness. Beyond its permanence, friendship with God brings happiness for another reason. Like a tree, nature as a whole forms a unity in which all parts work together for a common end. Unlike a tree, nature's end is always realized:

> Know that every particular nature produces what is good to itself, unless something foreign disturbs or hinders it, either by overpowering and corrupting it within, or by violence from without. . . . If, therefore, every particular nature be thus constantly and unerringly true to itself, and certain to produce only what is good for itself and conducing to its own right state, shall not the general one, the nature of the whole, do full as much? Shall that alone miscarry or fail? Or is there anything foreign which should at any time do violence upon it or force it out of its natural way? (II, 106–7)

Because nothing is outside the system of nature, nothing can prevent it from attaining its end, the good of the whole. By willing God's end, the friend of God wills that which is certain to be realized—a point we also found in King, though, as we will see, Shaftesbury understands it very differently. Therefore, according to Theocles, the friend of God ought to "be pleased and rejoice at what happens, knowing whence it comes, and to what perfection it contributes" (III, 107). All happenings, in other words, are pleasing to the friend of God because all contribute to nature's good. Moreover, the friend of God, according to Theocles, can further rejoice in divine providence by recognizing that human beings have their good within their control. The realization that friendship with God is the human good forces one to admit that one's happiness is fully within one's control, depending only on one's affections: "How can we better praise the goodness of Providence than in this, 'That it has placed our happiness and good in things we can bestow on ourselves'?" (II, 149). The miserable have only themselves to blame.

The dialogue, we see here, addresses the worries about evil in a practical register. The point, for Theocles, is not to resolve the problem as one of theoretical speculation, though he does have a theoretical answer. The point, rather, is to teach his friend how to become a friend of God. In doing so, the theoretical problems posed by evil dissolve, and one learns to rejoice in all that happens.

One question the argument of *The Moralists* raises is how we are to understand our other social affections, which the *Inquiry* treats as the primary source of happiness: love of friends, family, country, humanity. How can the one who loves his friend rejoice in her misery? How can the one who loves her country rejoice in its downfall? These questions go unanswered in *Characteristicks*. Shaftesbury only explicitly addresses them in his private writings.[22] Here he denies that natural affections are the affections for those closest to us or for our country. In rational creatures, who can grasp their place in nature, the true natural affection is for the whole of nature: "If nature be a subject what can it be but the highest subject? If it be the highest subject, to be wanting in affection towards it, is to be most unnatural of all."[23] All other affections are to be "subdued" to this one.[24] We are to act for the good of our families and countries only insofar as they are consistent with our natural affection for the whole, which means that we must always be willing to give up particular objects of affection for the good of the whole: "Love all else than [the whole of] nature only as a part. This is the foundation. This is all."[25] In Miscellany IV of *Characteristicks*, Shaftesbury makes essentially the same point, which he emphasizes as "our Author's formal and grave sentiments":

> Since man has been so constituted, by means of his rational part, as to be conscious of this his more immediate relation to the universal system and principle of order and intelligence; he is not only by Nature sociable within the limits of his own species or kind, but in a yet more generous and extensive manner. He is not only born to virtue, friend-

ship, honesty, and faith; but to religion, piety, adoration, and a generous surrender of his mind to whatever happens from that supreme Cause or order of things, which he acknowledges entirely just and perfect. (II, 294–95)

The elevation of friendship with God, then, radically transforms all other affections, including those otherwise seen as the highest and best.

Recall that the *Inquiry* is meant to convince its readers to be realists about morality because realism in morality entails realism in divinity. In this account of the *Inquiry*, the harmony of the affections, with its constant appeal to affections for particular objects or particular others, is intended primarily to establish the plausibility of finding happiness in virtue, even for the atheist or skeptic. It leads one to see the key role of the social affections that establish our harmony with larger systems. The ultimate aim, however, is achieved in *The Moralists* when this line of reasoning leads to the recognition of a higher affection that absorbs and transforms all others. The harmonious nature of our affections—the fact that they lead us naturally into society and mutuality with other human beings and larger systems—points to a higher truth. In *Askêmata*, Shaftesbury continues to maintain the beautiful harmony of the lesser natural affections. Yet he says that living by these natural affections alone is appropriate only to "animals and men-animals."[26] For the one who grasps the harmonious whole, to continue to live by these lesser affections is to debase oneself, to lower oneself below one's station. After discussing the importance of compassion in animals, Shaftesbury writes:

> But in another order of life, in another species, and in respect of another, a higher relation, nothing can be more dissonant than this; nothing more inconsistent with that true affection, which in a mind soundly rational is, as it were, in the place of all. To act by temper simply is, in such a one, the greatest degeneracy; a sinking down into a lower species of nature; a betraying of that higher one and of that relation into which he is assigned.[27]

Human beings partake of the reason by which God governs the whole. We can thus join our affections with God's, loving all things for the sake of the whole. Greater happiness is found in social affections than private affections, but true happiness is found only in the most social of all affections, the affection for the whole.

Shaftesbury's theological and ethical vision, we see here, shares the central features of the consequentialist moral cosmology, even if his cosmic holism makes it a bit odd to call him a consequentialist.[28] For Shaftesbury, God's end is the greatest good, the good of the cosmic whole. God wills all things for the sake of this single end. Rational creatures, too, ought to act for the sake of the good of the cosmic whole. Moreover, while God and rational creatures share this same moral end, God's perfect wisdom, knowledge, and goodness entail that God's will ought to reign in all things. Rational creatures ought to conform their wills to God's will, rejoicing in all things as elements of the good of the whole.

Yet while Shaftesbury embraces a view that broadly mirrors the consequentialist moral cosmology, he also departs from More and Cumberland in important respects. Responding to Bayle, Shaftesbury denies the existence of evil: nothing is ill with respect to the whole. He instead embraces a cosmic holism in which the cosmos forms a single system with a provident mind. All apparent evil is simply the necessary subordination of parts to the whole and thus part of the universal good. Those who lament the evils that beset the human race fail to recognize that human beings, too, are parts of the whole. To complain about our subordination to the larger system is to falsely imagine that all of creation is for us. While Shaftesbury's view resolves some of the problems regarding evil, it also creates new problems. Unlike King, Shaftesbury does not allow human and divine ends to come apart. He maintains a strong view of a moral community between God and human beings. Human beings ought to will precisely the same end as God for the same reason: its goodness. Yet Shaftesbury's response to Bayle's critiques about evil, I will now argue, creates a tension in his moral vision that ultimately renders his view of divine and human moral ends untenable.

Human and Divine Ends: The Necessity of Vice

Shaftesbury's response to Bayle's arguments about evil is quite effective. For Bayle, all of creation is beautiful and harmonious except for human beings. Shaftesbury observes that creation is full of the sacrificial subordination of one creature for the good of another. Why should humanity be excepted? The idea that only human beings spoil creation is an anthropocentric picture, one that arises from our refusal to see ourselves as parts of a larger whole. If we were mice, we would see owls as a flaw in creation; if we were deer, we might reject divine providence because of the existence of wolves. As it is, we complain about the evils that beset human beings. But once we recognize that we, like mice and deer, are parts of a larger whole, we will see that our complaints falsely presuppose that we are the ends of creation.

Notice that Shaftesbury's response does not appeal to the freedom of human beings and thereby avoids many of Bayle's most forceful arguments. The "evils" that human beings do and suffer are not a product of their ability to will against the good. These, too, are components of the larger system, which are part of its good. Indeed, Shaftesbury's view of the cosmos, with its insistence that all things always occur for the good of the whole, leaves no room for individual freedom to do otherwise. Human beings will always do that which is necessary for the good of the whole, whether intentionally or unintentionally, virtuously or viciously. In a theistic cosmos, every part functions perfectly for the good of the whole, and human action is no exception.

Despite the effectiveness of Shaftesbury's response to Bayle, a tension lurks in his thought, one that undermines the possibility that human beings can will the same end as God—and thus the possibility of human friendship with God. It stems from an implication of his rejection of the existence of evil that he never makes explicit, namely, that human vice, when it occurs, is also a necessary part of the good of the whole and is for that reason willed by God.

Shaftesbury's response to Bayle is well designed to address what King calls the evil of imperfection and natural evil. In each case, we recognize that our limitations and sufferings are necessary for the good of the whole. Joining our wills with God's in friendship, we can will not only the good of the whole but even our own limitations and sufferings for the sake of that higher good. But moral evil presents a different set of challenges. Moral evil, for Shaftesbury, must also be necessary for the good of the whole. I must accept and even rejoice in the vice of my friend, which is a component of the good of the whole. Doing so presents challenges but is not in principle more difficult than accepting the other evils that may befall a friend. More problematically, I must also accept that my vice may be necessary for the good of the whole. But how can I do this? In joining my will to God's, can I will that I become vicious for the sake of the good of the whole? The problem is that virtue consists of acting according to our highest social affection, while vice consists of deviation from our highest social affection. To will that I become vicious for the sake of the cosmic good would be to will that I not will the cosmic good for the sake of the cosmic good—or, in simpler terms, to be virtuously vicious—a practical contradiction.

While Shaftesbury never addresses this problem in his published writings, he was aware of it. In his private *Askêmata*, Shaftesbury raises the problem explicitly. The passage is worth quoting in full:

If I were conscious (says Epictetus) of what was decreed me, and could be certain of what were to happen before it happened, I would will that and that only; suppose it sickness; suppose it infamy, suppose it death . . . if I knew how this was to be controlled; if I knew what else was appointed: I would turn to this; and this should be the object of my aim; this I would affect, and nothing but this. But (says one) if may thus happen, that I may also will that I be wicked. Not if there were a possibility left of its being any otherwise; but if no possibility, I will however be pious and good (that is to say I will be happy) as long as is allowed me, as long as I possibly can be so. If I cannot be so the moment that follows, at least I will remain so this present moment that precedes, and will join my applause to what God has for the best decreed. For to will against that which is best, and to will what is impossible, what else were this but to be wicked and miserable? Now that every creature should seek its good and not its misery, is necessary in itself; nor can it be supposed the will of God that a creature should do otherwise than thus, for this is contradictory and consequently impossible even with God. So that my will towards virtue is irrefragable and immutable; but towards life, death, poverty, riches, and all other exterior things it is variable upon occasion.[29]

For Shaftesbury, if I knew my vice was necessary, I should still will the general good while I can. And when I become vicious, as I must, I continue to will my good, as is necessary, but I no longer believe that my good lies in virtue—and thus I fail to be happy.

This answer very well may be the best one Shaftesbury can give, but it threatens the idea that we can join our wills to God's in the way *The Moralists* suggests. As limited creatures, we cannot know what the general good requires. We do know, however, that it may require the one thing we cannot will. For this reason, we cannot will the good of the cosmos as such. Rather, we can only will it conditionally on its not including our vice and thus our misery. And if this is true, we do not truly will the same end as God; we cannot fully conform our minds to the general mind, as Theocles claims. Friendship with God, at least in the full sense envisioned by Theocles, is not possible for us.

Creatures, according to Shaftesbury, are not the only ones who cannot will their misery; the same is true of God. But of course, no case can arise in which the general good conflicts with God's happiness. God, unlike us, is not a part of the whole. God, willing only the good of the whole, treats every part as what it is: a part. But we, as parts, cannot, in the end, treat ourselves as parts. We can accept the subordination of our bodies, our loved ones, even our species to the general good—but we cannot accept the subordination of our wills to the general good. Yet the subordination of our wills is necessary—they are, after all, parts of the whole—and God requires it of us. Our friendship with God, then, is undermined by the fact that God treats us as parts in a way that we cannot treat ourselves.

As a result, Shaftesbury, in the end, fails to show that human beings can share in God's end. The very structure of the consequentialist moral cosmology rests on the claim that God and creatures must both work to achieve the same end, the realization of the greatest good. While Shaftesbury affirms this view, his denial of the existence of evil ultimately undermines it. In doing so, it also undermines his argument for the possibility of happiness, which, for Shaftesbury, can be found only in friendship with God.

I have argued that *The Moralists* addresses two separate issues: the question about evil raised by Palemon and the question of the human good raised by Philocles. Both, in the end, are answered through the notion of friendship with God. Friendship with God is the human good; it is also the practical solution to the problem of evil. We can now see that Shaftesbury is unable to hold these two positions together. If we accept the nonexistence of evil, we cannot truly will the same end as God; if we do truly will the same end as God, we must reject the idea that it could include our vice.

Shaftesbury and the Consequentialist Moral Cosmology

Shaftesbury's importance in intellectual history is often attributed to the unique ethical role he assigns to the affections. This story has several variants: he is the first to found ethics on psychological experience; he is the first to interpret virtue as psychological fitness to one's environment; he is the first to argue for the possibility of self-governance by nonrepresentational affections.[30] Shaftesbury is no doubt influential in the role he assigns to affection, though it is not obvious that he intended to be innovative on this point. His *Pathologia* is explicitly Stoic and Platonic, and the role he assigns to affect closely mirrors that of Henry More. More's boniform faculty is an affective faculty that is also rational in its love of the highest good. While there are no doubt differences, Shaftesbury's natural affection for the whole plays effectively the same role in his ethics as More's boniform faculty plays in *Enchiridion ethicum*.[31]

When he is situated in the tradition of More and Cumberland, Shaftesbury's most important innovation—which is also a partial return to the Stoics—is his solution to (or dissolution of) the problems raised by Bayle: his denial of the existence of evil. His dissolution, if it can be made plausible, is certainly effective. It rationally reconciles the world to the existence of a single good principle, and it does so while maintaining that God and rational creatures share the same end: the realization of the greatest good. Yet, as we have just seen, a tension lurks just beneath the surface of Shaftesbury's published writings, one that emerges explicitly in his unpublished *Askêmata*. Human beings can share God's end only conditionally on it not including their vice, something they cannot know in advance. Human and divine moral ends, therefore, cannot truly align. King, I argued in the previous chapter, gave up the idea that human beings can share God's reasons for pursuing the best end in order to better explain moral evil. Shaftesbury holds to it tightly, but, as I just concluded, cannot do so consistently. In King and Shaftesbury, we see two quite different examples of the problems the consequentialist moral cosmology faces in confronting Bayle's arguments about evil.

While King and Shaftesbury offer the earliest systematic treatments of evil in Britain in the wake of Bayle's *Dictionnaire*, the concern with evil remained central for much of the eighteenth century. The resources generated by King and Shaftesbury were developed and redeployed—and in the process often combined in creative ways. One prominent and influential instance is found in the work of Francis Hutcheson. Hutcheson, like King and Shaftesbury, develops an approach to morality that is integrally bound up with theodicy and that maintains the core tenets of the consequentialist moral cosmology. In doing so, he draws from both King and Shaftesbury.

Hutcheson will be our final instance of an attempt to resolve Bayle's critiques within the broad framework of the consequentialist moral cosmology. Hutcheson, I will argue, does successfully retain the idea that God and human beings ought to both act for the realization of the greatest possible goodness in creation. His ability to do so stems from the fact that he sharply diminishes the role of reason in morality. In doing so, I argue, he ends up with a position that verges on ethical voluntarism. This result prepares the way for the unexpected return of ethical voluntarism in the consequentialist tradition, which I address in part III.

Theodicy and the Moral Affections in Francis Hutcheson

In the years following his death, Shaftesbury's insistence on the goodness of human nature, more than any other aspect of his thought, sparked intense debate. Shaftesbury was targeted by a number of critics unwilling to grant that human affections are anything but various modifications of self-love. The most notorious critique came from Bernard Mandeville in his infamous work *The Fable of the Bees*. The 1723 edition of *Fable* caused a particular stir and generated a series of published responses. Among them was Francis Hutcheson's *Inquiry into the Original of Our Ideas of Beauty and Virtue* (1725), the subtitle of which was: *In Which the Principles of the Late Earl of Shaftesbury Are Explain'd and Defended, against the Author of the Fable of the Bees: And the Ideas of Moral Good and Evil Are Establish'd.*[1]

While Hutcheson's early treatises defend Shaftesbury against Mandeville, they do not reproduce Shaftesbury's views. In this case, as Laurent Jaffro rightly states, the negation of the negation is not identical to the affirmation.[2] The true aim of Hutcheson's early treatises is not the vindication of Shaftesbury but the vindication of human nature. Hutcheson seeks to demonstrate that human nature includes affections that are entirely other-directed without a trace of self-love. To do so, he develops ideas from Shaftesbury into an original moral psychology, which includes a variety of internal senses and basic desires that together explain why we are naturally benevolent and naturally approving of benevolence. Hutcheson's earliest treatises focus on moral psychology and moral motivation. As his thought matures in subsequent editions and later works, he increasingly recognizes that his moral philosophy, like Shaftesbury's, depends upon a theologically informed cosmology. Indeed, his final work, *A System of Moral Philosophy*, which he originally conceived as his magnum opus, has been called a work of theodicy.[3] While this designation is somewhat misleading, it rightly calls attention to the fact that Hutcheson's ethics ultimately requires a defense of the benevolence of God and the goodness of the created order.

Hutcheson's approach to theodicy, however, does not follow the model of Shaftesbury's. While Hutcheson rarely explicitly distances himself from Shaftesbury, he nevertheless quietly drops Shaftesbury's cosmic holism.[4] For Hutcheson, the whole is as perfect as it can be, but it is not free of evil. Hutcheson substitutes Shaftesbury's organic whole for a mechanistic one and seeks to reconcile Shaftesbury's ethics with a more orthodox theology. In doing so, he draws upon King's *De origine mali*, a book which he rates "above all others on this subject" and calls a "most ingenious Book."[5]

Hutcheson sees himself and Shaftesbury as participants in a tradition leading back to Henry More. In 1743, Hutcheson edited and published an edition of More's *Divine Dialogues*. In the preface, Hutcheson praises More, and he notes More's influence on Shaftesbury as well.[6] Moreover, Hutcheson's works follow the outlines of the consequentialist moral cosmology.[7] He argues that only benevolence—that is, acting with the end of realizing the greatest possible happiness of all rational creatures—is morally good.[8] God's moral perfection ensures that God acts perfectly for this end. Human beings, too, ought to seek this end. Moreover, in a passage on divine authority that closely mirrors More's *Divine Dialogues*, Hutcheson writes:

> For as it must tend to the universal good that a being of perfect wisdom and goodness should superintend human affairs, assuming to himself to govern their actions, and to declare his pleasure about them; so it must undoubtedly tend to the universal good that all rational creatures obey his will. This shows his right of moral government. For the ultimate notion of right is *that which tends to the universal good*; and when one's acting in a certain manner has this tendency, he has a right thus to act. The proper foundation of right here is the infinite goodness and wisdom.[9]

In all these ways, Hutcheson sounds like More, echoing the consequentialist moral cosmology. But Hutcheson's focus on the affections, especially when combined with his approach to evil, leads to a quite different version of the consequentialist moral cosmology.

While Hutcheson seems originally interested in defending human nature rather than divine goodness, his work is increasingly shaped by the same concerns about evil that preoccupied King and Shaftesbury. Hutcheson develops his own innovative solution, which, I argue, is in some key respects a synthesis of the approaches of King and Shaftesbury. Hutcheson does not follow Shaftesbury's denial of evil. Instead, he accepts King's view of the origin of metaphysical and natural evils. When it comes to moral evil, however, Hutcheson's commitment to Shaftesbury precludes the embrace of King's radical agential voluntarism. Instead, Hutcheson extends King's approach to natural evil and applies it to moral evil, arguing that moral evil is a necessary byproduct of the best possible psychological laws.

In this way, Hutcheson can affirm until the very end that human beings and God naturally pursue and approve the very same end: the realization of the most possible natural goodness. Yet Hutcheson's version of the consequentialist moral cosmology differs from that of More and Cumberland in one crucial respect. For Hutcheson, the shared end is not determined by reason. Reason, for Hutcheson, is solely instrumental. The end, rather, is determined by the affective responses of our senses and desires. These affections are implanted in us by God so that we can share God's end. But why does God seek this end? Hutcheson argues that God, too, must have an analogous set of senses and desires. Ultimately, there is no reason for God or rational creatures to pursue the shared end, no sense in which it is objectively best. Everything stems from the arational preferences of divine nature. Hutcheson, then, ends up with a view that is almost indistinguishable from ethical voluntarism—the very thing that More and Cumberland sought to defeat.

Hutcheson's Moral Psychology

In order to understand Hutcheson's approach to morality and moral psychology, let us begin where he does: with the defense of human benevolence in response to Mandeville's critique of Shaftesbury. Hutcheson's first major work, *Inquiry into Beauty and Virtue*, argues that we morally approve only of benevolence and that we do so without any concern for our own self-interest. His argument develops Shaftesbury's account of moral judgment as a sentiment about sentiments into a theory of "internal senses," which is modeled in part on John Locke's account of the senses in *An Essay Concerning Human Understanding*. All agree, according to Hutcheson, that we have a fixed number of external senses. Through the external senses, we passively receive ideas as well as pleasure or pain from objects. When two sensations are completely different from one another, we divide the power of receiving the sensations into two different senses (e.g., sight and taste). If we experience sensations that can be explained by no external sense, Hutcheson argues, then we must posit the existence of internal senses. One example is a sense of beauty. We receive, according to Hutcheson, an immediate, passive pleasure upon the perception of anything beautiful.

Beauty is not itself in the things perceived as beautiful. As with the objects of other senses, like color or sound, the object of the sense of beauty is a secondary quality produced in us, not a reality existing in things. Color does not exist in a flower, but some feature of the flower (the wavelength of the light it reflects, as we now know) is responsible for our perception of color. Likewise, he thinks, we can find in objects some feature that explains our perception of beauty, namely, "uniformity amidst variety."[10] Upon the perception of uniformity amidst variety, we receive an immediate pleasure. Hutcheson emphasizes that this pleasure has nothing to do with our desires or interests. The fact that we take pleasure in beauty will give rise to desires for beauty, but the desires are subsequent to the sense of beauty.

Why do we take pleasure in uniformity amidst variety? The answer is simple: Because we have this particular sense of beauty. If we ask why we have this sense of beauty, we are asking why God gave us the constitution we have. The sense of beauty, after all, is simply a faculty that is pleased by a particular feature of the world. Hutcheson acknowledges that God could have just as easily given us pleasure in deformity: "There seems to be no necessary connection of our pleasing ideas of beauty with the uniformity or regularity of the objects, from the nature of things, antecedent to some constitution of the author of our nature, which has made such forms pleasant to us."[11] Indeed, he suggests, other creatures likely have a different sense of beauty than we do. So why has God given us our particular sense of beauty? In short, because it conduces to our happiness, both as a source of pleasure and as an additional motive in the pursuit of other goods. In other animals, a different sense of beauty will serve the same function.[12]

Human beings also possess an internal moral sense. The moral sense, too, is a power of passively receiving ideas and pleasure or pain upon the perception of particular objects—in this case, human affections, whether one's own or those of others. The moral sense gives rise to the idea of moral goodness. In addition to pleasure, it also elicits approval and esteem for the morally good.[13] As with beauty, moral goodness and badness are not found in the objects perceived. Moral goodness and badness are secondary qualities in the mind of the perceiver. And as with beauty, we can identify the features of the object that cause the ideas: the perception of benevolent affections by the moral sense causes the idea of moral goodness as well as pleasure and approval.[14]

Once Hutcheson has presented his position conceptually, the challenge is to demonstrate its superiority to Mandeville's. Mandeville agrees that we morally approve of benevolence. According to Mandeville, we approve or disapprove of the conduct of others based on how that conduct affects us. Our approval of benevolence arises from the simple fact that benevolence in others is good for us.[15] By arguing that moral approval and disapproval arise from a passive internal sense, Hutcheson is attempting to show that moral approval and disapproval are completely independent of all desire and volition—and therefore also of self-love. Both views are psychologically possible, and neither can prove the falsity of the other on a priori grounds. The argument against Mandeville takes the form of an appeal to the experience of the reader. And on these grounds, Hutcheson has some good arguments. We approve and disapprove of many actions that have no relationship to us: actions in distant countries, actions in history, actions in works of fiction. Moreover, we disapprove of actions that do benefit us. We disapprove, for example, of tyrants and misers, though some tyrants may do us good and some misers may leave their inheritance to us. In every case, he argues, what we approve is the benevolent motivation of the actor, not our own benefit.

Moral approval, then, is independent of self-love. What about virtue, which, according to Mandeville, also stems ultimately from self-love?[16] While Hutcheson addresses this objection in the *Inquiry*, a fuller treatment of it comes in his *Essay on the Nature and Conduct of the Passions and Affections*, published three years later and intended in part as a response to criticisms by the psychological egoist John Clarke of Hull.[17] In this work, which presents a more developed moral psychology, Hutcheson argues for two additional internal senses: a public sense and a sense of honor.[18] The former takes pleasure in the happiness of others and pain in their unhappiness; the latter takes pleasure in honor and pain in dishonor. Together with the external senses, the sense of beauty, and the moral sense, Hutcheson now has five classes of sense. Each sense, he argues in the *Essay*, gives rise to a corresponding desire or affection for its object. There are, therefore, five basic classes of desire or affection, the objects of which correspond to the five basic classes of sense.[19] In addition, Hutcheson makes a second division of desires or affections.[20] This second division concerns the subject for whom we desire a good. Desires for a good for oneself are called selfish; desires for a good for others are called benevolent. This division cuts across the previous one. Goods of every kind can be desired either for oneself or others.

The public sense addresses the motive to virtue. It takes pleasure in the good of others and gives rise to desires for the good of others. As in the *Inquiry*, the plausibility of Hutcheson's argument rests largely on its capacity to account for our experience, and Hutcheson again raises numerous cases in which we do seem to care about others for their sakes. Intuitively, Hutcheson seems to be right in his rejection of egoism. But there is a subtler problem that Hutcheson recognizes, one which he cannot avoid addressing given his reliance on Locke's psychology. The problem arises from Locke's theory of desire. Desire, according to Locke, is "the uneasiness a man finds in himself upon the absence of anything, whose present enjoyment carries the idea of delight with it."[21] The strength of desire, he argues, is a function not of the perceived goodness of the object of desire but of the uneasiness produced by its absence. The importance of desire, for Locke, is that it alone determines the mind to action. Though the mind is not moved automatically by desire—it can pause and reflect on the objects of desire—the mind will ultimately be moved by what turns out on reflection to be the strongest desire.[22] Human action, then, is motivated not directly by the attainment of goods but indirectly by the avoidance of uneasiness.

Mandeville relies on Locke's theory of desire and action to argue that every natural action is reducible to self-love.[23] Even the most selfless of actions, according to Mandeville, stems from Lockean desires. The pity we feel at the suffering of others causes us pain, and our seemingly selfless acts of compassion are in fact efforts to relieve this pain.[24] Mandeville applies the same logic in case after case. This view of desire and action fits well with the idea that every action, no matter how other-directed, is actually a form of self-love.

Hutcheson's response is twofold. The first response, which is present already in the *Inquiry*, is to argue that even when we do feel uneasiness in the absence of some good, we do not act in order to remove the uneasiness. In the case of compassion or pity, if our only concern were to alleviate uneasiness, we would be indifferent between eliminating the suffering of the other or eliminating our knowledge of it. Yet given the choice between these two options, no person feeling compassion would choose the latter.[25] The uneasiness may provide an additional motivation, but its existence presupposes a prior concern for the other. And more generally, Hutcheson argues that the idea that all actions aim primarily at the satisfaction of desire for its own sake is absurd. For Hutcheson, we only have desires because of a determination of our nature to certain ends. The realization of these ends, and not the satisfaction of the desires themselves, is the aim of our actions.

The second and more important response is to reject Locke's theory of desire. For Hutcheson, the identification of desire with uneasiness is a category mistake. Desire, he argues, is "as distinct from any sensation, as will is from the understanding or senses."[26] This distinction can be seen, Hutcheson argues, in the fact that we can speak of desiring to remove the uneasy sensation. In its pure form, desire is completely independent of any sensation. It is simply an inclination toward some end. Many desires are also mixed with sensations. Hutcheson calls desires without sensations calm desires or calm affections. Desires mixed with sensations are passions. The sensation of passions arises from the fact that passions, unlike calm desires, include a change in bodily constitution.[27] We have two foundational calm desires: a calm desire for our own good and a calm desire for the public good. These desires are psychologically basic. No sensation explains or accompanies them.

What is the good we desire for ourselves and others? For Hutcheson, natural good is pleasure and natural evil is pain. Happiness consists of pleasure and the absence of pain.[28] Calm selfish desire is for our pleasure, and calm benevolent desire is for the pleasure of others. And natural goodness, according to Hutcheson, can be quantified. The quantity of any natural good, which he calls "the moment of good," can be calculated in a formula that echoes Henry More's axioms.[29] The moment of good is "in compound proportion of the duration and intenseness." Calm desire can also be quantified. Hutcheson argues for a set of "general laws" of calm desire, which he compares to the Newtonian laws of motion.[30] These laws, too, echo More's axioms, except that what is self-evident and morally normative in More becomes contingent and descriptive in Hutcheson. According to the "natural laws of calm desire," the strength of a calm desire is directly proportional to the moment of good expected from its object. In the case of private good, the strength of calm selfish desire is directly proportional to the moment of good for oneself. In the case of a public good, the strength of calm benevolent desire is directly proportional not only to the moment of good but also to the number of people to whom it extends.[31]

With his natural laws of desire, Hutcheson displays an aspiration also espoused by King: to understand the operations of the intellectual world by analogy with the physical world.[32] King doubts his capacity to grasp these laws with sufficient precision, but Hutcheson is bolder. Hutcheson also quantifies the approval of the moral sense, introducing formulas to show that its approval tracks precisely with calm benevolent desire.[33] Hutcheson's general aim of demonstrating that we naturally approve of benevolence and have naturally benevolent desires does not require mathematical laws. He wants to demonstrate in addition that our minds are perfectly ordered by God. This is clear from the fact that he moves immediately from the mathematical laws to a potential objection: If desire does not require sensation, and if our calm desires are so perfectly attuned to the moment of good, why would God give us the passions, which constantly interfere with calm desire?[34]

Because there is no necessary connection between desire and sensation, there is no reason to think we must have passions or to think that our particular passions are necessary. Some creatures, for Hutcheson, likely have no passions, while others have passions very different from ours.[35] Since passions are not necessary for motivation, we must look to other aspects of our nature to see their value. The value of the passions, according to Hutcheson, arises from the limits of our understanding.[36] We understand so little of the human constitution, he argues, that we would be unable to determine when to eat, how much to eat, and what to eat without pleasurable and painful sensations to guide us. Likewise, without painful sensations, we would not know how to avoid bodily harm or overexertion. And once sensations are introduced to guide us in one sphere of activity, other desires will require sensations to balance them out.[37] For example, given that a painful aversion to excessive labor is necessary to teach us the limits of our bodies, we need strong counter-sensations to induce us to undertake the exhausting task of raising offspring (e.g., sexual desire, parental love). Likewise, given these passions for private goods like food, drink, and sex, we need others to maintain balance with public goods, such as a passion for honor.

Some passions, then, guide us in cases in which our knowledge is inadequate. Other passions counteract the force of those passions, ensuring a balance between our various motivations, especially between the selfish and benevolent:

> With this balance of public passions against the private, with our passions toward honor and virtue, we find that human nature may be as really amiable in its low sphere, as superior natures endowed with higher reason, and influenced only by pure desires; provided we vigorously exercise the powers we have in keeping this balance of affections, and checking any passion which grows so violent, as to be inconsistent with the public good.[38]

Hutcheson admits that, given the effects of custom, education, habits, and company, few people achieve this precise natural balance. Nonetheless, he argues, if we apply ourselves, nothing prevents us from attaining a natural "economy" of the passions.[39]

Affection, Reason, and Ends

One of the most striking features of Hutcheson's ethics—especially when we read it in continuity with More and Shaftesbury—is the sharply limited role of reason. The moral sense, like all other senses, operates independently of reason. Reason does play a role in inferring motives, but it plays no role in approval or disapproval.[40] Hutcheson's motivation for restricting reason in the *Inquiry* is clear enough. He thinks that if reason is allowed to play a role, then moral approval could be construed as a rational inference about how a motive or action furthers our self-interest. The immediate passive approval of an internal sense best insulates moral approval from interference from self-love.

Hutcheson likewise argues in the *Essay* that benevolent desires are independent of reason. Reason, again, has a role, this time in determining means to ends. But the end of benevolence—natural good to some other or others—is simply given by natural desire. In fact, Hutcheson believes that reason is incapable of setting practical ends for action. Practical reason is exclusively instrumental reason. Why does Hutcheson believe this?[41] The argument occurs in *Illustrations on the Moral Sense*, a work written in response to his rationalist critics. In *Illustrations*, Hutcheson appeals to Aristotle's claim in *Nicomachean Ethics* that we deliberate about means but not about ends. The rationality of actions, he argues, lies not in the ends sought but in the conduciveness of the actions to those ends. No reasons can be given for our ends. Ask a man why he desires wealth, Hutcheson says, and he will say that it brings pleasure and happiness. Ask why he desires pleasure and happiness and "one cannot imagine what proposition he could assign as his *exciting reason*."[42] He can give no reason because his pursuit of happiness is instinctual. An appeal to instinct provides a reason of a sort, but "it is not this reflection on his own nature, or this *proposition* which excites or determines him, but the *instinct itself*."[43]

While Hutcheson appeals to the authority of Aristotle in this argument, he does not agree with Aristotle that we have a singular final end called happiness. The reason, I want to suggest, is similar to the reason that led Cumberland to reject Aristotelian eudaimonism. Hutcheson implicitly assumes a productivist picture of agency: the object of desire and action is always taken to be the realization of some outcome or state of affairs.[44] We can see this assumption in his treatment of calm desire. The strength of calm desire, according to Hutcheson, is always proportional to the moment of good of the object of desire. And the moment of good—as the product of the intensity of pleasure, its duration, and the number of enjoyers—is conceived as a feature of states of affairs. As with Cumberland, when the object of desire and action is assumed to be an outcome or state of affairs, the claim that happiness is our final end is interpreted to mean that we desire every outcome only for its contribution to the realization of our own happiness. Eudaimonism becomes indistinguishable from egoistic hedonism, the view Hutcheson is combating. The only way, in this view, to permit the possibility of true benevolence is to add another ultimate end: the happiness of others.[45]

The Aristotelian tradition, however, does not conceive of the desire for happiness as purely affective or in productivist terms. The desire for happiness in Aristotle is the manifestation in human beings of a more general phenomenon of all beings seeking to actualize their form. It is not a desire for one outcome among others; it is a metaphysical condition of agency. The pursuit of happiness is, in essence, the activity of being the sort of thing one is. It in no way precludes seeking outcomes that have nothing to do with oneself or one's pleasure. One cannot give a reason for desiring happiness because that would be like giving a reason for being a human being. For Hutcheson, by contrast, ends are whatever we instinctively desire to bring about. Indeed, given the fact that Hutcheson sees desire, which is an instinctive disposition to bring about some end, as entirely distinct from sensation, he can give no reason in principle why God could not have implanted in us a desire for our own misery. If God were malevolent, God could replace our current desires and passions with a calm desire to sit on burning logs or to drop large stones on our feet. In such a world, we would quite literally have no reason not to continually cause ourselves pain—and that without making the pain any less bad for us. The fact that pleasure is a natural good and pain is a natural evil does not itself give us any reason to do anything. Hutcheson's argument, then, is simply that exciting reasons must end somewhere. We can give no reason why we pursue private or universal happiness; therefore, we pursue them instinctually. Moreover, instincts are conceived as fundamentally arbitrary. Nothing about the metaphysics of organisms or agency requires us to have any particular ends. Ends are just states of affairs that we instinctually seek.[46]

The claim that ends are arational plays an important role in Hutcheson's defense of human nature against Mandeville. Nonetheless, it has the somewhat bizarre implications just enumerated. Can anything else be said about why Hutcheson accepts it? One way to see its appeal is to compare it to live alternatives in early eighteenth-century British ethics. The egoistic option of Locke and Mandeville is obviously unacceptable to Hutcheson, and we have already seen why eudaimonism appears to him indistinguishable from egoism. The other principal option, expressed by John Balguy in the exchange that sparked Hutcheson to write *Illustrations*, is the rationalist option. For Balguy, following Samuel Clarke, the rational grasp of the fitness or lack of fitness of actions explains both obligation and moral motivation.[47] Hutcheson's stated reason for rejecting this view is simply that fittingness only applies to means, not ends. Perhaps Hutcheson really cannot make sense of the idea that one end is more fitting or rational than another. But there is another reason that Hutcheson is dissatisfied with the rationalist view, a reason that emerges in *Illustrations* VI and becomes more defined in the *System*, namely, that the rationalist view requires a picture of human freedom that Hutcheson finds unappealing. For the rationalist, we have rational motives to do what is fitting, and we have other motives to do what is pleasurable or useful. Rational fitness binds morally, but other motives can overcome moral motives. Hutcheson sees this account of the freedom to choose between incommensurable motives as problematic because it turns the will into a "capricious" power that we would be better off without, a power that a morally good God would not give us.[48] Though Hutcheson does not cite Bayle at this point, he is clearly motivated by the same concerns as King and Shaftesbury: to avoid concluding that God has given us the power to unnecessarily act against what is best. To substantiate this claim, I turn to the *System*.

God, Freedom, and Evil

Hutcheson never seems bothered by the worry that his view renders ends arbitrary. He does, however, begin to worry about a related problem. If multiple ends are set by our various implanted instincts, how do we choose between them? Since the ends are not subject to rational evaluation, the only available answer seems to be that we choose on the basis of the strength of desire. But given that desires and passions are heterogeneous, how does agency cohere? In the *Essay*, Hutcheson's only answer is that our desires naturally form a balanced economy. Yet he recognizes how rarely this balance is maintained after custom and habit shape human constitution. And once the balance of our affections is overthrown, Hutcheson supplies no psychological mechanism capable of correcting the damage.

Hutcheson addresses this problem in his *A System of Moral Philosophy*, a work that circulated during his lifetime but was only published posthumously in 1745. He originally conceived of the work as his magnum opus, though he was never satisfied with the result. The question of how the *System* relates to Hutcheson's other writings has been a subject of debate. James Moore argues that it should be read as a theodicy that Hutcheson wrote in part as a response to Edmund Law's translation of King's *De origine mali*.[49] Moore's thesis is intriguing. Calling the work a theodicy, however, is misleading. The *System* is precisely what it presents itself as: a systematic treatment of virtue and happiness. Moore is certainly right that Hutcheson's systematic moral philosophy is integrated with a theodicy. But as James Harris observes, the same is true of Hutcheson's early treatises.[50] The integration of theodicy and moral philosophy is basic to Hutcheson's thought, just as it was to Shaftesbury's. The *System* provides a developed theodicy, not for the sake of theodicy alone, but because nothing short of a theodicy allows for a systematic defense of his ethics and a full answer to the question of the coherence of agency.

The aim of moral philosophy, Hutcheson begins, is "to direct men to that course of action which tends most effectually to promote their greatest happiness and perfection."[51] To do so, the moral philosopher must inquire into the constitution of the species, especially its perceptive and active powers and their objects, "since happiness denotes the state of the soul arising from its several grateful perceptions or modifications."[52] What follows is an enumeration of the now familiar internal senses, passions, and calm desires. As in previous work, Hutcheson sees this complex set of heterogeneous desires and passions as naturally harmonious. But in the *System*, unlike in previous writings, he explicitly considers the problem of conflicts of desire, especially between the two calm desires, selfish and benevolent. He writes:

> Here arises a new perplexity in this complex structure, where these two principles seem to draw different ways. Must the generous determination, and all its particular affections, yield to the selfish one, and be under its control? Must we indulge their kind motions so far as private interest admits and no further? Or can we suppose that in this complex system there are two ultimate principles which may often oppose each other, without any umpire to reconcile their differences?[53]

The author of nature, he says, plainly intends the good of the whole and the good of each part insofar only as it is consistent with the good of the whole. But unlike in previous works, he is not satisfied with this response. We must also ask "from what determination of soul, from what motive, are we to comply with the divine intentions."[54]

Hutcheson addresses the problem by slightly amending his conception of the moral sense. The moral sense, he says, "from its very nature appears designed for regulating and controlling all our powers."[55] He gives two arguments for this claim. First, he says, we immediately recognize a higher dignity in the objects approved by the moral sense.[56] This argument, however, does not solve the problem, for Hutcheson's psychology recognizes only strength of motive, and dignity has no obvious connection with strength. The second argument is more promising. Choice is ordinarily between competing desires whose strengths are independent of one another. If we must choose between satisfying the sense of beauty and satisfying the external senses, the strength of the desire for each will be proportional to the suitability of the object to the sense. If an object increases or decreases in its suitability to its corresponding sense, then the balance of desire will shift. The moral sense is different. While the moral sense does often compete with other senses, its strength is responsive to the benevolence of an action, which increases when the sacrifice involved increases. If an act of benevolence requires a sacrifice of external pleasure, the moral sense will approve of it even more. Increasing the degree of the pleasure sacrificed will not change the balance, because the higher the sacrifice, the greater the approval of the moral sense. For this reason, the desire for the morally good action is always capable of a strength that exceeds the strength of all other desires.[57] In this way, Hutcheson can defend the primacy of the moral sense in a manner reminiscent of Joseph Butler—and Hutcheson even uses the language of the authority of the moral sense[58]—even while he maintains that the moral sense is purely affective and operates, like all other motives, in a field of competing desires.[59] Without the moral faculty, Hutcheson concludes, "a species endowed with such a variety of senses and of desires frequently interfering must appear a complex confused fabric." With the moral faculty, all its powers may conspire harmoniously in one direction.[60]

We now have an account of the moral sense that explains how we achieve psychological coherence in virtue. At this point, a new set of questions arises. If the moral faculty ensures that virtue can prevail in a field of desires competing purely by strength, why do we so often fail to be virtuous? What is the source of moral evil? The traditional theological answer, we have seen, is the misuse of the creaturely will. Hutcheson has a quite different view of the will both from the Augustinian tradition and from King. For Hutcheson, the will is not a particular appetite among others; it is the affective faculty as a whole, which includes all the desires and passions.[61] Hutcheson grants little attention to the question of its freedom. In *Illustrations*, he addresses the topic of merit and argues that merit is compatible with acting from instinct.[62] His only sustained discussion of freedom of the will comes in his *Metaphysics*. Given the pedagogical function of Hutcheson's Latin works, as well as the fact that they often borrow in structure and content from similar pedagogical models written by others, it is never entirely safe to base one's interpretation of Hutcheson on these works. The discussion of will in the *Metaphysics*, for example, distinguishes rational and sensitive desire, following other such texts.[63] Nonetheless, in this case, Hutcheson puts his own spin on the traditional distinction, aligning it with that between calm desires and passions. When it comes to the freedom of the will, Hutcheson dismisses the idea that we have a power indifferent in its choice between greater and lesser goods. Such a power, he says in an echo of Bayle, would be "useless and capricious."[64] Instead, he suggests, freedom can be thought of as "a power of doing what we wish and of refraining when we do not wish."[65] The discussion ends in a somewhat indeterminate manner, though Hutcheson seems inclined to the view just quoted. In any case, this view is most consistent with his moral psychology as a whole, given the absence of any decision-making faculty independent of competing desires.

If we lack such a "useless and capricious" freedom, why do we commit moral evils? Hutcheson's primary explanation appeals to the association of ideas, a notion Hutcheson draws from Locke. In a chapter added to the fourth edition of his *An Essay Concerning Human Understanding*, Locke introduces the notion of the association of ideas. While some ideas have a natural connection with one another, other ideas are associated through accidental circumstances like chance, custom, or education. Locke uses this notion to explain a few psychological phenomena—the difficulty of finding errors in our own reasoning, the existence of intellectual habits— but leaves it largely undeveloped. He does, however, comment that the association of ideas "might be the most significant factor in setting us awry in our actions, as well moral as natural, passions, reasons, and notions themselves."[66] Hutcheson picks up on precisely this thought.

According to Hutcheson, while our desires and passions are naturally harmonious and ordered to the good of the whole, we often develop accidental associations between unrelated ideas that disorient our affections. One might, for example, associate an action with the public good that does not actually promote it. Or one might associate an action with honor that once brought it by an accidental result. Associations explain how the limited number of desires corresponding to the five classes of sense is compatible with the seemingly unlimited objects of human desire. The more that desires and passions are moved by accidental rather than natural associations, the more the economy of affections will be disordered.[67]

The association of ideas is not the only cause of our vices. Hutcheson also points to false opinion as a cause of vice. A false opinion does not directly harm our affections, but it has important indirect effects. A false view of the consequences of actions can cause us to approve of actions that we should not approve. A false opinion about the comparative pleasures of the internal and external senses can cause us to prefer the latter to the former. His chief target is a false view of the relationship between happiness and virtue. For Hutcheson, benevolence is natural to us. The only thing that can prevent our benevolence is the belief that it stands in opposition to self-interest. The false opinion that pits benevolence against happiness, he thinks, is the primary source of vice in many.[68]

For Hutcheson, then, vice lies not primarily in our affections but in our opinions and associations. Our affections are fundamentally sound; the problem is intellectual. When false opinions and associations are removed, "nature itself will incline us to benevolence."[69] The obvious follow-up question is: Why do we associate ideas? Hutcheson's response, first stated in the *Essay* and repeated in the *System*, is that both language and memory depend upon the capacity to associate ideas.[70] Without the association of ideas, we would lose the capacity for speech and memory. And false opinions are a necessary consequence of the limitation of our rational capacities—the same limitation that explains the need for the passions to guide us.

Hutcheson, then, treats the origin of moral evil in the same way King treats the origin of natural evil. For Hutcheson, the mind is a mechanical structure in which the various parts work together for an end, namely, for the good of the whole and the good of the individual as a subordinate part. Like the rest of nature, it operates by natural laws that can be expressed in mathematical form. As with the larger mechanism of the universe, the fact that the mind operates by general laws means that unavoidable but justified negative outcomes will occur. The mind follows general laws of mental association, which are necessary for the operations of memory and language. These laws have the side effect of creating associations that misdirect our affections. This side effect is unfortunate but a necessary result of the laws that produce greater goods.

Moral evil, therefore, is necessary for the same reason that natural evil is necessary. Hutcheson also goes further, arguing that both natural and moral evils are instrumentally good as well. The goodness of virtue is only possible for an agent facing a world of natural and moral evils. One must, for example, face pain to be courageous and wrongs to be forgiving.[71] No creature whose good lies in social actions and affections, as ours does, could be without "imperfection, indigence, pain, and moral evil."[72] Again, Hutcheson justifies natural and moral evil in the same terms.

Like those of King and Shaftesbury, Hutcheson's innovations solve some important problems but also create new ones. By treating moral evil as a kind of natural evil of the mind, Hutcheson seems to make moral evil natural to us. Doing so raises at least two problems. The first concerns our responsibility for it. If moral evil is a result of natural mental processes, can we really be said to be responsible for it? The second concerns his claim that virtue is natural. If the mechanical processes of the mind, in their natural operation, give rise to both virtue and vice, in what sense can we say virtue is natural and vice is not? Regarding the first problem, Hutcheson simply dismisses the idea that merit and demerit require the freedom to act against our desires.[73] On the second, he has more to say.

The issue arises from the ambiguity of the word "natural" in a context in which teleology is reinterpreted in mechanistic terms. In Aristotelian philosophy, nature is identified with perfection. Hutcheson continues to assume this notion of nature when he refers to virtue as natural. But with the rise of mechanical philosophy, nature is also associated with the outcomes of mechanistic processes. For Hutcheson, virtue is natural in the former sense, while both virtue and vice occur naturally in the latter sense. Insofar as these two senses of "natural" presuppose competing descriptions of nature, how are we to think about their interrelation?

Hutcheson notices this problem by the time he publishes *Illustrations* in 1728. He ends *Illustrations* with a delineation of various senses of "natural."[74] But he does not treat the question fully until his inaugural lecture at the University of Glasgow, and he repeats the same view in the *System*. The argument is based on an analogy with objects of human art. It is possible, he argues, to discern the end for which any artificial construction is intended. When we determine the end, we can see how the various parts conspire together to the end. The same is true even of broken artifacts. If we see an old and decaying house—even one that is missing parts—we can generally see its intended purpose and the way the parts are supposed to conspire together for that purpose. If the house is old, its decay is, in a sense, natural, though decay is not natural in the sense of being part of the design or end of a house. Even the fact that every house eventually decays does not entail that decay is natural to a house in the latter sense. By analogy, human constitution conspires together to a particular end, though it, too, is subject to weakness, decay, and effects outside the purpose of its design:

> Therefore you would not say that everything that happens to a thing is natural however it happens, even if it happens to each and every object of that kind, provided there is nothing in the structure of the object that was designed to bring about precisely that effect. Or, as I would not want to argue about a word, I would call some things, in order to distinguish them, natural, because of their weakness. These are things which are the way they are because God, the maker of all things, did not wish them to be stronger or more enduring than they are. The weakness of our nature appears to have been willed by the good and great God in the excellent wisdom of his counsel; yet all our innate desires strive against that weakness and declare that such weakness is not the end of our duties, much less the goal which nature has set for our actions.[75]

Virtue, then, is natural in the proper sense, whereas vice can be said to be "natural according to our weakness." The latter arises as a byproduct of proper operations and stems from the overall weakness of our natures, a weakness seen in the limitations of our understanding, the fragility of bodies, and the corruptibility of our affections.

Hutcheson repeats this argument in the *System*. Given the new context of the *System*, he is forced to address a follow-up question: why has God given us such a weak nature? To this Hutcheson, following King, replies that it is highly probable that "the best possible constitution of an immense system of perceptive beings may necessarily require a diversity of orders, some higher in perfection and happiness, and some lower."[76] Hutcheson does not use the term "evil of imperfection," but the appeal is essentially the same. We are weak because of our place in a hierarchy of beings that together is the best possible system.

One final objection remains: Bayle's claim that the evils of the world are so great that if they are unavoidable, and if this is in fact the best possible world, then God should not have created anything. Hutcheson spends little time on this worry, asserting that the goodness of the world far outweighs the bad. Rather than taking the objection seriously, he turns it on Bayle. The fact that we are so concerned about the natural and moral evils of the world is further proof of the goodness of our natures. The pleasures of this world far exceed the pains. Pain stands out to us only because of the strength of our public sense, which is strongly moved by the suffering of others. Likewise, most people are far more virtuous than vicious. We only think otherwise because our moral faculty is created with such a high standard of virtue.[77]

Hutcheson and the Consequentialist Moral Cosmology

Beginning with Hutcheson's early moral psychology, we have followed him through the problems it creates and the solutions he proposes. The full development of his moral psychology ultimately leads to a robust theodicy. At this point, we can see more clearly why Hutcheson must hold that our ends are arational and fixed by instinct: it plays a key role in his explanation of the compatibility of perfect divine goodness with the existence of moral evil. By accounting for ends as instinctual, Hutcheson can explain how God created human minds as "well-tuned instruments" that naturally pursue the greatest public good while at the same time accounting for the necessity of moral evil as a byproduct.

Hutcheson, I noted above, locates himself in a tradition that includes More and Shaftesbury. Though he is not a consequentialist—the moral goodness of acts is explained by the motive, not the consequences—his views conform to the broad structure of the consequentialist moral cosmology. God acts only for the sake of the public good, understood as the greatest possible sum of the happiness of creatures. Human beings ought to act for the same end. And God's authority over creatures is grounded in the fact that God is the one best able to direct creatures in their pursuit of the public good. At the same time, Hutcheson's rejection of the rationality of ends marks a crucial disagreement with More and Cumberland.

Hutcheson, like More and Cumberland, sees himself as an opponent of ethical voluntarism. He raises the traditional critique that ethical voluntarists cannot meaningfully affirm the moral goodness of God since they define moral goodness as whatever God wills. He even echoes More by asserting that the precepts of the law of nature are "immutable and eternal."[78] Yet his opponents argued that Hutcheson's position was subject to the same problem as ethical voluntarism.[79] It is true that Hutcheson can give an account of our moral approval of God and God's laws that is not immediately tautological. We do not, in Hutcheson's picture, approve of God's actions and commands simply because God wills them. But for Hutcheson, we do not approve of God because God is morally good, either. The opposite is true: God is morally good because we approve of God. And we only approve of God because God implanted a faculty in us that approves of God's end.

Hutcheson's critics were right to worry that his view introduces an arbitrariness very much like that of ethical voluntarism. And the matter is not resolved by asking why God made us to morally approve of benevolence. The answer to that question cannot be that benevolence is morally good independent of our approval. The only available answer is that making us approve of benevolence is part of the way God achieves God's end. Making us to morally approve of benevolence is part of how God realizes maximal happiness in creation. Our moral and public senses, in other words, are willed by God as a means to God's end.

Human benevolence, then, is explained by divine benevolence. Why is God benevolent? For Hutcheson, ends are no more rational for God than they are for us. How, then, does God determine an end? Hutcheson assumes that God's moral psychology must be analogous to our own: "We must conceive in a deity some perceptive power analogous to our moral sense, by which he may have self-approbation in certain affections and actions rather than the contrary."[80] God's ends, like ours, depend on God's affections—or at least something analogous to our affections. Without such affections, God could have no reason to act. How, then, can we know that God's affections are benevolent? Hutcheson makes no a priori appeal to perfection or any other metaphysical or theological category. Because ends are arational, no end could be more perfect than another. Our only option is to infer God's ends from creation.[81] God, Hutcheson argues, could only have three possible ends: God's own happiness, universal happiness, or universal misery.[82] It is quite striking that Hutcheson does not include the common answer discussed in chapter 1—that God is God's end—among the possible options. This omission appears to be another point at which his implicit productivism about agency shapes his thought.

Because divine happiness is eternally secure, God's happiness cannot explain creation and thus cannot be God's end. Only universal happiness and universal misery remain. Hutcheson then argues from the character of the created world that God's end must be universal happiness rather than universal misery.[83]

Is this ethical voluntarism? It is certainly not ethical voluntarism in the usual sense. Morality is determined by our nature, not by divine commands. God could not change what is morally good and evil without changing our nature, a claim generally associated with intellectualism. At the same time, God could change what is morally good and evil by changing just one thing about our nature, our moral sense. All other implanted senses and desires could remain the same. In such a world, we could have, for example, all the same reasons (beyond the moral one) not to want to be hated, but hatred—and even hatred of God—could be morally good. This sort of result is generally associated with ethical voluntarism.

Moreover, God's decision of which moral sense to give us is not constrained by any prior moral or rational standards. The particular constitutions of our moral sense can only be explained by God's affection, which, in Hutcheson's terminology, is the same as saying that it is explained by God's will.[84] Yet God's will, while it is not guided by any logically prior intellectual standard, is not exactly arbitrary. The standard of divine action is a divine affective moral sense. Why does God's moral sense approve of benevolence? Hutcheson provides no answer. Since God's moral sense is not a perfection—or is at least no more a perfection than a moral sense that approves malevolence—it is difficult to avoid the conclusion that we just got lucky that God approves benevolence and desires our happiness. We can explain our ends in terms of our senses and desires, our senses and desires in terms of God's ends, and God's ends in terms of God's (analogous) senses and desires. But God's senses and desires remain, in the logic of Hutcheson's position, brute facts—no less so than facts about God's will do in ethical voluntarism.

The fact that Hutcheson takes a big step toward ethical voluntarism is not necessarily a problem on his own terms. If he is willing to ground all morality in an inexplicable divine sense, he can hold his view coherently. But the fact that Hutcheson's version of the consequentialist moral cosmology drifts toward ethical voluntarism further illuminates the problems evil poses for More's and Cumberland's views. King and Shaftesbury lose the notion that God and human beings will the same ultimate end. Hutcheson maintains it but denies that they do so rationally. Hutcheson's step toward ethical voluntarism is partial. The future of theological consequentialism, as we will see in part III, lies in a full embrace of ethical voluntarism.

Epilogue to Part II

The eighteenth century has been called "the golden age of theodicies" and "the century of theodicy."[1] Many factors contributed to the central role of theodicy in eighteenth-century European thought. In the British intellectual context, I have highlighted one factor in particular: the rise of the consequentialist moral cosmology in the latter half of the seventeenth century. With the invention of consequentialist moral rationality and its application to God, the existence and extent of evil in the world became problematic in a new way. The appearance of Bayle's *Dictionnaire historique et critique* in 1697 brought the issue of evil to the fore. It is unsurprising that Britain, where More and Cumberland were particularly influential, produced several prominent responses to Bayle in the early seventeenth century.

In chapter 4, I argued that "the problem of evil" is not a singular or timeless problem. The tensions between theism and the existence of evil, if and when they arise, depend on a number of related ideas. For our purposes, the most important ideas concern the nature of morality and its relationship to God. The figures discussed in the last three chapters, like More and Cumberland before them, believe that God's moral perfection requires God to realize the greatest good in creation—whether this good is understood as the good of the cosmic whole, as in Shaftesbury, or the maximization of the total good to individuals, as in King and Hutcheson. And all of these figures assert—with varying degrees of success—that human moral perfection requires human beings to will the same end as God.

Without these views about divine and human morality, the story would be quite different. The ethical voluntarist, I argued, can avoid the most significant problems posed by evil altogether. And those ethical intellectualists who reject the idea that God shares our morality can often achieve a similar, if less extreme, result. I used Aquinas as an example in chapter 4. In the eighteenth century, Joseph Butler expresses doubts that God shares human morality, and his writings on evil are quite different from those discussed in previous chapters.[2] But even among those who believe that moral principles apply in the same way to God and rational creatures, the challenge posed by the existence of evil depends on the moral principles endorsed. Consider the work of John Clarke. Clarke is the younger brother of the more famous Samuel Clarke, the great early eighteenth-century representative of the view that morality consists of acting according to the eternal fitness of things. In his Boyle Lectures, Samuel Clarke writes:

> The true Ground and Foundation of all Eternal Moral Obligations, is this; that the same Reasons, *vis*: the forementioned necessary and eternal *Different Relations* which *Different Things* bear one to another; and the consequent *Fitness or Unfitness* of the Application of different Things or Different Relations one to another, unavoidably arising from the Difference of the Things themselves; these same Reasons, I say, which always and necessarily *do* determine the Will of God, as hath been before shown; *ought* also constantly to determine the Will of all Subordinate Intelligent Beings.[3]

There could be no stronger statement of the identity of human and divine morality. John Clarke, a defender of his brother's ethical views, delivered his own Boyle Lectures, published as *An Inquiry into the Cause and Origin of Evil*, which respond to Bayle's arguments about evil. In many ways, including in the taxonomy of evils and in many particular arguments, Clarke echoes King. But Clarke's differing views about divine morality alter the nature of his case. For Clarke, God and rational creatures are morally bound by the same set of eternal moral truths. But those truths, as Clarke understands them, do not determine the ends for which one acts. Clarke accepts that God must seek to express the divine nature and communicate happiness, but he does not see these purposes as setting determinate ends. In fact, he claims that we do not know God's ends in creation.[4] We know only that God acts in all things in perfect conformity to the eternal fitness of things. And this fact, Clarke argues, can be seen in all created things; there is "a manifest *Fitness* in every one of *These*, to their proper and Respective *Ends*."[5]

When it comes to moral evil, Clarke addresses Bayle's arguments that the gift of freedom and the imposition of divine law cause more harm than benefit, but he does not respond to the arguments on their own terms. Clarke insists that nothing requires God to create free and rational creatures but that it is "reasonable and fit" for God to do so.[6] And having created free and rational creatures, God acts toward them fittingly. God,

Clarke writes, "has done everything that was fit for infinite Wisdom and Goodness to do to prevent [sin]," but God will not interfere with their freedom, which would be unfitting.[7] God governs them by imposing sanctions, which, again, is "fit and reasonable."[8] On Clarke's account, the gift of freedom and the imposition of divine law could cause more harm than benefit without God having done anything unfitting.

The situation, as we have seen, is quite different for those who believe that divine moral perfection requires God to maximize the good in creation. Nothing in Clarke's response to Bayle puts pressure on his view that God and rational creatures share the same moral principles. For King, Shaftesbury, and Hutcheson, the challenge is much greater. The reason is simple. Due to their views about divine morality, every facet of the world, including divine law and human psychology, has to be conducive to the realization of maximal goodness. Human morality and moral psychology are thus remade under the pressure of a maximizing theodicy.

Under the pressure of a maximizing theodicy, the idea that human beings can share God's end and God's principles of action becomes difficult to maintain. We see this tension especially in King and Shaftesbury. King maintains that we ought to conform our wills to God's, willing the realization of maximal goodness as God does. But the reason we are to do so, on his account, is that it is the best way to make ourselves happy. Our concern with the realization of maximal goodness is thus subordinated to our desire to attain happiness—and God, whose goal is our happiness, wants it to be thus. For Shaftesbury, the denial of the existence of evil entails that human vice—which, in his view, is also human misery—is necessary for the good of the cosmic whole. Human beings are to share God's end, willing only the good of the cosmic whole. Yet because they cannot, according to Shaftesbury, will their own misery, they can finally only share God's end conditionally on it not including their vice. Few people, it would seem, get so lucky.

Unlike King and Shaftesbury, Hutcheson does successfully maintain the view that God and human beings share an end and moral principles of action. Hutcheson does so by arguing that God and human beings possess a similar moral sense, which arationally approves the same thing: the pursuit of maximal public happiness. As we have seen, the difficulty with Hutcheson's view is that, by treating all ends as arational, it renders God's benevolent end inexplicable. In the end, Hutcheson, despite his anti-ethical-voluntarist commitments, explains all morality by an ultimately arbitrary state of divine affections.

While the consequentialist moral cosmology was invented as a new alternative to ethical voluntarism, we see in Hutcheson an unintentional turn back toward ethical voluntarism. The trajectory that leads to Hutcheson is not accidental. The idea that ends are arational plays a key role in this theodicy. Hutcheson moves the broadly consequentialist tradition back toward ethical voluntarism. The full embrace of ethical voluntarism in the consequentialist tradition occurs among a group of like-minded scholars, who, in the 1720s and 30s, were reading the works of King, Shaftesbury, and Hutcheson together with the works of John Locke. Continuing to merge theodicy and moral theology, they seek a new path forward. In their writings—the most important of which is a translation of King's *De origine mali* with extensive notes—we find the earliest articulation of the dominant eighteenth-century tradition of consequentialism, Anglican utilitarianism.

Rather than continuing to hold onto the consequentialist moral cosmology, the Anglican utilitarians, who also wrestle deeply with the existence of evil, abandon it. In its place, they embrace a quasi-Hobbesian version of ethical voluntarism: we are to obey God only because God has complete power to grant us happiness or misery. Yet even while they abandon the consequentialist moral cosmology, they continue to employ consequentialist moral rationality. Indeed, as we will see, they largely take for granted the idea that God acts for the sake of maximal happiness and commands us to do so as well. Consequentialist moral rationality, as we have seen, was invented to combat ethical voluntarism. In the Anglican utilitarians, we see that it continues and thrives even beyond the context that first motivated its development.

PART III

The Anglican Utilitarian Synthesis

8

John Gay's "Preliminary Dissertation"

The Cambridge tradition of theological utilitarianism is usually dated to the publication of John Gay's "Preliminary Dissertation Concerning the Fundamental Principle of Virtue or Morality" in 1731. According to Ernest Albee, "the whole outline of Utilitarianism, in its first complete and unencumbered form" can be found in Gay's "Dissertation."[1] Colin Heydt echoes this claim with his assertion that "the key themes of Anglican utilitarianism" are all expressed by Gay.[2] And Getty Lustila writes of Gay: "He is the first utilitarian."[3] Even Élie Halévy, who considers Gay's theological presuppositions "foreign to the spirit of the doctrine," admits that Gay is "the true founder of . . . Utilitarian morality."[4]

More recently, Patrick Connolly has argued that Susanna Newcome, an accomplished author and intellectual living in Cambridge and married to a Cambridge scholar, has a better claim to be the earliest utilitarian.[5] Connolly may well be correct, though as he admits, claims to priority are difficult, especially in this case, when Gay's "Dissertation" circulated in an unpublished form. Newcome's view can certainly be called utilitarian, and her 1728 text, *An Enquiry into the Evidence of the Christian Religion*, bears fascinating similarities to Gay's "Dissertation," which I discuss below.

There is no doubt, though, that Gay's text is the one that became canonical in the Anglican utilitarian tradition, and, following many others, I will focus on it as a foundational text for theological utilitarianism.[6] Unlike many others, though, I will insist that Gay's "Dissertation" not be read in abstraction from the context of its publication. Gay did not publish the "Dissertation" himself, and we do not know when it was written. Instead, Edmund Law published it as a preliminary treatise attached to his own translation of William King's *De origine mali*, which was titled *An Essay on the Origin of Evil* (1731). Law did not attribute the "Dissertation" to Gay until the fourth edition in 1758, though Gay's authorship was known at Cambridge.[7] Law's translation also included many other supplements in addition to Gay's treatise. Later editions added Law's own essays on ethical theory and a couple of sermons by King. Moreover, Law supplemented the translation with sprawling notes—notes that together far exceed the length of the translated text. The notes are generally but not always friendly to King. Often, they further develop points or respond to objections. And they frequently cite and discuss the works of other authors, creating a conversation among dozens of thinkers. The massive apparatus of notes and attached essays was neither accidental nor arbitrary. Law intended the text to be a "*Compendium of Metaphysics*, or speculative Divinity."[8]

Niall O'Flaherty is correct to assert that "the prime mover in the development of Christian Utility was Edmund Law."[9] Gay's "Dissertation" and its reception should not be treated in isolation but rather as part of Law's larger project in natural theology—not to downplay Gay's contribution but to properly contextualize it. The Cambridge tradition of theological utilitarianism is not simply a set of ideas in ethical theory. It is a larger project of natural theology, and Law is its primary early source.

Following Colin Heydt, I will call the Cambridge tradition inaugurated by Gay and Law "Anglican utilitarianism." The term is meant to pick out not simply a set of ideas but also a larger institutionalized tradition of natural theology and ethics.[10] Similar ideas were in the air at this time—in part, as we will see, as a result of attempts to develop what Locke left unfinished—and Gay and Law are not the only early eighteenth-century thinkers plausibly described as theological utilitarians.[11] Nonetheless, Gay and Law are no doubt the most influential, and the account of theological utilitarianism developed in Law's *An Essay on the Origin of Evil* inaugurated the Cambridge tradition that culminated in the works of William Paley.

By using the term "utilitarianism," I intend to mark the emergence of an explicitly hedonistic and maximizing form of consequentialism. If the views discussed so far have been quite strange from a contemporary perspective, we find a view in Gay and Law that, despite its robustly theological character, begins to sound much like the view we now call classical utilitarianism. Anglican utilitarianism is the dominant form of utilitarianism in the eighteenth and early nineteenth centuries, and it decisively marks British utilitarianism to this day.

The task of part III is to tell the story of the emergence of Anglican utilitarianism at Cambridge in the first half of the eighteenth century. When Gay's "Dissertation" is read in its larger context within Law's "*Compendium*," I argue, Anglican utilitarian ethical theory appears as a development within the larger set of issues discussed in part II. Law's aim is to present a comprehensive, rational approach to theology, the central task of which is to explain the existence of evil. The concerns that preoccupied Bayle, King, Shaftesbury, and Hutcheson remain front and center, and Law seeks a new way forward. The work of ethical theory has to be read as an element within this larger task.

The last three chapters have demonstrated that those attracted to a moral vision like that of the consequentialist moral cosmology struggle in new ways with the existence of evil. King, Shaftesbury, and Hutcheson all defend the view that God, being morally perfect, will realize maximal goodness in creation. The pressures of a maximizing theodicy reshape human morality and human moral psychology in ways that make it difficult to maintain the idea that human being share God's moral ends and principles of action. Hutcheson, I argued, was able to maintain this sort of moral community between God and human beings, but only by rejecting the rationality of ends—and, in doing so, effectively abandoning the ethical intellectualism that was so important to More and Cumberland. It is not hard, then, to understand why Gay and Law both reject ethical intellectualism, embracing instead a slightly tempered version of ethical voluntarism.

Consequentialism, I argued in part I, began as an innovative response to ethical voluntarism. The fact that the dominant eighteenth-century consequentialist tradition, Anglican utilitarianism, is explicitly ethical voluntarist is on its face surprising. Those who have read part II, though, should not be surprised. Gay and Law inherit the issues raised by Bayle and the responses of King, Shaftesbury, and Hutcheson. Rather than struggling to maintain ethical intellectualism or the consequentialist moral cosmology, Gay and Law follow a new path. In abandoning the consequentialist moral cosmology, however, Gay and Law do not leave consequentialist moral rationality behind. Most of the key innovations found in More and Cumberland—innovations in the nature of goodness, agency, ends, and causation—remain. Thus while Anglican utilitarianism, in one sense, represents an endpoint for the consequentialist moral cosmology, I will argue for a deeper sense in which it marks a further development in the tradition of More and Cumberland. Consequentialist moral rationality becomes, among the Anglican utilitarians, too obvious to need a defense.

While the aim of part III is to show how Anglican utilitarianism emerges from the debates discussed in part II, we must begin with a figure who has thus far figured into the story only marginally: John Locke. Locke's influence has certainly already shaped the story. King wrote one of the first replies to Locke's *Essay on Human Understanding*, a reply that likely influenced Locke's later editions;[12] Shaftesbury was Locke's pupil-turned-critic; and Hutcheson explicitly develops Lockean epistemology. But we have yet to address Locke's ethical writings directly.

Gay and Law can be described with little qualification as Lockeans. One of the only descriptions we have of Gay comes from Law, who said that no one knew scripture or the works of John Locke better.[13] And Law himself edited and published Locke's collected works. Indeed, Law has been described as "the most convinced adherent of Locke's philosophy in eighteenth-century England."[14] Yet to say that Gay and Law are Lockeans is not to say that they uncritically adopt Locke's theological or ethical views. Locke's ethical views were plagued with difficulties, both interpretive and philosophical. He never published his early ethical writings or completed his late ones, and his various published comments on morality are difficult to hold together. This chapter begins, therefore, with a short overview of Locke's published statements about morality along with the controversy surrounding them, which sets the context for Gay's reception and development of Locke's views. Gay, I argue in the remainder of the chapter, uses Lockean resources to modify the moral philosophy of Francis Hutcheson. He does so in a manner that Law sees as compatible with the theology and ethics of William King. The next chapter situates Gay's "Dissertation" within Law's larger project.

John Locke and the Natural Law

Interpretive controversies have surrounded Locke's ethical views from their earliest publication. The central area of controversy is the ethical voluntarist/intellectualist issue: the extent to which Locke thinks morality depends on God's will.[15] Part of the difficulty stems from the fact that Locke never published a treatise devoted to morality. His views are scattered throughout his writings, and doubts are sometimes raised about his commitments to some of his published views. Rather than trying to resolve interpretive and philosophical difficulties in Locke's moral philosophy, I intend to trace the main outlines of his explicitly stated ethical views. The difficulties facing his readers are more important for my purposes than any definitive answer about his own views. These difficulties explain why even those committed to Locke's larger philosophical program, like Gay and Law, were required to rethink the nature of morality.

The work that poses the most difficult interpretive questions—and the work most important to Gay's "Dissertation"—is *An Essay Concerning Human Understanding*. The *Essay*, first published in 1689, originated from conversations about ethics, but it addresses epistemology in general.[16] Locke argues that all human knowledge has its source in experience, and he categorically rejects any notion of innate ideas, including practical or ethical ideas. Importantly, the rejection of innate practical ideas does not entail the rejection of innate practical principles. Locke writes: "Nature, I confess, has put into Man a desire of Happiness, and an aversion to Misery: these indeed are innate practical Principles, which (as practical Principles ought) do continue constantly to operate and influence all our Actions, without ceasing."[17] From this innate and unceasing disposition to happiness and away from misery, Locke proposes the rough outlines of a moral philosophy. Our notions of good and evil arise immediately from the experience of pleasure and pain. That which causes pleasure or diminishes pain is called good; that which causes pain or diminishes pleasure is called evil.[18] Locke's point here is about the origin of our ideas, but he also embraces hedonism normatively and descriptively. Happiness, understood as maximal pleasure, is the human good. Only private pleasure and pain can motivate us: "*Pleasure* and *Pain*, and that which causes them, Good and Evil, are the hinges on which our *Passions* turn." (II.xx.3).

Good and evil are simple ideas, derived immediately from passive experiences of pleasure and pain. Moral good and evil, by contrast, are complex ideas. A complex idea, for Locke, is one derived from the combination of simple ideas. In the formation of complex ideas, the mind is active, making choices about which simple ideas to combine. The combinations are not required by nature but are made by human choice for the accomplishment of human purposes. The idea of moral good and evil first requires ideas about actions. Locke treats ideas about actions as a category of complex ideas called mixed modes. Modes are complex ideas that "contain not in them the supposition of subsisting by themselves, but are considered as Dependences on, or Affections of Substances."[19] Mixed modes are modes that contain multiple simple ideas of different types. The human mind combines a set of simple features to come up with ideas about act-types. Act-types like lying or murder, Locke argues, are mixed modes. Nothing about human action requires these particular ideas formed by their particular combinations of simple ideas. We form them for practical purposes. For Locke, "the greatest part of the Words made use of in Divinity, Ethicks, Law, and Politicks" are mixed modes.[20]

The ideas of moral good and evil themselves fall under a different category of complex ideas: relations. Moral good and evil "is only the Conformity or Disagreement of our voluntary Actions to some Law, whereby Good or Evil is drawn on us, from the Will and Power of the Law-maker."[21] Locke then claims that there are three different "*Moral Rules*, or *Laws*" by which people judge actions: the divine law, the civil law, and the law of opinion or reputation. Divine law arises from the command of God with its corresponding sanctions; it determines duty and sin. Civil law arises from the rule of the commonwealth with its corresponding sanctions; it determines innocence and criminality. The law of opinion arises from the common judgments of a community about virtue and vice. Its sanctions are the praise and blame of one's community. Conformity to the law of opinion is virtue, and deviation from it is vice. For Locke, each is a law because it is a way the demands of others influence our actions by reward and punishment, but divine law alone is "the true touchstone of *moral Rectitude*."[22]

Locke undoubtedly embraces legislative voluntarism.[23] Moral good and evil in the proper sense depend on the legislative will of God, which lays down the divine law with sanctions. The further question is whether he embraces ethical voluntarism. The account of moral good and evil could easily lead us to assume that he would. The act-types that are commanded or prohibited by divine law are, as we have seen, constructions of the mind, not real essences (III.iv.5). It is difficult to see, then, how acts could have any intrinsic properties of goodness or badness prior to God's commands. Yet Locke does not embrace this seemingly straightforward implication of his view. In the *Essay*, Locke famously writes:

> The *Idea* of a supreme Being, infinite in Power, Goodness, and Wisdom, whose Workmanship we are, and on whom we depend; and the *Idea* of our selves, as understanding, rational Beings, being such as are clear in us, would, I suppose, if duly considered, and pursued, afford such Foundations of our Duty and Rules of Actions, as might place *Morality amongst the Sciences capable of Demonstration*: wherein I doubt not, but from self-evident Propositions, by necessary Consequences, as incontestable as those in Mathematicks, the measures of right and wrong might be made out, to any one that will apply himself with the same Indifferency and Attention to the one, as he does to the other of these Sciences. (IIII.iii.18)

The only example Locke gives of a demonstrable moral truth is, "*Where there is no Property, there is no Injustice*," which, he says, "is a Proposition as certain as any Demonstration in *Euclid*" (IIII.iii.18).

The idea that morality is demonstrable seems to sit uncomfortably with the idea that our moral categories are merely mental constructions. For Locke, however, the two points are integrally linked. Demonstration is possible because our ideas are purely nominal.[24] No empirical knowledge is necessary; demonstration concerns the relationship between ideas (e.g., property and justice). Yet this point does not solve the real issue. Even if the relationship between ideas allows one to construct demonstrably true propositions, we seem to be demonstrating nothing beyond the internal logical relationship between our moral ideas. If our moral ideas are merely pragmatic constructions, why should we think that the logical relationships between them constitute true moral knowledge, that is, knowledge about what God commands and forbids?

Various proposals have been put forward to answer this question. Some point out that Locke thought highly of the ethical writings of the great German natural lawyer, Samuel Pufendorf. While Locke does not do the work of systematically deriving the content of the natural law, they argue that he would likely have followed the outlines of Pufendorf's broadly Grotian view, deriving the content of the natural law from our self-interested but sociable nature.[25] Others argue that Locke's hedonism allows him to derive the content of morality from what brings pleasure and pain. According to Elliot Rossiter, Locke believes that God has annexed pleasure and pain to actions in order to teach us the moral law. While the pleasures and pains that follow from any particular action or course of life do not themselves make the action or course of life obligatory, they reveal God's legislative will, a view much like Cumberland's. In this way, ordinary pleasures and pains "function as signposts of divine intent."[26] Following a similar argumentative line, A. P. Brogan has even argued that Locke is a utilitarian.[27]

One reason Locke does not provide an explicit demonstration of the content of the natural law may be that he has doubts about our capacity to do so. To say that morality is demonstrable is not to say that anyone knows how to demonstrate it.[28] Locke's doubts about our capacities in this regard are particularly clear in *The Reasonableness of Christianity*, where he argues for the importance of revelation. For Locke, we can much more easily recognize the truth of Jesus's moral teachings than demonstrate them for ourselves.[29]

However Locke intends to determine the content of morality, he evidently intends to deny ethical voluntarism. Morality depends upon God's will, but God's will is not arbitrary. The content of morality follows from God's nature and ours.[30] He also claims that God's will determines our moral obligation not only due to God's power to reward and punish but also due to God's legitimate authority:

That God has given a Rule whereby Men should govern themselves, I think there is no body so brutish as to deny. He has a Right to do it, we are his Creatures: He has Goodness and Wisdom to direct our Actions to that which is best: and he has Power to enforce it by Rewards and

Punishments, of infinite weight and duration, in another Life: for no body can take us out of his hands. (II.xxviii.8)

For God to have a right to govern us, however, is for us to have an obligation to obey God, an obligation which cannot itself be explained by God's commands. We have seen how Cumberland navigates this issue, arguing that God's right and our obligation are grounded in the shared end to which we and God are rationally bound. Locke provides no such account of God's authority. If he did, he would have to explain how we can have an obligation to obey God that is not itself a product of divine law. Daniel Layman has offered one possible Lockean account, arguing that Locke's view of divine authority is analogous to the authority of parents over children.[31] Layman's interpretation is plausible, but it raises many other questions. In Layman's view, the moral obligations, including those between parents and children and creators and creatures, are natural. Locke's insistence that moral good and evil depend on the relationship of acts to divine law becomes difficult to understand.[32]

Locke's explicit views on ethics fall in the broad tradition of Suárez, Culverwell, Cumberland, and Pufendorf, all of whom embrace legislative voluntarism while rejecting ethical voluntarism.[33] God's commands are necessary for moral obligation, but God's commands also necessarily conform to the truth of what is naturally good and bad for human beings to do. J. B. Schneewind has noted that "after Locke no major thinker tried to work out a Grotian theory of natural law in [legislative] voluntarist terms."[34] The reason, according to Schneewind, is that Locke's epistemology, which was a development of an empiricist view that he shared with other Grotian natural lawyers, ultimately rendered him unable to defend God's authority. While Locke's moral philosophy depends upon God's authority and right to command, his epistemology undermines any attempt to justify God's authority. In the end, Schneewind argues, Locke cannot avoid a Hobbesian reduction of divine authority to divine power. Even if one or more of the reconstructions of Locke's view cited above is correct, Schneewind is right that Locke's work marks the endpoint of a popular seventeenth-century tradition of combining legislative voluntarism with an empirically discernible natural law.

My aim in this section has been to briefly sketch the main outlines of the position Locke defends and to raise some of the many philosophical and interpretive difficulties it generated for Locke's successors. Locke's views about ethics, I have suggested, occupy familiar terrain, defending legislative voluntarism but not ethical voluntarism. Locke's ethical innovations are primarily epistemological, and these innovations introduce many ethical complications. As Timothy Stanton has written,

> A great deal of eighteenth-century British philosophy can be seen, without too much distortion, as a single (if very complicated) sequence of arguments over the implications for Christianity and natural jurisprudence of the analyses of human knowledge and language that Locke had worked out in the Essay. Locke's successors were not usually content to take his positions as they found them—his writings rarely functioned straightforwardly as objects of assent—but he raised the problems in a form in which later philosophers, even those who dissented from him, found it fruitful to address them.[35]

Francis Hutcheson, with his introduction of the internal senses, has already provided one instance of the creative use of Lockean epistemology in ethics. Gay and Law will provide another. In both cases, Locke's epistemology serves a new purpose. Neither Hutcheson nor Gay and Law seek to remain true to Locke's explicit views about morality. Gay and Law aim to rethink morality in a manner consistent with Locke's epistemology and with their broader theological commitments.

John Gay on the Criterion of Virtue

Gay's "Preliminary Dissertation" presupposes Locke's account of the origin and character of our moral ideas. He creatively deploys Lockean epistemology in an argumentative approach that would be repeated by nearly all theological utilitarians in the eighteenth century. It begins with the observation that moralists have generally agreed about which actions are virtuous while disagreeing about both what makes them virtuous and what motivates people to act virtuously. Gay calls the former a disagreement about the criterion of virtue and the latter a disagreement about the principal or motive of virtue. He contends that agreement about the content of virtue despite disagreement about the criterion of virtue suggests one of two things: either moralists are not actually employing their criteria in their judgments about virtue, or their disagreements about the criterion are merely verbal. Gay favors the latter explanation. Drawing on Locke's Essay, he argues that different moralists are relying on different combinations of simple ideas to build their moral terminologies. In any debate centered on complex ideas, he thinks, verbal disagreement is bound to arise when precise definitions are not given. This argument allows Gay to avoid directly criticizing other accounts of the criterion of virtue, such as reason, truth, and the fitness of things. He aims to demonstrate that linguistic precision can dissolve what seem to be intractable disagreements (xi–xii).[36]

Before a criterion of virtue can be determined, Gay argues, we first need a definition of virtue. A definition, as in Locke, is about our construction of ideas. A criterion, by contrast, is "a Rule or Measure by a Conformity with which any thing is known to be of this or that sort, or of this or that degree" (xv). According to Gay, we have the idea of particular virtues before we have an abstract notion of virtue. The question is what unites them into a single complex idea called "virtue." Gay's definition of virtue comes primarily from Hutcheson. He highlights two features: (1) virtue is always to be approved (Hutcheson's "justifying reason"); (2) virtue is always an object of choice (Hutcheson's "exciting reason"). To say that virtue is always to be approved is to say that we always have a sufficient motive to approve it. To say that virtue is always an object of choice is to say that we always have a sufficient motive to act virtuously. The latter feature is particularly important. For Gay, the motive for virtue must always, when fully considered, override all competing motives. Only in this way can virtue become obligatory. In this regard, too, Gay agrees with Hutcheson, who explains the obligation to virtue in the *System* with an account of the moral sense as an overriding motivation.

The problem with Hutcheson, according to Gay, is that he solves the problem of the criterion and the problem of the motive by positing the existence of implanted instincts: the moral sense for the former and the public sense bolstered by the moral sense for the latter. To posit the existence of implanted instincts, for Gay, is not to explain but to give up on explanation. Hutcheson's account "seems still insufficient, rather cutting the Knot than untying it, and if it is not a-kin to the Doctrine of *Innate Ideas*, yet I think it relishes too much of that of *Occult Qualities*" (xiv). Hutcheson defends the internal senses on Lockean grounds, and Gay contests them on the same grounds. At stake here is in part what counts as an adequate explanation.[37] For Gay, as for Locke, an adequate explanation of anything affective or conative requires derivation from our only innate practical principle: the desire for private happiness, which is the desire to obtain pleasure and avoid pain.

Despite these disagreements about explanation, Gay borrows heavily from Hutcheson's picture of the content of virtue, and he offers the following definition: "Virtue is the conformity to a rule of life, directing the actions of all rational creatures with respect to each other's happiness; to which conformity everyone in all cases is obliged; and everyone that does so conform is or ought to be approved of, esteemed and loved for so doing" (xvii).[38] It is important not to lose sight of the fact that virtue is for Gay a complex idea. This combination of simple ideas is not required by anything in the ideas or in the world. This set of simple ideas will, if properly constructed, pick out certain things in the world that are useful for human purposes. The success of Gay's definition depends on its capacity to pick out only those acts ordinarily taken to be virtuous.

Once we have a definition of virtue, the next question is about the criterion of virtue. The distinction between definition and criterion is crucial for Gay. We can see why by returning to the problems with Locke's ethics. For Locke, demonstration is possible in morality because moral ideas are constructed by the mind. Moral truths can be proved by demonstrating the conceptual relations between our ideas: without property, there is no injustice. But as we have seen, this type of demonstration leaves open the question of how we know that our ideas have any relation to that which actually determines the content of morality: the divine will. Gay addresses this issue with his distinction between definition and criterion. The definition remains at the level of the internal relationships between ideas. It tells us what we mean when we call an act virtuous but does not itself provide information about which acts are virtuous. A criterion is still needed to specify which acts make up the "rule of life" of virtue. With the criteria, Gay seeks to explicitly connect our ideas to that which truly determines what is morally good or evil.[39]

The question, then, is which criterion can explain how the acts we call virtuous have all the qualities of Gay's definition. Gay begins with the aspect of the definition that he sees as the shortest route to a criterion, the motive of virtue. Gay takes the notion of obligation to be that of having a decisive motivating reason to act. And for Gay, a decisive motivating reason can only come from the necessity of some act for the end of achieving private happiness: "Obligation is the necessity of doing or omitting any action in order to be happy" (xviii). Like Locke and Hutcheson, Gay understands happiness as the attainment of private pleasure and the avoidance of private pain. Anything that contributes to private happiness or the avoidance of private misery imposes an obligation to some degree. Building on Locke, Gay lists four sources of obligation: the natural consequences of actions, the esteem or contempt actions produce in other people, the civil sanctions attending actions, and the divine sanctions attending actions (xviii). This list combines Locke's three kinds of moral law with their three attendant sanctions (opinion, civil, divine) and a variant of Cumberland's law with natural consequences as sanctions. While natural consequences, social opinions, and civil sanctions are all relevant to happiness, only divine sanctions can completely determine happiness and misery. Only divine law, then, constitutes a "full and complete obligation," which means that divine will is the only possible criterion of virtue (xix).

Gay thus eliminates all options except for the will of God on the grounds that no other criterion can explain virtue's universal obligation. What, then, about his argument that disagreements about the criterion are merely verbal? To see how Gay incorporates all other criteria into his own, we have to consider the content of the will of God. To this massive theological question, Gay responds with a simple argument, which we will consider in more depth below, the upshot of which is that God wills the universal happiness of human beings. The will of God is the ultimate criterion of virtue, but Gay now adds a proximate criterion: the happiness of mankind. Those who say that the criterion of virtue is the happiness of mankind or the common good of mankind, according to Gay, are both right and wrong. Materially, they are right. The happiness of mankind as a criterion picks out the correct acts of virtue. In fact, however, the happiness of mankind succeeds in doing so not because it is the immediate criterion of virtue but because it is the criterion of the will of God. The happiness of mankind alone as a criterion cannot explain the universal obligation to virtue.

Even while the happiness of mankind is not the immediate criterion of virtue, Gay can explain why it gives materially correct results and affirm it as a proximate criterion, that is, as the criterion of the criterion. And Gay simply repeats this move for the other possible candidates for the criterion of virtue. Each one is a more remote criterion. How can we discover which acts promote the happiness of mankind and which do not? By the fitness of things. Following Hutcheson, Gay considers fitness without relation to an end scarcely intelligible (xii). Fitness can only mean fitness to an end, namely, to the happiness of mankind. The fitness of things, then, is the criterion of the happiness of mankind. And what is the criterion of the fitness of things? Reason. Moreover, reason, when outwardly expressed, is called truth. Both reason and truth are criteria of the fitness of things (xx). In this way, Gay can explain the appeal of competing criteria without affirming them. He can also explain why formal disagreements about criteria do not lead to material disagreements about the content of virtue.

Gay's approach to explaining away other criteria would be highly influential among the Anglican utilitarians. While Newcome uses the argument quite differently, a similar argument can be found also in her *Enquiry into the Evidence of the Christian Religion*, which was published three years before Gay's "Dissertation."[40] Newcome, too, explains fitness, reason, and truth in terms that ultimately lead back to the tendency to promote happiness. Newcome's use of the argument, though, is different, as I explain below.

The Psychology of Virtue

Even if Gay is right that only the will of God can provide an adequate motive for virtue, he still needs to show that the will of God can also account for the other features of virtue. In particular, he needs to explain why we approve of virtue and love the virtuous. The proximate criterion, universal happiness, begins to explain why we approve of virtue. We are motivated only by our own happiness, and approving virtue in others is equivalent to approving their efforts to further universal happiness. But Gay, like Hutcheson, avoids appealing to any sort of explicit calculation. Instead, he introduces a story about developmental psychology.

The story, which is perhaps his most lasting innovation, goes like this. Pleasure is the only thing we pursue for its own sake, and pain is the only thing we avoid for its own sake. We call good that which brings pleasure (or reduces pain) and evil that which brings pain (or reduces pleasure). Reflecting upon those things that cause pleasure elicits desire, and reflecting upon those things that cause pain elicits aversion. From desire and aversion arise love and hatred toward the sources of pleasure and pain (xxii–xxiii). This account is rather straightforward when the objects in question are not rational agents. When the objects are rational agents, further nuance is required. In this case, the process is similar but with a modification. Unlike other sources of pleasure and pain, rational agents act on us voluntarily. They cause us pleasure only by the concurrence of their wills with ours. For this reason, we naturally approve of whatever is apt to cause this concurrence. Because others are motivated in the same way as we are, nothing can cause their wills to move one way or another but the prospect of private pleasure or pain. We, therefore, approve not only of their actions that concur with our wills but also of their receiving pleasure for those actions, since their hope of pleasure is what elicited the acts. Gay goes on: "Because what we approve of we also desire . . . hence also we *desire* the Happiness of any Agent that has done us good. And therefore *Love* or *Hatred*, when placed on a rational Object, has this difference from the Love or Hatred of other things, that it implies a desire of, and consequently a pleasure in the Happiness of the Object beloved" (xxiv). This psychological process, which moves from desire for pleasure by the concurrence of another's will to the approval of virtue and love of the virtuous, explains the justifying reason of virtue.

The combination of his account of divine will and the above psychological process allows Gay to derive from egoistic hedonism a picture of virtue indebted to Hutcheson. In so doing, Gay grounds the explanation of virtue in the one innate practical principle in human beings: the natural desire for pleasure and aversion to pain. He makes no appeal to "*Occult Qualities.*" A single basic human desire, developing through a complex causal process, gives rise to all Hutcheson's moral affections. Yet even if Gay gains a certain explanatory high ground over Hutcheson, the plausibility of his position depends upon its ability to answer Hutcheson's many objections to egoism.

One of Hutcheson's most important objections is that moral approval cannot be explained by complex calculations of self-interest because it is immediate. Gay's response to Hutcheson, unlike that of other egoists, simply accepts moral experience as Hutcheson describes it. His response begins: "The Matter of Fact contained in this Argument is not to be contested" (xxix). How, then, can the "Matter of Fact" be made consistent with the foregoing argument? The answer comes from a different use of one of Hutcheson's key psychological doctrines, which he found in Locke and developed: the association of ideas. Recall the central role of the association of ideas in Hutcheson's moral psychology. The mind, for Hutcheson, naturally associates ideas that are regularly connected, whether the connection is natural or accidental. This capacity of the mind is necessary for both language and memory, but it also has negative side effects. Most importantly, the association of ideas has the effect of misdirecting our passions and desires and disturbing our natural harmony of affections. If, for example, through accidental circumstances, we associate theft with the public good, we will approve of theft, whether or not it actually conduces to the public good. If we associate someone else's achievements with our own failures through competition, we will disapprove of her achievements and hate her. The association of ideas is a key mechanism by which Hutcheson explains how our naturally balanced economy of passions can end up in disarray and vice.

Gay's use of the association of ideas is, in a sense, the opposite of Hutcheson's. Hutcheson begins from natural benevolence and uses the association of ideas to explain how vice disrupts our natural tendency to virtue. In this way, Hutcheson's use of the association of ideas parallels Locke's own. Locke writes that the wrong association of ideas "has such an influence, and is of so great force to set us awry in our Actions, as well Moral as Natural, Passions, Reasonings, and Notions themselves, that, perhaps, there is not any one thing that deserves more to be looked after."[41] Gay, by contrast, gives the association of ideas a positive and essential role in morality. Beginning from a desire for private pleasure, Gay uses the association of ideas to explain how we come to care about virtue and the good of others. He argues that we naturally associate those things that bring us pleasure with our happiness. This association itself has the effect of annexing pleasure to whatever is associated with our happiness. Because the virtue of others conduces to our happiness, we associate it with our happiness and annex pleasure to it. Once this association is formed, we immediately approve it, even apart from any consideration of its effects. Gay uses the example of the love of money. Money has no value except as a means of procuring other things. When we experience the power of money to bring us happiness, we naturally associate money with happiness and annex pleasure to it. This association, once it is established, no longer depends upon the power of money to bring happiness. Instead, we simply love money for its own sake, like the miser who wants money more than the goods that made money desirable in the first place. The same is true with virtue. We make the association because the virtue of others brings us happiness, but once the association is formed, we immediately take pleasure in the virtue of others. And, according to Gay, we approve whatever brings us pleasure. The approval, too, is immediate because the object that brings pleasure, once the association is formed, is the virtue itself, no matter its effects. Over time, we tend to forget that we are pleased by and approve of some things only by association. Just as, Gay thinks, we forget the source of many of our most basic ideas and convince ourselves that they are innate, so we often forget the associations that form basic affections and believe the affections to be innate (xxx). Tracing desire from its "resting places" to its ultimate source is difficult. It is much easier to see the various resting places of desire as innate and psychologically basic.

If Gay can, in this way, explain our immediate approval of virtue, he faces a more difficult challenge with a second objection. For Hutcheson, our moral approval and disapproval are always of the ends of actions, and we only approve benevolent ends. If Hutcheson is right, we would never approve of the actions—even the seemingly virtuous actions—of Gay's moral agent, who always acts for private pleasure. Because Gay takes Hutcheson's description of moral experience for granted, he must explain how benevolence is possible when all actions are motivated only by private happiness. The explanation, again, appeals to association. As we have seen, we receive pleasure from voluntary beings by the concurrence of their wills with ours. The best way to elicit this concurrence is to treat them in such a way as to earn their favor, that is, to act benevolently toward them. When, through benevolent acts, we earn the favor of others and thus procure private pleasure, we build an association between our benevolent acts and our pleasure. In this way, we annex pleasure to our own benevolent acts. This strategy allows Gay to explain how hedonistic egoists come to desire and perform benevolent acts for their own sake. Yet Hutcheson would surely object. Gay may have explained benevolent acts, but he has not explained benevolence. Insofar as the end of the act is private pleasure, as Gay thinks it must always be, no possibility exists for what Hutcheson would call benevolence.

Gay understands this concern but refuses to recognize it as a liability. To allow Hutcheson's benevolence would be to lose the ability to explain all behavior from a single innate practical principle. Gay argues that Hutcheson fails to distinguish between an inferior end and an ultimate end. Each of us has only one ultimate end: private happiness. While every action has the same ultimate end, each action also has its own inferior end. The inferior end, according to Gay, is "the thing which, if possess'd, we would not undertake that Action" (xxv). The ultimate end of study is, like all other actions, private happiness; the inferior end is knowledge. Likewise, the ultimate end of exercise is private happiness; the inferior end is health. Because the ultimate end is not chosen, Gay argues that it is not subject to moral evaluation. Against Hutcheson, he contends that the moral evaluation of action concerns only inferior ends. Any action that takes the happiness of another or the pleasure of God as an inferior end is meritorious (xxvi). The happiness of others will always be a means to the agent's private happiness, but the key question, for Gay, is the kind of means–end relationship. My action only counts as meritorious if another's happiness is my inferior end, that is, if another's happiness is that which, if it were already achieved, would make my action unnecessary. If, by contrast, my action produces another's happiness but not as its inferior end, it is not meritorious. In this latter case, the action is not undertaken on the other's account.

Christian Maurer has written of David Hartley what is also true of Gay, from whom Hartley drew inspiration:

> In the framework of Hartley's psychology, we can note a shift in attention with regard to the selfish hypothesis. Rather than explicitly insisting on self-interested analyses of all affections, he explores their psychological origin and development from the agent's experiences of pleasure and pain. In his discussion of the other-directed pleasures and pains of sympathy, for example, Hartley draws attention to their psychological origins in self-interested mechanisms.[42]

Gay is not trying to show that we always self-consciously seek our own pleasure. He wants to show how we can come to act for the sake of the happiness of others without any additional innate principles. In this sense, one might think Gay embraces a kind of self-effacing approach in which we are drawn to virtue for the sake of pleasure but eventually come to value it for its own sake. Yet to think this would be a mistake. For Gay, we must recognize our binding obligation to virtue, which is only possible when we recall that the one thing we truly want, private happiness, depends entirely on our conformity to the will of God. The fact that the pursuit of pleasure naturally leads us to acts of benevolence and the approval of virtue is an indication of divine design. Ultimately, however, the security of virtue depends on our rational commitment to our own ultimate end and the recognition of its dependence upon God. Gay's disagreement with Hutcheson is not simply about the source of our moral and public senses. It is also a substantive disagreement about our reason for being virtuous.[43]

Divine Will and Divine Authority in Gay

Let us now return to Gay's argument that God wills the happiness of all human beings. Recall that both More and Cumberland believe that God wills what Cumberland calls the *"best Effect"* because it is the greatest good. We find the same idea in Susanna Newcome: "The best End that any Being can propose is the Happiness of Beings."[44] And for Newcome, God wills this end because it is the best end. Thus while Newcome takes "fitness" to mean fitness to happiness, she does not, like Gay and Hutcheson, limit fitness to means. Ends can also be fitting, and the happiness of all beings is the most fitting end. Being perfect, God always wills the best end.

Human beings are also bound to will the best end. While Newcome believes that we should always do what makes us happy, she gives a different explanation: we should do what makes us happy because it is an indication of what God wills, and what God wills is maximal happiness and the means to it.[45] Willing our happiness is the way we will the best end. While she does not discuss divine authority, Newcome's overall view is in line with the consequentialist moral cosmology. On these points, though, Newcome differs substantially from Gay, a point Connolly also emphasizes.[46] If Newcome offers a utilitarian rendering of the consequentialist moral cosmology, Gay takes theological utilitarianism in a different direction, one that shapes the Anglican utilitarian tradition.

Gay's argument that God wills the happiness of all human beings is very different from Newcome's. The argument, which is crucial to his entire moral philosophy, is surprisingly short. He writes:

> Now, it is evident from the Nature of God, *viz.* his being infinitely happy in himself from all of Eternity, and from his Goodness manifest in his Works, that he could have no other Design in creating Mankind than *their* Happiness; and therefore he wills their Happiness; therefore the means of their Happiness: therefore that my Behavior, as far as it may be a means of the Happiness of Mankind, should be such." (xix)

Gay's argument echoes Hutcheson's argument that God is motivated by benevolence. As we saw in the previous chapter, Hutcheson lists the possible aims God could have in creation. He comes up with three: God's own happiness, universal happiness, or universal misery. The first is impossible because God's happiness does not depend on creation. The choice between the second and third is made on the basis of empirical evidence: creation appears to be designed for the happiness rather than the misery of creatures.[47]

Gay's argument has the same structure, determining God's end in creation by eliminating alternatives. Without listing the alternatives, Gay implicitly rules out the same options found in Hutcheson's list. First, Gay says, God's nature secures God's infinite happiness, meaning that God cannot be motivated to create by private happiness. God's motive must concern creatures. Next, God's works display God's goodness toward us, so God must not have created for malevolent purposes. Nothing else remains: God must will our happiness.

Though Hutcheson does not intend to embrace ethical voluntarism, his view, I argued, is very similar to it. No reason explains God's choice of universal happiness as an end. The choice stems from an arational divine appetite that, being arational, cannot be explained by God's perfection. It is, in the logic of Hutcheson's argument, no less arbitrary than an ungrounded act of divine will. Gay's brief argument invites the same interpretation. Moreover, Gay explicitly embraces legislative voluntarism, but he does not discuss ethical voluntarism. Indeed, he never raises the question of why God wills our happiness and whether God could have willed otherwise. He offers no positive reason for the content of the divine will, just a lack of alternatives. Thus while he does not explicitly embrace ethical voluntarism, Gay shows no interest in arguing for the independent rationality or goodness of the content of the divine law.[48]

In addition, Gay never raises the question of divine authority. This issue, as we have seen, causes problems for Locke. Locke explicitly states that God commands us by right and thus has authority to do so. Yet beyond his brief references to a creator's ownership of its creation, Locke gives no developed account of God's authority. There is, moreover, good reason to doubt that Locke could do so, which may be one reason that Gay does not seek to hold onto that aspect of the Lockean heritage. If God does not possess the authority to command, why then should we obey God? While Gay does not raise the question in these terms, his answer is clear: we are to obey God because God has the power to determine whether we are happy or miserable (xix). Gay makes this point explicitly, and no further reason is ever considered. Without stating it in so many words, Gay embraces the position of Hobbes: God's authority to command us is reducible to God's absolute power over us.[49]

Note that while Gay's argument that God wills universal happiness is almost identical to Hutcheson's, Gay uses the argument for a different purpose. Hutcheson, echoing More and Cumberland, uses it to show that God and human beings share the same end in order to justify God's authority to command us. God, who is not only perfectly benevolent but also omnipotent and omniscient, is best capable of directing creatures in seeking the end they are morally bound to pursue. The argument is not meant to determine *what* God commands but *why* we should obey God's commands. Gay, by contrast, shows no interest in divine authority. The point of Gay's argument is to tell us what God commands. Beyond the weakness already addressed in Hutcheson's argument, Gay's revised use of this argument faces serious problems. Let us consider three.

The first problem is found in Gay's assumption that if God creates for the sake of human happiness, God also wills that human beings act for the same end. The inference passes over a whole series of distinctions in philosophical theology. Consider, for example, the article "Will of God" in the *Encyclopédie ou Dictionnaire raisonné des sciences, des arts et des métiers*, published in Paris in 1765. The article, written by Diderot, lists the following distinctions: "the sign will and the good pleasure will, the antecedent will and the consequent will, the efficient will and the inefficient will, and the absolute will and the conditional will."[50] Such distinctions are common in technical theological writing. But no technical theology is needed to understand the problem. William Ames, in his widely read *The Marrow of Sacred Divinity* (1642), distinguishes the will of God as "powerfully effectuall, or ordaining," to which all creation is subject, from the will of God "which prescribes our duty to us."[51] To follow the former is not obedience; even devils are subject to it. Obedience is only to the latter. The importance of these distinctions is that an argument meant to establish God's intention in creation does not necessarily also establish the content of divine commands.

A second problem is this: while the fact that God wills the happiness of all does plausibly entail that God wills the means to the happiness of all, it does not entail that the best means is human beings intentionally acting for the sake of the happiness of others. It may be, as Mandeville argued so provocatively in *The Fable of the Bees*, that the greatest happiness of all requires the existence of vice. And many had argued what would, in the work of Adam Smith, become a commonplace view: that God has so designed the world that people acting solely for their own advantage could contribute to the good of society.[52] This sort of thought, which was well known in Gay's time, problematizes the inference from the thought that God creates for universal happiness to the thought that God commands us to seek universal happiness.

Finally, Gay simply asserts without explanation that if God wills us to seek the happiness of others, God will reward us for doing so and punish us for failing to do so. While the claim is not implausible, it is certainly not entailed by his premises. God, according to Gay, wills universal happiness. If, as Gay believes, the primary source of happiness or misery in any life comes after death, why would God not simply reward everyone? This is Bayle's objection against divine law with a twist. The happiness produced in the present life by the looming threat of sanctions is surely not greater than the happiness that would be produced by universal salvation. Gay's premises, then, give us at least as strong a reason to expect universal salvation as they do to fear divine sanctions.

It will be important to keep these problems with Gay's "Dissertation" in mind as we turn to the work of Edmund Law. Law seeks to revise the problematic aspects of Gay's position. Citing Gay and Paley, Colin Heydt comments:

It is worth reflecting for a moment on the idea—central to Anglican utilitarianism—that God wills our happiness: Why should we believe that God's principal goal in creation is the happiness of his creatures? Why shouldn't we think that this position overemphasizes God's benevolence (and does not acknowledge other features of God, like his vengefulness)? Or that God's ends are impenetrable to us—that God is mysterious? Or that God has lots of ends in designing humanity, only one of which is humanity's happiness? It is interesting how little effort seems to go into resolving these problems . . . This may indicate a general agreement concerning God's ends and our determination of those ends among readers of the Anglican utilitarians.[53]

Heydt's comment is perceptive. We find here an instance of what we set out to show: that which was by no means obvious is now essentially taken for granted. Yet Heydt's comment is too general. There is at least one Anglican utilitarian who took this problem seriously, Edmund Law. Indeed, if Gay's treatise is theologically thin, we must remember that it was not received in isolation. It was received as part of a larger theological treatise and was not identified as written by a separate author. Law does offer solutions to the problems in Gay's short argument. Nonetheless, while Law does dwell at length on the question of why God wills universal happiness, he is, as we will see, more committed to the view that God wills universal happiness than he is to any particular theological justification for the view, a fact which only further confirms Heydt's larger point.

In addition to addressing the three problems just named, we might also expect Law to reject Gay's reduction of God's authority to God's absolute power over us, a view that had been toxic since Hobbes first defended it. Indeed, as we saw in part I, the rejection of this view was an integral motivating factor in the development of consequentialism. Now, surprisingly enough, we find the view emerging in the consequentialist tradition in the work of a Cambridge descendant of More and Cumberland. Law, however, does not reject this view. Instead, he situates it within a larger philosophical and theological project meant to justify it. And that larger project is centered on developing a rational theology capable of resolving the issues regarding evil, a task that carries Law and the consequentialist tradition beyond the boundaries of the consequentialist moral cosmology.

Edmund Law and the Anglican Utilitarian Tradition

The first decades of the eighteenth century witnessed rapid change in the intellectual life of Cambridge University—an intellectual upheaval that mirrored the university's political upheaval. The unified Aristotelian curriculum had finally collapsed, and nothing consistent had replaced it. Edmund Law entered Cambridge during these years and became a voice for educational reform. By the time he was a young fellow at Christ's College in the 1720s, Law was at the center of an intellectual "circle" engaged in "a mass of philosophical activity."[1] John Gay was part of this circle, as were Daniel Waterland, John Clarke (not the brother of Samuel Clarke), Thomas Johnson, and Thomas Rutherforth. Newcome may have been connected to this circle as well.[2] Anglican utilitarianism, the philosophical and theological program developed by Law and his circle, would eventually fill the void left by the collapse of the Aristotelian curriculum.

The most important publication to emerge from this group was Edmund Law's *An Essay on the Origin of Evil*, a translation of William King's *De origine mali* filled with extensive notes. This text, representing the "first fruits" of the group's philosophical activity, included John Gay's treatise as a "Preliminary Dissertation."[3] Gay, an apparently reticent person, allowed Law to publish his "Dissertation," which Law was evidently eager to make public. While Gay's authorship seems to have been an "open secret" in Law's circle, the published version included no mention of his name.[4] The arrangement of the title page of the first edition, which was changed in subsequent editions, even tends to imply Law's authorship of the "Dissertation." Only twenty-seven years later, in the fourth edition of 1758, was the work attributed to Gay. The reception of Gay's "Dissertation," then, is inseparable from its position in *An Essay on the Origin of Evil* and thus from Law's larger theological project.

Edmund Law has been called "the most influential Cambridge theologian of the mid-eighteenth century."[5] On many points, Law was an original thinker, but his primary contribution to theology and ethics comes by way of synthesis. Law is a generous thinker, embracing what he takes to be true in the works of others and stitching together the contributions of many thinkers. In his biography of Law, Law's mentee William Paley writes: "The life of Dr. Law was a life of incessant reading and thought, almost entirely directed to metaphysical and religious inquiries . . . No man formed his own conclusions with greater freedom, nor treated those of others with greater candor and equity."[6] The generosity of Law's work— his tendency to foreground the ideas and contributions of others—has obscured his intellectual importance. Law's *An Essay on the Origin of Evil* is a major constructive work, which is achieved primarily through the synthesis of, and commentary on, the works of others. Law's notes are filled with citations and extensive quotations. But the two most important figures whose work Law recommends and seeks to improve upon are William King and John Gay. Indeed, as I will argue, one of the major achievements of Law's *Essay* is to integrate Gay's psychology and ethics with King's theology. For Law, King's theology corrects weaknesses in Gay's theological arguments, while Gay's treatise strengthens and completes King's psychology and ethics. In Law's work, we first discover the combination of natural theology and ethics that marks Anglican utilitarianism over the next century.

Law is for good reason considered a "convinced adherent of Locke's philosophy."[7] He was, for example, a prominent defender of Locke's view on personal identity. He also edited Locke's collected works. While Law embraced Locke's philosophy, however, he did so, as Victor Nuovo writes, "not uncritically and not without modification."[8] This is especially true in natural theology and ethics. Law is Lockean in the same mold as Gay, committed to some fundamentals but always looking to innovate. And if we look to his self-description, Law is no less a "Kingian" than a Lockean. Law borrows widely from others in forming his own views.

This chapter demonstrates the constructive work performed by Law's *An Essay on the Origin of Evil*. I show how Law uses Gay's psychology and ethics to strengthen King's theology and King's theology to reinforce Gay's psychology and ethics. I then highlight Law's own constructive contribution to lingering issues regarding God and morality. The result is an impressively comprehensive vision that addresses major issues in theodicy and ethics and forms a new synthesis beyond the consequentialist moral cosmology. Law's *Essay* is the publication that launches the Anglican Utilitarian tradition, and Law remains instrumental to its growth, especially at Cambridge, for many decades. The final section looks ahead to the spread of Anglican utilitarianism after Law's *Essay*.

The Project of Law's *An Essay on the Origin of Evil*

An Essay on the Origin of Evil is Law's first major work. As Victor Nuovo has written, "Edmund Law entered the republic of letters by responding to a crisis precipitated by Pierre Bayle."[9] Though Law was not yet born when Bayle published the *Dictionnaire*, the issue of evil remained central. The full subtitle of Law's translation reads: "Translated from the *Latin*, with large *Notes*; tending to explain and vindicate some of our Author's Principles Against the Objections of *Bayle*, *Leibniz*, and the Author of a *Philosophical Enquiry Concerning Human Liberty*; and others." Law here expresses his intention to go beyond mere translation. He wants to vindicate "some of the Author's Principles" against those who had since criticized them, including Bayle in his *Réponse aux questions d'un provincial* (1706), Leibniz in the appendix attached to *Théodicée* (1710), and Anthony Collins in his *Philosophical Enquiry* (1717). Uta Golembek, in her study of the reception of *De origine mali* across Europe, argues that Law's translation was essential to the success of King's treatise in the English-speaking world.[10]

But even the intention of vindicating King does not fully express Law's ambitions. He is doing more than contributing to the "crisis precipitated by Pierre Bayle." In the fifth edition, he adds an explanation of the genesis of the project:

> At my first entrance on the study of Philosophy, of morals in particular, it was my principal endeavour to get a competent knowledge of the several systems then in vogue, as well as of the general powers, and properties of human nature, and the rules by which they ought to be directed; taking Mr. Locke for one of my chief guides in such enquires. During some progress made in this study, and consulting such authors as might be of most service on the occasion, about the year 1723, I met with Archb. King's *Essay on the Origin of Evil*, in which there appeared to be so many useful points of Theology, comprised in something like a consistent Theory, as deserved my more particular attention, and at length determined me to pursue the like plan, and try to digest its several parts in such order, as to set the whole in a proper light; resolving that if I should ever be tempted to offer any thing to the public on those subjects, it should be done by shewing a due piece of gratitude to this my original instructor, in carefully reviewing his positions, and adding such illustrations as seemed to be more immediately requisite, instead of borrowing his materials to erect a pompous edifice in my own name, according to the usual mode of authorship.[11]

Law's project was highly ambitious in scope. He sought to provide a comprehensive "consistent theory" that would include almost every subject of natural theology and philosophy. Uta Golembek notes that Law's commentary "takes on the scope of its own work *in nuce*."[12] Even this perhaps understates Law's achievement. Law's work in the *Essay* is primarily synthetic but still highly constructive. Law does not simply follow King's views any more than he simply follows Locke's. He sometimes criticizes King and often, without making what he is doing explicit, "projects how King 'really' should have argued."[13] What differentiates Law's *Essay* from other major works of natural theology and ethics is not the scope of the work but the approach. Rather than developing his own system, Law worked by way of commentary on King's treatise—not only by adding his own ideas but also by drawing together those of many other authors, citing dozens of other texts and often quoting them at length. Law's notes were so extensive that, despite being printed in small, densely packed characters, they "increased the length of his chosen text twice over."[14]

As Law goes on to explain, his ambition even went beyond the development of theory. He contextualizes his project in a time of educational reform at Cambridge. Aristotle had recently fallen out of favor, and mathematics dominated the curriculum. The limited space left to metaphysics and ethics went to Samuel Clarke and John Locke, though the two were at odds with one another. Then, Law tells us, after about twenty years of this state of affairs, Clarke's doctrine of absolute fitness "fell into disrepute, and was generally given up."[15] This event, which Law never explains, "sunk the credit of that whole science; as to the certainty of its principles, which thereby received so great a shock, as is hardly yet recovered."[16] The result was an even greater dominance of mathematics. Law frames himself as an educational reformer, seeking to rehabilitate the Cambridge educational system by saving the study of metaphysics and ethics. As we will see, the character of theology and ethics at Cambridge in the following century suggests that Law achieved his aim.

While the format was unusual, Law intended the *Essay* to gather together the best work in theology and philosophy into a coherent and systematic whole. In the preface to the second edition, responding to the criticism that his approach is tedious, he writes:

I can only answer that the Notes and References together, were intended to point out a sort of *Compendium of Metaphysics* or speculative Divinity; by directing the Reader to a Set of true Notions on the various Subjects which our Author touched upon; and which could not be found in any one particular Book, nor collected from several, without

much Trouble and Confusions, and unnecessary reading. I chose rather
to quote the very words of the Authors than either use worse of my own
or pretend to discover what had been discovered before . . . A Writer
often does more good by shewing the Use of some of those many Volumes which we have already, than by offering new ones; tho' this be
of much less Advantage to his own character. I determin'd therefore
not to say anything myself where I could bring another conveniently
to say it for me.[17]

Law's text was widely read, especially at Cambridge, going through five
editions over the course of fifty years.[18] As a "*Compendium of Metaphysics*
or speculative Divinity," it became part of the Cambridge curriculum, a position it held for most of the eighteenth century.[19]

Law's influence on Cambridge in the eighteenth century is unmistak-
able. Nonetheless, his intellectual importance has largely been overlooked
in large part due to the form of his major work. The choice to make his
contributions in the form of commentary spread throughout hundreds
of pages of notes makes Law's arguments difficult to find and organize,
especially for modern readers. As Nuovo writes, "given the nature of his
literary productions, [Law's] philosophical scheme must be discovered
in the details. Few seem to have had the patience for this."[20] But it is not
simply a matter of patience. The work is easy to overlook because it takes
the form of a translation. The practice of doing philosophy through commentary had lost its appeal by this time in European intellectual life. The
remainder of this chapter draws out the insights scattered throughout
Law's notes, attached essays, and editorial choices.

Law's Synthesis

The question of why Law attached Gay's dissertation to the *Essay* has
received little sustained attention. Nuovo and O'Flaherty both emphasize Law's interest in completing Locke's unfinished work of developing
a moral philosophy compatible with his epistemological principles.[21] This
claim is surely true, but as an approach it treats the "Dissertation" as an
addition unrelated to the task of the *Essay*. Uta Golembek considers this
question at greater length. She agrees that Law wants to show that Lockean
morality is possible, which she sees as part of a larger effort to establish
Locke as the philosopher of English Protestantism. But she also considers the relationship between the "Dissertation" and the rest of the text.
There is, she writes, "no such compelling thematic connection between
the question of the origin of evil in the world and that of the fundamental

principles of virtue and morality that one could claim that the Preliminary Dissertation closes a gap in King's writing on theodicy." Nonetheless, even if it does not fill an obvious gap, Gay's dissertation addresses a theme that is integrally related to King's treatise:

> The question of the foundations of virtue and morality can be under-stood not only as an object of ethics in the narrower sense, but also as a side piece of theodicy. The foundation of a theonomic morality, the basis of moral laws, the question of orthopraxy, and the question of the criteria of the moral or God-pleasing way of life reach into the topic of theodicy.[22]

Golembek is right to highlight the fact that morality and theodicy are in-tegrally related, especially when morality depends, as it does for both Gay and King, on the end that God seeks in creating. Gay's moral philosophy ultimately depends on a defensible account of the benevolence of God, while King's theodicy is vulnerable if its account of morality cannot be made plausible. Even if Gay's "Dissertation" does not exactly fill a hole, it certainly does strengthen King's theodicy. Conversely, King's theodicy strengthens Gay's moral philosophy. In Law's synthetic project, the two works become mutually reinforcing.

Let us begin with how King's theology bolsters Gay's moral philoso-phy. Recall the three flaws in Gay's argument recounted in the previous chapter. First, Gay assumes that an argument meant to establish God's intention in creation also establishes what God commands us to do. But this is to conflate two different senses of "the will of God" without argu-ment. Second, Gay argues that because God wills human happiness, God wills that we intentionally promote human happiness. The inference is not valid. God might will that we do our part in serving God's aims by following a strict set of rules that, as far as we can see, has no reference to happiness. God might even will that we do our part simply by seeking our own worldly pleasure at all costs. Without a fully developed account of how each part of creation and providence fits into the realization of the greatest possible happiness, we cannot know that our role is to intention-ally promote human happiness as a whole. Third, Gay argues: God wills us to promote human happiness; therefore, God will reward or punish us based on our efforts to promote human happiness. Gay simply assumes that God's commands will be enforced with sanctions. But why make this assumption? After all, God's aim is the realization of maximal happiness. Why not reward all human beings? Given its duration, the pleasures and pains of the afterlife are far greater than the pleasures and pains of this life.

If God's end is the realization of maximal human happiness, surely God would not subject human beings to eternal misery for failing to adequately promote fleeting earthly happiness.

How does King's theology solve these problems? Gay takes God's intention in creation to also be a form of divine legislation and simply assumes the existence of sanctions. King provides an account of divine law according to which God's legislative will and the existence of sanctions are further manifestations of the same intention behind creation. He does this by reinterpreting the nature of divine law. Briefly, King's account, discussed in chapter 5, goes as follows: God creates the world to operate according to general rules that are on the whole maximally conducive to creaturely happiness. Those same rules, however, inevitably also produce some negative consequences—including negative consequences after death. Divine positive law is simply God informing us of these consequences, which God cannot eliminate without changing the world for the worse. Divine law is not, for King, an act of legislation properly speaking—that is, it is not a command grounded in God's authority. Rather, it is the revelation of how we can achieve the happiness that we want and that God wants for us. And the "sanctions" attached to divine law are not rewards and punishments. They are natural consequences. Following King, Law rejects Gay's assumption that God would ever intentionally reduce the happiness of a creature as a punishment, an assumption Bayle had rendered problematic. God, Law thinks, is merely trying to warn us of the natural effects of sin. Divine laws, he writes, "cannot properly bring us a worse state than we should have been without them."[23]

Law further develops King's view in his notes, arguing that benevolence is the whole of moral goodness. Divine goodness, by which he means benevolence, is the foundation of all other divine moral attributes, including justice:

> Thus we conceive his justice to be exerted on any being no farther than his goodness necessarily requires, in order to the making that being, or others, sensible of the heinous nature and pernicious effects of sin; and thereby bringing either it, or some others, to as great a degree of happiness as their several natures become capable of. His holiness hates and abhors all wickedness, only as the necessary consequence of it is absolute and unavoidable misery; and his veracity of faithfulness, seems to be no farther concerned for truth, than as it is connected with, and productive of the happiness of all rational beings; to provide the properest means for attaining which great end is the exercise of his wisdom.[24]

Whereas Gay, in his assumption that God will reward and punish according to obedience, seems to presuppose some notion of justice that is independent of benevolence, Law interprets all God's moral qualities as products of one and the same quality of benevolence, that is, the same desire to maximize creaturely happiness. Because perfect benevolence is the whole of God's moral perfection, the success of Law's argument requires him to show that all divine actions, including the imposition of sanctions, can be derived from divine benevolence. Law uses King's account of divine law to achieve this aim, ensuring that divine law and its "sanctions" flow immediately from God's intention to maximize happiness.

This account of divine law resolves the issue of sanctions. Negative consequences are unavoidable. God cannot reward everyone, so God uses the divine law to warn us about the natural consequences of our actions. It also addresses the issue of the different senses of divine will by providing a reason to think that God's intention in revealing the divine law is identical to God's intention in creating. No foreign standard of justice intervenes. Everything God does with respect to creation stems solely from benevolence. The issue of whether we best promote universal happiness by doing so intentionally cannot be so quickly addressed, but King provides enough detail about how God maximizes happiness to make it plausible to think that we can participate. King's theology, therefore, strengthens Gay's ethics.

The reverse is also the case: Law uses Gay's ethics to bolster King's theology. I will highlight two ways in which he does so. The first concerns the relationship between individual appetites and universal happiness. Recall that for King, animal appetites and other affections are necessary for the survival of creatures, but they are also necessarily frustrated. The frustration of natural appetite and affection is natural evil, and thus natural evil is necessary. Animal appetite and other affections, in King's understanding, are ordered to the good of the individual creature—or, in the case of the appetite to procreate, to the good of the species. With Shaftesbury, we get instead an account of natural affections as ordered to the good of larger systems. This picture, developed by Hutcheson, fits nicely with the view that God designs all things for the greatest possible happiness of all. Yet for Shaftesbury and Hutcheson, human beings naturally possess benevolent affections, a point that puts them at odds with King.

Gay provides a way to reconcile an account of the harmony of creaturely affections, designed by God for the good of all, with King's (and Locke's) view that private happiness is the end of each creature. The association of ideas, designed by God, explains how creatures concerned only with their own private happiness will, in the natural development of human affections, act benevolently and further the happiness of all. At the same time, Gay can explain much better than Hutcheson why the obligation to virtue remains even in cases in which the natural affections fail to achieve their intended end, as King's theology implies that they must sometimes do.

Second, Law relies on Gay to make King consistent with Lockean epistemology, a requirement that Law takes for granted. King had explicitly rejected the epistemology of Locke's *Essay*.[25] King argues that God aims to realize the maximal satisfaction of appetites and other affections. Our good lies in the complete satisfaction of our appetites. But in Locke's account, the good, like all other concepts, is known by experience. We do not experience ourselves as being moved by the maximal satisfaction of appetite. We are moved, rather, by pleasure. Law follows Locke in conceiving of pleasure as the only good. He writes:

> Now a *sensible* being, or one that is made capable of sensitive happiness or misery, can reasonably propose to himself no other end than the perfection of this being, i.e. The attainment of the one and avoidance of the other. He can have no reason or motive to pursue that which does not at all relate to him; and it is evident that nothing does relate to him, but that which has relation to his happiness.[26]

Sensitive beings, including human beings, can ultimately care about nothing but their own sensitive happiness or misery, that is, pleasure or pain. Gay's moral psychology allows Law to reconcile King's theological architecture with Locke's single innate practical principle.

In addition to the ways that King and Gay bolster one another, Law sees the synthesis of King and Gay as able to account for the strengths of Hutcheson's position and avoid its weakness. Law appears to have originally been attracted to Hutcheson's moral sense. In the first edition, he refers to the moral sense without explicitly tracing it back to private pleasure. But if he was originally convinced, this soon changed.[27] The strength of Hutcheson's position, as Gay recognized, lies largely in its capacity to make sense of ordinary moral experience. Indeed, the primary grounds of Hutcheson's arguments for his own position are its capacity to make sense of moral experience. Why do we intuitively admire and praise the benevolence of others, even when we do not benefit from it? Why do we care about the good of others, including distant others we encounter in the news and fictional others we encounter in literature, when their happiness can have no possible implications for our own? Hutcheson has a clear answer to these questions. Gay, as we have seen, provides a way to account for these moral experiences without giving up the view that nothing moves us but private pleasure.

Tracing all motivation back to private pleasure, for Law, has a further advantage over Hutcheson: it provides a better account of the obligation to virtue. Hutcheson explains our obligation to virtue by the fact that the moral sense approves it. Rejecting legislative voluntarism, Hutcheson argues that obligation is nothing but a "determination without regard to our own interest, to approve actions, and to perform them."[28] Even granting Hutcheson's notion of the moral sense, this account of the obligation to virtue is doubtful. For Hutcheson, action is caused by the strongest affection. In his earlier essays—those written before the first edition of Law's translation—Hutcheson gives no reason to think that we always have a decisive motive for virtue. Gay's position remedies this problem. The process of psychological association reconciles hedonistic egoism with Hutcheson's account of moral experience while also explaining why divine command provides a decisive motivation to virtue and thus an obligation.

Hutcheson, as we have seen, remedies the fault in later writings by devising a new account of the moral sense according to which its strength grows in proportion to the strength of competing motives.[29] While this solution is not entirely implausible—approval of virtuous actions does often seem to increase in proportion to the sacrifices involved in them—the result is that our strongest motive is always for virtue. Vice, then, must come from false associations and other accidental psychological processes by which we misconstrue virtue. At this point, Hutcheson's position begins to look psychologically implausible. Do we really never intentionally act viciously? Are our moral failures really only failed attempts at virtue? Gay's position can ensure the obligation to virtue without this implausible picture of motivation.

There is at least one other way in which the synthesis of Gay and King seems to take the best of Hutcheson while leaving behind its weaknesses. Gay's account of psychological association is able to explain both our benevolent desires and our approval of benevolent desires. Moreover, while these psychological features are not innate, they result from a natural process. They can be said, therefore, to be natural to us. Gay achieves this result without one of the most implausible features of Hutcheson's psychology: the lack of any internal connection between desire and natural goodness. For Hutcheson, desire is simply an inclination to some end, which could be but does not have to be related to happiness. There would be no contradiction in God giving us a desire for our own misery. Gay avoids this implication by grounding all desire in the ultimate end of private happiness.

Law on Freedom and the Goodness of God

Law's project, I have argued, is primarily synthetic, weaving together the insights of Gay and King (among many others) into a consistent account of natural theology and ethics. But Law is also an innovator himself, and the position of his *Essay* depends at key points on his unique contributions. I will consider two of the points on which Law, building on King, Hutcheson, and Gay, offers his own further insights. The first concerns the nature of human freedom. Gay makes no mention of freedom in the *Preliminary Dissertation*. D. L. Le Mahieu suggests that, at least in contrast to later writers in his own school of thought, Gay's moral psychology is rather mechanistic.[30] The features that make Gay's psychology sound mechanistic are the same as those found in Hutcheson. Neither Gay nor Hutcheson makes any appeal to a capacity to choose freely between different motives. And tellingly, David Hartley writes in the preface to *Observations on Man, His Frame, His Duty, and His Expectations* that his project began from an attempt to develop Gay's insights about association and eventually led him, against his wishes, to reject the freedom of the will.[31] Gay may very well have agreed with Locke that our freedom lies in our capacity to suspend action, but he gives us no reason to think he would have any interest in a stronger account of free will.

Law, by contrast, is quite convinced by King's view of freedom: "Our author," Law writes in the preface, "seems to be the first that has proposed the true Notion of human Liberty, and explained it consistently."[32] Law seeks to reconcile Gay's moral psychology and ethics with the existence of King's free appetite. For Law, Gay's moral psychology only concerns fixed appetites. Gay's development psychological story gives an account of the fixed appetites that explains why the satisfaction of our fixed appetites usually aligns with virtue. But Law agrees with King that only a free appetite can ultimately account for both moral responsibility and human experience and also resolve problems in theodicy. Morality and liberty, he writes, "must stand and fall together, and can, I think, only be secured effectually upon the Principles laid down by our Author."[33] He also thinks that King provides the only reasonable account of why God would choose to create free creatures.

Law understands freedom negatively as the absence of prior determination. He considers but rejects the possibility that freedom only requires the absence of external determination. His argument relies on King's distinction between active and passive powers. Passive powers are those with a fixed object. Sight spontaneously takes in light. Hunger is spontaneously moved by food. Even the intellect, according to King, is passive

in its judgments. Law argues that passive powers are free of external constraint, yet they are not free. He even assimilates Hutcheson's internal
senses (suitably reconstructed by Gay) to King's psychology. The internal
senses, too, are passive powers. The moral sense is spontaneously pleased
by benevolence, just as thirst is spontaneously pleased by drink. The same
is true of the public sense and the sense of beauty. For Law, Hutcheson
and Gay offer a purely passive psychology, because no appetite or power
chooses its object. But Law thinks that Gay's quasi-Hutchesonian passive senses, if combined with King's free appetite, provide a compelling
moral psychology.

Hutcheson, of course, disagrees that the existence of King's free appetite is desirable. He calls it capricious. Moreover, he contributes an
important objection against its possibility. In *Illustrations*, Hutcheson directly addresses King's account of freedom. In the course of his argument
that all ends are determined by instinct, he considers the possibility that
ends could be determined by "mere Election, without prepollent Desire
of one Action or End rather than its opposite," a view which sounds like
that of King.[34] But in a footnote, Hutcheson points out that this is not in
fact King's view. King, he insightfully notes, "does not represent *Freedom*
of Election, as opposite to all *Instinct* or *Desire*; but rather as arising from
the *Desire* of that *Pleasure supposed to be connected with every Election*."[35]

Law embraces Hutcheson's point. All human action has as its sole end the
attainment of pleasure and the avoidance of pain. The freedom of the will is
not a freedom from this instinctual end implanted by God. Law agrees that
an appetite that was free to pursue anything other than our happiness would
not have been a good gift of God. Freedom does not lie in the ultimate end
of the will. Private happiness is our ultimate and unchosen end. Freedom
lies, rather, in the possibility of attaining this end in different ways by taking
pleasure in whatever we choose. Moreover, Law uses Hutcheson's point as a
way to avoid the objection that free will is mere arbitrary choice. No choice
is arbitrary since we always have private happiness as our end. Summarizing notes from King, Law writes: "For the will to choose a thing in order
to please itself in the choice, is no more to choose without reason, than to
build a house in order to preserve one from the inclemency of weather, is
to act without reason."[36] One is indifferent in that one can take pleasure in
anything, but one does not choose without a reason. Rather, one always has
a reason to choose that which one knows, either by human reason or divine
revelation, to be most conducive to the attainment of pleasure. The most
conducive choice, King argues, is to will what God wills.

For Law, then, we always have a reason to choose that which is most
conducive to our happiness. Freedom does not concern ends. The im-

portance of freedom is that it allows us to reach a high degree of private happiness in the adverse circumstances that are unavoidable even given the best possible general laws. In arguing that freedom of choice is not arbitrary, Law is not disagreeing with King, but he is able to make the point more clearly and more convincingly by embracing Gay's hedonism and Hutcheson's clarification about King. Rather than treating the satisfaction of appetite as itself the point, Law argues that the sole end of every action is pleasure. The will is not a faculty that chooses ends. The will is a faculty that freely conforms itself to whatever allows one to achieve the end of private pleasure. The possibility of merit and demerit lies in this free conformity.

The second subject on which Law seeks to improve upon all previous authors is the argument for the claim that God takes the happiness of creatures as God's end. The question of why God wills the happiness of creatures is a crucial one. For More and Cumberland, the reason is simple: the greatest happiness of creatures is the best end and thus rationally binding. This account, I have argued, appears to many to be problematic after Bayle. The objective goodness of the end of the greatest happiness raises troubling questions about why God would have given us the freedom to act against the good. For similar reasons, Law wants to avoid any conception of a best end that is itself rationally or morally binding. The difficulty is to explain why God chooses this end if God lacks a decisive reason to do so. Hutcheson thinks we can know empirically that God has chosen this end, but his argument suggests that it just happens to conform to God's moral sense.[37] Gay's argument is no better. Without any argument for the rational or moral superiority of the end of the happiness of creatures, these accounts effectively collapse into ethical voluntarism: promoting the end of creaturely happiness is morally good because God chooses it, whether from instinctual desire, lack of options or arbitrary choice. And ethical voluntarism is not easily combined with the high degree of confidence (based on reason rather than revelation) about what God wills that these authors espouse. King likewise resists any moral or rational necessity in God's choice, arguing that nothing is good prior to God's free choice, but he also develops a more sophisticated argument about what is logically presupposed by God's creative volition. Law never tells us what he thinks of King's argument. The fact that he never mentions it suggests that he is not convinced. King presupposes a very robust view of logical or metaphysical entailment that would not sit well with Law's Lockean sympathies.

Law, likewise, wants an account according to which we can know that God wills the happiness of all creatures without that choice being morally or rationally binding on God (or on rational creatures apart from God's commands). After a very weak argument in the first edition, which seeks to improve Hutcheson's similarly weak argument, Law includes an additional note in the second edition that returns to the subject.[38] The second edition employs a new argument meant to show that God necessarily acts for creaturely happiness even though nothing is good prior to free divine choice.

The argument relies on a distinction between the natural and moral perfections of God.[39] Natural perfections include necessary existence, eternity, omnipotence, omniscience, and so on. Moral perfections concern God's will and actions. Law thinks that God's existence and natural perfections can be proved simply from the existence of finite creatures.[40] He does not think, however, that God's moral perfections are part of God's nature. Nevertheless, he seeks to show that if God creates, God does so in a morally perfect way. According to Law, God's will is nothing more than God's self-determination, which means that God always acts in a manner consistent with God's nature, that is, with God's natural perfections. Acting in conformity with the divine nature entails that if God chooses to create, God will communicate God's own perfections to creatures. Happiness is one of God's natural perfections and will thus be communicated. The other perfections, which will also be communicated, are not the same as happiness. Yet they are, Law argues, "the Foundation of *Happiness* to the Being possess'd of them, and therefore when communicated to other Beings, they must produce that Happiness, which is founded in and naturally results from them."[41] Everything God communicates, then, is also the communication of happiness. Therefore, when God creates, God will do so in a manner that communicates happiness. This is not to say that the communication of happiness is morally good before God chooses it. It is just to say that God, if God freely chooses to act *ad extra*, necessarily communicates happiness. God's moral perfection is established on these grounds. Law writes:

> The *voluntary* Communication of the Divine Happiness by the free exercise of every such Perfection as is productive of it, will constitute all those which we call moral Attributes: a voluntary, designed Production of Happiness or Misery being all that to me seems required to make any action *Moral* in God or Man. And that an absolutely powerful, intelligent, free and happy Being, intending to communicate some degree of these Perfections, needs no other *Objective Rule* than what is contain'd in these Perfections themselves; that so long as he is pleased to exercise them in pursuance of this general intent, he can never do amiss or go wrong in the exercise of them, tho' there be ten thousand equal ways

of exercising them, and consequently no objective Rule to direct which
he shall actually choose: Because perfect Knowledge, Power and Happiness *can never produce any thing in the main repugnant to Knowledge,
Power and Happiness,* i.e. to *themselves.* (312–13n53)

God requires no rule beyond God's nature to voluntarily communicate
happiness. And once God takes the universal happiness of creatures as
God's end—if this is an accurate way of describing what God does[42]—
God will approve of and reward us for joining God in seeking this end.
Seeking universal happiness becomes morally good.

Law goes on to argue that God not only communicates happiness but
does so maximally. Defending his position against the argument, commonly raised against ethical voluntarism, that his view undermines any
meaningful sense in which God can be called good, Law argues:

> This I apprehend to be far from subverting the ground of Morality, or
> making it ever equally agreeable to the Deity to have acted for no End
> at all, or for a bad one, since it supposes that he was always determin'd
> to pursue the very best End, and by the best means, (wherever there
> was room for *better* and *worse*) tho' *why* he was so determin'd I cannot
> pretend to shew; and in what sense this was *better* and *fitter* for him who
> could receive no addition of Happiness from it, I must confess I do not
> understand. (311–12n53)

Law echoes Cumberland's language, arguing that God is determined to
pursue the "very best End," by which he means maximal creaturely happiness. At the same time, he confesses not knowing why God does so. Law
makes this point frequently. We do not know *why* God acts benevolently
toward us: "Why he is good, or inclined to act in this manner, we know
not" (307n53). Here we see more clearly the payout of Law's argument.
We can explain God's end by appealing to God's nature, but we cannot
give a *reason* for God's choice. A reason to act would have to connect the
act to God's happiness, and God requires nothing to be perfectly happy.
Nothing, therefore, is morally or rationally required of God. God's will is
the ultimate and undetermined source of all morality. Nonetheless, we
can have confidence—even if, as Law admits, it is finally only probable
and not certain—that God wills the happiness of creation, since creating
is nothing other than communicating God's perfections, all of which are
or are conducive to happiness.[43]

As a result, Law can hold that God wills the happiness of all creatures
without presupposing that God has a moral reason to do so. All moral

reasons to seek the happiness of creatures are subsequent to God's will. Our reason to do so is that our private happiness depends upon the will of God, which intends the happiness of all creatures. Law thus holds both legislative and ethical voluntarism. To the objection that his view entails that virtue is no better than vice prior to God's free choice, Law expresses no concern: "there is no harm in it."[44] Still, Law holds that if God chooses to create, God cannot do other than communicate happiness.

Strikingly, Law displays little concern to protect the freedom or sovereignty of God. This point highlights the fact that Law's reasons for embracing ethical voluntarism are quite different from those of earlier ethical voluntarists. Ethical voluntarism is generally understood to have its roots in concerns about divine freedom and omnipotence.[45] If God is constrained by independent moral considerations, then God, being morally perfect, may be the most constrained of all agents. Ethical voluntarism protects divine freedom and omnipotence against any limitations imposed by other divine perfections. God, for the ethical voluntarists, could have made a different world or imposed a different law.

Law's motives are quite different. One can hardly imagine Law celebrating the freedom of God to command malevolence or hatred. Law does everything he can (short of rejecting ethical voluntarism) to argue that God maximally communicates happiness. He even uses the language of God being "determin'd to pursue the very best End" in the quotation above. And while, as an ethical voluntarist, Law could have dismissed many of Bayle's arguments about evil, contending that whatever God wills is good, Law instead spends hundreds of pages defending divine benevolence. In fact, Law, as best as I can tell, is motivated to hold onto ethical voluntarism, despite his commitment to the view that God is perfectly benevolent, precisely in order to better maintain the benevolence of God in the face of evil. To say that maximizing the happiness of creatures is morally best independent of God's will would, Law believes, mean that human beings, too, are morally bound by the same end. If there is by nature a morally best end, human freedom becomes a problematic feature of creation that potentially undermines the benevolence of God. Throughout part II, we saw those responding to Bayle abandon traditional notions of freedom for the sake of theodicy. It is for this reason that Law works so hard to hold together the view that maximizing creaturely happiness is not morally good before God chooses it with the view that God necessarily chooses it.

Law's argument is not without problems. Most pressingly, the argument does not establish that God intends to communicate happiness, only that God does in fact communicate happiness. Consider my recent foray into building simple wooden furniture. My creations reflect aspects of my character such as my lack of attention to detail. It does not follow that my aim is to make pieces that lack attention to detail. My aims are, for example, to make shelves for storage and desks for my kids to do their work when school goes virtual. Likewise, the fact that anything God makes will necessarily possess some of God's perfections does not entail that communicating those perfections is God's aim—and it certainly does not entail that communicating one of those perfections, happiness, is God's overriding end. Communicating perfections could be a means to an end or even just a byproduct. Even if Law is right that God cannot create without communicating God's perfections, all of which are or are conducive to happiness, he has not established that creaturely happiness is God's ultimate end. And without establishing God's ultimate end, he cannot be certain that God maximizes creaturely happiness or intends for us to do the same. Even so, Law's argument is a creative attempt to patch an argumentative weakness inherited from his sources.

Let us note, finally, a problem lingering in Law's synthesis of King and Gay, which only comes to light later. Gay claims that God "could have no other Design in creating Mankind than *their* Happiness."[46] From here, he argues that we ought to judge all human action by its promotion of this end. Yet even if God's design "in creating Mankind" is human happiness, God's larger aim may be something beyond human happiness. By placing Gay's ethics in the context of King's theology, Law must show how Gay's ethics is compatible with the view that God's aim is not just human happiness but the greatest happiness of all creatures, some of which are higher than humans. In *Free Inquiry into the Nature and Origin of Evil* (1756), Soame Jenyns is only elaborating on possibilities latent in King's work when he argues that human suffering may be necessary for the happiness of higher creatures, just as the suffering of nonrational animals is necessary for our happiness.[47] When Gay's ethics is combined with King's theology, virtue should consist not of promoting human happiness alone but of promoting the happiness of all creatures. While this result could be embraced without contradiction, Law does not seem to recognize it.[48] Law's definition of virtue, which would be repeated verbatim by William Paley, is *"the doing good to mankind, in obedience to the will of God, and for the sake of everlasting happiness."*[49] There is, as far as I can tell, no justification for Law's restriction of virtue to doing good "to mankind" rather than doing good to all creatures.[50]

This problem in Law's thought is highlighted by the work of another member of Law's circle, Thomas Rutherforth's *An Essay on the Nature and Obligations of Virtue* (1744). Rutherforth affirms without hesitation that

God created the world with the sole aim of communicating happiness to creatures, a fact which, he says, has been adequately proved "with great industry and sagacity" by others.[51] And this fact, he sees, causes a problem for Gay's argument. It is true, he writes, that God has no other aim in creating mankind than their happiness. Then he adds:

> But why should you stop here? why will you limit our duty within the bounds of our own species, when your own principles will extend it much farther? . . . For if you prove from God's having worked for the good of man, that he could have no design in creating us but our happiness; you may prove, by the same argument, that he could have no design but the happiness of brutes in creating them: and then whether you will agree to call the behaviour, which tends to prevent their misery and to promote their happiness, by the name of *virtue* or not, yet by the same sort of inference you must conclude that God requires this behaviour of us and will reward us for it. Why is not it therefore as criminal to warm ourselves with *the fleece of our sheep* as with *the fleece of the fatherless?*[52]

Rutherforth sees the problem clearly. One seemingly easy solution would be to accept that we do have duties to all creatures and that our notion of virtue ought to be expanded. This solution would present some real problems. For example, significant revision would be required to Gay's argument that the process of association, which is a product of divine providential design, provides motives to be virtuous and to approve virtue in others. Nothing in Gay's current version can account for the wider set of affections needed for an expanded picture of virtue. Still, because God's will and God's will alone determines our obligations, Anglican utilitarianism is perfectly consistent with the expansion of virtue to include promoting the happiness of all creatures. Rutherforth rejects this option, arguing that God has not tied our happiness to our treatment of non-human creatures.[53] Law, as far as I know, never addresses the issue, which remains a lingering problem for the synthesis of King and Gay.

The Tradition of Anglican Utilitarianism

Law's *Essay* may have been, as John Stephens writes, the "first fruits" of the wave of philosophical activity at Cambridge in the 1720s and 1730s, but it was followed by many other publications.[54] Thomas Johnson published two works on natural religion and ethics in the 1730s. His 1736 work *A Summary of Natural Religion*, an explicit attempt to systematize

Law's work in the *Essay*, was the first work to develop Gay and Law's ideas into an account of the various duties of the natural law in the tradition of Pufendorf. In 1744, Thomas Rutherforth developed very similar ideas in a slightly different direction, publishing *An Essay on the Nature and Obligations of Virtue*. In 1749, David Hartley, a fellow at Cambridge during the same period as Law and Gay, published his influential two-volume work *Observations on Man, His Frame, His Duty, and His Expectations*. Inspired by Gay's "Dissertation," Hartley develops a sophisticated account of human psychology as well as a detailed natural theology and ethics. Hartley, who was widely read in and beyond Britain, became an important source for the dissemination of Anglican utilitarian ideas. Abraham Tucker, the most important contributor to the tradition not to be associated with Cambridge, published the first two volumes of *The Light of Nature Pursued* in 1668 under the pseudonym Edward Search. With Tucker, the focus turns increasingly to the practical task: putting Anglican utilitarian ideas about association and utility to work in order to shape virtuous citizens.[55]

Meanwhile, Anglican utilitarianism grew particularly pervasive at Cambridge. In 1745, Rutherforth was named the prestigious Regius Professor of Divinity. In 1764, Law was named the similarly prestigious Knightbridge Professor of Moral Theology and Casuistical Divinity. Law's *Essay* was adopted as a textbook at Cambridge, a position it held for most of the eighteenth century. Law's increasingly powerful positions in both the university and church granted him the power to support and elevate those with similar views. No one was more important in this regard than William Paley. Law was Paley's "patron and mentor," securing his major appointments at the university and in the church and encouraging the publication of his work.[56] Paley, in turn, adopted and developed Law's ideas, dedicated his major work in ethics to Law, and wrote Law's biography.

The most significant event in the further development and dissemination of the Anglican utilitarian tradition was no doubt the publication in 1785 of William Paley's *The Principles of Moral and Political Philosophy*. Paley's *Principles* was a revision of a set of lectures on the same topic that he gave at Cambridge in the 1770s. Law was instrumental in pushing Paley to publish them. When Law was putting together the fifth edition of his *Essay* in 1781, he even expressed the wish to his son that Paley's *Principles* would be published simultaneously with his fifth edition.[57] When Paley's book was eventually published in 1785, it quickly became one of the most widely read texts in England and the United States. It went through fifteen editions in Paley's lifetime, not counting the numerous abridgments and student primers. In England, *Principles* was for over a half century "cited by writers and politicians as an unrivalled authority on a host of moral and political questions." [58] And across the Atlantic, Paley's works were "as well known in American colleges as were the readers and spellers of William McGuffrey and Noah Webster in the elementary schools."[59]

Paley's *Principles* functioned primarily to popularize the work of the Anglican utilitarians. Rather than addressing the areas of dispute or ongoing uncertainty, Paley presents the tradition in its most straightforward and compelling light. This is not to say, however, that Paley makes no substantive contributions. Not only does Paley further develop the more practical side of the tradition, which goes beyond argumentation and tries to form readers in virtue; he also develops Anglican utilitarianism into a fully fledged political program, crafting original arguments about many of the most pressing political controversies of the day.

Unsurprisingly, Paley's intellectual influence was especially notable at Cambridge. *Principles* was adopted as a textbook at Cambridge just two years after its publication—the same year as Edmund Law's death—and it remained mandatory reading for undergraduates until the 1840s.[60] In 1852, over 120 years after the publication of the first edition of Law's *Essay*, Law's distant successor as Knightbridge Professor, William Whewell, wrote that the position first developed by Gay and Law was "*the* Scheme of morality which has been taught in this University for the last century."[61]

Shortly after the publication of Paley's *Principles*, the secular, reformist version of utilitarianism began its career in England. In 1789, Jeremy Bentham published *An Introduction to the Principles of Morals and Legislation*. The evidence suggests that Bentham developed his views primarily from reading the French *philosophes* and without knowledge of the writings of Gay, Law, Johnson, Rutherforth, and Tucker. He was even reportedly concerned—almost comically in retrospect—that Paley had plagiarized the principle of utility, which he believed himself to have invented.[62] Bentham may indeed have "invented" utilitarianism without reading the earlier sources, but Albee is surely right that "utilitarianism had been so distinctly in the air for more than a generation before he published his *Principles of Morals and Legislation* that he could not possibly have failed very substantially to profit by the fact."[63]

Despite the current stature of Bentham's *Principles of Morals and Legislation*, the book was notoriously unsuccessful. While Bentham was recognized for his work on politics and legislation, his book "was almost completely ignored for decades."[64] It was not reprinted until the 1820s. Well into the nineteenth century, the critics of utilitarianism targeted Paley as its major proponent, not Bentham.[65] It was not until the 1830s that John Stuart Mill and William Whewell began to rehabilitate the works of

Bentham.[66] The currently popular story of Jeremy Bentham is a creation of the mid-nineteenth century.

So many of the considerations that led to the development of Anglican utilitarianism are theological: concerns about divine ends in creation, about evil, about human freedom, about divine morality and its relation to human morality. When utilitarianism severs its theological roots, these motivating concerns largely disappear. The philosophical and rhetorical grounds of the debate surrounding utilitarianism shift. New arguments become prominent, and new objections are raised. The consequentialism-deontology debate of today emerges from this context.

The story of "classical" utilitarianism is beyond the scope of this book. It has been told elsewhere.[67] In the conclusion, though, I discuss problems that arise when utilitarianism is uprooted from its theological context and treated as a self-standing, secular moral theory. Many of the standard objections to utilitarianism, I argue, arise precisely due to the severing of its theological roots. One way to address the objections is to return to a theological version of utilitarianism. I argue that a better way forward is to rethink the early modern innovations regarding goods, ends, agency, and causation that led to utilitarianism in the first place.

Epilogue to Part III

In 1736, Thomas Johnson, a member of Law's circle at Cambridge, published a short treatise called *A Summary of Natural Religion*. The treatise undertakes two main tasks: first, to establish the existence and attributes of God; second, to explain and justify the duties of the natural law. These tasks, Johnson notes in the preface, have been performed numerous times, including by very well-known thinkers such as Pufendorf, Thomasius, and Wilkins. Why, then, contribute another version? Johnson explains:

> Since them [Pufendorf and others] a very ingenious Writer (whom the Reader will find I have been much indebted to in the course of these papers) has thrown a great deal of Light on several very important and nice Points which fall within the compass of our Enquiry: It were to be wish'd that He had given us a set Treatise on the Subject, rather than interspersed his Notions here and there occasionally, or thrown them into a Corner where scarce any body will think of looking for them. Had he done so, my Labours might well have been spared, as the World would have been furnish'd with a much better Treatise on the Subject before us, than I can pretend to give them.[1]

Johnson's *Summary* is an attempt to organize Law's views into a series of axioms, propositions, and corollaries, arranged logically and sometimes deductively. Johnson follows Law's argument for the existence and natural perfections of God. He also recites Law's argument for God's moral goodness, although, following the pattern we have noted, he, too, invents a new argument to make the case stronger.[2] And Johnson agrees with Law that God's moral goodness is simply benevolence. All other moral perfections—wisdom, justice, holiness, veracity, faithfulness—are nothing more than the effects of God's benevolence: "so many emanations from the same source, diversified indeed by the several channels through which they flow, but not distinct attributes existing apart from or counter to his goodness."[3]

These arguments, for Johnson, establish that God wills universal happiness. As our private happiness depends entirely on the will of God, we are obligated by the will of God to act for universal happiness. From this foundation, Johnson derives the content of the natural law—that is, he derives our moral duties. He writes, "Those propositions, which express what particular actions will introduce the greatest moment of happiness into human life, are the true laws of human nature."[4] Johnson goes on to discuss the standard topics of treatises on the natural law: duties of government and citizens, duties of spouses, duties of parents and children, duties of masters and servants, and duties to God. The arguments are utilitarian and the conclusions broadly Lockean.

Johnson is the first to systematize Law's principles into the form of a standard treatise on the contents of the natural law. Having covered the standard topics, Johnson ends his *Summary* with a chapter called "Containing Some General Rules of Action." Here he abstracts from particular relationships and realms of life and considers general moral principles. The chapter, consisting of thirteen axioms and several corollaries, is quite reminiscent of the axioms of Henry More's *Enchiridion ethicum*. More's axioms, I argued in chapter 2, were the first articulation of consequentialist moral rationality. The appearance of a set of axioms among the Anglican utilitarians invites an opportunity to step back and consider how the theological consequentialist tradition has changed.

I noted in chapter 2 that More's first axiom is quite vague in its definition of the good: "Good is that which is grateful, pleasant, and congruous to any Being, which hath Life and Perception, or that contributes in any degree to the preservation of it."[5] By Johnson's time, More's definition appears to be conflating the two major alternatives: the good as defined by that which is pleasurable and the good as defined by the objective fitness of one thing to another. Both sides of the debate tend to agree that the fitting is also that which produces pleasure, but the question is which quality makes an act good. Johnson, together with all the consequentialists of his time, answers that it is the pleasure. Objective fitness is associated with Samuel Clarke's rationalism, which we would now call deontological. Beyond this difference, however, More and Johnson use very similar language about the good. It can, for both, be calculated as the product of weight or intensity and duration. For both, the value of a good does not depend on its temporal distance from the present. Probabilistic considerations have a more important role in Johnson, though they are present also in More. Moreover, both agree that the good of every person ought to be part of our consideration. Johnson uses Hutcheson's language of "the moment of good" to make the point. The moment of good of any action, he writes, "is in a compound Ratio of the degrees of Good in the Action and the number of Enjoyers."[6] This is a more formal way of expressing the idea that More expressed through examples (i.e., if it is good for one person to live happily, it is twice as good for two people to do so, three times as good for three people, and so on).[7]

There are, of course, differences between the two sets of axioms. Johnson's axioms are in several ways more sophisticated. He not only provides a fuller analysis of the role of probability but also considers our relations to other persons and the effects of our actions on the capacity of others to do good. In addition, Johnson provides a clear decision procedure for cases in which we must choose one person's happiness over another, prioritizing one's relations and people of moral importance.

The overall resemblance is striking, but this should not lure us into thinking that little has changed. The most important difference between More and Johnson is not found in the content or logic of the axioms. It is found, rather, in the nature and function of the axioms. For More, the axioms are immutable, self-evident principles of practical reason. All rational beings, both divine and human, are bound to act according to them. For Johnson, the axioms are the principles of divine will. They are not self-evident or rationally or morally binding. God acts according to them not because of their truth or inherent goodness but, as far as we can understand, because God's natural perfections preclude God from acting in any other way. Our confidence that God acts according to these principles is enhanced by the structure of creation. Ultimately, though, we do not know why God acts according to them. And lacking God's natural perfections, we do not naturally act in the same way as God. Rather, we act according to the principle that God, seeking to maximize our happiness, implanted in us, namely, a desire for private happiness. The axioms only bind us because God wills them, and we, in order to attain private happiness, must please God.

In Johnson's view, our reasons for acting on the axioms are not the same as God's. Johnson makes this point one of his central arguments against the rationalist alternative of Clarke—an argument that, we can add, could just as easily be used against More. He writes:

> But, were it true that [the eternal relations of things] were such a Rule to the Deity, does it therefore follow, that the same Rules of acting are common to us with him? This would be either to raise human Nature to the same Eminence with the Divine, or to bring down the Divine

Nature to a Level with ours. But the Truth is, God being absolutely
Perfect, his Creatures, however numerous they be, can neither augment
nor lessen his Happiness; and therefore what may be a Rule of Action to
him, cannot be so to Men, who have not like him their Happiness from
within . . . These Gentlemen therefore, who pretend that the same Reasons which determine the Deity to command, also oblige us to obey,
would do well to let us know why we are obliged to act in concert with
him: for, as the Matter stands above, the Case betwixt us and the Deity
will not admit of any Parallel.[8]

Johnson finds it inconceivable to imagine that God and human beings act
according to the same principles. The differences between God and us, especially regarding the sources of happiness, are too great for a shared principle of action. For Johnson, the outcomes of divine goodness and human
virtue are the same—both promote universal happiness—but the reason
God promotes universal happiness must be different from the reason we
do. We must always act for our private happiness. God, being necessarily happy, need not do so. In stark contrast to More, Johnson argues that
God's reason for imposing the law on us, whatever it is, "is no Ground or
Reason for our Obedience."[9] Despite the similar axioms, Johnson is a long
way from the consequentialist moral cosmology.

*****

In part I, I introduced Henry More's innovations in part by contrasting
More's view with that of his friend and colleague Ralph Cudworth. Both
More and Cudworth argue that the good is eternal, immutable, and independent of the divine will (though not, of course, of the divine nature).
God's very center is goodness, and God's knowledge and power operate
according to divine goodness. Both also make an analogy between God
and human beings on this point. Human beings, like God, have the love of
goodness at their center. But More and Cudworth disagree about how to
conceive the human analogy. For Cudworth, following the Platonic tradition, our love of the good is different from God's. God's is not a "love of
indigent desire, but a love of overflowing fulness and redundancy, communicating itself." Human beings, by contrast, "by reason of the *penia* which
is in them, are in continual inquest, restless desire, and search, always pursuing a scent of good before them and hunting after it."[10] Because God has
no need, God's relation to the good is to overflow with it, communicating
it endlessly to creatures. We, on the other hand, are needy and driven by
our lack to an erotic pursuit of unity with the good.

More breaks with this standard Platonic picture. For More, our love of the good is the same as God's. More defends this view by positing the existence of a divine faculty in our souls, a faculty by which we take pleasure in conforming to the same eternal principles that guide divine action. More thus creates a single moral standard for both God and human beings—and thereby, in his view, defeats ethical voluntarism. His revised picture of the relationship between God and human beings, together with his consequentialist conception of how we are to pursue the good, gives rise to a new teleological moral cosmology with a new account of the end of moral action and a new justification of divine authority: the consequentialist moral cosmology. This view, as we have seen, struggled with problems regarding the nature and origin of evil. Over the course of part II, I noted indications of trouble. Here, in the works of Johnson, following Law, we see an explicit rejection of More's key move. The Anglican utilitarians deny that God and rational creatures have the same moral reasons or moral ends.

In rejecting More's key move, the Anglican utilitarians echo Cudworth. It is important to recognize, though, that they do not return to Cudworth's view about the moral relationship between God and human beings. Though Cudworth does not think that God and human beings act according to the same principles, he does think that God and human beings act for the sake of the same goodness, namely, God's own goodness. On this point, Cudworth agrees with Aquinas and Ames. For Cudworth, God and creatures share an ultimate object of love (and thus an end) but, due to their different relationships to it, act differently for the sake of it. A kind of moral community between God and rational creatures can be found in a shared love of God's goodness, though it is not a community founded on shared moral principles of action. When the Anglican utilitarians reject shared principles of action, they, unlike Cudworth, reject any notion of moral community between God and creatures. Johnson even denies that we can attributes virtue to God, for "the Manner, Reasons, Motives, &c. of God's Actions must be as different from those of Men as Heaven is from Earth."[11] For Law and his circle, we ought to obey God because of God's absolute power.

Since More's initial articulation of the consequentialist moral cosmology, the intellectual concerns and pressing questions had changed. More's reason for asserting the existence of immutable moral principles shared by God and human beings was to combat ethical voluntarist views according to which arbitrary divine will is the source of all morality. In rejecting the existence of such principles, the Anglican utilitarians are not seeking to defend absolute and arbitrary divine power. Indeed, the entire project of

King's *Essay*, which is the foundation of Law's work, is to defend God's perfect moral goodness by consequentialist standards. If not to elevate God's absolute power even over morality, why reject moral community between God and creatures?

There are a number of reasons, including shifting standards of what counts as a successful explanation and the increasingly widening gap between reason and affection in the early eighteenth century. Yet none of these reasons necessitates rejecting shared divine-human moral principles. Samuel Clarke and Thomas Balguy, the chief targets of the Anglican utilitarians, maintained that God and rational creatures share the same moral principles determined by the eternal fittingness of things. Notably, non-consequentialists maintain shared divine-human moral principles, while consequentialists reject them.[12] The reason that I have highlighted is that God's moral goodness, when understood in consequentialist terms, is best secured against Bayle's critiques by abandoning the idea that God and rational creatures are subject to eternal moral truths.[13]

Strikingly, the Anglican utilitarians do not reject moral community with God in order to elevate God above human moral standards, which is how Schneewind characterizes ethical voluntarism. They are deeply concerned with proving that God is perfectly benevolent and thus meets utilitarian moral standards. They give up on divine-human moral community in large part in order to protect divine benevolence. Indeed, their arguments aside, it is quite clear that they take for granted that moral goodness consists of promoting universal happiness and that God must do so perfectly. If promoting universal happiness were not good until God freely chose to condition our happiness on it, as they explicitly affirm, then one would expect them to be firmly convinced by a foundational, nonmoral argument that establishes the content of God's will. Getting this point wrong, after all, would be getting morality as a whole wrong. As it turns out, we find weak and constantly shifting arguments in support of their view that God promotes universal happiness and commands us to do the same. Their commitment to the moral goodness of promoting universal happiness is certainly more basic than any proof to support it.

It is perhaps better—though somewhat misleading—to say that the Anglican utilitarians reject divine-human moral community not by elevating God above morality but by morally diminishing human beings. God is capable of acting solely for the happiness of others, but we are not. And we are not capable of it because a perfectly benevolent God would not burden us with that capacity. Human beings, in the Anglican utilitarian tradition, are hedonistic egoists. All appearances to the contrary—for example, the appearance of sacrificial love—are explained either by the association of ideas that annexes pleasure to benevolent acts or by the motivational power of postmortem sanctions. Both egoism and hedonism are unexpected occurrences with little pedigree in the Christian theological and moral tradition. If egoism has any place, it is usually a result of original sin, not a basic feature of human nature. The strangeness of finding these views in texts in Christian ethics was one of the curiosities that first sparked my interest in these figures. Unexpected as their views are, though, they make good sense within the larger theological context, especially given the approach to theodicy.

*****

In an important sense, Law's *An Essay on the Origin of Evil* marks an endpoint in the tradition of the consequentialist moral cosmology. Yet in another and perhaps more profound sense, it simply marks one further development in the legacy of More and Cumberland. Consequentialist moral rationality not only continues but thrives. Indeed, I have suggested that it is effectively axiomatic for Gay, Law, and Johnson. The ever-shifting arguments in support of the idea that God wills us to promote universal happiness are attempts to justify what appears transparently true. Law's extensive citations of others who support the same view of divine morality are good evidence that the Anglican utilitarians were not alone in this view.[14] And despite the fact that the Anglican utilitarians reject moral community between God and creatures, they continue to believe that rational creatures, in conformity to the will of God, should maximize universal happiness.

A productivist picture of agency, moreover, is taken for granted, a fact which is clear from the list of ends that Hutcheson, Gay, and Law believe God might seek. That God could be God's own end is never even considered. That God's glory might be God's end in some sense other than as a state of affairs to be realized in creation is likewise absent. Indeed, any notion of teleology that is not productivist is almost entirely eclipsed. As a result, the only live alternatives to consequentialism beyond egoism are non-teleological. Moreover, the notion that virtue is causally productive of universal happiness drives new inquiries into the causal relationships between human actions and social outcomes, inquiries that presuppose and further reinforce Cumberland's views about the moral significance of efficient causality. For all of these reasons, the consequentialist moral cosmology's failure marks not the end but simply one further stage of consequentialism's long and evolving historical influence.

Conclusion

Consequentialism, I have argued, has its roots in seventeenth-century debates about divine ethics and its relationship to human ethics. Consequentialist moral rationality was invented to serve as an innovative, rational approach to ethics—divine and human—in opposition to ethical voluntarism. Seeking to move beyond scholastic Aristotelian ethics, which was becoming increasingly problematic for philosophical elites, Henry More and Richard Cumberland reached for newly ascendant paradigms of thought, the geometric and the mechanistic, and developed a new picture of moral rationality. More and Cumberland, moreover, argued that both God and rational creatures ought to conform to the same consequentialist standards. In doing so, they developed a larger theological and ethical view, the consequentialist moral cosmology, which was similar to but also importantly different from the theocentric moral cosmology it displaced. According to this new view, God and all creatures ought to pursue the realization of maximal goodness in creation. Their ultimate end is, in Cumberland's terminology, the "*best Effect.*"

The consequentialist moral cosmology, despite its widespread influence, quickly came under substantial pressure due to its difficulty accounting for the existence and extent of evil in the world. This pressure, I argued in parts II and III, ultimately led to its demise. But the end of the consequentialist moral cosmology was by no means the end of consequentialist moral rationality. Indeed, over the course of the century following the major works of More and Cumberland, consequentialist moral rationality was increasingly taken for granted by many ethicists. In the works of Gay, Law, Johnson, and Rutherforth, the arguments meant to support consequentialist conclusions are clearly constructed to justify what appears evident prior to justification.

One of the more striking features of the narrative of this book is how quickly ideas move from innovative conceptual developments to commonplaces requiring little or no argument. Consequentialist moral rationality—with its picture of goods, ends, agency, and causation— follows this trajectory, as does the assumption that God must be a perfect consequentialist. The view that God's end in creation is to maximize uni-versal happiness became widespread in Anglophone theology and ethics. While this view does not itself entail that human morality must take the same form—Joseph Butler argues in his *Dissertation upon the Nature of Virtue* that God maximizing happiness does not entail that we should—it is natural to think that our moral actions ought to reflect God's, even if our moral reasons do not.

Defenders of non-consequentialist principles for human moral-ity often end up with explanations of human morality that look rule consequentialist—since our moral principles must ultimately be condu-cive to God's ends—even though they are not. We may be obligated by a moral sense, conscience, or divine commands, but the reason God has created these obligations must ultimately be traced back to God's desire for universal happiness. Adam Smith, for example, argues that God "is determined, by his own unalterable perfections, to maintain in [the uni-verse], the greatest possible quantity of happiness." He does not believe that human beings ought to do the same: "The administration of the great system of the universe, however, the care of the universal happiness of all rational and sensible beings, is the business of God and not of man. To man is allotted a much humbler department, but one much more suitable to the weakness of his powers, and to the narrowness of his comprehen-sion."[1] Even still, Smith argues repeatedly that maintaining our "humbler department" contributes to universal happiness.

I am not suggesting that Butler and Smith are consequentialists or that they embrace the consequentialist moral cosmology. Neither believes that we are independently bound to realize maximal goodness or that God's authority lies in God's capacity to guide us to this end. I am only calling attention to the widespread influence of the idea that God maximizes hap-piness and the effect it has, even for non-consequentialists. Jacob Viner was not exaggerating when he wrote, "There was, nevertheless, an impor-tant measure of utilitarianism of some species in practically all of British eighteenth-century moral philosophy."[2]

It is not surprising, then, that nineteenth-century British moral philoso-phy, as Schneewind writes, "centred on the attempt to determine whether or not there is a rational basis for setting moral limits to the principle of utility."[3] This question became especially pressing as the secular version of utilitarianism became predominant over the course of the nineteenth century. Anglican utilitarianism appealed to divine providence to explain the link between conventional standards of virtue and the promotion of universal happiness. Anglican utilitarianism was occasionally revisionary but usually sought to explain widely shared moral judgments by reference to utility. Without divine providence, secular utilitarianism could be far more revisionary and reform-oriented, sometimes placing judgments about utility directly at odds with ordinary morality. The more utilitarianism was seen as an alternative to commonsense morality rather than an explanation of it, the more attractive limits to the principle of utility became.

The contemporary Anglophone moral conversation is no longer that of the nineteenth century. Yet if the popularity of trolleyology is any indication, questions about the limits of consequentialist moral rationality remain among our most puzzling moral issues. In this book, I have sought to open up some distance from these questions by attending to the history in which consequentialist moral rationality was invented and through which it came to have such a prominent place in moral reasoning. How can this history help us think better about consequentialism today?

* * * * *

Contemporary debates about consequentialism look somewhat different when seen in light of consequentialism's theological history. In particular, the history sheds new light on common critiques—both long-standing and more recent—of consequentialism. Because utilitarianism has for several centuries been the dominant form of consequentialism, I will focus on the major critiques of utilitarianism, many but not all of which apply to consequentialism more generally. Most of the standard critiques of utilitarianism, I will argue, arise precisely from the fact that contemporary utilitarians have almost entirely dropped the theological premises that originally motivated the development of utilitarianism.

The most important theological premise is divine providence. All of the theological consequentialists treated in this book assume, in one way or another, that divine providence ensures that the actions generally taken to be virtuous cause good consequences, at least on the whole. Consequentialism, as they conceive it, is not a morally revisionary project; it is a justification for moral virtue. Their primary question is not: Which actions maximize the good? Their primary question is: What makes virtuous actions morally good? Their answer: Virtuous actions maximally realize natural goodness (e.g., happiness). The worry, for example, that theft or deceit might sometimes cause more good than evil can be dismissed by appeal to divine providence. One does not have to worry about apparent exceptions. One also does not have to worry about distant and impossible-to-measure consequences. In their providential universe, virtue is sure to be for the best.

Without these premises regarding divine providence, the situation is quite different. One can no longer be confident that actions widely considered virtuous do in fact maximize the good. Utilitarianism becomes a revisionary project, as it was in Bentham's hands. The secularization of utilitarianism certainly made it more interesting, and it contributed to ethical developments that are rightly lauded today. Yet the loss of theological premises created new and very difficult problems, which we can see by considering how the most influential contemporary objections to utilitarianism arise from the loss of theological premises.

Consider first the objection to utilitarianism known as the "problem of cluelessness."[4] Critics of utilitarianism have long raised epistemic worries about our capacity to know the consequences of our actions. Shelly Kagan states that this sort of epistemic objection is "the most common objection to consequentialism."[5] Utilitarians have generally dismissed this objection with the claim that probabilistic knowledge is sufficient. In recent decades, critics have gone further, arguing that we are not merely unsure about the results of our actions but almost entirely clueless about whether any action will cause more good or evil.

A common way to address the standard epistemic worry is to admit that we cannot foresee all the consequences of our actions but to argue that we can learn by experience—our own and that of human beings more generally—which types of actions cause good and bad results. According to the cluelessness objection, we cannot learn by experience because some portion of the consequences of an action—plausibly the largest portion by far—is completely invisible to us. James Lenman, who first put the objection in these terms, points in particular to "identity-affecting actions," that is, killings and engenderings. He asks us to consider a man who, several millennia ago, chooses not to kill a woman who turns out to be a very, very distant ancestor of Hitler. Such a scenario is not at all improbable when one considers the enormous number of people whose bloodlines produced Hitler. The man who chooses not to kill Hitler's ancestor has as one consequence of his action the Holocaust. Does his act of mercy then turn out to be wrong? We cannot say. The Holocaust is obviously a horrific evil included on the negative side of the column when adding up the consequences of his action. Yet we still have no clue how many other events are attributable to his action or what would have happened had he chosen otherwise. Moreover, the results of his actions are still ongoing, since his choice not to kill continues to have massive implications for who exists in the world. Most of its consequences, in Lenman's terms, are not only unforeseen or even unforeseeable but invisible. We cannot discern them even in retrospect.[6]

A utilitarian can still insist that the foreseeable consequences of actions provide sufficient grounds for a utilitarian decision procedure. Objective utilitarianism may be absolutely unworkable in practical terms, but subjective utilitarianism—an approach that sees the right action as the one with the greatest expected value based on available knowledge—may be salvageable. Even this response faces significant problems.[7] But my point here is simply to demonstrate that these problems can be seen as products of a particular history in which utilitarianism became detached from the theological premises with which it was originally accompanied. These problems only arise in the absence of an omniscient and provident God.

We can add to the problem of cluelessness a second epistemic objection: even if we knew all the consequences of an action, we would still have no idea how to quantify and sum up pleasure and pain. Here, again, the Anglican utilitarians can simply appeal to divine omniscience. If a sum of pleasures and pains is intelligible, then surely God knows the quantities and can do the math. We know enough to see roughly how the causal lines run, but we do not need to make detailed calculations. God has providentially arranged the world so that the actions we naturally approve are also those that produce the greatest total happiness.

These epistemic objections—the cluelessness objection and the objection about the impossibility of the necessary calculations—are one clear result of the rejection of theological premises. Other prominent objections to utilitarianism also arise for the same reason. A third common objection is that utilitarianism permits and even requires abhorrent actions. I discussed Anscombe's version of this objection in the introduction. According to Anscombe, the very fact that the utilitarian must weigh the consequences before deciding whether or not to execute an innocent person renders the theory untenable. Some actions must simply be off the table.

We can see this third objection, too, as a product of the rejection of divine providence. The opponents of Anglican utilitarianism in the eighteenth century raised no similar objection. If they had, the objection could have been quickly dismissed. Our sense that certain actions are abhorrent is, for the Anglican utilitarians, a product of a divinely designed psychological process. The fact that some acts are widely seen as abhorrent is a result of the common experience that they cause more evil than good. If a situation arises in which some abhorrent action appears necessary to maximize the good, one should trust divine providence rather than one's own very uncertain calculations.

The objection that utilitarianism sometimes requires abhorrent actions is related to a fourth well-known objection: utilitarianism has no place for justice. John Rawls famously argued for the inadequacy of a utilitarian theory of justice on the grounds that utilitarianism "does not take seriously the distinction between persons."[8] Utilitarianism, according to Rawls, treats separate persons as if they were a single person, maximizing total utility without considering its distribution across separate individuals. It is perfectly reasonable for an individual to sacrifice one good to achieve another, but utilitarianism applies the same logic to society, allowing the sacrifice of the good of some people for the sake of the greater total happiness achieved by others.

This objection cannot be quite so easily dismissed by the Anglican utilitarians. While they can appeal to divine providence to avoid the result that one must sometimes violate justice for the sake of greater happiness, they cannot avoid the rejoinder that—at least at the level of ultimate justification—they do not respect the distinction between persons. Anglican utilitarianism does, however, have an answer unavailable to its secular counterpart. The answer appeals to an additional theological premise, namely, the reality of a final judgment in which individuals receive rewards or punishments for what they have done. Here the distinctiveness of persons is built into the very heart of the larger theological vision: each individual stands as an individual before the judgment seat of God and receives what they are due.

A fifth common objection, developed especially by Bernard Williams, is that the demands of utilitarianism undermine an individual's ability to pursue his own projects and commitments, which are often the very core of his being, "what his life is about." Utilitarianism, according to this objection, undermines personal integrity. One may spend decades protecting wildlife or teaching a community's children, but if an opportunity to do more good arises, one must abandon one's life work and pivot. Likewise, much of one's life may be devoted to one's family, but one can only remain so devoted if other activities do not do more good. He writes:

> It is absurd to demand of such a man, when the sums come in from the utility network which the projects of others have in part determined, that he should just step aside from his own projects and decisions and acknowledge the decision which utilitarian calculation requires. It is to alienate him in a real sense from his actions and the source of his

action in his own convictions . . . It is thus, in the most literal sense, an attack on his integrity.[9]

Williams's critique gets its force from the seeming absurdity of laying down one's central commitments to satisfy the impersonal demands of "utilitarian calculation." But the notion that "utilitarian calculation" makes the demands would only occur after the rejection of theological premises. For the Anglican utilitarians, the demands of "utilitarian calculation" are not impersonal. They are the commands of God. And the idea that one ought to submit all one's personal projects and commitments to one's commitment to God and the project of uniting one's will to God's is not absurd. It is a central teaching of most theistic traditions. Subordinating one's own projects, for theistic traditions, is not a loss of integrity; it is how one gains the only kind of integrity that has lasting value.

A sixth and final common objection to utilitarianism is known as the "demandingness objection." According to this objection, utilitarianism demands too much. It requires that every person do as much as possible to maximize universal happiness. One can only cease giving more of one's efforts and resources to increasing total happiness when one is so depleted that giving more begins to decrease total happiness. Every self-indulgence is swamped by the overwhelming demands of morality. Utilitarianism, the objection goes, leads to a completely implausible picture of the demands of morality.

This sixth objection, too, follows directly from the rejection of theological premises. As we have seen, explaining the motivation for virtue is paramount for the Anglican utilitarians. Appealing to divine providence, they provide a psychological explanation of why acts of virtue tend to be pleasurable for the virtuous person such that moral demands do not generally cut against one's desires. This psychological explanation, however, imagines a local context for the exercise of virtue and would be hard to extend into the globalized world that the demandingness objection presupposes. Even so, the Anglican utilitarians were well aware of the general problem, and their solution is crucial to their case for the superiority of their view over that of their rationalist competitors. Central to their project is the claim that we must never lack a motive for virtue. While they explain the motive to virtue with ordinary psychology in most cases, they appeal to divine sanctions to cover cases in which ordinary psychology looks insufficient. Morality may indeed be very demanding, but, according to the Anglican utilitarians, it never asks us to do anything that is not ultimately for our happiness. Every act of virtue will be rewarded with sufficient abundance to ensure its worthwhileness to the agent.

Without an overriding motive, the Anglican utilitarians believe that virtue cannot be obligatory. Even beyond the worry about demandingness, the question of motive has loomed over the secular utilitarian tradition. Bentham retained Gay's hedonistic egoism without his religious sanction, leaving a motivational gap to be filled (if it could) by legislation and education.[10] John Stuart Mill, wrestling with the question of motivation, finally suggested that hope in an afterlife might be justified, even if theism could not be demonstrated philosophically. Sidgwick thought the choice between egoism and utilitarianism was rationally undecidable without theism. John Hare has traced this genealogy and argued convincingly that the problem persists.[11]

*****

One does not have to see these objections as products of a theological history to recognize their force. Nonetheless, the history illuminates the objections. Contemporary utilitarianism, we can see, bears the traces of its history. Its persistent problems are not accidental. They arise from the particular path it has taken, a path of theological development followed by the rejection of core theological premises. The rejection of the theological premises occurred while leaving almost everything else in place. The result is a theory with notable gaps, which significant effort has gone into patching or closing.

If the most important objections to contemporary utilitarianism are products of the rejection of its original theological premises, should contemporary utilitarians seriously reconsider theological utilitarianism? Moreover, if theological utilitarianism can address the major critiques of contemporary secular utilitarianism, then theological ethicists have good reason to revisit it. Does it provide a promising contemporary option for theological ethicists?

Based on what I have said thus far, it might at first appear obvious that theological utilitarianism is a more promising option than its nontheistic counterpart and a promising option for theological ethics. Simply by appealing to divine providence and divine sanctions, the theological utilitarian can answer most of the standard objections. Under greater scrutiny, however, the matter looks somewhat more complicated. Some of the objections listed above are indeed solved by the return of theological premises. The first two objections—the problem of cluelessness and the problem of calculation—carry little or no weight given divine providence and divine omniscience. God knows what is best and can ensure that we do as well. William King, for example, recognized that "it was impossible for nature to acquaint us with all the consequences which attend our actions in an infinite train and continuance of things."[12] But for King, as for the others, God can ensure that we know which acts have the best consequences. Yet some of the theological answers to the objections above prove less successful than they first appear, either because they can be applied to God or because the theological solution proves inadequate upon further examination.

Consider, for example, how we might further develop the third objection about abhorrent actions such that it becomes a problem for the Anglican utilitarians. Their response to the initial objection is to insist that we can trust divine providence that the actions we find abhorrent are not, on the whole, for the best. We can then ask: Why do you think God will ensure that commonsense moral judgments correspond with utility? To be consistent, the Anglican utilitarian can only give one answer: God will do so in order to maximize happiness. As we have seen, they believe maximizing happiness is God's only end. But there is a problem with this answer. How can we know that providentially ensuring that those actions we consider abhorrent are not sometimes the means to the greatest happiness is the best way for God to maximize happiness? If human beings are weak or corrupt, perhaps God maximizes happiness by using our vices, as Bernard Mandeville argued. There are certainly reasons one might want to insist that God does not permit abhorrent actions to be for the best, but these reasons are about justice or fittingness. In the Anglican utilitarian picture, such reasons get no purchase. God cares only for maximizing happiness, and God will arrange the world in whatever manner achieves this end. We can, therefore, have little confidence that divine providence solves the problem of abhorrent actions.

Indeed, this line of argument undercuts much of the work done by divine providence. Even the two epistemic objections, which fail when applied to God, now reappear. God certainly knows which actions maximize happiness, but God would not tell us unless doing so would maximize happiness—and, as far as we can know, it very well may not. Likewise, the idea that we naturally have a sufficient motive in most cases also becomes doubtful since we cannot be sure how God arranges our psychology to maximize happiness. The demandingness and integrity objections can thus reappear in a new guise.

The Anglican utilitarians do have another means of addressing these objections. Even if part of the response to the demandingness and integrity objections fails, the Anglican utilitarians can still appeal to divine sanctions to align morality with happiness and thus with an ultimate religious project. Yet, as I noted in part III, the assertion about rewards and punishments is quite vulnerable. Gay provides no argument for it, and his view is liable to the objection that eternal punishments are an infliction of pain that cannot possibly be outweighed by the happiness produced in this life. We cannot be sure how God maximizes happiness, but the imposition of eternal punishment seems like an odd route. Law seeks to solve this problem by appealing to King's idea that divine "sanctions" are just facts about the necessary consequences of actions. Even the best possible world cannot avoid negative consequences, including after death. Yet this argument, too, is vulnerable to similar responses. Perhaps sanctions are just the inevitable consequences of actions in the best possible world. Even so, unless we know exactly how universal happiness is best maximized, we have no clear reason to think that sanctions (negative consequences for the agent) will always follow moral evil (acts that produce negative consequences on the whole). Once again, God will only design the world in such a way that sanctions follow moral evil if doing so maximizes total happiness. Unless we can understand the whole, we cannot know whether and how sanctions relate to moral evil.

Further, we can raise some of these objections in a new way by applying them to divine morality. The Anglican utilitarians seem faced with the prospect that God will sometimes perform abhorrent actions. God, for example, might damn the innocent in order to maximize happiness, a highly unattractive view. The only way to avoid this conclusion would be to argue that damning the innocent could never maximize happiness. It is unclear whether such an argument is possible. Even if it were, the Anglican utilitarians would still have to admit that God would damn the innocent under counterfactual conditions.

These issues provide reason to doubt that Anglican utilitarianism can resolve all the problems facing contemporary utilitarianism, even if it does resolve some of them. Still, many of these critiques arose long after the decline of Anglican utilitarianism, and no one has really tried to respond on Anglican utilitarian grounds. The prospects of a revised version of Anglican utilitarianism are unclear, and further exploration is justified. Anglican utilitarianism, moreover, is not the only theological option. Theological consequentialists of other stripes have other options available, which may be more promising. Henry More and Richard Cumberland, for example, offer a more expansive picture of goodness that God maximizes. God maximizes not only pleasure but also perfection. They also offer a different account of motivation according to which we can be directly motivated by the good. These differences may make the view more plausible, though they do not address every objection.

Many more consequentialisms—theological and secular—remain available. The above objections will likely cause problems for any maximizing version of consequentialism with a relatively simple picture of the good to be maximized, but one can tweak one's view about what is good and how much one is required to promote it in order to get more satisfying responses to the objections. Philosophers have become increasingly interested in recent years in testing out consequentialist views with an expanded list of natural goods—beauty, friendship, integrity, justice, knowledge, autonomy—and with less stringent requirements (e.g., satisficing rather than maximizing views). Consequentialism, in this way, can begin to churn out results that look more intuitive.[13] Indeed, some argue that any view in ethics can be "consequentialized" because some version of consequentialism can be constructed that produces identical results.[14] Yet the more one tweaks consequentialism to make its conclusions appear more plausible, the more convoluted it becomes. Its original simplicity— deriving all morality from the single principle of maximizing happiness, perfection, or, more recently, preference satisfaction—has been its great strength. The more one multiplies intrinsic goods, the more difficult it becomes to imagine doing the necessary calculations. All views may be consequentializable in one way or another, but the point of consequentializing them is unclear. As Campbell Brown argues, an approach that tries to make consequentialism work by consequentializing other views renders consequentialism effectively empty.[15]

*****

If consequentialism faces all of the above objections, what explains its persistent appeal? Mark Schroeder points to the fact that consequentialism is the only moral theory able to capture what he calls the Compelling Idea: "It is always permissible for every agent to do what will lead to the outcome that is best."[16] It seems bizarre to think that one could do wrong by acting to bring about as much good as possible. Why? Ultimately, I think, the appeal of consequentialism comes from the enduring sense that bringing about as much good as possible is the most rational course of action. Samuel Scheffler expresses the point aptly: consequentialism, he writes, is so appealing because it follows from "the canons of rationality we most naturally apply."[17]

Scheffler's language is telling. Consequentialist moral rationality is not the only form of rationality one can apply to human action. It is the kind of rationality we most "naturally" apply. But the fact that we naturally apply consequentialist moral rationality to human action does not make it appropriate. The application feels natural due to inherited ways of thinking, a partial history of which I have just provided. In reflecting on this history, we have the opportunity to distance ourselves from what otherwise seems natural.

Recall my critique of J. B. Schneewind in the first chapter. Schneewind rightly argues that the roots of utilitarianism can be found in seventeenth-century efforts to defeat ethical voluntarism. To provide an alternative to ethical voluntarism, he argues, the anti-voluntarists needed an account of divine rationality. He goes on:

> A teleological model of rationality was the only model available. We act rationally when we act deliberately to bring about some good end. If God acts rationally, that is what he does as well. When one possible action promises more good than the alternatives, the rational course is to pursue the greater good. If some single course of action produces more good than any of the others, then the most rational action is the one that maximizes good. If God is rational, then he wills to bring about the greatest good. And if morality requires us to do what God necessarily does, then we are on the road to utilitarianism.[18]

Schneewind, too, finds it natural to apply consequentialist moral rationality to divine action. In fact, he suggests that consequentialist moral rationality is the only form of teleological rationality. The problem here, as I have already argued, is that Schneewind, misled by the seeming naturalness of applying consequentialist moral rationality, presupposes the existence of what he is supposed to explain. The early consequentialists do not draw from an already available form of rationality; they invent a new one. In the seventeenth century, the "canons of rationality" most naturally applied to human action may have been teleological, but they were certainly not consequentialist.

Perhaps, then, we can learn from the wider field of alternative approaches to teleological rationality available in the seventeenth century, approaches that have largely been occluded by the dominance of consequentialist moral rationality. The dominant approach to teleological rationality in the seventeenth century, I argued in the first chapter, is one according to which the end to be sought is not an outcome or state of affairs but an object to which one is drawn by its goodness or value. I surveyed Thomistic, Reformed, and Platonic traditions. The first question, for these traditions, is not: What is the best possible state of affairs? The first question is: What is the best thing? The answer—qualified, of course, by

the fact that God is not properly speaking a "thing"—is God. The rationality of action is determined by proper orientation toward what is best, and the final end is attained when one achieves perfect relation to what is best.

Modern readers, habituated to a productivist approach to agency, find it difficult not to immediately translate what I have just said into productivist terms in which the end is ultimately a state of affairs. Saying that God is one's final end is seen as a shorthand for saying that friendship with God or enjoyment of God is one's final end. This interpretation is not entirely unreasonable. For these traditions, one does indeed attain the final end ultimately through relationship with God. Nonetheless, as we have seen, something important changes in the translation. When the final end is seen as the best thing and highest object of love, then God is the final end. When the final end is seen as a state of affairs, one suddenly begins to worry that one's own friendship with God is not the best state of affairs. Should the best state of affairs not also include goods for all others? One is then on the way to consequentialism.

Limits to consequentialism are often described by contemporary philosophers as "agent-relative constraints." These constraints place limits on what one can do to achieve the best consequences. For example, many believe that one should never violate someone's rights, even if doing so produces better results. The difficulty, though, is justifying a constraint that seems to contradict natural "canons of rationality" for action. According to the alternative forms of teleology one finds in the seventeenth century, however, one does not need to impose "constraints" on one's pursuit of the good in order to explain why one should never act in certain ways. Certain kinds of acts are simply incompatible with acting for the sake of the final end. Moreover, while these traditions identify God as the highest good and final end, they apply a similar logic to lesser goods and subordinate ends. One must relate appropriately to these goods as well. Indeed, doing so is necessary to relating appropriately to God.

One could, of course, avoid the problems with consequentialism by abandoning teleological approaches to moral rationality, arguing for a priority of the "right" or for a "deontological" approach to morality. Theist traditions have a long history of treating divine commands as ultimate imperatives to which one must submit regardless of any ends one may have in view. But for those attracted to teleological forms of moral rationality, one lesson of the story told in this book is that teleological rationality is quite a bit broader than is commonly recognized.

It may be worth, then, rethinking how we understand goods, agency, and the relations among them. If, contra productivism, ends are not (or not only) states of affairs, then perhaps the rationality of

should not be judged solely by the states of affairs it realizes. Perhaps the Compelling Idea is only compelling when one assumes a particular picture of goods, acts, and ends that is currently but not historically widespread and that is not necessary.

If a very different picture of teleological rationality—or, better, a family of such pictures—was pervasive in the seventeenth century, why was it displaced? For the early defenders of consequentialism, the reason seems to largely be the attempt to distance themselves from scholasticism and assimilate human action to newly ascendant paradigms of thought. In particular, More seeks moral principles that are self-evident in the same manner as mathematical principles. This search leads to the idea that the goods at stake in human action ought to be subject to quantitative analysis. And Cumberland, building on More, seeks to reconstruct human action according to the paradigm of mechanical philosophy. Cumberland redescribes human action in efficient causal terms with ends conceived as outcomes—outcomes whose goodness can be calculated mathematically.

More's and Cumberland's innovations were reasonable attempts to rethink moral philosophy in the wake of an upheaval in natural philosophy. Aristotelian natural philosophy had evidently fallen short in light of new experimental results, and geometric and mechanistic explanations had demonstrated their great explanatory potential. But even if More and Cumberland were reasonable in their attempts to apply new paradigms of thought to human action, we now have good reason to question the results. In a surprising turn that More and Cumberland would not have anticipated, Aristotelianism is now back in many areas of philosophy, including ethics.

To say that Aristotelianism is back is not to suggest that a simple return to seventeenth-century views is possible or even desirable. It is simply to indicate that the reasons for moving away from earlier forms of teleology and toward consequentialism are, once again, up for grabs. Seventeenth-century natural philosophy is certainly no longer viable, a fact which any attempt to draw from seventeenth-century ethics must recognize. Theologians and ethicists have too often sought to sidestep such issues. Nonetheless, the fact remains that the reasons for rejecting the dominant seventeenth-century intellectualist traditions and inventing consequentialist alternatives are no longer as compelling as they once were.

There is good reason, as Scheffler recognizes, to assess human action teleologically. Yet when one assumes a productivist picture of human agency, consequentialism appears to be the most rational approach to morality, even if some of its results are widely seen as unpalatable. Returning to the

seventeenth century and the early development of productivism and consequentialism illuminates a wider field of options for thinking teleologically.
Because these options are developed in theological terms, their appeal to
religious ethicists is most obvious.[19] But given the problems with consequentialism and the attractiveness of teleological rationality, their appeal
should be more general. Indeed, some of the best work in nontheistic moral
philosophy in recent decades has begun to move in this direction, rethinking moral teleology by rethinking the nature of goods, ends, and agency.
Elizabeth Anderson and Talbot Brewer, for example, have both argued persuasively that construing all ends as states of affairs cannot make sense of
human agency or of the goods for which we act and by which we are drawn.[20]

*****

I began this book by asking what we can learn from the intellectual and
cultural prominence of the trolley problem. Let us conclude by returning
to the trolley problem. We can now further develop the lessons we learn
from its current prominence. In the trolley problem, we see a fixation on a
particular moral issue: the issue of whether or not there are limits to what
we can do to produce the best outcome and, if so, what those limits are.
The same issue is the focus of other frequently discussed ethical quandaries such as ticking timebomb cases.

This moral issue is no doubt important, but the history told in this
book ought to make us suspicious of the way it is commonly framed. The
framing, as we see in the trolley problem, directs our attention to the goodness or badness of outcomes. The question of which outcome is better
is not supposed to be in doubt. Generally, quantitative differences (e.g.,
the number of people who will die) are used to ensure that one outcome
appears obviously better than the other. The good to be desired, then, is
the best available state of affairs. The only means to that state of affairs is
an action that is widely perceived to be morally wrong. We are then in a
bind: do we abide by widely accepted moral principles (deontology) or
bring about the best outcome (consequentialism)?

In addition to framing the goods (or, really, the less-bads) at stake in
a particular way, trolley cases also embody a particular way of imagining
moral agency. Moral agents, in this picture, stand outside the situation of
risk and possess the capacity to change the outcome. Lives are in the balance, and their choice determines the result. They are active in a world of
passive and silent sufferers, discerning whether there are moral limits to
how they can exert their power to achieve the best outcome.

This vision of goods and agents is the one bequeathed to us by More, Cumberland, and their successors. Human action is imagined as a causal intervention in the world intended to make a difference, and the central moral focus is what kind of difference it makes. Goodness and badness figure into action as attributes of outcomes, and the differences between the goodness or badness of different possible outcomes are treated quantitatively. When considering how to act, the agent views himself as active and all others as passive recipients. When the actions of others are a necessary part of the relevant causal sequences, they are often treated mechanistically. The resulting moral agent, as I have observed, is not a genuinely political agent insofar as he never truly acts together with others. His actions aim at the social good, but they do so as individual actions that give rise to their own singular causal sequences, the consequences of which are attributable to him. To center trolley cases in discussing and teaching ethics is to continue to implicitly reinscribe this picture of agency, ends, goods, and causation.

The alternative picture I discussed sits uncomfortably with a trolley approach to ethics, but we could still ask what would happen if we were to apply it to trolley cases. What if, for example, the goods for the sake of which the agent acts are not states of affairs but the people (or animals or other objects) we hypothetically place on trolley tracks or footbridges? In a theological register, we might also include the goodness of God, though God is not one good among others to be weighed in one's calculations. For the theocentric traditions discussed above, properly valuing God as one's ultimate end means properly valuing the many goods of the world, each of which participates in the divine goodness in its own distinctive way.

What difference would it make, then, to treat the people as the relevant goods in the standard trolley cases? At first, one might think it makes no difference. If what matters is the people, then we still have a trade-off: whose lives do we prioritize? But valuing people is not the same as valuing the continuation of their lives. The trolley problem imagines the good to be achieved as an outcome in which more people live longer. And certainly that outcome is, all other things being equal, valuable. Yet, to state the obvious: it is valuable because people are valuable. And the question of what the value of people requires of the agent is not simply that she always seeks to prolong their lives. There are innumerable ways to value people: to treat them with respect, to listen to them, to avoid interfering with their plans, to grieve their pain, to support their dreams, to give them gifts, and so on. While trolley cases sharply limit the ways in which the agent can value the people on the tracks, we can still ask which ways of valuing them remain.

Even taking their good and their rights into account in one's deliberation about what to do is a way of valuing them. And there are more: crying out in alarm, calling for help, and frantically searching for alternative solutions; trying to save everyone involved while potentially risking oneself in the process, even if one sees that doing so will almost certainly fail (as the trolleyologists require it must); rushing into the aftermath, looking for signs of life, and calling for emergency personnel; and, of course, grieving their deaths, supporting their loved ones, and seeking to honor them in how one carries on with one's life.

These many ways of valuing the people at risk in trolley cases are almost never considered, yet they are crucial to a morally appropriate response, whatever one chooses concerning switches and footbridges. Imagine a person noticing the oncoming trolley and the switch in front of her, calmly deliberating, deciding to turn the train onto the side track, watching as it hits the one person instead of the five, feeling satisfied that her choice was correct, and walking away to carry on with her day. Such a person, I think, should not be praised for acting well, even by those who think her choice was correct. She may have caused a better outcome, but her grasp of the value of the people on the tracks is questionable at best. We might contrast her with the person who decides not to pull the switch but engages in all the other modes of valuing listed above. Even if their choice is wrong, I am confident that they have grasped something about the value of human beings that the first person has not. The almost-exclusive focus on outcomes and the permissibility of the means to them renders invisible the multitude of ways that we ought to value persons (among other goods).

I am not claiming here to resolve trolley cases. In fact, I am doubtful that we can or should identify a single, timelessly correct way to value people and other goods abstracted from their social contexts.[21] I am only seeking to reframe how we think about and employ them in ethical reflection and pedagogy. The usefulness of trolley cases is supposed to lie in the way they illuminate real moral choices that we might face. Everyone recognizes that the real-world cases are much more complex and include doubt and uncertainty and a much larger range of possible choices. The thought experiments that strip away uncertainty and other complexities are supposed to get to the heart of the issue. Trolley cases, though, can just as easily obscure the heart of the issue. In real-life situations, the more expansive range of ways that human beings (among other goods) can and should be valued is—given uncertainty, a wider range of options, and other complexities—even more important to a morally appropriate response. The idea that we gain deep insight into the appropriate way to act in situations in which goods are at risk by answering "yes" or "no" to pulling the switch is, as most undergraduate students instinctively know, extremely simplistic.

Those who share my skepticism that the best way of framing our moral options is consequentialism versus deontology have long been critical of "quandary ethics," that is, an approach to ethics that assumes that we gain special insight by focusing on the most difficult quandaries. I am quite sympathetic to this critique. The idea that moral insight is found especially in the hardest cases—no matter how abstract or artificial those cases are— is doubtful. Still, approaching ethics by reflecting on moral dilemmas is attractive for other reasons. It tends to generate more interest and motivate students, and I do think we can learn by reflecting on particularly hard cases. My skepticism about the insightfulness of the trolley problem does not extend to all moral quandaries. Other cases more adequately highlight the many ways in which we ought to value others—including but not limited to seeking to bring about outcomes in which they survive—while also keeping in view the fact that we are almost always acting together with others for the sake of goods we value together.

We do not have to look far for examples. Considered Jean-Paul Sartre's famous example of a situation faced by one of his students in 1940.[22] The student's father had recently abandoned his mother, and his only sibling, an older brother, had been killed in a German offensive. His mother was in great pain from the losses, and he was her only source of comfort. The student was torn between two options. He could stay and care for his mother, or he could seek to join the Free French Forces and avenge his brother.

Sartre describes the dilemma as a choice between "two kinds of morality"—and thus a choice with no correct answer.[23] That is one interesting way to think about the situation, but it is not the only one. The situation, I think, is better described as one in which the student ought to value two different goods but seemingly cannot adequately value both. One good is his mother, whose need is great. As her only surviving child, he is both uniquely able to care for her and especially responsible for her care. The other good, as Sartre describes the case, is his deceased brother, who, the student believes, is best honored through vengeance. In the case of his brother, the student is not uniquely capable, but he is, once again, especially responsible. There are, of course, other moral reasons to resist the Nazis, and these ought to inform his choice, even if they are not prominent in Sartre's characterization.

What makes this case especially illuminating is that the choice is not focused on better and worse outcomes. As the student fully understands, a choice to join the battle may make no difference whatsoever. He could easily die on his way to join the forces. Even if he made it, his chances of making a real difference in the war effort are slim. And even if he somehow makes a meaningful difference in the war, the difference does not affect the brother who he is honoring. Nonetheless, the effort would be undertaken to honor his brother. With his mother, he can more obviously make a concrete difference, though the difference is much more complicated than life versus death.

The choice, then, is not best seen as a choice between outcomes but between the pull of competing demands to value particular goods in particular ways. And while the situation does demand a choice, it does not require an artificial either-or. Both goods must be valued in some way, and the situation invites complex deliberation. Could he, for example, stay and care for his mother while working to subtly undermine the German occupation from home? In doing so, would he fail to honor his brother? Or could he join the war effort while doing his best to avoid the front lines and promising to write daily to his mother, whom he entrusts to the care of extended family members or close friends? Would that course of action sufficiently value his mother? And, we must add, what difference does it make what his mother prefers or demands or accepts? No realistic treatment of the case can take her to be a purely passive sufferer like a person on a trolley track. In addition, we must ask: who else cares about his mother and brother such that they might act together with him to ensure each is properly valued? Any attempt to properly value all the goods at stake, as is almost always the case, will require acting together with others who are responding to similar values.

In addition, a case like Sartre's, because it highlights the fact that valuing is a social enterprise, illuminates the role of social critique in ethical reflection. For example, the student is convinced that vengeance is the way to honor his brother. This conviction, presumably, reflects his social context. Given this social context, he may feel not only that vengeance is required but also that anything less than vengeance will fail to bestow honor as others understand it. Yet there are ethical reasons to question whether vengeance is the right way to honor a soldier killed in battle. This line of reflection may lead to an attempt to honor his brother in new ways that implicitly or explicitly criticize established norms for honoring those killed in battle.

The fact that the trolley problem is our standard moral dilemma makes sense in light of the history told in his book, a history in which a consequentialist picture of goods, ends, agency, and causation is increasingly assumed. To center trolley cases in ethical pedagogy is to continue to reinscribe this picture. By critiquing the intellectual and cultural prominence of the trolley problem, I do not mean to deny the importance of the fundamental question it highlights: are there limits to how we should act to make the world better? Indeed, the widely espoused desire to make the world better is one of the great inheritances of the consequentialist tradition, one that ought to be encouraged. Given that desire, we will necessarily have to reflect on what is and is not permissible in our pursuits of a better world. The problem is not the question but the way it is posed as a clash between consequentialism and deontology and as an apolitical choice in which one acts alone and the agency and preferences of others are excluded. Those who express a desire to make the world better are rarely thinking about sums of pleasure and pain or any other simplistic measurement of the goodness of states of affairs. They are thinking about the things that matter to them: people, animals, ecosystems, artifacts, practices, traditions, social and political structures, and so on. When we focus our attention on these goods and the other people together with whom we value them, then we can have a richer conversation about how they are to be valued, including when they are to be valued by seeking particular outcomes and when they are to be valued in other ways.

Acknowledgments

Before writing this book, I did not realize how much lies behind the single name printed on a book's cover. While I wrote the text, this book is the product of more friends, colleagues, mentors, authors, and institutions than I can list. I began this project at Yale University. I am deeply grateful to Jennifer Herdt. She was (and is) a thoughtful and generous mentor who has encouraged and guided me at every step. Her influence can be seen throughout this book. My intellectual debt to her is enormous, as is my personal debt. John Hare and Kathryn Tanner read an early version of the project, and their guidance made it much better than it would have been otherwise. My thinking has been shaped by so many other teachers and faculty members from the multiple universities that have formed me: David Clairmont, Adam Eitel, Norrie Friesen, Clifton Granby, Willie Jennings, Willis Jenkins, Gerald McKenny, Kevin Miller, Jean Porter, John Sanders, Steven Schweitzer, Fred Simmons, Miroslav Volf, and Todd Whitmore. This work was also made possible by the intellectual community and friendship of many others at Yale: Ryan McAnnally-Linz, Andrew Forsyth, Brad East, Ross McCullough, Jamie Dunn, Janna Gonwa, Matt Croasmun, Roger Baumann, Justin Hawkins, Jane Abbottsmith, Graedon Zorzi, Awet Andemicael, Wendy Mallete, Samuel Loncar, Calli Micale, and Kathy Chow.

This book was completed during the three years I spent as a Postdoctoral Research Associate at the University Center for Human Values at Princeton University. UCHV was a valuable, interdisciplinary scholarly community with supportive faculty and a wonderful group of fellow postdocs. I am especially grateful to Andrew Chignell, Lara Buchak, and the Princeton Project in Philosophy and Religion (3PR). Emerging from Andrew's vision and leadership, 3PR was just the kind of intellectual space for this book. The weekly 3PR working group read and commented on several portions of the manuscript. My fellow 3PR postdocs and fellows—Daniel

Rubio, Elizabeth Li, Alex Englert, Kamal Ahmed, and Toni Alimi—were excellent intellectual interlocutors as well as good friends. I am grateful to Eric Gregory, who was an important mentor at Princeton and remains a mentor and friend. Many others at Princeton commented on and contributed their insights to the book, including Dan Garber, Gabriel Citron, Liz Harmon, Jonathan Gold, and Mark Johnston.

In addition to UCHV and 3PR, the Religion and Critical Thought workshop was a significant source of intellectual community and friendship in Princeton. The group provided valuable feedback on parts of this project. I want to thank Mary Nickel, Judah Isseroff, Aysenur Guc, Darren Yao, Candace Jordan, and Yoav Schaefer. I owe a particular debt of gratitude to Enoch Kuo, who not only talked with me for many hours about the book but also generously read the entire manuscript. I am also grateful for the support of the Princeton Center for Culture, Society and Religion, which supported my work for the 2020–2021 academic year. The Religion and Public Life Seminar run by Johnathan Gold gave some of the most detailed feedback I've received on the introduction.

I want to thank Kyle Wagner, my editor at Chicago, who skillfully and insightfully guided the book through the review process. The three anonymous reviewers offered what now feels like indispensable commentary and guidance, and the book is significantly stronger due to their careful and insightful feedback. During the final revisions, Layne Hancock read the entire manuscript and provided the most detailed and comprehensive feedback I received anywhere. Portions of the book are significantly indebted to his insights.

My children, Clara, Calvin, and Rosalie, contributed to this book largely by continually getting in its way, which, at many points, was precisely what I needed. I am grateful for them every day. Their love and boundless energy have been a much-needed balance to the solitude and silence of long days of research and writing. That having three young children—and especially twins—while writing did not derail this book entirely is due in significant part to Laura Sanchez Carrillo and Misikir Adnew, each of whom spent two years as part of our family. I am so grateful to them both. Dwight and Natalie Brautigam, my parents-in-law, supported me and my family unceasingly and often in tremendously practical ways through the long writing process. I am so fortunate to have them as family.

Most importantly, I want to thank Katie, whose love and companionship is the happiest part of my life. Her support through the long and economically precarious process of writing, even when it went against her best instincts, is a gift for which I am deeply grateful.

Finally, I want to thank my parents, Kevin and Kathy Darr, to whom I dedicate this book. From my early obsession with physics and cosmology to my more recent interests in theology and philosophy, they have always patiently listened to my latest ideas and encouraged my passions. Their support has also been extraordinarily practical in recent years, including many weeks and months spent caring for my children, especially in the desperate months after the twins were born. Thank you for everything.

Notes

Introduction

1. Elizabeth Anscombe, "Modern Moral Philosophy," *Journal of the Royal Institute of Philosophy* 33, no. 124 (January 1958): 17.

2. J. J. C. Smart, "An Outline of a System of Utilitarian Ethics," in *Utilitarianism: For and Against*, eds. J. J. C. Smart and Bernard Williams (Cambridge: Cambridge University Press, 1973): 6.

3. Philippa Foot, "The Problem of Abortion and the Doctrine of Double Effect," *Oxford Review* 5 (1967): 5–15.

4. Google Scholar search of "The Trolley Problem" on October 14, 2022.

5. David Edmonds, *Would You Kill the Fat Man? The Trolley Problem and What Your Answer Tells Us about Right and Wrong* (Princeton, NJ: Princeton University Press, 2014); Thomas Cathcart, *The Trolley Problem, or Would You Throw the Fat Guy Off the Bridge? A Philosophical Conundrum* (New York: Workman Publishing, 2013).

6. See, for example, the popular Facebook page "Trolley Problem Memes": https://www.facebook.com/TrolleyProblemMemes/. For many other references to the trolley problem in popular culture, see Frank G. Bosman, "Five Shakespeares versus One Santa Clause: Self-Sacrifice and the Trolley Problem in the Series 'The Good Place,'" *Religions* 11, no. 7 (2020): 3.

7. Around 90 percent of people respond this way. See Marc Hauser, *Moral Minds* (New York: HarperCollins, 2006): 139.

8. Joshua Greene, *Moral Tribes: Emotion, Reason, and the Gap Between Us and Them* (New York: Penguin, 2013), 128.

9. *Moral Tribes*, 202.

10. On some views, the actions themselves can be among the good and bad outcomes.

11. Samuel Scheffler, *Consequentialism and Its Critics* (Oxford: Oxford University Press, 1988): 1.

12. One could, of course, point to even earlier conceptual work that contributes to consequentialism. Doing so would take us back to ancient philosophy—above all to Plato's *Protagoras*. The limits of this study require a somewhat more proximate starting point.

13. Leslie Stephen, *The English Utilitarians*, vol. 1 (London: Duckworth and Co., 1900): 1.

14. Stephen, *English Utilitarians*, 2.

15. Ernest Albee, *A History of English Utilitarianism* (New York: Collier Books, 1962): 12.

16. Albee, *History of English Utilitarianism*, 182.

17. Leslie Stephen, *History of English Thought in the Eighteenth Century*, vol. I (London: Smith, Elder, and Co., 1876): 105.

18. Élie Halévy, *The Growth of Philosophical Radicalism*, trans. Mary Morris (Clifton, NJ: A. M. Kelley, 1972): xxviii.

19. "Our study," he writes, "is of Utilitarianism as a whole." Halévy, *Growth of Philosophical Radicalism*, xxvii.

20. Halévy, *Growth of Philosophical Radicalism*, 7.

21. John Plamenatz, *The English Utilitarians* (Oxford: Blackwell, 1966): 51.

22. See Julia Driver, "The History of Utilitarianism," *Stanford Encyclopedia of Philosophy*, revised September 22, 2014, https://plato.stanford.edu/entries/utilitarianism-history/.

23. Fredrick Rosen, *Classical Utilitarianism from Hume to Mill* (New York: Routledge, 2003): 143. This sort of approach to Paley can be found as early as Thomas Rawson Burks's *Modern Utilitarianism* (London: Macmillan and Co., 1874).

24. Philip Schofield, "*Utilitarianism in the Age of Enlightenment: The Moral and Political Thought of William Paley*, by Niall O'Flaherty," *English Historical Review* CXXXV, no. 577 (December 2020): 1601.

25. For Crimmins's work, see, for example, James E. Crimmins, "John Brown and the Theological Tradition of Utilitarian Ethics," *History of Political Thought* 4, no. 3 (1983): 523–50; "Religion, Utility and Politics: Bentham versus Paley," in *Religion, Secularization, and Political Thought: Thomas Hobbes to J. S. Mill*, ed. James Crimmins (New York: Routledge, 1990): 130–52.

26. Crimmins has collected and published works of eighteenth-century theological utilitarians in *Utilitarians and Religion* (Bristol: Thoemmes Press, 1998).

27. Niall O'Flaherty, *Utilitarianism in the Age of the Enlightenment: The Moral and Political Thought of William Paley* (Cambridge: Cambridge University Press, 2018).

28. I am especially grateful to a blind reviewer for pressing me on this point.

29. John Milbank, *Theology and Social Theory* (Malden, MA: Wiley-Blackwell, 2006).

30. Elizabeth Anscombe, "Modern Moral Philosophy," *Philosophy* 33, no. 124 (1958): 1–19.

31. Alasdair MacIntyre, *After Virtue* (Notre Dame, IN: University of Notre Dame Press, 2007): 69.

32. Brad Gregory, *The Unintended Reformation* (Cambridge, MA: Harvard University Press, 2015): 184.

33. Gregory, *Unintended Reformation*, 15.

34. See Jeremy Waldrom, ed., *Nonsense upon Stilts: Bentham, Burke, and Marx on the Rights of Man* (New York: Methuen, 1987).

35. John Perry, "Where Did Utilitarianism Come From?," in *God, the Good, and Utilitarianism*, ed. John Perry (Cambridge: Cambridge University Press, 2014): 24.

36. See the conclusion for more on this point.

37. J. B. Schneewind, "Voluntarism and the Origins of Utilitarianism," *Utilitas* 7, no. 1 (May 1995): 87. Broad definitions like this one can be useful for rhetorical purposes but are of little practical use to the scholar of the history of ethics.

38. The term "consequentialism" was first coined by Elizabeth Anscombe to mean a view that makes no moral distinction between intended and foreseen consequences. See Anscombe, "Modern Moral Philosophy," 12. Since Anscombe's initial definition, however, the term has taken on a new usage, which I follow.

39. This example comes from Walter Sinnott-Armstrong, "Consequentialism," *Stanford Encyclopedia of Philosophy*, revised June 3, 2019, https://plato.stanford.edu/entries/consequentialism/.

40. In some cases, the act might itself be a realization of value—if, for example, certain kinds of acts are taken to be valuable in themselves. In this case, the language of causal

promotion could be misleading. Still, we can say that the act causally promotes the realization of value by instantiating value.

41. As Heydt notes, others develop similar ideas from similar sources. Bishop Berkeley is the most prominent example. But I will focus on the dominant stream. See Colin Heydt, "Utilitarianism before Bentham," in *The Cambridge Companion to Utilitarianism*, eds. Ben Eagleston and Dale E. Miller (Cambridge: Cambridge University Press, 2014): 16–37.

Chapter One

1. Colin Heydt, "Utilitarianism before Bentham," in *The Cambridge Companion to Utilitarianism*, eds. Ben Eagleston and Dale E. Miller (Cambridge: Cambridge University Press, 2014): 16–37, at 16.

2. Epicurus and Jesus have been cited as early utilitarians. This classification relies on a very broad picture of utilitarianism, one that is too broad to lead to much historical insight. It is also sometimes said that Mo Tzŭ (or Mozi), the ancient Chinese philosopher, is a utilitarian. I am unqualified to judge this assertion. Even if it were true, it would not change the fact that utilitarianism had to be invented independently in early modern Europe. See Geoffrey Scarre, *Utilitarianism* (New York: Routledge, 1996); Katarzyna de Lazari-Radek and Peter Singer, *Utilitarianism: A Very Short Introduction* (Oxford: Oxford University Press, 2017).

3. Francis Oakley, *Natural Law, Laws of Nature, Natural Rights: Continuity and Discontinuity in the History of Ideas* (New York: Continuum, 2005): 45–46.

4. Oakley likely exaggerates the importance of Aquinas in causing the backlash. Central to the story is the condemnation of a series of propositions, some of which applied to Aquinas but none of which were aimed at him. See Tobias Hoffman, "Intellectualism and Voluntarism," in *Cambridge Companion for Medieval Philosophy*, ed. Robert Pasnau (Cambridge: Cambridge University Press, 2010): 414–27.

5. Oakley, *Natural Law*, 52.

6. Oakley, *Natural Law*, 52–60. Cf. Michael Allen Gillespie, *The Theological Origins of Modernity* (Chicago: University of Chicago Press, 2008): 19–30. Gillespie writes that the late medieval notion of divine omnipotence "was responsible for the demise of realism" (22).

7. John Milbank, *Theology and Social Theory* (Malden, MA: Wiley-Blackwell, 2006): 15.

8. Milbank, *Theology and Social Theory*.

9. Daniel Horan, *Postmodernity and Univocity: A Critical Account of Radical Orthodoxy and John Duns Scotus* (Minneapolis, MN: Fortress Press, 2014): 59–96.

10. Michael Gillespie, *Nihilism Before Nietzsche* (Chicago: University of Chicago Press, 1995): xii. See also Gillespie, *Theological Origins of Modernity*, 12–16.

11. Gillespie, *Nihilism Before Nietzsche*, xiii.

12. J. B. Schneewind, "Voluntarism and the Foundation of Ethics," in *Essays on the History of Moral Philosophy*, by J. B. Schneewind, 202–21 (Oxford: Oxford University Press, 2009): 213.

13. Heiko A. Oberman, *The Harvest of Medieval Theology*, 3rd. ed. (Durham, NC: Labyrinth Press, 1983): 63.

14. Davey Henreckson, *The Immortal Commonwealth: Covenant, Community, and Resistance in Early Reformed Thought* (Cambridge: Cambridge University Press, 2019): 17.

15. On the origins of the term, see Eilert Herms and Caroline Schröder-Field, "Voluntarism," in *Religion Past and Present* (Leiden: Brill, 2011). Cf. Jan Van Vliet, *The*

Rise of the Reformed System: The Intellectual Heritage of William Ames (Eugene, OR: Wipf and Stock Publishers, 2013): 59.

16. For an insightful discussion of some related but quite different meanings of the term, see Margaret Osler, "Triangulating Divine Will: Henry More, Robert Boyle, and Descartes on God's Relationship to the Creation," in *"Mind Senior to the World": Stoicismo e origenismo nella filosofia platonica del Seicento inglese*, ed. Marialuisa Baldi (Milano: FrancoAngeli, 1996): 75–87.

17. The reason is straightforward. If God's will were indifferent to God's judgments about the good to be done, God could act badly. Those who think that truths about good and evil precede divine will generally think that God necessarily (though also freely) wills the good. If, however, God's will is constitutive of the good, then God's will can be said to be indifferent prior to its own free choice without threatening God's goodness. In this case, God's will is not indifferent to the judgments of reason, since there is nothing to judge; it is simply unconstrained.

18. A view would not be a form of ethical voluntarism if it held that the good to be done and the evil to be avoided depend on divine will because they depend on human nature, which was created by divine will. It must hold that God could in principle change what is to be done or avoided without changing human nature.

19. On these many nuances, see Terence Irwin, *The Development of Ethics: A Historical and Critical Study*, vol. 2 (Oxford: Oxford University Press, 2008): 224–25. Irwin attributes the first position to Richard Cumberland and the second to Francisco Suárez. In addition, he attributes to Culverwell the view that there is a natural obligation that does not depend on divine will but that moral obligation does. There are too many possible nuances here for a neat spectrum, but my definition classifies all of these figures as legislative but not ethical voluntarists.

20. There are many issues here that I do not want to address, especially regarding the doctrine of sin.

21. This section, including separating out the term "soteriological voluntarism," is especially indebted to conversations with Layne Hancock.

22. J. B. Schneewind, "Voluntarism and the Origins of Utilitarianism," *Utilitas* 7, no. 1 (May 1995): 87.

23. See Descartes's "Reply to the Sixth Set of Objections," in René Descartes, *The Philosophical Writings of Descartes*, vol. 2, trans. John Cottingham, Robert Stoothoff, and Dugald Murdoch (Cambridge: Cambridge University Press, 1984). Commenting on Descartes, Margaret Osler offers the helpful clarification that Descartes is a voluntarist regarding God's absolute power but not God's ordained power. I am passing over this nuance. See Osler, "Triangulating Divine Will," 80–81.

24. Thomas Hobbes, *On the Citizen* (Oxford: Clarendon Press, 1983): XV.5.

25. The translation is from Richard Ward's *The Life of Henry More*, eds. Sarah Hutton, Cecil Courtney, Michelle Courtney, Robert Crocker, and A. Rupert Hall (Dordrecht: Kluwer Academic Publishers, 2000): 15.

26. Ward, *Life of Henry More*. Cf. Henry More's "The Preface General," in his *A Collection of Several Philosophical Writings* (London, 1662): x.

27. Henry More, *Divine Dialogues*, vol. 1 (London, 1668): 407. Cf. Henry More, *Annotations upon the Two Foregoing Treatises* (London, 1682): 62.

28. J. B. Schneewind, *The Invention of Autonomy* (Cambridge: Cambridge University Press, 1998): 510. See also Jennifer Herdt, "The Invention of Modern Moral Philosophy:

A Review of *The Invention of Autonomy* by JB Schneewind," *Journal of Religious Ethics* 29, no. 1 (2001): 141–73.

29. Schneewind, "Voluntarism and the Origins of Utilitarianism," 89.

30. On this point and many others, I am indebted to Jennifer Herdt, "Affective Perfectionism: Community with God without Common Measure," in *New Essays on the History of Autonomy: A Collection Honoring J. B. Schneewind*, eds. Natalie Brender and Larry Krasnoff (Cambridge: Cambridge University Press, 2004): 30–60.

31. Cambridge was not unique in this regard. Despite the hostility of some of the earliest reformers to scholastic thought, many Protestant universities developed rich scholastic traditions. See, for example, Willem J. Van Asselt, *Introduction to Reformed Scholasticism* (Grand Rapids, MI: Reformation Heritage Books, 2011); Willem J. Van Asselt and Eef Dekker, eds., *Reformation and Scholasticism: An Ecumenical Enterprise* (Grand Rapids, MI: Baker Academic, 2001); Carl R. Trueman and R. Scott Clark, *Protestant Scholasticism: Essays in Reassessment* (Eugene, OR: Wipf and Stock Publishers, 2007).

32. William Costello, *The Scholastic Curriculum at Early Seventeenth-Century Cambridge* (Cambridge, MA: Harvard University Press, 1958): 113.

33. John Patrick Donnelly, "Calvinist Thomism," *Viator* 7 (1976): 454.

34. John K. Ryan, in his survey of the influence of Aquinas on seventeenth-century English Protestant thought, writes, "The seventeenth century opens with the pre-eminence of Aquinas among scholastic thinkers recognized in widely differing circles and with his works known and available to students." See *The Reputation of St. Thomas Aquinas among the English Protestant Thinkers of the Seventeenth Century* (Washington, DC: Catholic University of America Press, 1948): 5. David Sytsma documents the way Aquinas was classified a "sounder scholastic" and thus allowed to have an increasing influence on Reformed theology. See "Sixteenth-Century Reformed Reception of Aquinas," in *The Oxford Handbook of the Reception of Aquinas*, eds. Matthew Levering and Marcus Plested (Oxford: Oxford University Press, 2021).

35. It is worth noting that the position of Duns Scotus, which was also highly influential, especially among Franciscans, shares many of the features of Thomism discussed below. A fuller treatment of the alternatives to ethical voluntarism would include Scotus as well. See Duns Scotus, *Duns Scotus on the Will and Morality*, ed. Allan B. Wolter, O. F. M. (Washington, DC: Catholic University of America Press, 1997).

36. Thomas Aquinas, *Summa contra gentiles*, trans. Vernon J. Bourke (Notre Dame, IN: University of Notre Dame Press, 1956): I.72.

37. Thomas Aquinas, *Summa theologica*, trans. Fathers of the English Dominican Province (Westminster, MD: Christian Classics, 1981): I.25.6.

38. The point is not that God must will that all creatures attain their end in God, only that God must will that God is their end. God could not create a human being whose end is another creature.

39. Mark Johnston has argued quite persuasively that maximizing approaches to ethics cannot be held together with this sort of theistic picture of the good in which the good is already as fully realized as possible given the existence of God. See Mark Johnston, "Why Did the One Not Remain within Itself?" *Oxford Studies in Philosophy of Religion* 9 (2019): 106–64.

40. Aquinas, *Summa theologica*, I–II.1.8.

41. Aquinas, *Summa theologica*, I–II.1.8.

42. For a more developed version of Aquinas's alternative picture of teleological

rationality, see Ryan Darr, "For the Sake of the Final End: Eudaimonism, Self-Orientation, and the Nature of Human Agency," *Journal of Religious Ethics* 48, no. 2 (2020): 182–200.

43. With the caveat, of course, that God's freedom precludes precise specification of what God will do in a manner analogous to free creatures.

44. *Summa theologica*, I.3.

45. There is, according to Aquinas, one self-evident moral principle, the first principle of practical reason and of the natural law: "Good is to be done and pursued, and evil is to be avoided" (I–II.94.2). While Aquinas only discusses this principle in discussing the natural law, which is unique to rational creatures, we can presumably apply this principle to all agents, including even God. In this very limited sense, there is a principle of action that applies to God and creatures. Yet this principle is completely empty without the content provided by the nature of the acting entity. It is in reality nothing more than a highly formal statement of the entire view just described.

46. Jennifer Herdt, "Affective Perfectionism," 30. While I borrow the term from Herdt, I use it to name a somewhat different (though related) view.

47. See Richard Muller, *After Calvin: Studies in the Development of a Theological Tradition* (Oxford: Oxford University Press, 2003).

48. Francis Turretin, *Institutes of Elenctic Theology*, vol. 2, trans. George Musgrave Giger (Philsberg, NJ: P and R Publishing, 1994): XI.2. I am grateful to Layne Hancock for pointing me to this passage.

49. The importance of dispensations lies primarily in how to explain the fact that God appears to command immoral actions in scripture. Turretin is picking up here on a long tradition of debate.

50. A partial exception to the division is the commandment to observe the Sabbath. While it is of natural right that one is to worship God, it is of positive right that one is commanded to do so on any particular day.

51. Turretin, quite reasonably, considers the opinion of Duns Scotus as an intermediate view. But it is worth noting—especially given the crucial role assigned to Scotus as a source of voluntarism in many of the big narratives of modern thought—that Scotus would not qualify as an ethical voluntarist according to my definition. In fact, Scotus offers another view that shares the general structure of the Thomist, Reformed, and Platonic views described in this chapter. Scotus believes that it is self-evident to both God and rational creatures that God is to be loved above all things. God and all rational creatures are all bound to love God above all things. In this way, God and rational creatures form a single moral community. What makes Scotus sometimes sound like an ethical voluntarist is that he believes God has some discretion over *how* this love is to be practiced. To love God above all else is to conform one's will to God's, and Scotus believes that God has discretion to determine how we are to act given that there is more than one fitting way. So God does issue commands, and some of those commands could have been otherwise. These commands apply to us and not to God. In this sense, how we are to love God differs from how God loves Godself. Nonetheless, we and God necessarily share a sort of moral community—one without common measure—founded on loving the same object above all else.

52. Turretin, *Institutes of Elenctic Theology*, vol. 2, XI.2.10, 10.

53. Turretin, *Institutes of Elenctic Theology*, vol. 2, XI.2.11, 10.

54. Turretin, *Institutes of Elenctic Theology*, vol. 2, III.14.5–8.

55. Peter Sedgwick, *The Origins of Anglican Moral Theology* (Leiden: Brill, 2018): 288.

56. William Ames, *The Marrow of Sacred Divinity* (London, 1642): II.ii.13, 225.

57. Ames, *Marrow of Sacred Divinity*, II.ii.15, 226.

58. Ames, *Marrow of Sacred Divinity*, I.vii.12, 27.

59. Ames, *Marrow of Sacred Divinity*, I.viii.21, 38.

60. Ames, *Marrow of Sacred Divinity*, I.vii.12, 27.

61. We find this sort of worry in William King, the subject of chapter 5.

62. *The Westminster Confession of Faith* (1646): II.2. See "The Westminster Confession of Faith," Center for Reformed Apologetics, accessed on October 31, 2022, https:// reformed.org/master/index.html?mainframe=/documents/wcf_with_proofs/contents.html.

63. See the Westminster Larger Catechism, chapters 82, 83, 86, 90. Available online at "Larger Catechism," Orthodox Presbyterian Church, accessed February 10, 2023, https:// opc.org/lc.html.

64. In fact, Ames's account of God's soteriological action fits perfectly within his more general ethical intellectualist account of divine action. Predestination, for Ames, is God's decree from eternity "of manifesting his special glory in the eternal condition of men" (*Marrow of Sacred Divinity*, I.xxv.3, 116). Note the assertion, which recurs throughout his treatment of the issue, that God's decree in the case of predestination, like all of God's decrees, is for the sake of the same end, God's glory. Predestination is "properly an act of Gods Will, whereby it is exercised about a certaine object which it determines to being to a certaine end by certaine means" (*Marrow of Sacred Divinity*, I.xxv.12, 118). God does not elect at whim but as a means to the same end as all God's other acts. Yet while Ames specifies the end to which God orders this divine decree, he also insists on multiple occasions that the decree "depends not upon any reason," but solely upon the will and good pleasure of God (*Marrow of Sacred Divinity*, I.xxv.9,11, 118–19). Yet one cannot read ethical voluntarism into this claim. The thought seems to be something like this: God's glory is achieved by both displaying justice in punishing sinners and by displaying mercy in saving sinners. Since all have sinned and God does not owe mercy to anyone, nothing constrains God's choice. God can act on mercy or justice as God pleases and will perfectly achieve glory either way.

65. Aquinas, *Summa theologica*, I.23.4.

66. Ward, *Life of Henry More*, 18.

67. Ward, *Life of Henry More*, 19.

68. This stance may sound like a prioritization of the will over the intellect. More does prioritize affect over rationality. As we will see in the next chapter, however, he locates the relevant affect not in the will but in a new faculty, which he calls the boniform faculty.

69. *The Theologica Germanica of Martin Luther*, trans. Bengt Hoffman (Mahwah, NJ: Paulist Press, 1980): chapter 12.

70. Plato, *Timaeus*, 29e1–4 in *Plato: Complete Works*, ed. John M. Cooper (Indianapolis, IN: Hackett Publishing Company, 1997): 1236.

71. Plato, *Timaeus*, 30d2–3.

72. Plotinus, *The Enneads*, trans. Lloyd Gerson (Cambridge: Cambridge University Press, 2017): V.2.1.

73. Plotinus, *Enneads*, V.4.1.

74. Plotinus, *Enneads*, IV.8.6. On the development of this idea, see Arthur Lovejoy, *The Great Chain of Being* (Cambridge, MA: Harvard University Press, 1964).

75. Plotinus, *Enneads*, III.2–3.

76. Pseudo-Dionysius, *The Divine Names*, 708A–B, in *Pseudo-Dionysius: The Complete Works*, trans. Colm Luibheid (Mahwah, NJ: Paulist Press, 1987): 79–80.

77. On Pseudo-Dionysius's Christian transformation of the role of love in Neoplatonic philosophy, see Dimitrios Vasilakis, *Eros in Neoplatonism and Its Reception in Christian Philosophy: Exploring Love in Plotinus, Proclus, and Dionysius the Areopagite* (New York: Bloomsbury Academic, 2021).

78. Marsilio Ficino, *Platonic Theology*, trans. Michael Allen with John Ward (Cambridge, MA: Harvard University Press, 2001): book II, chapters 12–13.

79. More, "Preface General," xxii. See Origen, *On First Principles*, trans. John Behr (Oxford: Oxford University Press, 2020). More flirts with Origenist universalism in *Divine Dialogues*, but he does not ultimately appear to embrace it. His view seems to be that eternal punishment is potentially compatible with divine goodness, but that God nonetheless may ultimately choose to forgive all sin. For a nuanced discussion of this argument, see D. P. Walker, *The Decline of Hell: Seventeenth-Century Discussions of Eternal Torment* (Chicago: University of Chicago Press, 1964): 127–34; Robert Crocker, "Henry More and the Preexistence of the Soul," in *Religion, Reason, and Nature in Early Modern Europe*, ed. Robert Crocker (Boston: Kluwer Academic Publishers, 2001): 87–89.

80. It is true that one frequently finds in Christian Platonism the idea that all beings imitate God and seek to become like God. Yet the idea that creatures imitate God does not mean that they act in the same manner as God. Aquinas agrees that all things imitate God, but each does so in its own way according to its kind. Nothing can imitate all God's perfections, but each part of creation can imitate some aspect of the divine.

81. Pseudo-Dionysius, *Divine Names*, 708B, 79.

82. Pseudo-Dionysius, *Divine Names* , 700B, 75.

83. Ralph Cudworth, *A Treatise Concerning Eternal and Immutable Morality*, ed. Sarah Hutton (Cambridge: Cambridge University Press, 1996): I.1.5, 14.

84. Cudworth, *Treatise Concerning Eternal and Immutable Morality*, I.iii.8, 27.

85. Ralph Cudworth, *The True Intellectual System of the Universe*, vol. 3 (London, 1845): chapter 5, section V.

86. Cudworth never finished his ethical writings, and what he finished does not supply any of the moral truths that he insisted are eternal and immutable. It is possible that Cudworth's moral truths would have mirrored More's. In fact, there is evidence from Cudworth's letters that he did not finish his ethical writings in part because of the publication of More's. I make no claim to know how Cudworth's completed works would have compared to More's. But I do think that there is evidence in the above-cited passages that Cudworth would have been hesitant to assimilate divine and human morality. The relevant letters can be found in *The Diary and Correspondence of Dr. John Worthington*, ed. James Crossley (Manchester, 1860). For the relevant passages, see Thomas Birch's *An Account of the Life and Writings of Ralph Cudworth, D.D.* published as part of Cudworth's *True Intellectual System of the Universe.*

87. Ralph Cudworth, *A Treatise on Freewill*, in *Treatise Concerning Eternal and Immutable Morality*, 172.

88. I am arguing here that More is innovating against the background of the major alternatives, but this innovation does not make his position unprecedented. A related view can be found, for example, in Cicero, who argues in *De legibus* that "men have Law also in common with the gods," which means that we also share justice and a commonwealth with the gods. See *On the Republic, On the Laws*, trans. C. W. Keyes (Cambridge, MA: Harvard University Press, 2000): 323.

Chapter Two

1. This comment comes from Reid's review of Robert Crocker's biography of More. See Jasper Reid, "Review of Robert Crocker, *Henry More, 1614–1687: The Biography of a Cambridge Platonist,*" *Notre Dame Philosophical Reviews* 4 (September 2004), https://ndpr.nd.edu/news/henry-more-1614-1687-a-biography-of-the-cambridge-platonist/. See also Jasper Reid, *The Metaphysics of Henry More* (New York: Springer, 2012).

2. William Whewell, *Lectures on the History of Moral Philosophy* (London, 1852): 37.

3. On the Cambridge Platonists, see Ernst Cassirer, *The Platonic Renaissance in England* (Austin: University of Texas Press, 1953); Gerald R. Cragg, *The Cambridge Platonists* (Oxford: Oxford University Press, 1968); Charles Taylor, *Sources of the Self: The Making of Modern Identity* (Cambridge, MA: Harvard University Press, 1989); John Tulloch, *Rational Theology and Christian Philosophy in England in the Seventeenth Century*, vol. 2 (London: William Blackwood and Sons, 1872); D. P. Walker, *The Ancient Theology: Studies in Christian Platonism from the Fifteenth to the Eighteenth Century* (Ithaca, NY: Cornell University Press, 1972); *Revisioning Cambridge Platonism: Sources and Legacy*, eds. Douglas Hedley and David Leech (Cham, Switzerland: Springer, 2019).

4. Henry More, *Enchiridion ethicum* (London, 1667): I.ii.7. The translation is Edward Southwell's from 1690. The translations will be Southwell's unless otherwise stated. See Henry More, *An Account of Virtue: Or Dr. Henry More's Abridgement of Morals*, trans. Edward Southwell (London, 1690).

5. More, *Enchiridion ethicum*, I.ii.5.

6. More, *Enchiridion ethicum*, I.ii.6.

7. More, *Enchiridion ethicum*, I.ii.7.

8. Sarah Hutton, "Henry More's Moral Philosophy: Self-Determination and Its Limits," *Studia z Historii Filozofii* 8, no. 3 (2017): 11.

9. For details, see Sarah Hutton's "Introduction," in Ralph Cudworth, *A Treatise Concerning Eternal and Immutable Morality*, ed. Sarah Hutton (Cambridge: Cambridge University Press, 1996): ix–xxx.

10. As far as I know, until the last five years, the most recent article on More's ethics was Grace Dolson's "The Ethical System of Henry More," *Philosophical Review* 6, no. 6 (November 1897): 593–607. In the last five years, two have been published: Hutton, "Henry More's Moral Philosophy," and James Bryson, "A Philosophy of Love: Henry More's Moral Philosophy," *Neue Zeitschrift für Systematische Theologie und Religionsphilosophie* 61, no. 1 (2019): 84–106.

11. Robert Crocker, *Henry More: 1614–1687: The Biography of a Cambridge Platonist* (Dordrecht: Kluwer Academic Publishers, 2003): 29.

12. Crocker, *Henry More*, 45–58.

13. Henry More, *An Explanation of the Grand Mystery of Godliness* (London, 1660), Preface, viii.

14. More, *Grand Mystery*, preface, viii.

15. More, *Grand Mystery*, preface, viii.

16. More, *Grand Mystery*, II.iv.1.

17. In *Conjectura Cabbalistica* (London, 1653), More reads the fall in Genesis 3 as both a literal historical fall of human beings and a symbolic representation of the fall of preexistence human and angelic souls from the reign of the divine life to the unregulated pursuit of animal pleasure.

18. More, *Grand Mystery*, VIII.i.1.

19. More, *Grand Mystery*, II.ix.3.

20. More, *Grand Mystery*, II.ix.1.

21. More, *Grand Mystery*, II.ix.3.

22. More, *Grand Mystery*, II.ix.3.

23. More, *Grand Mystery*, II.ix–x.

24. More, *Grand Mystery*, II.xi.1.

25. More, *Grand Mystery*, II.xi.4–5.

26. More, *Grand Mystery*, II.xii.1.

27. More, *Grand Mystery*, II.xii.1–10. More here echoes the scholastic notion of the infused cardinal virtues. Yet for More, in contrast to the scholastics, both the acquired and the "infused" virtues are natural because the divine principle is natural to the soul.

28. Augustine, *City of God*, trans. Henry Bettenson (New York: Penguin Classics, 2003).

29. More, *Grand Mystery*, II.v.1.

30. More, *Grand Mystery*, II.v.2.

31. More, *Grand Mystery*, III.xix.2; see also V.vi.8.

32. More, *Grand Mystery*, VIII.xix.1. For the seven powers of the gospel, see book VIII, chapters 1–18.

33. More, *Grand Mystery*, II.vii.5.

34. More, *Grand Mystery*, II.xii.2.

35. More, *Enchiridion ethicum*, preface.

36. He explains the latter fact by saying that he means to shame Christians for taking virtue less seriously than pagans. More, *Enchiridion ethicum*, preface.

37. More, *Enchiridion ethicum*, preface.

38. More, *Enchiridion ethicum*, I.i.1.

39. More, *Enchiridion ethicum*, I.ii.2: "*Beatitudo est voluptas quam animus percipit ex sensu virtutis recteque (ad virtutius norman) factorum conscientia.*"

40. More, *Enchiridion ethicum*, I.ii.3. Though he recognizes that this stance is at odds with some things Aristotle says, More argues, citing *Magna Moralia*, that Aristotle ends up basically equating happiness with the pleasure that completes the operation of virtue.

41. More, *Enchiridion ethicum*, I.ii.5.

42. Aristotle, *Nicomachean Ethics* (Indianapolis, IN: Hackett Publishing Co., 1999): X.7, 1177a13–18.

43. I owe this neat summary to personal conversation with Adam Eitel. For a very helpful account of the reasons for the increasing concern with the will in this period, see Bonnie Kent, *Virtues of the Will: The Transformation of Ethics in the Late Thirteenth Century* (Washington DC: Catholic University of America Press, 1995).

44. For a very detailed account of medieval debates about the priority of intellect or will in human and angelic agency, see Tobias Hoffmann, *Free Will and the Rebel Angels in Medieval Philosophy* (Cambridge: Cambridge University Press, 2020).

45. For Aquinas's view, see Thomas Aquinas, *Summa theologica*, trans. Fathers of the English Dominican Province (Westminster, MD: Christian Classics, 1981): I-II.3.4. For Scotus's view, see Duns Scotus, *Duns Scotus on the Will and Morality*, ed. Allan B. Wolter, O. F. M. (Washington, DC: Catholic University of America Press, 1997): 153–66, 275–92.

46. More, *Enchiridion ethicum*, I.ii.6.

47. More, *Enchiridion ethicum*, III.i.10.

48. More, *Enchiridion ethicum*, III.i.2.

49. The first reference is in More, *Enchiridion ethicum*, I.iii.3. The second, among other places, is in I.iii.4. I am not following the translations of Southwell, who tends to exaggerate the divinity of the boniform faculty.

50. More, *Enchiridion ethicum*, I.ii.5. This translation is mine.

51. More, *Enchiridion ethicum*, I.ii.7.

52. More, *Enchiridion ethicum*, I.iii.10.

53. More, *Enchiridion ethicum*, II.ix.15.

54. More, *Enchiridion ethicum*, I.iii.1.

55. More, *Enchiridion ethicum*, I.iii.5.

56. Aristotle, *Nicomachean Ethics*, III.4, 1113a22.

57. Aristotle does not actually use the language of "good in some respect" in the passage in *Nicomachean Ethics* at III.4. However, he elsewhere makes it clear that the good to those in an imperfect condition can be called good in some respect. See *Nicomachean Ethics*, VII.12, 1152b26. See also Aristotle, *Eudemian Ethics*, VII.2, 1235b30–1236a7, in *The Complete Works of Aristotle*, ed. Jonathan Barnes (Princeton, NJ: Princeton University Press, 1984).

58. Thomas Aquinas, *Summa contra gentiles*, trans. Vernon J. Bourke (Notre Dame, IN: University of Notre Dame Press, 1956): III.108.6. At least one reason that Aquinas (along with More) needs this distinction is that he (unlike Aristotle) needs to explain how sin is possible for those created without defect of character. See *Summa theologica*, I.5.1ad1.

59. More, *Enchiridion ethicum*, I.iii.5.

60. Circles of this kind are not necessarily problematic, but More criticizes Aristotle for precisely this kind of circle. *Enchiridion ethicum*, II.ix.10.

61. More, *Enchiridion ethicum*, I.v.6–7.

62. More, *Enchiridion ethicum*, I.iii.4.

63. More, *Enchiridion ethicum*, I.iii.5.

64. More, *Enchiridion ethicum*, II.ii.6.

65. More, *Enchiridion ethicum*, I.iv.2.

66. More, *Enchiridion ethicum*, I.iv.2.

67. More, *Enchiridion ethicum*, II.ix.16. From the intellectual love of the boniform faculty "arise[s] all the Shapes and Modes of Virtue and of doing: And 'tis into this again, that all of them may, by a due and unerring Analysis, be resolv'd."

68. The axioms are in More, *Enchiridion ethicum*, I.ix. All translations of the axioms are mine.

69. The first is the definition of Aquinas. The second comes from Suárez. The third was rejected by all the scholastics, but the return of Epicureanism made it a live option, defended on the continent by Gassendi and in England by Walter Charleton. More's definition of happiness reveals a certain degree of sympathy with it. See Aquinas, *Summa theologica*, I.6; Suárez, *Metaphysical Disputation* X, in *The Metaphysics of Good and Evil according to Suárez*, eds. Jorge J. E. Gracia and Douglas Davis (München: Philosophia Verlag, 1989); Walter Charleton, *Epicurus's Morals* (London, 1656); Thomas Franklin Mayo, *Epicurus in England* (Dallas: Southwest Press, 1934).

70. His examples are telling. Goods are not food or a home but *that* a man have wherewithal to live well and happily (*Noema* XVII). His example of an evil is *that* a man should live in want and calamity (*Noema* XIX). See More, *Enchiridion ethicum*, I.iv.3.

71. Plato, *The Complete Works of Plato*, ed. John Cooper (Indianapolis, IN: Hackett Publishing Co., 1997): 353ff.

72. More, *Enchiridion ethicum*, I.v.8. The argument here is presented as binding with a

hypothetical necessity: *if* preservation is so valuable, *then* these conclusions follow. This argument is so constructed because it is directed against Hobbes. In the context, it is unclear if More means this claim to be merely a hypothetical conclusion to which Hobbes is committed or a substantive truth. In any case, More does not think that what we are bound to do is contingent on what we judge to be good, since judgments about good and evil are true or false.

73. The reference to "neighbor" is, of course, the biblical neighbor, that is, everyone.

74. More, *An Antidote against Atheisme* (London, 1653): I.v.

75. John Locke ridicules the notion of innate ideas but misconstrues how most advocates understand it. See John Locke, *An Essay Concerning Human Understanding*, ed. Peter Nidditch (Oxford: Clarendon Press, 1979): book I.

76. More, *Antidote against Atheisme*, I.v. A similar argument is made by Socrates in *Theaetetus*. More does not mention Plato but would certainly have known this text. Cudworth does cite it in his related argument discussed below.

77. More, *Antidote against Atheisme*, I.v. He gives two arguments that these ideas cannot be a product of sense experience. First, these ideas can be produced in relation to a subject even when that subject undergoes no physical alteration, as when the same two-pound block of lead is first compared to a four-pound block (producing the notion "half") and then to a one-pound block (producing the notion "double"). Second, opposite relative notions can be applied to the same physical object at the same time—again, "half" and "double" both apply when the two-pound block is between the one- and four-pound blocks.

78. More, *Antidote against Atheisme*, I.v.

79. Cudworth, *Eternal and Immutable Morality*, IV.ii.5.

80. Cudworth, *Eternal and Immutable Morality*, IV.vi.4.

81. More, *Enchiridion ethicum*, II.i.

82. More, *Grand Mystery*, II.ix.3.

83. More, *Enchiridion ethicum*, I.vi.8.

84. See René Descartes, *The Passions of the Soul*, in René Descartes, *The Philosophical Writings of Descartes*, vol. 1, trans. John Cottingham, Robert Stoothoff, and Dugald Murdoch (Cambridge: Cambridge University Press, 1984): 325–404.

85. More, *Enchiridion ethicum*, I.viii.1.

86. See More, *Enchiridion ethicum*, I.vi–xiii. While More often contrasts his views with Stoicism, his arguments are quite similar to those of the Stoics.

87. More, *Enchiridion ethicum*, II.v.4.

88. More, *Enchiridion ethicum*, I.iii.11.

89. More, *Enchiridion ethicum*, I.iii.5.

90. More, *Enchiridion ethicum*, II.iv.6.

91. Henry More, *Divine Dialogues*, vol. 1 (London, 1668): 14–15.

92. More, *Divine Dialogues*, vol. 1, 177.

93. Henry More, *The Immortality of the Soul* (London, 1659): II.xii.7, 242–43.

94. More, *Divine Dialogues*, vol. 1, 159.

95. More, *Divine Dialogues*, vol. 1, 237–38.

96. More, *Divine Dialogues*, vol. 1, 179–80.

97. More, *Grand Mystery*, II.xii.1.

98. More, *Divine Dialogues*, vol. 2 (London, 1668): 18.

99. More, *Divine Dialogues*, vol. 2, 14–15.

100. More, *Divine Dialogues*, vol. 2, 24–25. The priority of goodness over wisdom and power is clear from Philotheus's claim that "to infinite, permanent, and immutable goodness of right belongs as well omnisciency as omnipotency, the one as her secretary the other as her satellitium" (24).

101. More, *Enchiridion ethicum*, I.iii.6.

102. More, *Divine Dialogues*, vol. 2, 14–15.

103. For a more detailed treatment of productivist accounts of agency, see Ryan Darr, "For the Sake of the Final End: Eudaimonism, Self-Orientation, and the Nature of Human Agency," *Journal of Religious Ethics* 48, no. 2 (2020): 182–200, at 186–91.

104. For a definition, see pages 16–17.

Chapter Three

1. Jon Parkin, *Science, Religion, and Politics in Restoration England* (Rochester, NY: Boydell Press, 1999): 176. Knud Haakonssen argues the same in "The Character and Obligation of the Natural Law according to Richard Cumberland," in *English Philosophy in the Age of Locke*, ed. M. A. Stewart (Oxford: Oxford University Press, 2000): 29–48.

2. Albee, for example, calls him the "true founder of English Utilitarianism." Ernest Albee, *A History of English Utilitarianism* (New York: Collier Books, 1962): 19.

3. Linda Kirk, *Richard Cumberland and the Natural Law: Secularization of Thought in Seventeenth-Century England* (Cambridge: James Clarke and Co., 1987). She is not alone in this perspective. Ernest Albee, in his *A History of English Utilitarianism*, argues that Cumberland can rightly be called the first utilitarian because his arguments about divine commands are mere "scaffolding."

4. Parkin, *Science, Religion, and Politics in Restoration England*, 108. See also the response of Haakonssen, who points to other textual evidence that shows that what was added to the definition at the last minute was already assumed by Cumberland to be implicit in it. Cumberland's detailed exposition of the definition, which was not changed, includes discussion of the ethical voluntarist elements. Haakonssen, "Character and Obligation of the Natural Law," 37–38.

5. See John Maxwell, "Translator's Preface," in Richard Cumberland, *A Treatise of the Laws of Nature*, trans. John Maxwell, ed. John Parkin (Indianapolis, IN: Liberty Fund, 2005): 5.

6. Hugo Grotius, *De jure belli ac pacis* (Paris, 1625); Robert Sharrock, *De officiis secundum naturae jus* (London, 1660).

7. Richard Cumberland, *Treatise of the Laws of Nature*, Intro.ii–iii. Further references to this work will be cited parenthetically in the text. I follow Maxwell's translation unless otherwise noted.

8. John Selden, *De jure naturali et gentium* (London, 1640).

9. J. B. Schneewind, *The Invention of Autonomy* (Cambridge: Cambridge University Press, 1998): 70–73.

10. Schneewind, *Invention of Autonomy*, 72.

11. Schneewind agrees. He sees Cumberland as working at least in part in continuity with the perfectionist natural law tradition of the scholastics, but adds that Cumberland wants to "bring this view up to date" (Schneewind, *Invention of Autonomy*, 102).

12. In my terminology, Suárez is a legislative voluntarist but not an ethical voluntarist.

280 NOTES TO PAGES 76-80

13. Francisco Suárez, *A Treatise on Law and God the Lawgiver*, I.3.3, in Suárez, *Selections from Three Works*, ed. Thomas Pink (Indianapolis, IN: Liberty Fund, 2015).

14. Suárez, *Treatise on Law and God the Lawgiver*, II.6.8.

15. Nathaniel Culverwell, *An Elegant and Learned Discourse on the Light of Nature* (Indianapolis, IN: Liberty Fund, 2001).

16. Part of Cumberland's reasoning is also ad hominem. He argues that Hobbes, the target of his critique, has already shown himself unwilling to take scripture seriously (*Treatise of the Laws of Nature*, Intro.xxvii).

17. Thomas Aquinas, *Summa theologica*, trans. Fathers of the English Dominican Province (Westminster, MD: Christian Classics, 1981): I-II.1-5.

18. Aquinas, *Summa theologica*, I-II.1.1. Human behaviors that do not proceed from a deliberate will (e.g., sneezes, reflexes, etc.) are called "actions of a man" rather than "human actions."

19. Aquinas, *Summa theologica*, I-II.1.8. This quote from the Fathers of the English Dominican Province translation does not appear to be in the original Latin text. It is, however, an adequate statement of Aquinas's view.

20. Aquinas, *Summa theologica*, I-II.1.4; Aristotle, *Nicomachean Ethics* (Indianapolis, IN: Hackett Publishing Co., 1999): I.2, 1094a18-22.

21. For Aquinas, the internal act of will relates to the external act of the body as form to matter (*Summa theologica*, I-II.18.6). Cumberland rejects the Aristotelian metaphysical assumptions behind this picture. An action is a bodily movement, and moral philosophy can safely bracket the activity of soul. Thus, while Cumberland is a perfectionist, he is strictly speaking only giving an account of the perfection of the movements of the body and asking what qualities of soul would produce those movements of body.

22. Frank Spaulding also notes this shift in terminology and attributes it to a desire for ethics to be as valid as natural science. I do not disagree, but I am highlighting a further aim. See Spaulding, *Richard Cumberland als Begründer der englischen Ethik* (Leipzig: Gustav Fock, 1894): 18.

23. The Latin term *facultates* includes a number of possible English translations that exceed the meaning of "faculties": means, abilities, skills, opportunities, chances, resources, supplies. For simplicity, I will stick with "faculties," but the broader meaning should be kept in mind.

24. See Francisco Suárez, *Metaphysical Disputation X*, in *The Metaphysics of Good and Evil according to Suárez*, eds. Jorge J. E. Gracia and Douglas Davis (München: Philosophia Verlag, 1989). Both Suárez and Cumberland use *convenientia*. Gracia and Davis argue that "agreeability" is a better translation than "agreement" because it indicates a characteristic of something rather than an act. See *Metaphysics of Good and Evil according to Suárez*, 23–29. This argument, I think, holds true for Suárez but not Cumberland. I will later emphasize the differences between Cumberland and Suárez on this point.

25. Thomas Hobbes, *Leviathan*, ed. Edwin Curley (Indianapolis, IN: Hackett Publishing Co., 1994): I.xv.40.

26. The primary mystery is why Cumberland excludes nonrational beings from the highest good. Presumably, a more inclusive aggregate is possible: all living beings, perhaps, or even all beings. He only notes briefly that he does not deny that we should care for nonrational beings, but that their perfection is to be sought only insofar as it serves the common good of all rationals (*Treatise of the Laws of Nature*, V.viii).

27. Whether aggregates are genuine wholes in a metaphysical sense remains unclear. His description of aggregation suggests that it is an abstraction performed by intellect.

Nonetheless, it must pick out something unified enough to have a proper order and its own proper goods. Some interpreters have been misled by the language of summation. Cumberland never says he is summing the happiness of individual rational beings. He is summing the particular things that are good for this aggregate as an aggregate.

28. *De legibus*, III.iv. Cumberland cites this sentence from Thomas Hobbes, *On the Citizen* (Oxford: Clarendon Press, 1983): I.ii.

29. For detailed treatment of these contrasts, see Terence Irwin, *The Development of Ethics: A Historical and Critical Study*, vol. 2 (Oxford: Oxford University Press, 2008): 224–25. Irwin also discusses the material treated in the next several paragraphs, but he fails to recognize the important break Cumberland makes with Suárez and Culverwell on the relationship between moral goodness and rational nature.

30. There are too many nuances here for my terminology to be particularly helpful. What exactly counts as "obligation" gets difficult to discern. Is natural *honestas* obligatory? My definitions will not do full justice here since the terminology itself is shifting. I do think, however, that calling each of these figures a legislative voluntarist but not an ethical voluntarist is generally a helpful way of understanding them.

31. Suárez, *Disputation* X.i.12, in *Metaphysics of Good and Evil according to Suárez*, 111.

32. Suárez, *Disputation* X.ii.31, in *Metaphysics of Good and Evil according to Suárez*, 138.

33. Culverwell, *Elegant and Learned Discourse*, 55.

34. Cumberland seems to assume without argument that the individual's happiness is necessarily contained in the common good of all rationals. Even if the assumption were warranted, the common good of all rationals would still be what defines virtue.

35. This distinction is true not only of contemporary usages, but also of Latin usage before Cumberland. See, for example, Aquinas's contrast between benevolence and concupiscence as two different ways to love someone (*Summa theologica*, II-II.32.1).

36. Cf. Parkin, *Science, Religion, and Politics in Restoration England*, 176–77; Spaulding, *Richard Cumberland als Begründer*, 21–23. Maxwell, Cumberland's earliest English translator, also notes the odd use of the term. See note 8 on pages 297–98 of *A Treatise of the Laws of Nature*.

37. He says that he has "not been so happy as to learn the laws of nature in so short a way" as by innate ideas. At the same time, it is clear that he is trying not to alienate the "Platonists," to whom he attributes this approach. He instead seems to be trying to show that their ideas about morality do not require the philosophically doubtful appeal to innate ideas. See Cumberland, *Treatise of the Laws of Nature*, Intro.v.

38. See also Stephen Darwall, *The British Moralists and the Internal 'Ought'* (Cambridge: Cambridge University Press, 1995): 84–85.

39. Albee, *History of English Utilitarianism*, 47; Frank Chapman Sharp, "The Ethical System of Richard Cumberland and Its Place in the History of British Ethics," *Mind* 21, no. 83 (1912): 377–78; Schneewind, *The Invention of Autonomy*, 113–14. Albee recognizes that Cumberland refuses to prioritize pleasure over perfection explicitly but thinks he does so implicitly. Schneewind's argument for Cumberland's hedonism—that he is forced into it by his need to treat God as a member of the moral community—is very interesting but, I think, ultimately mistaken.

40. Almost every aspect of this argument is traditional. Platonic, Aristotelian, and Stoic influences are evident. But the idea that happiness is a reward for (rather than constitutive of) virtue changes the character of the argument. Cumberland acknowledges that happiness is "so *intimately* connected with [virtue] as to be *inseparable* from it." But he argues that because "this Reward may be *distinguish'd*, in Thought at least, from Virtue,

and is *proper* to it, and may be *foreseen* as a *Reward*, it seem'd necessary to consider it under the Notion of a *Sanction* annex'd" (*Treatise of the Laws of Nature*, V.xxxv). In passages like this one, Cumberland wrestles with the oddity of describing the happiness of the virtuous as an effect of their actions, especially because his account of happiness includes perfection. But two features of Cumberland's position lend a certain plausibility to this picture: (1) his formal distinction between the natural goodness of virtuous action itself and the natural goodness of virtuous action to the agent and (2) his productivist account of agency.

41. A lot of attention has been given to the fact that Cumberland rarely mentions sanctions after death. But Haakonssen is exactly right on this matter. The point of his emphasis on this-worldly sanctions is to prove the existence of the natural law. He is perfectly clear that there are also sanctions after death. Indeed, these play a crucial role in correcting for natural contingencies—a feature which will play an important part in future uses of Cumberland's argument. But they cannot be proved by the natural sciences Cumberland is citing. See Haakonssen, "Character and Obligation of the Natural Law," 39–40.

42. The claim about probability does have another function. It allows Cumberland to argue that even though there is no necessary connection in this life between virtue and happiness, virtue remains the path most likely to cause happiness.

43. For Cumberland, the whole of humanity operates like the body of an animal. Each part is for the good of the whole, and the good of each part is found in the good of the whole. When individual agents pursue the common good, their own happiness is served. But disorders can occur in both the bodies of animals and the "body" of humanity as a whole. "We must confess, however, that many things may happen, by means whereof this general *Care of the Whole* may not *always* produce the propos'd Happiness of Individuals, without allay; as breathing and eating, however necessary to the whole Body, do not ward off *all* Diseases and Accidents. For, as well by an *irregular Behavior of our Fellow-Citizens*, like an *indisposition in the Bowels*, as by *foreign Invasion*, good Men may be depriv'd of some of the Rewards of their good Actions, and may suffer Evils from without" (*Treatise of the Laws of Nature*, Intro.xxii). The existence of irregularities in human society—of, for example, individuals who subvert the good acts of others for their own gain and thereby disrupt proper social functioning—no more undermines the nature of human society than the existence of disease undermines the nature of the animal body (*Treatise of the Laws of Nature*, Intro.xxii). Just as we do not determine the nature of an animal or its parts by studying a diseased body, we do not determine the natural course of human social life with reference to its disordered elements. The will of the first cause is known by nature, meaning the ordinary and healthy operation of human social life. Disordered elements may further derail the natural proportioning of sanctions, but they do not undermine the expressed command of God.

44. Henry Sidgwick, *Outlines of the History of Ethics* (Indianapolis, IN: Hackett Publishing Co., 1998): 175; Albee, *History of English Utilitarianism*, 53–54; Sharp, "Ethical System of Richard Cumberland," 382–83; Stamatios Tzitzis, "La loi et le châtiment chez Richard Cumberland, adversaire de Hobbes," *Revue historique de droit français et etranger* 65, no. 2 (1987): 233–52.

45. In particular, see Darwall, *British Moralists*, 105–6; Irwin, *Development of Ethics*, vol. 2, §539.

46. This a summary of my reading of Cumberland, *Treatise of the Laws of Nature*, VII. vi–vii.

47. Darwall, *British Moralists*, 91, 105–6.

48. Irwin, *Development of Ethics*, vol. 2, §539, 235.

49. On Cumberland's influence on Pufendorf, see Parkin, *Science, Religion, and Politics in Restoration England*, 205–12. Samuel Pufendorf, *De jure naturae et gentium libri octo*, ed. J. B. Scott (Oxford: Clarendon Press, 1934).

50. James Tyrrell, *A Brief Disquisition of the Law of Nature* (London, 1693); Samuel Parker, *A Demonstration of the Divine Authority of the Law of Nature and the Christian Religion* (London, 1681). Tyrrell's version had the secondary aim of convincing John Locke that Cumberland's argument could provide the missing grounds for Locke's expressed belief that morality, while founded on the command of God, was capable of rational demonstration.

51. On the productivist picture of agency, see page 71.

52. See, for example, G. E. M. Anscombe, *Intention* (Cambridge, MA: Harvard University Press, 2000).

53. For more on this point, see Ryan Darr, "For the Sake of the Final End: Eudaimonism, Self-Orientation, and the Nature of Human Agency," *Journal of Religious Ethics* 48, no. 2 (2020): 182–200, at 186–91.

54. Jorge Gracia and Douglas Paul Davis, "Introduction," in *The Metaphysics of Good and Evil according to Suárez*, eds. Gracia and Davis, 23–29.

55. Hence when Cumberland asserts the scholastic dictum that the adequate object of the will is the good, he takes this to mean that any effect can be willed in which something is preserved or perfected.

56. Cf. Spaulding, *Richard Cumberland als Begründer*, 29.

Epilogue to Part I

1. Henry Sidgwick, *Outlines of the History of Ethics* (Indianapolis, IN: Hackett Publishing Co., 1998): 169–75.

2. Cumberland is responding directly to Hobbes. More's ethical writings are not usually directly engaged with Hobbes, but I have argued that his attacks on Calvinism are often better understood as attacks on Hobbes's views.

3. Sidgwick, *Outlines of the History of Ethics*, 170.

4. For Cumberland, as discussed in the previous chapter, the principle of the natural law binds both divine and human will and action, though it does not bind them in the same way. It is not strictly morally binding on God since God has no superior. Nonetheless, Cumberland says that God's judgments are like a law to God, and God's judgments bind God to pursue the same end as rational creatures.

5. More's attempt to model morality on mathematics fits with a common ambition of the era. Mordechai Levy-Eichel has recently published a history of the attempt to integrate mathematical calculation into ethics. In Levy-Eichel's story, Shaftesbury introduces the term "moral arithmetic," and Francis Hutcheson is the first to formalize it into equations. Both Shaftesbury and Hutcheson, I argue in part II, are indebted to More, and the form of Hutcheson's equations can be seen as a formalization of the mathematical logic of More's axioms. See Mordechai Levy-Eichel, " 'The Moral Arithmetic': Morality in the Age of Mathematics," *Intellectual History Review* 31, no. 2 (2021): 267–82.

6. I noted in the introduction that I am calling views according to which the goodness of actions consists in their causal promotion of good outcomes consequentialist even when they include the caveat that divine command is necessary for obligation.

7. James Tyrrell, *A Brief Disquisition of the Law of Nature* (London, 1693): 85–90.

Chapter Four

1. Susan Neiman, *Evil in Modern Thought: An Alternative History of Philosophy* (Princeton, NJ: Princeton University Press, 2002): 2–3.

2. Neiman, *Evil in Modern Thought*, 11.

3. Citations come from the edition published in Paris in 1820: Pierre Bayle, *Dictionnaire historique et critique* (Paris: Desoer, 1820). Translations are my own.

4. For a good overview of the debates about evil between a few of the major philosophers and theologians of the seventeenth century, see Steven Nadler, *The Best of All Possible Worlds: A Story of Philosophers, God, and Evil in the Age of Reason* (Princeton, NJ: Princeton University Press, 2010).

5. Or, more recently, it is often framed as two problems: the logical problem of evil and the evidential problem of evil.

6. Amelie Oksenberg Rorty, "From Passions to Emotions and Sentiments," *Philosophy* 57, no. 220 (1982): 160.

7. Lactantius, "The Wrath of God (*De ira rei*)" in *The Minor Works*, trans. Sister Mary Francis McDonald, OP (Washington, DC: Catholic University of America Press, 1965), excerpted in *The Problem of Evil: A Reader*, ed. Mark Larrimore (Malden, MA: Blackwell, 2001): 50.

8. See Larrimore, *Problem of Evil*, xx–xxiv.

9. Larrimore, *Problem of Evil*, xx–xxiv. On the different arguments from evil, see also Michael Hickson, "A Brief History of Problems of Evil," in *The Blackwell Companion to the Problem of Evil*, eds. Justin P. McBrayer and Daniel Howard-Snyder (Malden, MA: Wiley Blackwell, 2013): 3–18.

10. Manicheanism is different from Marcion's Gnosticism, and I do not mean to conflate the two. But for my purposes, it is sufficient to treat them as two versions of a dualistic explanation of evil. Bayle, as we will see, does the same.

11. Plotinus, *The Enneads*, trans. Lloyd Gerson (Cambridge: Cambridge University Press, 2017): I.8. See also Dominic J. O'Meara, "Explaining Evil in Late Antiquity: Plotinus and His Critics," in *Evil: A History*, ed. Andrew Chignell (Oxford: Oxford University Press, 2019): 129–54; O'Meara, *Plotinus: An Introduction to the Enneads* (Oxford: Oxford University Press, 1993): ch. 8.

12. This way of making the distinction comes from Samuel Newlands. O'Meara gives a slightly different reading of Plotinus. See Samuel Newlands, "The Problem of Evil," in *Routledge Companion to Seventeenth-Century Philosophy*, ed. Dan Kaufman (New York: Routledge, 2017): 536–62.

13. See "Translator's Introduction" to Augustine, *On Free Choice of Will*, trans. Anna Benjamin and L. H. Hackstaff (Upper Saddle River, NJ: Prentice Hall, 1964): ix.

14. Augustine, *On Free Choice of Will*, 3.

15. Augustine, *On Free Choice of Will*, 3.

16. Augustine, *On Free Choice of Will*, 84. Book III raises a host of issues including the cause of the will's act, the compatibility of freedom and divine foreknowledge, and the justice of inherited sin. I am passing over this material.

17. See, for example, G. R. Evans, *Augustine on Evil* (Cambridge: Cambridge University Press, 1990); William Mann, "Augustine on Evil and Original Sin," in *The Cambridge Companion to Augustine*, eds. Eleonore Stump and Norman Kretzmann (Cambridge: Cambridge University Press, 2001): 98–107; Eleonore Stump, "Augustine on Free Will," in *The Cambridge Companion to Augustine*, eds. Stump and Kretzmann, 166–86.

18. Jesse Couenhoven, "Augustine's Rejection of the Free-Will Defense: An Overview of the Late Augustine's Theodicy," *Religious Studies* 43, no. 3 (2009): 279–98.

19. See Michael Hickson, "A Brief History of Problems of Evil," 9–10; Brian Davies, *Thomas Aquinas on God and Evil* (Oxford: Oxford University Press, 2007), 5–7

20. See Hickson, "Brief History of Problems of Evil," 11–12.

21. Bayle, "Pauliciens," Remark F, in *Dictionnaire historique et critique*, 488.

22. Thomas Hobbes, *Of Liberty and Necessity*, in *Hobbes and Bramhall on Liberty and Necessity*, ed. Vere Chappell (Cambridge: Cambridge University Press, 1999): 22.

23. Thomas Aquinas, *Summa contra gentiles*, trans. Vernon J. Bourke (Notre Dame, IN: University of Notre Dame Press, 1956): I.14.2.

24. I am obviously simplifying quite a bit here. The goal is simply to illuminate More and Cumberland's vision and its relation to evil more clearly through contrast. For much more on Aquinas and evil, see Davies, *Thomas Aquinas on God and Evil*; Herbert McCabe, *God and Evil in the Theology of St. Thomas Aquinas* (New York: Continuum, 2010).

25. Thomas M. Lennon, *Reading Bayle* (Toronto: University of Toronto Press, 1999): 9–10.

26. Jean-Pierre Jossua, *Bayle ou l'obsession du mal* (Paris: Aubier-Montaigne, 1977).

27. See Elisabeth Labrousse, *Bayle*, trans. Denys Potts (Oxford: Oxford University Press, 1983).

28. For a useful summary of the state of scholarship on this question, see Mara van der Lugt, *Bayle, Jurieu, and the* Dictionnaire Historique et Critique (Oxford: Oxford University Press, 2016). For the most interesting recent attempt to resolve the Bayle enigma, see Dmitri Levitin, *The Kingdom of Darkness: Bayle, Newton, and the Emancipation of the European Mind from Philosophy* (Cambridge: Cambridge University Press, 2021).

29. Van der Lugt, *Bayle, Jurieu, and the* Dictionnaire Historique et Critique, chapter 4.

30. Pierre Jurieu, *Traité de la natura et de la grâce*, quoted in van der Lugt, *Bayle, Jurieu, and the* Dictionnaire Historique et Critique, 169.

31. Bayle, "Manichees," Remark D, in *Dictionnaire historique et critique*, 196–97.

32. Bayle, "Manichees," Remark D, in *Dictionnaire historique et critique*, 199.

33. Bayle, "Manichees," Remark D, in *Dictionnaire historique et critique*, 198.

34. The term "freedom of indifference" can mean different things, and I use it with some hesitancy. But Bayle uses the term, and I specify here how I understand its meaning. On the different senses of "indifference" in early modern thought, see Thomas M. Lennon, "Descartes and the Seven Senses of Indifference in Early Modern Philosophy," *Dialogue* 50 (2011): 577–602.

35. In my typology of voluntarisms related to ethics in chapter 1, I defined agential voluntarism as the perspective in which the will in itself is indifferent to the judgments of reason about the good to be done and the evil to be avoided. There is no strict incompatibility between this view and determinism. Thus the freedom of indifference must include not only agential voluntarism but also libertarian freedom.

36. Bayle, "Manichees," Remark D, in *Dictionnaire historique et critique*, 198.

37. Bayle makes this argument quickly and does not discuss any real attempts to reconcile the two. He does treat this issue in more detail elsewhere in response to criticism from Isaac Jacquelot. See Pierre Bayle, *Réponse aux questions d'un provincial* (La Haye: La Compagnie des Libraires, 1737): vol. 2, ch. 141. Leibniz also criticizes Bayle on this point. See G. W. Leibniz, *Theodicy: Essays on the Goodness of God, the Freedom of Man, and the Origin of Evil* (Eugene, OR: Wipf and Stock Publishers, 2001): §388–93. For discussion, see Jean-Pascal Anfray, "Continuous Creation, Occasionalism, and Persistence: Leibniz

on Bayle," in *Physics and Metaphysics in Descartes and in his Reception*, eds. Delphine Antoine-Mahut and Sophie Roux (New York: Routledge, 2018): 213–24.

38. On clear and distinct ideas, see René Descartes, *Meditations on First Philosophy* in *The Philosophical Writings of Descartes*, vol. 2, trans. John Cottingham, Robert Stoothoff, and Dugald Murdoch (Cambridge: Cambridge University Press, 1984): 1–62. On free will, see *Principles of Philosophy* in *The Philosophical Writings of Descartes*, vol. 1, trans. Cottingham, Stoothoff, and Murdoch, 177–291.

39. Bayle, "Pauliciens," Remark E, in *Dictionnaire historique et critique*, 482–83.

40. Bayle's theological opponents are not without possible responses. Perhaps the saints in heaven retain the possibility of sin in other circumstances but not in the beatific vision. Perhaps their infallible choice of the good stems from the immediate presence of the highest good together with the absence of temptation. Bayle recognizes this possibility, but he does not think it provides any better answer. God could remove temptation on earth as well. If, as the Molinists think, God respects free will but puts individuals in circumstances in which God knows they will or will not sin, God is morally responsible for all moral evil. A Molinist theory of free will and divine decree, Bayle thinks, still must accept that God could have providentially ordered the world in such a way as to prevent sin from ever occurring. Perhaps a Molinist account explains why human beings freely sin and thus deserve the consequences of sin. Bayle's primary worry is elsewhere. Such an account, he claims, still does nothing to morally justify God for allowing the existence of evil.

41. Bayle, "Marcionites," Remark E, in *Dictionnaire historique et critique*. See also book III of Cicero's *De natura deorum*, which Bayle cites. See Cicero, *On the Nature of the Gods*, trans. Francis Brooks (London: Methuen, 1896).

42. Bayle, "Pauliciens," Remark E, in *Dictionnaire historique et critique*, 485.

43. Bayle, "Pauliciens," Remark F, in *Dictionnaire historique et critique*, 487–88.

44. Bayle, "Pauliciens," Remark M, in *Dictionnaire historique et critique*, 505.

45. Bayle, "Pauliciens," Remark E, in *Dictionnaire historique et critique*, 479–80.

46. Bayle, "Pauliciens," Remark E, in *Dictionnaire historique et critique*, 483–84.

47. See, for example, his dispute with William King on whether dualism really addresses the issue of the good principle's willingness to allow evil. King argues that the good principle still would have foreseen the evils of the world and judged it worth creating in the first place. Bayle responds that had the good principle refrained from creating, the evil principle would have created a horrific world. Thus the good principle has no choice in a dualistic view. In a theistic view, by contrast, God could simply refrain from creating. See Bayle, *Réponse aux questions d'un provincial*, vol. 2, ch. 75.

48. Bayle, "Manichees," Remark D, in *Dictionnaire historique et critique*, 199.

49. See Leibniz, *Theodicy*.

50. Samuel Newlands has shown how privation theory, which remained prominent in the work of Descartes, slowly declined over the course of the seventeenth century. A fuller treatment of evil in this period would address this line of argument more fully. I have decided not to do so primarily because the kind of worry that privation theory was meant to answer becomes less significant and attention turns much more to God's moral reasons for permitting or causing evil. Samuel Newlands, "Evils, Privations, and the Early Moderns," in *Evil: A History*, ed. Andrew Chignell (Oxford: Oxford University Press, 2019): 273–306.

51. Paul Rateau is thus not entirely correct when he writes, in the opening lines of his essay on Leibniz's *Theodicy*, "The way Leibniz tackles the problem of evil is original, as it

is explicitly connected with the theme of justice. The first question evil raises is not 'Why does it exist?' or the traditional 'Where does it come from?' (*Unde malum?*), but rather 'Who is responsible for it?' The issue is first moral and juridical, because it is the question of imputation that is at stake." Leibniz's explicit moral framing of the question is, at least in part, a response to Bayle's framing. See Rateau, "The Problem of Evil and the Justice of God," in *The Oxford Handbook of Leibniz*, ed. Maria Rosa Antognazza (Oxford: Oxford University Press, 2018): 100.

52. Bayle, *Réponse aux questions d'un provincial*, vol. 3, part 2, ch. 81, section XVI (my translation).

53. Leibniz makes this point about Bayle as well. In his *Dissertation on the Conformity of Faith with Reason*, Leibniz complains that Bayle puts God on trial via the ordinary means by which a human being would be tried. Nicola Stricker responds by pointing to the following line from Bayle: "Il ne faut point se promettre de mesurer à la même aune la conduite de Dieu & la conduite des hommes." But the response is misleading. While Bayle does ultimately refuse to measure God by human moral standards, he insists that any *rational* account of the existence of evil would have to do so. His ultimate refusal to do so is one with his embrace of fideism. See Nicola Stricker, "Les Stratégies Argumentatives d'une (Anti-) Théodicée: Bayle et Leibniz," *Études théologiques et religieuses* 81, no. 4 (2006): 484.

54. Labrousse, *Bayle*, 90.

55. Justin Champion, "Bayle in the English Enlightenment," in *Pierre Bayle (1647–1706), le philosophe de Rotterdam: Philosophy, Religion and Reception*, eds. Wiep van Bunge and Hans Bots (Leiden: Brill, 2008): 178–79.

Chapter Five

1. Justin Champion, "Bayle in the English Enlightenment," in *Pierre Bayle (1647–1706), le philosophe de Rotterdam: Philosophy, Religion and Reception*, eds. Wiep van Bunge and Hans Bots (Leiden: Brill, 2008): 183.

2. Uta Golembek, *Willensfreiheit und Gottes Güte: Kings Lösung des Theodizeeproblems und ihre Rezeption in der deutschen Aufklärung* (Würzburg: Königshausen & Neumann, 2013): 10. Translations of this text are my own.

3. Sean Greenberg writes, "Although *On the Origin of Evil* is little-read today, it was quite significant in its own time and it proved immensely influential on latter writers." See Greenberg, "Leibniz on King: Freedom and the Project of the 'Theodicy,'" *Studia Leibnitiana* 40, no. 2 (2008): 207.

4. Marion Hellwig, *Alles ist gut: Untersuchungen zur Geschichte einer Theodizee-Formel im 18. Jahrhundert in Deutschland, England und Frankreich* (Würzburg: Königshausen & Neumann, 2008): 79–80.

5. For an extensive treatment of King's reception, which focuses on Germany but treats other realms for the sake of contrast, see Uta Golembek's *Willensfreiheit und Gottes Güte*.

6. Arthur O. Lovejoy, *The Great Chain of Being* (Cambridge, MA: Harvard University Press, 1964): 211–12. This conclusion, according to Golembek, is valid only for the English-speaking realm. See Golembek, *Willensfreiheit und Gottes Güte*, 54.

7. Joseph Richardson, "William King—European Man of Letters," in *Archbishop William King and the Irish Anglican Context, 1688–1729*, ed. Christopher J. Fauske (Dublin: Four Courts Press, 2004): 112. See also Victor Nuovo, "Introduction," in *The Collective Works of Edmund Law*, ed. Victor Nuovo (London: Thoemmes Press, 1997): xiv; R. R. Hartford, "William King, the Man and His Work," *Theology* 48 (1945): 59. Golembek,

by contrast, argues that King is seen as an opponent of Bayle not because he intentionally wrote against Bayle but because Bayle responded to him. See *Willensfreiheit und Gottes Güte*, 39.

8. See the introduction for a discussion of how utilitarianism relates to consequentialism.

9. Though King is committed to the rational project of natural theology, he elsewhere defends a rather strong doctrine of analogy. In his widely circulated and debated sermon "Divine Predestination and Foreknowledge, consistent with the Freedom of Man's Will," King argues that all language about God is analogical. King's account of analogy appeals to contemporary science and its understanding of secondary qualities. According to modern atomism, secondary qualities like color and heat are not in objects but are produced in us by the way that the matter and motion of objects affect our senses. For King, we do not know the actual nature of objects or how they produce their effects on our senses. Nonetheless, the knowledge of our senses is sufficient for all practical purposes. The same, he argues, is true of our knowledge of God. Just as we do not know what fire is or how it produces the sensation of heat, we do not know what God is or how God does what God does. At the same time, we do know enough about fire to understand its importance for human life, and the same is true of God. Our knowledge of God, like our knowledge of fire, is practical. This way of understanding analogy gives King the confidence to say that even though we do not know what it means about God to say that God is good, we do know what it means about how God acts towards creation, namely, that God always acts for the good of creatures. Hence, for King, to say that God is good is to say that God will create a "world with the greatest goodness." In this way, King's doctrine of analogy actually makes divine aims more transparent than they might otherwise be. See William King, *Divine Predestination and Fore-Knowledge, Consistent with the Freedom of Man's Will* (Dublin, 1710).

10. William King, *An Essay on the Origin of Evil*, 1st ed., ed. and trans. Edmund Law (London, 1731): I.iii.10. Quotations are from Edmund Law's translation unless otherwise noted. All further references to this work will be cited parenthetically in the text.

11. The Latin is: "Per Bonum hic intelligo quod conveniens & commodum est, quod appetitui cujusq."

12. As discussed in part I, Cumberland uses *convenientia* to define the good. More uses several terms, one of which is *congruentia*. Nothing in King's text suggests that he means anything different by *convenientia*, *commoditate*, and *congruentia*. They seem to function as synonyms, blending terminology from More and Cumberland.

13. This threefold distinction, according to Maria Rosa Antognazza, was first introduced by Leibniz in *Tractatio de Deo et Homine*, though Leibniz's *Tractatio* was published the same year as *De origine mali*. Leibniz distinguishes between metaphysical, natural, and moral evil. See "Metaphysical Evil Revisited" in *New Essays on Leibniz's Theodicy*, eds. Larry M. Jorgensen and Samuel Newlands (Oxford: Oxford University Press, 2014): 112–34.

14. King here echoes Lovejoy's "principle of plenitude." Lovejoy, however, fails to recognize that the rationale is actually somewhat different. King does not argue that there is good simply in the realization of every level of being. God's aim is to create as many creatures as God can in such a way that those creatures form a single system. Why a single system? The thought, as far as I can tell, is that a system is how God ensures that each is ordered in such a way as to ensure the satisfaction of all as far as is possible. God does want more creatures, but realizing levels of being is not the point. The point, rather, is the

maximal satisfaction of appetite, and having beings of multiple levels improves the system's capacity to do this. Thus I do not think King's point here is Platonic.

15. Pierre Bayle, *Réponse aux questions d'un provincial* (La Haye: La Compagnie des Libraires, 1737): vol. 2, ch. 75.

16. In the second edition, Law adds a note from King's unpublished papers written in response to some of his critics. King writes that confusion arises when the words "good, better, and best [are taken for] for absolute qualities inherent in the nature of things, whereas in truth they are only relations arising from certain appetites. They indeed have a foundation; but yet they themselves imply nothing more than a Relation of Congruity between some Appetite and its Objects, as appears from hence, that the same Object when applied to an Appetite to which it has a congruity is good, and Vice versa, bad." King, *An Essay on the Origin of Evil*, 2nd ed. and trans. Edmund Law (London, 1732): note Q.

17. As quoted in chapter 2, More argues that the "*Incompossibilities* and *Lubricities* of *Matter*" are such that certain evils are unavoidable. See Henry More, *Divine Dialogues*, vol. 1 (London, 1668): 179–80.

18. I am here disagreeing with Maria Antognazza. See Maria Rosa Antognazza, "Metaphysical Evil Revisited," 118.

19. In his response to King, Bayle is extremely critical on this point, arguing that there are no necessary principles determining how souls and bodies must interact. God did not have to make anything painful. He could have achieved the same result through varying degrees of pleasure. See *Réponse aux questions d'un provincial*, vol. 2, chs. 76–77.

20. Thomas Aquinas, *Summa theologica*, trans. Fathers of the English Dominican Province (Westminster, MD: Christian Classics, 1981): I-II.18.1.

21. John Locke, *An Essay Concerning Human Understanding*, ed. Peter Nidditch (Oxford: Clarendon Press, 1979): II.xx.

22. See also Greenberg, "Leibniz on King," 214.

23. See chapter 1 above for the definitions of the various species of voluntarism.

24. The idea that creation satisfying a fixed appetite in God entails that creation is necessary is not necessarily true. The views discussed in chapter 1 would say something different. God does have what King would consider a fixed appetite for the good, which is perfectly satisfied because God in Godself is the highest good. Creation is not necessary for divine happiness. But God has discretion in how God acts for the sake of Godself. God chooses to do so by creating and orienting creatures to Godself. King never considers this sort of option, perhaps because of its congruence with scholastic notions of the will.

25. Hellwig, *Alles ist gut*, 82–83.

26. The will can overpower the other appetites, producing, in King's example, six units of pleasure against the appetite's two units of pain. The result is a net benefit, yet one that remains short of perfect happiness (V.ii.6). Leibniz is very critical on this point. For Leibniz, if the will is free to take pleasure in any object, it is also free to take as much pleasure as it wants. How, then, could anyone ever be unhappy? King seems to imagine a somewhat weaker power. The will can take any object as good, but the pleasure it can take in that good is limited. See Leibniz's response to King in the appendix to *Theodicy: Essays on the Goodness of God, the Freedom of Man, and the Origin of Evil* (Eugene, OR: Wipf and Stock Publishers, 2001): 423–24.

27. Kathryn Tanner, *God and Creation in Christian Theology: Tyranny or Empowerment?* (Minneapolis, MN: Fortress Publishers, 2005).

28. In arguing for this position, King does not mean to rule out grace. Free will, he

argues, can be vitiated through misuse. When it is, God's grace can act to restore the will to freedom. Grace cannot, however, determine the will to good (V.v.iii.3).

29. In an argument that anticipates themes that would be developed at length by Bernard Mandeville, King adds that God has so ordered the universe that even undue elections can ultimately benefit the whole. This point is somewhat puzzling because King considers elections undue merely on the grounds that they might cause natural evil. King does not provide a satisfactory explanation here, but his thought is clear enough. Vice is vice because it produces natural evil, but God limits the evils primarily (though not exclusively) to the vicious actor and others who deserve harm. For the system as a whole, however, God manages to bring about greater natural goods. King's example is a classic case: A man raises an immense sum of money and squanders it on luxury. Though the sum should have been given to the poor, the circulation of the money through luxurious spending may do just as much good (V.v.vi.9). In this way, God effectively neutralizes moral evils, limiting their negative effects in scope and turning the overall effect to greater natural good. Bayle discusses the same case, arguing that the mix of vice and good consequences is best explained by two principles. See Pierre Bayle, "Pauliciens," Remark G, in *Dictionnaire historique et critique* (Paris: Desoer, 1820).

30. John Hick, *Evil and the God of Love* (New York: Harper and Row, 1966): 153–54.

31. The frustration of appetite is not equivalent to subjective displeasure in the case of the fixed appetites, though it is hard to see why it is bad beyond its implications for subjective experience. In the case of the will, frustration of appetite is nothing other than subjective displeasure.

32. Bayle, *Réponse aux questions d'un provincial*, vol. 2, ch. 75 (my translation).

33. Jesse Couenhoven, "Augustine's Rejection of the Free Will Defense: An Overview of the Late Augustine's Theodicy," *Religious Studies* 43, no. 3 (2009): 279–98.

34. Aquinas, *Summa theologica*, I.48.6. The question in Latin is: "Quid habeat plus de ratione male, utrum poena vel culpa." Aquinas clarifies that *poena* includes not only the pain of sense but also any privation.

35. Henry More, as I have noted, had already suggested that some evils arise from the very nature of matter (*Divine Dialogues*, vol. 1, 179). But More does not use it to challenge the traditional structure of the explanation of evil. More explains our bodily composition—not the fact that we are embodied but the kind of bodies we have and thus the natural evils to which we are subject—as a penalty for the sins of preexistent souls (*Divine Dialogues*, vol. 1, 491).

36. King does try to stick a little more closely to the standard reading of Genesis 3 by suggesting that God could have protected Adam and Eve from all natural evils by a perpetual miracle. Having sinned, however, human beings can no longer expect miraculous protection (IV.ix.5).

37. Bayle calls attention to this reversal as well, arguing that the scholastic casuists would "cry out against" King's claim that natural evils are worse than moral evil: "They teach that sin, as an offense against the infinite being, is a worse thing than either plague or famine, and that it would not be permissible to stop these scourges if to do so one had to make a false oath or perform an idolatrous act." *Réponse aux questions d'un provincial*, vol. 3, part 2, ch. 82, section 20 (my translation).

38. See, for example, Bayle, "Pauliciens," Remark D, in *Dictionnaire historique et critique*.

39. Leibniz treats a "world" as a type of thing on the same logic. If God wills any world, God has to will all that is necessary to the perfection of that world. Leibniz, *Theodicy*, 428–29.

Chapter Six

1. Anthony Ashley Cooper, Lord Shaftesbury, "The Preface," in Benjamin Whichcote, *Select Sermons of Benjamin Whichcote* (London, 1693): xiii.

2. This common designation has been challenged by Robert Crocker. According to Crocker, it is the early philosophical poems of Henry More and not the sermons of Whichcote that are the first "manifesto" of Cambridge Platonism. See Crocker, *Henry More: 1614–1687: The Biography of a Cambridge Platonist* (Dordrecht: Kluwer Academic Publishers, 2003): 12.

3. Shaftesbury, "The Preface," x.

4. Shaftesbury, "The Preface," x.

5. There has been increasing attention to the relationship between Shaftesbury and the Cambridge Platonists in recent years. See Dirk Grossklaus, *Natürliche Religion und aufgeklärte Gesellschaft: Shaftesburys Verhältnis zu den Cambridge Platonists* (Heidelberg: Universitätsverlag C. Winter, 2000); Michael Gill, "From Cambridge Platonism to Scottish Sentimentalism," *Journal of Scottish Philosophy* 8, no. 1 (2010): 13–31; Insa Kringler, "Shaftesburys Natur- und Moralverständnis hinsichtlich der Rezeption des 'Cambridge Platonism,'" *Aufklärung* 22 (2010): 105–34; Sarah Hutton, "From Cudworth to Hume: Cambridge Platonism and the Scottish Enlightenment," *Canadian Journal of Philosophy* 42, no. 1 (2012): 8–26; Laurent Jaffro, *La couleur du gout: Psychologie et esthétique au siècle de Hume* (Paris: Librairie Philosophique J. Vrin, 2019).

6. Anthony Ashley Cooper, Lord Shaftesbury, *The Letters of Shaftesbury, Author of the Characteristics, Collected into One Volume* (Glasgow, 1746): 35.

7. Isabel Rivers, *Reason, Grace, and Sentiment: A Study of the Language of Religion and Ethics in England, 1660–1780*, vol. 1 (Cambridge: Cambridge University Press, 1991): 25–88.

8. Anthony Ashley Cooper, Lord Shaftesbury, to Jacques Basnages, January 21, 1707, quoted in Patrick Müller, "'Dwell with Honesty & Beauty & Order': The Paradox of Theodicy in Shaftesbury's Thought," *Aufklärung* 22 (2010): 204n9.

9. As Michael Gill writes, "If you had said to Shaftesbury that you could only read one of his books, *The Moralists* is what he would have given you. He thought of it as his magnum opus, the work that best captured both the essence and scope of his thought." See Gill, *The British Moralists on Human Nature and the Birth of Secular Ethics* (Cambridge: Cambridge University Press, 2006): 100.

10. There is, however, good reason to doubt that it was actually against his will, not least because he encouraged a French translation. See Alfred Aldridge, "Two Versions of Shaftesbury's *Inquiry Concerning Virtue*," *Huntington Library Quarterly* 13 (1950): 208–9.

11. Anthony Ashley Cooper, Lord Shaftesbury, *Characteristics of Men, Manners, Opinions, Times*, ed. John M. Robertson (Indianapolis, IN: Bobbs-Merrill Company, 1964).

12. Shaftesbury, *Characteristics*, vol. 1, 238. All further references to this work will be cited parenthetically by volume number and page number.

13. Another controversy surrounding Bayle's work was caused by his argument in *Pensées diverses sur la comète* (1682) that a society of atheists could be virtuous.

14. Laurent Jaffro has rightly noted that one of the most important contexts of Shaftesbury's writings—and the one most often missed—is the debate about deism. See Jaffro's account of the polemic context of Shaftesbury's work in "Ambiguïtés et difficultés du sens moral," in *Normativités du sens commun*, eds. Claude Gautier and Sandra Laugier (Paris: Presses universitaires de France, 2009): 303–18.

15. Henry More, *Divine Dialogues*, vol. 1 (London, 1668): 407.

16. Shaftesbury gives no argument for this claim beyond a few examples. A human being is neither good nor ill due to the effects of her plague spots or convulsive fits. The point seems to be the traditional one that one is virtuous or vicious by one's actions and not by that which is beyond one's control.

17. Timothy M. Costelloe, *The British Aesthetic Tradition: From Shaftesbury to Wittgenstein* (Cambridge University Press, 2013); Jerome Stolnitz, "On the Significance of Lord Shaftesbury in Modern Aesthetic Theory," *Philosophical Quarterly* 11, no. 43 (1961): 97–113; Dabney Townsend, "From Shaftesbury to Kant: The Development of the Concept of Aesthetic Experience," *Journal of the History of Ideas* 48, no. 2 (1987): 287–305.

18. For Shaftesbury's understanding of the passions, see his recently discovered *Pathologia* (1706), published in Lauren Jaffro, Christian Maurer, and Alain Petit, "*Pathologia*, a Theory of the Passions," *History of European Ideas* 39, no. 2 (2013): 221–40. For commentary, see Christian Maurer and Laurent Jaffro, "Reading Shaftesbury's *Pathologia*: An Illustration and Defence of the Stoic Account of the Emotions," *History of European Ideas* 39, no. 2 (2013): 207–20. See also Laurent Jaffro, *La couleur du goût*, 42–51.

19. In his defense of the *Inquiry* in *The Moralists*, Shaftesbury argues that the aim of the *Inquiry* is to convince readers of moral realism and then show them that realism in morality entails realism in divinity. As Isabel Rivers notes, the entire *Characteristicks* can be seen as following this method as well. But it is clear from the very first paragraph—in which he begins to develop his account of morality by defining what it is for a creature to be good—that he is implicitly presupposing the harmony of creation associated with theism. Without the truth of theism, the account of goodness and virtue could hardly get off the ground. As Rivers says, "The stages of Shaftesbury's argument from the part to the whole are designed to show that the realist in morality must be a realist in divinity, but they also show the converse, that unless one is a realist in divinity one cannot be a realist in morality." Isabel Rivers, *Reason, Grace, and Sentiment: A Study in the Language of Religion and Ethics in England, 1660–1780*, vol. 2 (Cambridge: Cambridge University Press, 2005): 141.

20. This aspect of his thought is picked up and developed by Joseph Butler in his first sermon preached at Rolls Chapel. See Butler, *Fifteen Sermons Preached at the Rolls Chapel and a Dissertation upon the Nature of Virtue* (London: G. Bell and Sons Ltd., 1958).

21. See Insa Kringler, "Shaftesburys Natur- und Moralverständnis," 109.

22. Patrick Müller has argued that it would be a mistake to assume that Shaftesbury's private notebooks are somehow truer to his view than his published writings, noting that Shaftesbury argues in "Soliloquy" for the exact opposite: that one should not present one's private thoughts and writings to the public as if there were something truer about one's half-formed or spontaneous thoughts. Shaftesbury clearly did what he recommends to others: put his thinking through a rigorous process of reflection and polishing before sharing it. See Müller, "Shaftesbury on the Psychoanalyst's Couch: A Historicist Perspective on Gender and (Homo)Sexuality in *Characteristicks* and the Earl's Private Writings," *Swift Studies* 25 (2010): 56–81. Michael Gill echoes the same point in "Shaftesbury on Politeness, Honesty, and Virtue," in *New Ages, New Opinions: Shaftesbury in His World and Today*, ed. Patrick Müller (Frankfurt: Peter Lang, 2014): 167–84. This perspective is one way of dealing with the seemingly contradictory viewpoints between Shaftesbury's published and unpublished writings. I think Mark-Georg Dehrmann, through his study of Shaftesbury's unpublished writings on Socrates, provides a better approach. According to Dehrmann, Shaftesbury's public writings engage in a kind of intentional double-speak meant to

lead those who would initially be offended by Shaftesbury's views into a recognition of their truth. This argument makes more sense of the diversity of writing styles and the development of thought over the course of *Characteristicks*, which may not sound Stoic in the early essays but does indeed move toward distinctly Stoic conclusions in *The Moralists*. See Dehrmann, "Shaftesburys stoischer Sokratismus," *Aufklärung* 22 (2010): 77–103. It is also worth noting that Shaftesbury works to make his ideas more palatable to what he sees as a degenerate age. On this idea, see Tim Stuart-Buttle, "Shaftesbury Reconsidered: Stoic Ethics and the Unreasonable of Christianity," *Locke Studies* 15 (2018): 163–213.

23. Anthony Ashley Cooper, Lord Shaftesbury, *The Life, Unpublished Letters, and Philosophical Regimen of Anthony, Earl of Shaftesbury*, ed. Benjamin Rand (New York: Macmillan, 1900): 10.

24. Shaftesbury, *Life, Letters*, 6.

25. Shaftesbury, *Life, Letters*, 11.

26. Shaftesbury, *Life, Letters*, 159.

27. Shaftesbury, *Life, Letters*, 159.

28. Shaftesbury believes that we always should (and in fact always do) act in harmony with the good of the whole, which is the greatest good. He does not frame his ethics in consequentialist terms, but it could be done. The great value of the good of the whole, to which our affections ought to be attuned, can and sometimes does explain why we ought to act in conformity with it (although it is also explained by the fact that we approve it when we reflect on our affections and by the fact that it is the best path to happiness).

29. Shaftesbury, *Life, Letters*, 91–92.

30. These are the arguments, respectively, of Henry Sidgwick, Ernest Tuveson, and J. B. Schneewind. See Sidgwick, *Outlines of the History of Ethics* (Indianapolis, IN: Hackett Publishing Co., 1998): 190; Ernest Tuveson, "The Importance of Shaftesbury," *ELH* 20, no. 4 (1953): 267–99; Schneewind, *The Invention of Autonomy* (Cambridge: Cambridge University Press, 1998): 285–309.

31. On the relationship between More's "boniform faculty" and Shaftesbury's "moral sense," see Laurent Jaffro, *La couleur du goût*, 18–30, 42–51; Insa Kringler, "Shaftesburys Natur- und Moralverständnis," 132–33.

Chapter Seven

1. Francis Hutcheson, *An Inquiry into the Original of Our Ideas of Beauty and Virtue*, ed. Wolfgang Leidhold (Indianapolis, IN: Liberty Fund, 2008).

2. Laurent Jaffro, "Francis Hutcheson et l'héritage shaftesburien: quelle analogie entre le beau et le bien?" in *Le beau et le bien*, eds. Carol Talon-Hugon and Pierre Destrée (Nice: Ovadia, 2011): 117–33.

3. James Moore, "Hutcheson's Theodicy: The Argument and the Contexts of *A System of Moral Philosophy*," in *The Scottish Enlightenment: Essays in Reinterpretation*, ed. Paul Wood (Rochester, NY: University of Rochester Press, 2000).

4. The only time that he distances himself from Shaftesbury, as far as I know, is in a passing remark about Shaftesbury's "prejudices against Christianity." See Hutcheson, *Inquiry*, preface.

5. Francis Hutcheson, *An Essay on the Nature and Conduct of the Passions, with Illustrations on the Moral Sense*, ed. Aaron Garret (Indianapolis, IN: Liberty Fund, 2002). See *Essay*, II.vi; *Illustrations*, V. For more on the relationship between Hutcheson and King, including the fact that Hutcheson sent his early essays to King, see Michael Brown,

"The Strange Case of Dr. King and Mr. Hutcheson," in *Archbishop William King and the Anglican Irish Context, 1688–1729*, ed. Christopher J. Fauske (Dublin: Four Courts Press, 2004): 135–47.

6. Francis Hutcheson, "The Editor to the Reader," in Henry More, *Divine Dialogues*, ed. Francis Hutcheson (Glasgow, 1743): i–iii.

7. Hutcheson also read Cumberland's *De legibus naturae* as part of his education in moral philosophy. See Darío Perinetti, "The Nature of Virtue," in *The Oxford Handbook of British Philosophy in the Eighteenth Century*, ed. James Harris (Oxford: Oxford University Press, 2013): 343.

8. Because only affections can be morally good or bad, Hutcheson would not technically qualify as a consequentialist. Practically, though, one should also act to realize as much happiness as possible.

9. Francis Hutcheson, *A System of Moral Philosophy* (London, 1745): II.iii.7.

10. Hutcheson, *Inquiry*, I.ii.3.

11. Hutcheson, *Inquiry*, I.v.1.

12. Hutcheson recognizes that in rendering beauty arbitrary, he is undermining any argument for the existence of God from the beauty of creation. He argues that he can get the same result, not from the beauty of creation, since there is no beauty beyond contingent senses, but from the way in which the sense of beauty functions for the sake of the happiness of creatures.

13. Hutcheson, *Inquiry*, II.i.1.

14. Hutcheson, *Inquiry*, II.iii.1.

15. Bernard Mandeville, *The Fable of the Bees* (New York: Penguin Books, 1989), 85–86.

16. Mandeville, *Fable of the Bees*, 81–86.

17. See John Clarke, *The Foundation of Morality in Theory and Practice* (York, 1726).

18. Hutcheson, *Essay*, I.i.

19. Hutcheson, *Essay*, I.ii.

20. Hutcheson, *Essay*, I.iii.

21. Locke, *An Essay Concerning Human Understanding*, ed. Peter Nidditch (Oxford: Clarendon Press, 1979): II.xx.

22. Locke, *Essay Concerning Human Understanding*, II.xx.

23. "Natural" is an important qualification. Mandeville always clarifies that his account of self-love only regards natural actions and not those made possible by grace. Mandeville, *Fable of the Bees*, 77.

24. Mandeville, *Fable of the Bees*, 91–92.

25. Hutcheson, *Inquiry*, II.ii.8.

26. Hutcheson, *Essay*, I.iv.

27. Hutcheson, *Essay*, II.vii.

28. Hutcheson, *Essay*, II.iii.

29. Hutcheson, *Essay*, II.iv.

30. Hutcheson, *Essay*, II.iii.

31. Hutcheson, *Essay*, II.iv. Though Hutcheson is here breaking with Lockean psychology, he remains committed to the rejection of innate ideas—at least as they are understood by Locke (see *Essay* II.ii). The proportionality of calm desire to the moment of good does not mean we have an innate idea of goodness as such or of the greatest aggregate of goodness to which calm desire is responsive. Rather, calm desire is automatically responsive to the moment of good prior to our conceptual grasp of this relationship. It is

by coming to rationally grasp the nature of our own desires that we develop the abstract notion of "moment of good."

32. William King, *An Essay on the Origin of Evil*, 1st ed., ed. and trans. Edmund Law (London, 1731): V.v.i.4.

33. Hutcheson, *Inquiry*, III.xi. Jaffro offers interesting nuance in his essay, "La mesure du bien. Que calcule le calcul moral de Hutcheson?" *Littérature et connaissance* 40, no. 1 (2013): 197–215.

34. Hutcheson, *Essay*, II.v.

35. Hutcheson, *Essay*, II.v.

36. Hutcheson, *Essay*, II.vi.

37. Hutcheson, *Essay*, II.vi.

38. Hutcheson, *Essay*, II.vii.

39. Hutcheson, *Essay*, II.vii.

40. Jürgen Sprute argues that moral judgment in Hutcheson (as in Shaftesbury) requires both reason and affection. He is right, but the conclusion is not particularly significant. It amounts, in my view, to the conclusion that only rational beings can make moral judgments because moral judgments approve or disapprove actions and motivations under some description. It does not mean, however, that reason has any role in determining what is approved and disapproved. And Sprute effectively recognizes this fact when he notes that there is no logical connection between the rational conceptualization of an object and the affective reaction of the moral sense. See Sprute, "Der Begriff des Moral Sense bei Shaftesbury und Hutcheson," *Kant Studien* 71, no. 2. (1980): 233. But even this minimal interpretation may go too far. As Laurent Jaffro has pointed out, Hutcheson does not presume that we know what object is pleasing to our internal senses. The analogy here is with the external senses. We do not need to know what it is about an object that makes it appear blue in order to see the color blue. It is an achievement—and one that not everyone reaches—to recognize what feature of actions elicits our approval. See Jaffro, "Francis Hutcheson et l'héritage shaftesburien," 177–33.

41. I do not think Terence Irwin is right to explain Hutcheson's account of ends as arational as a result of his internalism about obligation. According to the logic of *Illustrations*, the arationality of ends is what explains the internalism about obligation. See Terence Irwin, *The Development of Ethics: A Historical and Critical Study*, vol. 2 (Oxford: Oxford University Press, 2008): 399–420.

42. Hutcheson, *Illustrations*, I.

43. Hutcheson, *Illustrations*, I.

44. On this point, Hutcheson is closer to Cumberland than Shaftesbury.

45. There is another important difference that I am disregarding for the purpose of this discussion. For Aristotle, rationality requires a single organizing end. But Hutcheson goes on to deny that there is "*one great ultimate End*, with a view to which every *particular object* is desired" (*Illustrations*, I). For Hutcheson, there are two basic categories of desire: self-love and benevolence. Under these categories are many desires for many particular things: the pleasure of this good, the happiness of that person. Each of these particular desires sets an end for us. For Hutcheson, "each particular pleasure is desired without farther view" (*Illustrations*, I). Likewise, the happiness of each person is desired as an end in itself. Personal pleasures are not desired for the sake of personal happiness, and the happiness of others is not desired for the sake of universal happiness. But our selfish desires are proportional to the private moment of good, as our benevolent desires are

proportional to the public moment of good. Seeking the greatest possible pleasure is the best way to satisfy as many of our individual selfish desires as possible, and seeking the greatest possible public good is the best way to satisfy as many of our benevolent desires as possible. In this way, our many ultimate ends can be organized into two overarching pursuits.

46. In this way, Hutcheson also breaks from Hobbes and Locke, both of whom agree that we act only from instinctive desire but both of whom understand our desires in terms of the pleasure and pain that follow from the health or dissolution of bodies.

47. John Balguy, *The Foundation of Moral Goodness and of Our Idea of Virtue* (London, 1733); Samuel Clarke, *A Discourse Concerning the Unchanging Obligation of Natural Religion* (London, 1711).

48. Francis Hutcheson, *Logic, Metaphysics, and the Natural Sociability of Man*, ed. James Moore and Michael Silverthrone (Indianapolis, IN: Liberty Fund, 2006): II.iii.

49. Moore, "Hutcheson's Theodicy," 252–54.

50. James Harris, "Religion in Hutcheson's Moral Philosophy," *Journal of the History of Philosophy* 46, no. 2 (2008): 205–22.

51. Hutcheson, *System*, I.i.1.

52. Hutcheson, *System*, I.i.1.

53. Hutcheson, *System*, I.iii.6.

54. Hutcheson, *System*, I.iii.6.

55. Hutcheson, *System*, I.iv.6.

56. Commentators have noted the influence of Joseph Butler here. This observation seems right, though I do not think Hutcheson changed his basic position. See Joseph Butler, *Fifteen Sermons Preached at the Rolls Chapel and a Dissertation upon the Nature of Virtue* (London: G. Bell and Sons Ltd., 1958): sermon II. See also Henning Jensen, *Motivation and the Moral Sense in Hutcheson's Moral Theory* (The Hague: Martinus Nijhoff, 1971).

57. Hutcheson, *System*, I.iv.6.

58. Hutcheson, *System*, I.iv.6.

59. For Butler, by contrast, the superiority of conscience is founded on its authority rather than its strength. See Butler, *Fifteen Sermons Preached at the Rolls Chapel*, sermon II.

60. Hutcheson, *System*, I.iv.12.

61. Hutcheson, *System*, I.i.7.

62. Hutcheson, *Illustrations*, V.

63. For details on the relationship between Hutcheson's *Metaphysics* and other works, see the introduction by James Moore in Francis Hutcheson, *Logic, Metaphysics, and the Natural Sociability of Man*, ix–xxvii.

64. Hutcheson, *Metaphysics*, II.iii.

65. Hutcheson, *Metaphysics*, II.iii.

66. John Locke, *Essay on Human Understanding*, I.xxxiii.

67. Hutcheson, *System*, I.ii.8.

68. Hutcheson, *Essay*, Preface.

69. Hutcheson, *Inquiry*, VII.ii.

70. Hutcheson, *Essay*, I.ii; *System*, I.ii.8.

71. Hutcheson, *System*, I.ix.7.

72. Hutcheson, *System*, I.ix.7.

73. Hutcheson, *Illustrations*, V.

74. Hutcheson, *Illustrations*, VI.

75. Hutcheson, *Metaphysics*, 196–97.

76. Hutcheson, *System*, I.ix.6.

77. Hutcheson, *System*, I.ix.11.

78. Hutcheson, *System*, II.iii.11.

79. See, for example, John Balguy's *Foundations of Moral Goodness*. See also the discussion in Terence Irwin, *The Development of Ethics*, vol. 2, 452–59.

80. Hutcheson, *System*, I.ix.5.

81. We might expect Hutcheson to appeal to scripture. Yet, as Shaftesbury repeatedly insists, the trustworthiness of scripture depends upon a prior conviction of the goodness and trustworthiness of God (e.g., *Characteristics*, II, 92). Because Hutcheson accepts that God's end might be our misery, he cannot trust scripture until he can rule out this possibility.

82. Hutcheson, *System*, I.ix.5.

83. Hutcheson, *System*, I.ix.5.

84. As I noted above, Hutcheson takes the will to be the affective faculty as whole. Hutcheson, *System*, I.i.7.

Epilogue to Part II

1. See, respectively, John Hick, *Evil and the God of Love* (New York: Harper and Row, 1966): 145; Carl-Friedrich Geyer, "Das 'Jahrhundert der Theodizee,'" *Kant-Studien* 73, no. 4 (1982): 393–405.

2. Butler maintains that we must be careful in what we assert about divine morality. At best, our knowledge of God and God's morality is by analogy with the knowledge we can gain from creation. See Joseph Butler, *The Analogy of Religion* (New York: Harper and Brothers, 1898).

3. Samuel Clarke, *A Demonstration of the Being and Attributes of God* (London, 1705): 255–56.

4. John Clarke, *An Inquiry into the Cause and Origin of Evil* (London, 1720): 114–15.

5. Clarke, *Inquiry into the Cause and Origin of Evil*, 225.

6. John Clarke, *An Inquiry into the Cause and Origin of Moral Evil* (London, 1721): 188–89.

7. Clarke, *Inquiry into the Cause and Origin of Moral Evil*, 294.

8. Clarke, *Inquiry into the Cause and Origin of Moral Evil*, 312.

Chapter Eight

1. Ernest Albee, *A History of English Utilitarianism* (New York: Collier Books, 1962): 90.

2. Colin Heydt, "Utilitarianism before Bentham," in *The Cambridge Companion to Utilitarianism*, eds. Ben Eagleston and Dale E. Miller (Cambridge: Cambridge University Press, 2014): 16–37, at 26.

3. Getty Lustila, "John Gay and the Birth of Utilitarianism," *Utilitas* 30, no. 1 (2018): 87.

4. Élie Halévy, *The Growth of Philosophical Radicalism*, trans. Mary Morris (Clifton, NJ: A. M. Kelley, 1972): 7.

5. Patrick J. Connolly, "Susanna Newcome and the Origins of Utilitarianism," *Utilitas* 33 (2021): 384–98.

6. Connolly's article was published during the final stages of this book, and I was not able to incorporate it fully. Because I am focused in this chapter on the reception and

transformation of the consequentialist moral cosmology among the Anglican utilitarians, claims of priority are not of central importance. Gay's "Dissertation" is at the heart of the Anglican utilitarian tradition. But Connolly's claim is intriguing, and Newcome's contribution deserves further study.

7. It is also possible that Law contributed to the writing of the "Preliminary Dissertation." When he does attribute the dissertation to Gay in the fourth edition, he says that it was "primarily written by John Gay." I will attribute the text to John Gay. For commentary, see Uta Golembek, *Willensfreiheit und Gottes Güte: Kings Lösung des Theodizeeproblems und ihre Rezeption in der deutschen Aufklärung* (Würzburg: Königshausen & Neumann, 2013): 81–86.

8. Edmund Law, in William King, *An Essay on the Origin of Evil*, 2nd ed., ed. and trans. Edmund Law (London, 1732): xvii.

9. Niall O'Flaherty, *Utilitarianism in the Age of the Enlightenment: The Moral and Political Thought of William Paley* (Cambridge: Cambridge University Press, 2018): 38.

10. See Heydt's explanation for the term in "Utilitarianism before Bentham," 33–34.

11. George Berkeley's essay "Passive Obedience" is also plausibly described as an early articulation of theological utilitarianism though, as James Crimmins notes, the label is "not unambiguous." See James Crimmins, *Utilitarians and Religion* (Bristol: Thoemmes Press, 1998): 8.

12. For analysis, see Stefan Storrie, "William King's Influence on Locke's Second Edition Change of Mind about Human Action and Freedom," *International Journal of Philosophical Studies* 27, no. 5 (2019): 668–84.

13. William Paley, *A Short Memoir of the Life of Edmund Law, D.D., Bishop of Carlisle* (Davis, Taylor, Wilks, and Chancery-Lane, 1800): 2.

14. B. W. Young, *Religion and Enlightenment in Eighteenth-Century England: Theological Debate from Locke to Burke* (Oxford: Oxford University Press 1998): 106.

15. For a very early version of this controversy between Thomas Burnet and Catharine Trotter, see Emilio Maria de Tomassio, " 'Some Reflections on the True Grounds of Morality'—Catharine Trotter in Defence of John Locke," *Philosophy Study* 7, no. 6 (June 2017): 326–39, http://doi.10.17265/2159-5313/2017.06.007.

16. J. B. Schneewind, "Locke's Moral Philosophy," in *The Cambridge Companion to Locke*, ed. Vere Chappell (Cambridge: Cambridge University Press, 1994): 202.

17. Locke, *An Essay Concerning Human Understanding*, ed. Peter Nidditch (Oxford: Clarendon Press, 1979): I.iii.3. This text, from which I will cite, is a version of the fourth edition, which was the most important for Gay.

18. Locke, *Essay Concerning Human Understanding*, II.xx.2.

19. Locke, *Essay Concerning Human Understanding*, II.xii.4.

20. Locke, *Essay Concerning Human Understanding*, II.xxii.12.

21. Locke, *Essay Concerning Human Understanding*, II.xxviii.5.

22. Locke, *Essay Concerning Human Understanding*, II.xxviii.8. In the *Essay*, Locke claims that moral truths can be determined by reason alone with mathematical certainty. In *The Reasonableness of Christianity*, he adds that it was too much for most or all human beings to attain certain knowledge of the divine law by reason alone. God sent Jesus to reveal the divine law and its sanctions. Once the law was revealed, we could recognize its certainty. Gay seems more optimistic about our rational knowledge of divine law. John Locke, *The Reasonableness of Christianity* (Oxford: Clarendon Press, 2000): §241.

23. Locke rarely speaks of obligation in the *Essay*, but he does say that our desires and passions place us under an obligation to pursue happiness. Presumably that obligation

becomes moral when the happiness is found by way of conformity to the divine law. Locke, *Essay Concerning Human Understanding*, II.xxi.52.

24. Andrew Israelsen, "God, Mixed Modes, and Natural Law: An Intellectualist Interpretation of Locke's Moral Philosophy," *British Journal for the History of Philosophy* 21, no. 6 (2013): 1111–32; Peter J. E. Kail, "Moral Judgment," in *The Oxford Handbook of British Philosophy in the Eighteenth Century*, ed. James A. Harris (Oxford: Oxford University Press, 2013): 316; Schneewind, "Locke's Moral Philosophy," 204–6.

25. Steven Forde, "'Mixed Modes' in Locke's Moral and Political Philosophy," *Review of Politics* 73, no. 4 (Fall 2011): 592–97; Hannah Dawson, "The Normativity of Nature in Pufendorf and Locke," *Historical Journal* 63, no. 3 (2020): 528–58; Schneewind, "Locke's Moral Philosophy," 209–12.

26. Elliot Rossiter, "Hedonism and Natural Law in Locke's Moral Philosophy," *Journal of the History of Philosophy* 54, no. 2 (April 2016): 210.

27. According to Brogan, all of the major features of theological utilitarianism can be found in Locke's ethics. The argument depends upon the claim that Locke's appeals to the common good, public good, or public happiness are appeals to the maximal sum of public happiness. Lacking explicit evidence that Locke intends to use these commonplace terms in a utilitarian manner, Brogan's argument is not particularly convincing. Nonetheless, his reading does raise the question of whether Locke's epistemology allows any other interpretation of public good. A. P. Brogan, "John Locke and Utilitarianism," *Ethics: An International Journal of Social, Political, and Legal Philosophy* 69, no. 2 (January 1959): 79–93.

28. Patrick J. Connolly, "Locke's Theory of Demonstration and Demonstrative Morality," *Philosophy and Phenomenological Research* 48, no. 2 (March 2019): 435–51.

29. Locke, *Reasonableness of Christianity*, §241–243.

30. See also Locke, *Reasonableness of Christianity*, §180.

31. Daniel Layman, "Accountability and Parenthood in Locke's Theological Ethics," *History of Philosophy Quarterly* 31, no. 2 (April 2014): 101–18.

32. Layman does have a story here, which is indebted to Stephen Darwall, about the link between obligation and accountability. I am passing over the details.

33. Terence Irwin, *The Development of Ethics: A Historical and Critical Study*, vol. 2 (Oxford: Oxford University Press, 2008): 269–70; Layman, "Accountability and Parenthood," 101–2. Cf. Francis Oakley, "Locke, Natural Law, and God: Again," *History of Political Thought* 18, no. 4 (Winter 1997): 634–51. Oakley agrees broadly with this reading but argues that it is consistent with the views of William of Ockham.

34. Schneewind, "Locke's Moral Philosophy," 222.

35. Timothy Stanton, "Locke and His Influence," in *The Oxford Handbook of British Philosophy in the Eighteenth Century*, ed. James A. Harris (Oxford: Oxford University Press, 2013): 22.

36. All citations of John Gay's "Preliminary Dissertation" come from the first edition of King's *An Essay on the Origin of Evil*, ed. and trans. Law, xi–xxxiii. Citations in this section will be parenthetical in the text.

37. On this point, see Irwin, *The Development of Ethics*, vol. 2, §863.

38. Gay says almost nothing in defense of the qualification that virtue concerns our actions with respect to each other's happiness. He seems to take it for granted.

39. Lustila, "John Gay and the Birth of Utilitarianism," 88–91.

40. Susanna Newcome, *An Inquiry into the Evidence of the Christian Religion* (Cambridge, 1728): 1–8.

41. Locke, *Essay Concerning Human Understanding*, II.xxxiii.9.

42. Christian Maurer, "Self-Interest and Sociability," in *The Oxford Handbook of British Philosophy in the Eighteenth Century*, ed. James A. Harris (Oxford: Oxford University Press, 2013): 306.

43. For this reason, I think it is somewhat misleading that O'Flaherty describes Gay as part of "the moral sense tradition." See Niall O'Flaherty, *Utilitarianism in the Age of Enlightenment: The Moral and Political Thought of William Paley* (Cambridge: Cambridge University Press, 2018): 43.

44. Susanna Newcome, *An Enquiry into the Evidence of the Christian Religion*, 2nd ed. (London, 1732): 19.

45. Newcome, *Enquiry into the Evidence of the Christian Religion*, 43. She does not state this position explicitly. The primary focus of the work is not to provide a detailed moral philosophy, and she does not answer every question we would like to put to her. But she definitely thinks that morality is prior to divine commands. She also reasons primarily by way of what brings us happiness because she believes a good God would annex happiness to good action. And she is clear that there is a best end that ought to be willed. My summary of her view is the best way I know to combine these views.

46. Connolly, "Susanna Newcome and the Origins of Utilitarianism," 396–98.

47. Francis Hutcheson, *A System of Moral Philosophy* (London, 1745): I.ix.5.

48. Discussing Gay's moral philosophy, O'Flaherty writes the following: "There is some question as to whether Locke was a strict voluntarist, or whether, as some of his statements appear to indicate, he did in fact believe in a natural law independent of God's commands with divine sanctions providing a 'condition for our obligation to act morally.' But whichever is the case, the principle of utility filled the void of normativity left by his virtual silence on the content of such laws, as it did with the intellectualist criteria" (*Utilitarianism in the Age of Enlightenment*, 51). The suggestion seems to be that by "filling the void of normativity," Gay avoids ethical and perhaps even legislative voluntarism. If Gay's intent was to fill this void, one would have expected at least some positive account of the goodness of the principle of utility independent of the fact that God wills it.

49. I am here disagreeing with Heydt, who states that Anglican utilitarians take over from Locke a theory of obligation founded not on the power of God but on the right or authority of a Creator. Heydt cites no evidence, so I am not sure of the reasons for his claim. I can see nothing in Gay or Law that suggests that God has any right to command. The power of God over pleasure and pain is continually emphasized. See Heydt, "Utilitarianism before Bentham," 20.

50. Denis Diderot, "Will of God," in *The Encyclopedia of Diderot & d'Alembert: Collaborative Translation Project* (Ann Arbor: Michigan Publishing, University of Michigan Library, 2013), https://quod.lib.umich.edu/d/did/.

51. William Ames, *The Marrow of Sacred Divinity* (London, 1642): II.i.3, 216.

52. See Jacob Viner, *The Role of Providence in the Social Order* (Princeton, NJ: Princeton University Press, 1972).

53. Heydt, "Utilitarianism before Bentham," 29.

Chapter Nine

1. John Stephens, "Edmund Law and His Circle at Cambridge," in *The Philosophical Canon in the 17th and 18th Centuries*, eds. G. A. J. Rogers and Sylvana Tomaselli (Rochester, NY: University of Rochester, 1996): 163. On Law's circle, see also B. W. Young, *Religion*

and Enlightenment in Eighteenth-Century England: Theological Debate from Locke to Burke (Oxford: Oxford University Press, 1998): 108–13.

2. Patrick J. Connolly, "Susanna Newcome and the Origins of Utilitarianism," *Utilitas* 33 (2021): 384–98, at 394–96.

3. Stephens, "Edmund Law and His Circle at Cambridge," 163.

4. Uta Golembek, *Willensfreiheit und Gottes Güte: Kings Lösung des Theodizeeproblems und ihre Rezeption in der deutschen Aufklärung* (Würzburg: Königshausen & Neumann, 2013): 83.

5. John Gascoigne, *Cambridge in the Age of Enlightenment: Science, Religion, and Politics from the Restoration to the French Revolution* (Cambridge: Cambridge University Press, 2002): 129. Cf. Victor Nuovo, "Review of *John Locke and the Eighteenth-Century Divines* by Alan P. F. Sell," *Journal of Theological Studies* 49, no. 1 (April 1998): 471; Golembek, *Willensfreiheit und Gottes Güte*, 74–75.

6. William Paley, *A Short Memoir of the Life of Edmund Law, D.D., Bishop of Carlisle* (Davis, Taylor, Wilks, and Chancery-Lane, 1800): 12–13.

7. B. W. Young, *Religion and Enlightenment in Eighteenth-Century England*, 106.

8. Victor Nuovo, "Introduction," in *The Collective Works of Edmund Law*, ed. Victor Nuovo (London: Thoemmes Press, 1997): x.

9. Nuovo, "Introduction," xiv.

10. Golembek, *Willensfreiheit und Gottes Güte*, 6.

11. Edmund Law, in William King, *An Essay on the Origin of Evil*, 5th ed., ed. and trans. Edmund Law (London, 1781): xvi.

12. Golembek, *Willensfreiheit und Gottes Güte*, 71.

13. Golembek, *Willensfreiheit und Gottes Güte*, 76.

14. Nuovo, "Introduction," xiv–xv.

15. Nuovo, "Introduction," xix.

16. Nuovo, "Introduction," xix.

17. Edmund Law, "Preface," in William King, *An Essay on the Origin of Evil*, 2nd ed., ed. and trans. Edmund Law (London, 1732): xvii.

18. James E. Crimmins, "John Brown and the Theological Tradition of Utilitarian Ethics," *History of Political Thought* 4, no. 3 (1983): 523–50, at 544.

19. Crimmins, "John Brown and the Theological Tradition of Utilitarian Ethics."

20. Nuovo, "Introduction," xix.

21. Nuovo, "Introduction," xxviii; Niall O'Flaherty, *Utilitarianism in the Age of Enlightenment: The Moral and Political Thought of William Paley* (Cambridge: Cambridge University Press, 2018): 45–50.

22. Golembek, *Willensfreiheit und Gottes Güte*, 86.

23. Edmund Law, in William King, *An Essay on the Origin of Evil*, 1st ed., ed. and trans. Edmund Law (London, 1731): 301n111.

24. Law, in King, *Essay on the Origin of Evil*, 1st ed., ed. and trans. Law, 49n18.

25. For King's comments on the first edition of Locke's *Essay Concerning Human Understanding*, see *The Correspondence of John Locke*, vol. 4, ed. E. S. de Beer (Oxford: Clarendon Press, 1979): 533–41.

26. Law, in King, *Essay on the Origin of Evil*, 5th ed., ed. and trans. Law, lxvi.

27. For discussion, see O'Flaherty, *Utilitarianism in the Age of Enlightenment*, 44–45.

28. Francis Hutcheson, *An Inquiry into the Original of Our Ideas of Beauty and Virtue*, ed. Wolfgang Leidhold (Indianapolis, IN: Liberty Fund, 2008): II.vii.1.

29. Francis Hutcheson, *A System of Moral Philosophy* (London, 1745): I.iv.6.

30. D. L. Le Mahieu, "Forward," in William Paley, *The Principles of Moral and Political Philosophy* (Indianapolis, IN: Liberty Fund, 2002): xvii.

31. David Hartley, *Observations on Man, His Frame, His Duty, and His Expectations*, vol. 1 (London, 1749): v–viii.

32. Law, in King, *Essay on the Origin of Evil*, 1st ed., ed. and trans. Law, ix.

33. Law, in King, *Essay on the Origin of Evil*, 1st ed., ed. and trans. Law, 155n61.

34. Frances Hutcheson, *An Essay on the Nature and Conduct of the Passions, with Illustrations on the Moral Sense*, ed. Aaron Garret (Indianapolis, IN: Liberty Fund, 2002): V.

35. Hutcheson, *Illustrations*, V.

36. Law, in King, *Essay on the Origin of Evil*, 2ond ed., ed. and trans. Law, 241nN.

37. Hutcheson, *System*, II.iii.3.

38. For the first argument, see Law, in King, *Essay on the Origin of Evil*, 1st ed., ed. and trans. Law, 45–50n18. For the second, see Law, in King, *Essay on the Origin of Evil*, 2nd ed., ed. and trans. Law, 301–14n53. Law's first attempt at an improved argument echoes ancient and medieval arguments in a manner that is not particularly consistent with the rest of his thought. Moral goodness, he says, is the intentional promotion of pleasure (or avoidance of pain) for another creature. Human beings naturally approve of this promotion. In the first edition, Law attributes our approval to the moral sense. In the second, he drops the reference to the moral sense but retains the claim that we naturally approve of moral goodness. In both editions, he notes that he wants to convince both those who accept a moral sense as implanted and those who see it as a product of the association of ideas. In either case, because we naturally approve of moral goodness, approving of moral goodness is a perfection in us. The key move is then to argue: "A Perfection found in some Degree in the Creature, must belong to, and be, in the highest Degree, in the Creator, who has been already prov'd to have all *natural* Perfections in an infinite or perfect Degree" (1st ed., n18). God, therefore, also approves of moral goodness. Because God has no inclination opposed to moral goodness, God will necessarily communicate the greatest possible happiness to creatures. The argument sits oddly in Law's larger project. But even as a standard argument of classical theism, Law's use of the argument is weak. It suggests an extremely simplistic picture according to which any capacity of a creature that is part of that creature's perfection is also part of God's perfection. God, it seems to follow, is also agile, poisonous, and brightly colored. Part of the problem for Law is that he wants to defend the radical freedom of God as King defines it—the goodness of what God wills follows from the fact that God wills it and not vice versa—while also ensuring that God always acts to promote and communicate happiness. If he can show that God's natural perfections include a natural approval of the promotion of happiness, then he can plausibly argue that God freely wills to create the greatest possible happiness in creatures. In this view, God, like rational creatures, has both a free appetite and at least one fixed appetite. The fixed appetite is the moral sense, which naturally approves of benevolent acts. The existence of this fixed appetite explains why God will always use God's free appetite benevolently.

39. The distinction, according to Sebastian Rehnman, is new in the eighteenth century. It appears in Samuel Clarke and Francis Hutcheson, though neither uses it in the same way as Law. See Rehnman, *Edwards on God* (New York: Routledge, 2020): 211n8.

40. Law, in King, *Essay on the Origin of Evil*, 1st ed., ed. and trans. Law, 47–49n18.

41. Law, in King, *Essay on the Origin of Evil*, 2nd ed., ed. an trans. Law, 302n53.

42. I raise some doubts about this below.

43. Law, in King, *Essay on the Origin of Evil*, 2nd ed., ed. and trans. Law, 311n53

44. Law, in King, *Essay on the Origin of Evil*, 2nd ed., ed. and trans. Law, 288nP.

45. Francis Oakley, for example, says that the late medieval voluntarists take "the omnipotence of God as their fundamental principle." See Francis Oakley, *Natural Law, Laws of Nature, Natural Rights: Continuity and Discontinuity in the History of Ideas* (New York: Continuum, 2005): 52. Margaret Osler says that voluntarists insist on "God's omnipotence and his absolute freedom of will." See Margaret Osler, "Triangulating Divine Will: Henry More, Robert Boyle, and Descartes on God's Relationship to the Creation," in *"Mind Senior to the World": Stoicismo e origenismo nella filosofia platonica del Seicento inglese*, ed. Marialuisa Baldi (Milano: FrancoAngeli, 1996): 77. Cf. J. B. Schneewind, "Voluntarism and the Origins of Utilitarianism," *Utilitas* 7, no. 1 (May 1995): 88.

46. Law, in King, *Essay on the Origin of Evil*, 1st ed., ed. and trans. Law, xix.

47. Soame Jenyns, *Free Inquiry into the Nature and Origin of Evil* (London, 1756).

48. Law clearly endorses the view that God's aim was the good of the whole, and that human beings are sometimes instruments of that larger good. He writes:

They who imagine that all things in this World were made for the immediate use of Man alone, run themselves into inextricable Difficulties. Man is indeed the Head of this lower part of the Creation, and perhaps it was design'd to be absolutely under his command. But that all things here tend directly to his own use, is, I think, neither easy nor necessary to be proved. Some manifestly serve for the food and support of others, whose Souls may be necessary to prepare and preserve their Bodies for that Purpose, and may at the same time be happy in a Consciousness of their own Existence. 'Tis probable, that they are intended to promote each others Good reciprocally: nay, Man himself contributes to the Happiness, and betters the Condition of the Brutes in several respects; by cultivating and improving the Ground, by watching the Seasons, by protecting and providing for them, when they are unable to protect or provide for themselves.

He concludes that all things conduce to the good of "the whole System, the general Good of which was the aim of its Creator" (Law, in King, *Essay on the Origin of Evil*, 2nd ed., ed. and trans. Law, 90–91n33).

49. Edmund Law, "Morality and Religion," in King, *Essay on the Origin of Evil*, 5th ed., ed. and trans. Law, liv.

50. One possible reading is that Law, like Gay, is trying to define the common notion of virtue. In this reading, God commands us to do good to all creatures, but we do not call it "virtue" unless the good is done to human beings. This reading, however, faces a serious problem: it would sometimes lead to the result that God commands us to act viciously (if, for example, we could do more good for the whole by harming some human beings).

51. Thomas Rutherforth, *An Essay on the Nature and Obligations of Virtue* (London, 1744): 241.

52. Rutherforth, *Essay on the Nature and Obligations of Virtue*, 251.

53. Rutherforth rejects this option. Instead, he leans on the point that we do not share God's end. Unlike God, we have no reason to care about the good of other creatures unless doing so brings us happiness. Rutherforth sees no reason that caring for other creatures would bring us happiness—unless, that is, God were to reward or punish us for it, which Rutherforth doubts. Instead, he reasons: Since God created us with our private happiness as our ultimate end, the most rational approach to determining our obligations is to

determine what most conduces to our earthly happiness, which, he argues, is promoting human happiness but not that of other animals. Ultimately, however, he concludes that we need the revealed will of God in scripture to know God's commands with confidence. Rutherforth, *Essay on the Nature and Obligations of Virtue*, 258–60.

54. Stephens, "Edmund Law and His Circle at Cambridge," 163.

55. On this point, I am indebted to Niall O'Flaherty's reading of Tucker. See *Utilitarianism in the Age of Enlightenment*, ch. 2.

56. O'Flaherty, *Utilitarianism in the Age of Enlightenment*, 18.

57. O'Flaherty, *Utilitarianism in the Age of Enlightenment*, 82

58. O'Flaherty, *Utilitarianism in the Age of Enlightenment*, 308.

59. Wilson Smith, "William Paley's Theological Utilitarianism in America," *William and Mary Quarterly* 11, no. 3 (July 1954): 402.

60. O'Flaherty, *Utilitarianism in the Age of Enlightenment*, 2.

61. William Whewell, *Lectures on the History of Moral Philosophy* (London, 1852): 137, quoted in Colin Heydt, "Utilitarianism before Bentham," in *The Cambridge Companion to Utilitarianism*, eds. Ben Eagleston and Dale E. Miller (Cambridge: Cambridge University Press, 2014): 16–37, at 25.

62. O'Flaherty, *Utilitarianism in the Age of Enlightenment*, 2.

63. Ernest Albee, *A History of English Utilitarianism* (New York: Collier Books, 1962): 162.

64. J. B. Schneewind, *Sidgwick's Ethics and Victorian Moral Philosophy* (Oxford: Oxford University Press, 1977): 122. Schneewind contrasts Bentham's work with that of his contemporary secular utilitarian reformer, William Godwin. While Bentham's book was largely ignored, "Godwin's received immediate acclaim, was at the centre of heated popular controversy for a few years, and then sank into an obscurity from which it has never recovered."

65. James Crimmins, "Religion, Utility and Politics: Bentham versus Paley," in *Religion, Secularization, and Political Thought: Thomas Hobbes to J. S. Mill*, ed. James Crimmins (New York: Routledge, 1990): 130–52, at 146. According to Schneewind, even those working with Bentham thought of utilitarianism as an invention of Paley. Schneewind, *Sidgwick's Ethics*, 129.

66. Schneewind, *Sidgwick's Ethics*, 151.

67. See especially Schneewind's *Sidgwick's Ethics*, Fredrick Rosen's *Classical Utilitarianism from Hume to Mill* (New York: Routledge, 2003), and Bart Schultz's *The Happiness Philosophers: The Lives and Works of the Great Utilitarians* (Princeton, NJ: Princeton University Press, 2017).

Epilogue to Part III

1. Thomas Johnson, *A Summary of Natural Religion* (London, 1736): preface.

2. The argument is that God cannot intend our misery as an end because God lacks knowledge of misery; this argument is meant to further eliminate possible options for divine ends, leaving only creaturely happiness. In the end, though, he accepts that empirical evidence of creation is our surest source of knowledge about divine ends.

3. Johnson, *Summary of Natural Religion*, 29.

4. Johnson, *Summary of Natural Religion*, 66.

5. Henry More, *Enchiridion ethicum* (London, 1667): I.iv.1.

6. Johnson, *Summary of Natural Religion*, 151.

7. More, *Enchiridion ethicum*, I.iv.3.

8. Johnson, *Summary of Natural Religion*, 54–55.

9. Johnson, *Summary of Natural Religion*, 80. Johnson does insist that we must trust the goodness of the lawgiver. The reason, however, is that without this trust, we would not be confident that God will reward us with private happiness. We care about the goodness of God not because we want assurance that the end of the laws is good, but because we want assurance of reward.

10. Ralph Cudworth, *A Treatise Concerning Eternal and Immutable Morality*, ed. Sarah Hutton (Cambridge: Cambridge University Press, 1996): 172.

11. Thomas Johnson, *An Essay on Moral Obligation* (London, 1731): 60.

12. For more on this point, see the epilogue to part II.

13. A God whose sole end is human happiness would not, King, Shaftesbury, Hutcheson, and the Anglican utilitarians believe, create Henry More's or Richard Cumberland's human beings: moral agents who can rationally grasp the good but who also have the freedom to act against it. This kind of freedom is not beneficial and so not befitting the gift of a perfectly benevolent God. What would God do instead? One option is to simply determine us to act in the best possible way. King and Law believe this answer cannot account for morality and human experience. There must be another reason that God would give us freedom. King provides the answer with his radical agential voluntarism: freedom permits pleasure even in naturally bad circumstances. Our sole end is private happiness, and freedom, far from allowing us to act against our end, vastly expands our options for attaining it. See the epilogue to part II for more.

14. See Edmund Law, in William King, *An Essay on the Origin of Evil*, 1st ed., ed. and trans. Law (London, 1731): 54n23.

Conclusion

1. Adam Smith, *The Theory of Moral Sentiments* (Indianapolis, IN: Liberty Classics, 1976): VI.ii.3.2,6.

2. Jacob Viner, *The Role of Providence in the Social Order* (Princeton, NJ: Princeton University Press, 1972): 62.

3. J. B. Schneewind, *Sidgwick's Ethics and Victorian Moral Philosophy* (Oxford: Oxford University Press, 1977): 9.

4. This problem can also be posed to non-consequentialist views that still rely on consequences, but it is obviously the greatest threat to consequentialism.

5. Shelly Kagan, *Normative Ethics* (Boulder, CO: Westview Press, 1998): 64.

6. James Lenman, "Consequentialism and Cluelessness," *Philosophy and Public Affairs* 29, no. 4 (2000): 342–70.

7. See Hilary Greaves, "Cluelessness," *Proceedings of the Aristotelian Society* CXVI, no. 3 (2016): 311–39.

8. John Rawls, *A Theory of Justice*, rev. ed. (Cambridge, MA: Belknap Press, 1999): 24.

9. Bernard Williams, "A Critique of Utilitarianism," in *Utilitarianism: For and Against*, eds. J. J. C. Smart and Bernard Williams (Cambridge: Cambridge University Press, 1973): 116–17.

10. On the difficulties of nailing down Bentham's position on this issue, see Hanna Fenichel Pitkin, "Slippery Bentham: Some Neglected Cracks in the Foundation of Utilitarianism," *Political Theory* 18, no. 1 (1990): 104–31.

11. John Hare, "Morality, Happiness, and Peter Singer," in *God, the Good, and*

Utilitarianism: Perspectives on Peter Singer, ed. John Perry (Cambridge: Cambridge University Press, 2014): 93–103. Hare's chapter includes the Bentham, Mill, and Sidgwick citations just mentioned.

12. William King, *An Essay on the Origin of Evil*, ed. and trans. Edmund Law (London, 1731): A.i.3.

13. See, for example, Douglas Portmore, *Commonsense Consequentialism: Wherein Morality Meets Rationality* (Oxford: Oxford University Press, 2011).

14. James Dreier, "Structures of Normative Theories," *Monist* 76, no. 1 (1993): 22–40; Douglas Portmore, "Consequentializing Moral Theories," *Pacific Philosophical Quarterly* 88 (2007): 39–73.

15. Campbell Brown, "Consequentialize This," *Ethics* 121, no. 4 (2011): 749–71. Portmore rejects Brown's claim, arguing that even if everything can be consequentialized, consequentializing is still meaningful because it changes the structure of the explanation of what is right and wrong. He is right. But finding views that fit widespread intuitions and then consequentializing them in order to shift the explanation of what is right and wrong is bizarre. If the goal is to match common sense, then why not stick with the commonsense explanation?

16. Mark Schroeder, "Teleology, Agent-Relative Value, and 'Good,'" *Ethics* 117, no. 2 (2007): 265–95, at 279.

17. Samuel Scheffler, *Consequentialism and Its Critics* (Oxford: Oxford University Press, 1988): 1.

18. Schneewind, "Voluntarism and the Origins of Utilitarianism," *Utilitas* 7, no. 1 (May 1995): 89.

19. Ryan Darr, "Teleology and Consequentialism in Christian Ethics: Goods, Ends, Outcomes," *Studies in Christian Ethics* 36, no. 4 (2023), forthcoming.

20. Elizabeth Anderson, *Value in Ethics and Economics* (Cambridge, MA: Harvard University Press, 1995); Talbot Brewer, *The Retrieval of Ethics* (Oxford: Oxford University Press, 2009).

21. For an excellent account of the irreducibly social and context character of valuing goods, see Elizabeth Anderson's *Value in Ethics and Economics*.

22. Jean-Paul Sartre, *Existentialism as Humanism*, ed. John Kulka (New Haven, CT: Yale University Press, 2007): 30ff.

23. Sartre, *Existentialism as Humanism*, 31.

Index

25, 28, 33, 111–12, 303n45; in William
King, 126–27, 130–44, 223–25, 288n9,
289n26, 289n28. *See also* agential
voluntarism
"free will defense," 109–10

Gay, John, 199–211; as Anglican utilitarian,
191–94, 202, 207; and consequentialist
moral cosmology, 20, 193; and consequentialist moral rationality, 193, 241,
243; and developmental psychology,
203–4; and divine authority, 209–11,
300n49; on divine ends, 202, 207–11; and
Edmund Law, 191–94, 210–11, 213–14,
217–25, 229–30, 298n7; and ethical voluntarism, 193, 208, 300n48; as first utilitarian, 191; and Francis Hutcheson, 194,
200–201, 204–9; on goodness, 193, 208,
300n48; on happiness, 200–211, 218–19,
299n38; and John Locke, 194, 199, 209;
and legislative voluntarism, 208, 300n48;
on moral sense, 200, 300n43; on obligation, 200–202, 207; and Pierre Bayle,
210; and Richard Cumberland, 201; and
Susanna Newcome, 191, 202–3, 207–8; on
virtue, 199–207, 221, 230, 299n38, 303n50;
and William Paley, 210
Gerson, Jean, 40
Gill, Michael, 291n9
Gillespie, Michael, 29–30, 269n6
glory: and Anglican utilitarianism, 241;
in Pierre Bayle, 119, 121; in William
Ames, 41–42, 48, 49, 273n64; in William King, 127
Gnosticism, 107–8, 284n10
God. *See* divine authority; divine commands; divine ends; divine morality
Godwin, William, 9, 304n64
Golembek, Uta, 126, 215–18
goodness: in Anglican utilitarianism, 193,
233, 235–38, 245; as attribute of states
of affairs, 6, 257, 262; in Augustine,
108–9; and consequentialist moral
cosmology, 16–18, 99–101, 113; and
consequentialist moral rationality, 6,
18, 98, 244; in Edmund Law, 193, 219,
221, 225–28, 240, 300n48, 302n38; and
ethical voluntarism, 29, 111, 270n17; in

Francis Hutcheson, 165–67, 168, 170–
74, 176, 181–82, 222, 294n31, 295n45; in
Henry More, 33–34, 52, 58–72, 97, 193,
238, 252, 258, 277n70, 279n100; in John
Gay, 193, 208, 300n48; in John Locke,
195–97; in modern morality, 11–13;
non-consequentialist, 255–62; in Pierre
Bayle, 115, 119, 121–22; in Platonism, 44–
48; in Plotinus, 108; as quantitative, 6,
100; in Ralph Cudworth, 46–48, 65–66,
239; in Richard Cumberland, 73, 76–77,
79–86, 90–92, 94, 97, 193, 252, 256, 258,
280n27, 281n40; in Shaftesbury, 147–48,
151–52, 158–60, 163–64, 292n19; shifting conceptions of, 106; and theocentric moral cosmology, 48–49, 254; in
Thomas Aquinas, 36–39, 77, 112, 130;
in trolley problem, 257–60; in William
Ames, 41–43; in William King, 125–29,
131–35, 138, 140–44, 288n9, 289n16
Gracia, Jorge, 94, 280n24
Greene, Joshua, 4–6
Gregory, Brad, 11–12
Grotius, Hugo, 74–76, 197–98

Haakonssen, Knud, 279n4, 282n41
Halévy, Élie, 8, 191, 268n19
happiness: in Anglican utilitarianism, 188,
236–38, 240–41, 244–49, 251–53, 303n53,
304n2, 305n9 (epilogue to part III),
305n13; and consequentialism, 15; in
Edmund Law, 218–30, 302n38, 303n48;
in Epicurus, 108; and eudaimonism, 16,
93; in Francis Hutcheson, 166, 168–69,
171, 173–76, 178–79, 181–83, 187, 294n8,
295n45; in Henry More, 57–59, 61,
64, 71, 276n40, 277n69; in John Gay,
200–211, 218–19, 299n38; in John Locke,
195, 298n23, 299n27; and modern natural law, 75; in Richard Cumberland,
77–78, 80–82, 84–90, 93, 281n34, 281n40,
282nn42–43; and Shaftesbury, 153–
60, 162–63, 293n28; in theological
consequentialism, 7, 15; in Thomas
Aquinas, 37; in utilitarianism, 5, 15, 244;
in William Ames, 42; in William King,
126–27, 131–33, 135–36, 138–41, 143–44,
187, 289n24, 289n26

51–52, 238; in Shaftesbury, 147, 154, 156, 158–59, 163; in Thomas Aquinas, 37, 281n35. *See also* benevolence; self-love

Lovejoy, Arthur, 126, 288n14

Lustila, Getty, 191

Luther, Martin, 110, 121

MacIntyre, Alasdair, 11–13

Mandeville, Bernard: and Francis Hutcheson, 165, 167–70, 174, 294n23; and John Gay, 210; on providence, 251; and William King, 290n29

Marcion, 107–8, 110, 114, 284n10

mathematics: and Anglican utilitarianism, 247; at Cambridge University, 216; in Francis Hutcheson, 171, 179, 283n5; in Henry More, 60, 62, 99, 236–37, 243, 256, 283n5; in John Locke, 196, 298n22; and moral rationality, 18; in Shaftesbury, 283n5; in Thomas Johnson, 236–37; and voluntarism, 30, 33

Maurer, Christian, 206

Maxwell, John, 92, 281n36

mechanical philosophy: in Francis Hutcheson, 166, 179–80; and John Gay, 223; and moral rationality, 18, 258; in Richard Cumberland, 77, 79, 89, 92, 94, 99, 243, 256; and William King, 129–30, 139

Milbank, John, 11–13, 28–30

Mill, James, 7

Mill, John Stuart, 7, 232, 250

modern morality: critique of, 11–14; history of, 11–14; and teleology, 13–14, 18; and voluntarism, 25–31, 48

Molinism, 286n40

Moore, James, 175

moral axioms: and Francis Hutcheson, 171; in Henry More, 52, 60–69, 98–100, 171, 236–38, 283n5; in Thomas Johnson, 235–38

moral community (divine-human): in Anglican utilitarianism, 20, 239–41; in Christian Platonism, 46–48; and the consequentialist moral cosmology, 17, 19, 99, 101; and Duns Scotus, 272n51; and ethical voluntarism, 11–13; in Francis Hutcheson, 166–67, 182–83, 187–88, 193; in Henry More, 19–20, 35–36, 48, 51–52,

56, 67–72, 111, 113, 122, 237–39, 243; in J. B. Schneewind, 26–27, 34–36, 111; in John Clarke, 186–87; and moral principles, 17, 27, 34–35; and problem of evil, 19, 111–13, 122; in Ralph Cudworth, 46–48, 239; in Richard Cumberland, 19–20, 90–92, 111, 113, 122, 243, 281n39; in Samuel Clarke, 186, 240; in Shaftesbury, 148, 157–60, 187–88; and theocentric moral cosmology, 39, 43, 48–49; in Thomas Aquinas, 38–39, 112; in Thomas Johnson, 237–39; and voluntarism, 26, 34–35; in William Ames, 42; in William King, 142–44, 148, 187–88; without common measure, 39, 111. *See also* divine morality

moral cosmology, 17, 99–100. *See also* consequentialist moral cosmology; theocentric moral cosmology

moral evil: in Anglican utilitarianism, 252; in Augustine, 108–10, 138–39; in Francis Hutcheson, 167–68, 177–81; in G. W. Leibniz, 288; in John Clarke, 186–87; in John Locke, 195–96, 198; in Pierre Bayle, 115–20, 286n40, 290n37; in Shaftesbury, 152, 161–65; in Thomas Aquinas, 112–13; in William King, 128–31, 136–40, 164, 290n29, 290n37. *See also* evil; natural evil; problem of evil

moral principles: and Anglican utilitarianism, 236, 239; and consequentialism, 3, 18, 240, 244, 257; and consequentialist moral cosmology, 16–17, 98; and ethical intellectualism, 34, 111; in Henry More, 51–52, 60–66, 71–72, 98, 111, 113, 239, 256; in John Clarke, 186–87; and moral community, 17, 27, 34–35, 48–49, 111; and problem of evil, 186–87, 193; in Richard Cumberland, 84–86, 98, 111, 113; in Samuel Clarke, 240; and theocentric moral cosmology, 49, 97, 111–12; in Thomas Aquinas, 38–39, 112, 139, 272n45; and trolley problem, 3, 18; in William Ames, 42

moral sense: and consequentialism, 244; in Edmund Law, 221–22, 224, 302n38; in Francis Hutcheson, 168–72, 176–77, 181–84, 187, 221–22, 224–25, 295n40; in

Tanner, Kathryn, 136
teleology: and Anglican utilitarianism,
241; Aristotelian, 12, 14, 256; in Christian Platonism, 45–48; definition of,
16; and diversity of options, 13–14, 16, 48–
49; in Francis Hutcheson, 180–81; in
Henry More, 49, 99, 239; in modern
morality, 11–14, 18, 29, 48; and moral
rationality, 26, 34–35, 48, 254–57; non-
consequentialist, 26, 254–62; in Platonism, 43–48; in Richard Cumberland,
76–81, 92–93, 99; in Thomas Aquinas,
37–39; in William Ames, 41–42
theocentric moral cosmology: and consequentialist moral cosmology, 17, 49,
243; description of, 48; and Henry
More, 71–72; and Richard Cumberland, 92; in seventeenth-century ethics, 27, 48–49, 258
theodicy: and Anglican utilitarianism,
241; coined by G. W. Leibniz, 120; and
consequentialist moral cosmology,
185–88, 193; in Edmund Law, 20, 214,
218, 223, 228; in the eighteenth century,
185; in Francis Hutcheson, 19, 164,
165–66, 175–81, 187–88, 193; after Pierre
Bayle, 120–22; in Shaftesbury, 154–63,
187–88, 193; in William King, 125–45,
148, 187–88, 193
Theologica Germanica, 44
theological consequentialism: in Anglican
utilitarianism, 21, 184, 188; and consequentialist moral cosmology, 18, 100–
101; critiques of, 250–53; developments,
17, 235–39; and divine command, 16;
and ethical voluntarism, 184, 188; and
modern morality, 14; as not revisionary, 18, 245–46. *See also* Anglican
utilitarianism; consequentialism;
theological utilitarianism
theological utilitarianism: beyond Anglican utilitarianism, 192, 298n11; and
Christian ethics, 20; critiques of, 250–
53; in the history of philosophy, 7–11;
and John Gay, 191–92, 199, 207. *See also*
Anglican utilitarianism; consequentialism; theological consequentialism;
utilitarianism

Thomasius, Christian, 235
Thomism: as ethical intellectualist, 36–39,
71; and Henry More, 26, 35; and moral
rationality, 36–39; and Platonism, 45–
46; and Reformed theology, 40; and
Richard Cumberland, 74, 78, 81, 83; and
teleology, 36–39, 111, 254–55; as theocentric moral cosmology, 48–49, 111
trolley problem, 1–4, 21, 245, 257–62
Tucker, Abraham, 231–32
Turretin, Francis, 40, 43, 272nn49–51
Tyrrell, James, 92, 100, 283n50

ultimate end. *See* final end
utilitarianism: classical, 5, 15, 100, 192,
232–33, 244, 302nn64–65; and consequentialism, 6, 15, 192, 288n8; and consequentialist moral cosmology, 16, 18,
100–101; critiques of, 21, 245–50; dates
of origin of, 25, 269n2; definition of, 14–
15; as development internal to Christian
ethics, 10; in history of philosophy, 5–11,
20–21, 244; in history of theology, 11–
14; and John Gay, 191; and John Locke,
197, 299n27; objections to, 245–50; as
reform project, 5–6, 13; and Richard
Cumberland, 73–74, 279n3; as secular
ethic, 5, 245–50; and Susanna Newcome, 191, 207; and trolley problem,
4; and voluntarism, 26–27, 32–35, 254;
and William King, 126, 140–41. *See also*
Anglican utilitarianism; consequentialism; theological utilitarianism

Vaughan, Thomas, 53
Viner, Jacob, 244
virtue: in Anglican utilitarianism, 229–30,
241, 245–46, 248–50; in Edmund Law,
218, 221–23, 228–29, 303n50; in Francis
Hutcheson, 169, 172, 175, 177–81, 221–22;
in Henry More, 54–67, 276n27, 277n67;
in John Gay, 199–207, 221, 230, 299n38,
303n50; in John Locke, 196; in modern morality, 11–13, 29; in Pierre Bayle,
118–19; in Richard Cumberland, 73–74,
76–77, 84–90, 281n34, 281n40, 282n42;
and Shaftesbury, 147, 149–54, 158–59,
161–64, 292n19; in Thomas Aquinas,